A Christian Student's Survival Guide

By Dr. Robert A. Morey
(B.A., M.Div., Ph.D., DLitt et Phil, D.Min., D.D.)

PRESS

About the Author

Dr. Robert A. Morey is the author of over 60 books, some of which have been translated into French, German, Italian, Dutch, Danish, Swedish, Spanish, Arabic, Farsi, Polish, and Finnish. He is listed in The International Authors and Writers Who's Who and Contemporary Authors.

It should be noted that Dr. Robert A. Morey as a young protégé with an IQ of 185 was selected by Yale University in the tenth grade of high school to become part of the School Mathematics Study Group (SMSG). Dr. Morey is also a Greek and Hebrew scholar and has debated some of the top scholars in the world who are against Christianity.

Education

He has earned the following degrees:

Date	Degree	Institution
1969	B.A. (Philosophy)	Covenant College
1972	M.Div. (Theology)	Westminster Theological Seminary
1989	D.Min. (Apologetics)	Westminster Theological Seminary
1996	D.D. (Honorary)	Faith Theological Seminary
2004	PhD. (Islamic Studies)	Louisiana Baptist University
2005	Culinary Arts (Chef)	Thompson Institute
2017	DLitt et Phil	The University of America

Professional Training

Dr. Morey was the Chairman of the membership committee of the Evangelical Theological Society for several years. Dr. Morey is recognized internationally as a professional apologist and theologian whose careful scholarship and apologetic abilities establish him as one of Christianity's top defenders. He is also adjunct Professor of Apologetics at Evangelical Theological Seminary and founder and past President of California Biblical University and Seminary (CBUS). He has studied alongside some great Christian theologians and apologists. They include Walter Martin (NYC, NJ CRI), Francis Schaeffer (Covenant College, L'Abri in Switzerland), Gordon Clark (Covenant College), Cornelius Van Til (WTS) and Hans Rookmaaker (NYC, Holland L'Abri).

Ministry Involvement (Past and Present)

- Adjunct professor at various seminaries.
- Lectured at seminaries, universities, colleges, and churches in 27 countries.
- Appeared on hundreds of radio and TV programs such as 700 Club, Coral Ridge Ministry, TBN, John Ankerberg Show, Moody Network, etc.
- Host of his own national talk show: *Bob Morey Live!*
- Executive Director of Faith Defenders Founder and Past President of California Biblical University and Seminary (CBUS)
- Pastor of New Life Bible Church 1977-1998
- Pastor of Faith Community Church 2005-2009

Recommendations For Dr. Morey's Ministry

Dr. Morey's speaking and writing ministry is recommended by some of the best- known Christian leaders in this generation.

Dr. D. James Kennedy (Coral Ridge Ministries)

"Dr. Robert A. Morey is an excellent speaker and writer on the subject of cults and the occult, His books are excellent resource tools on these -subjects. It is my pleasure to recommend him to churches everywhere throughout our land."

Dr. John Ankerberg (The Ankerberg TV Show)

"I have known Dr. Robert Morey for a number of years and welcome this opportunity to recommend him to you. Dr. Morey is a man with an excellent understanding of the historic Christian faith and a particular skill as a defender of the Faith. I heartily recommend him to you."

Dr. Stephen Olford (Dr. Morey's pastor for eight years)

"I praise the Lord that He has given you such a strategic ministry in the field of apologetics and theology. The Lord bless you richly."

Dr. Herbert Ehrenstein (Editor of Eternity Magazine)

"It is a genuine privilege for me to recommend Dr. Robert A. Morey as a competent Biblical scholar in the field of apologetics, Bible teaching and evangelism. I have known Dr. Morey for over 30 years and it has been a delight to me to see his developing a fantastic grasp of Biblical truth, and his unique ability to translate that exalted truth of God's Word into down-to-earth, meaningful and methodical ways his audiences can make use of it."

Dr. Kevin Johnson (Mount Carmel Outreach)

"Dr. Robert Morey is one of the finest Biblical scholars in the field of comparative religious studies (apologetics) in North America. His books and presentations have been tremendously useful. I highly recommend him to you."

Recommendations for Book

"*A Christian Student's Survival Guide* by Dr. Morey is the only book ever written for college and high school students that addresses a wide range of topics such as Creation Ex Nihilo, A Biblical Philosophy of Science, Evangelical Appraisal of Aristotle, Natural Theology, Apologetics, Cults, World Religions, etc. from a sound, intellectual and Biblical (Sola Scriptura) viewpoint – not from a secular humanist viewpoint that so many so-called 21st century Evangelical Christian apologists (they are really Thomists) that visit college campuses have adopted. This is why many of these Christian/humanist apologists visiting college campuses such as Princeton University loose the debate or argument when defending the faith. This is not the case with Dr. Morey's book—it will defeat even the most difficult intellectual arguments against the Bible with great clarity and bring glory to our Lord and Savior (Yeshua Ha-Mashiach)."

Didymus, President
New Jersey Institute for the Advancement of Truth (NJIAT)

"This is the best Student Guide that upholds Biblical Christianity. I wish I had it when a student at Princeton University. Invaluable."
Suthy MacLean, Missionary to Russia and the Ukraine

"One of the best books you have written."
Dr. George Hutchinson
(Princeton University, D. Phil. Oxford University)

Dedicated to Dr. Francis Schaeffer:
My Mentor, Friend, and Fellow Soldier
in the Cause of God and Truth.

Special thanks to Thomas F. Smith II,
John Morey, Jordan Worley, and
Rev. Timothy Gahles for their help
in preparing the manuscript.

Table of Contents

PART ONE

INTRODUCTION

The Cost Of Discernment

The Beheading of Apostle Paul by Enrique Simonet (1887)

One of the most important abilities a student must have as he attends college or university is DISCERNMENT. Discernment is the ability to distinguish, discriminate and judge between what is true and what is not true, what is good and what is evil.

In the Scriptures, discernment is referred to in such places as Gen. 31:32, where we are told to discern the difference between what belongs to us and what belongs to others. We are also to discern good from evil (II Sam. 14:17; 19:35; I Kgs. 3:9; Heb. 5:14), justice from injustice (I Kgs. 3:11), the holy from the profane, the clean from the unclean (Ezk. 44:23), the righteous from the wicked (Mal. 3:18) and those who serve God and those who do not serve God (Mal. 3:18).

Discernment also means understanding the times in which we live. This was the praise accorded to the men of Issachar "who understood the times and knew what Israel should do" (I Chron. 12:32). Discernment is the opposite of "gullibility." Gullibility is the naive and childish acceptance of whatever the professor or textbook teaches. It is the foolish assumption that if something were not true it would not be printed in a book. Or, if it were not true, the professor would not teach it.

In order to be discerning, we must understand the truth (I Kgs. 3:9, 11–14; Pro. 2:2). In order to have understanding, we need God's wisdom (Pro. 10:23). And, in order to have wisdom, we must learn to fear the God who made us (Pro. 1:7, 16:6; II Tim. 2:7).

The Fear of God is the missing note in modern theology and church life. Our seminaries do not teach it and, as a result, pastors do not preach it. If we can point to one main cause for all the ills of society and the church today, it is the lack of the fear of the Lord. I feel so strongly about this that I wrote *Fearing God*, available at www.faithdefenders.com. If you are a real Christian, you need to understand and practice the fear of the Lord in your daily life.

This means that no Christian student should be so gullible as to simply accept whatever the professor says or what the textbook teaches. It does not matter if he is on a Christian or secular campus. He must learn to discern the worldview that is being taught by the professor or textbook. This is what the Bible recommends in such places as Acts 17:11.

Some students lose their faith while at a Christian college because their professors taught them a humanistic worldview. Having spoken at many Christian colleges, it is obvious that much of what is called "Christian" education is nothing more than secular humanism sprinkled with a few religious terms. Just because the professor begins his class with prayer does not automatically mean that he is going to teach the Christian world and life view. A student must be discerning regardless of what college he attends.

Judge Not Lest Ye Be Judged

**Hunterdon Central High School, Flemington, NJ
Dedication Stone (Class of 1987) - 08/07/09**

"For we do not wrestle against flesh and blood, but against principalities, against powers, against the rulers of the darkness of this age, against spiritual *hosts* of wickedness in the heavenly *places*" (Ephesians 6:12, NKJV)

One of the rationalizations that some people use to escape their biblical responsibility to judge between truth and error is the popular saying, "Judge not lest ye be judged." The vague meaning that is sometimes given to this statement is that we should not judge anyone about anything. Thus when we judge that abortion is murder, the abortionists respond, "Judge not." When we judge that a certain professor is teaching humanism, he cries out, "Judge not." When we judge that unwed mothers are guilty of the sin of fornication, people cry out, "Judge not." We are told that we should never say anything negative about anyone, no matter what they have done.

The problem with a non-judgmental view of life is that it contradicts Scripture. When Jesus said not to judge in Matt. 7:1, He was not speaking to His disciples. He was speaking to the hypocrites who would condemn someone for doing something they themselves were doing (v. 5)! In other words, you don't have the moral right to stand up and condemn other people for being immoral if you are

4

immoral yourself! Jesus was condemning *hypocritical* judgments.

On the other hand, Jesus commanded His disciples to judge people as "false prophets" (Matt. 7:6–20) He told them to "judge a righteous judgment" in John 7:24. He Himself had no problem judging people (Matt. 23:13–39).

A non-judgmental view of life is also absurd. If we did not judge whether people were saved or not, no one could be baptized or join the church. There could be no church discipline if we did not judge people. No criminals would be tried or convicted. Lazy people could not be fired if we could not judge them as lazy. Sick people could not be treated unless we judged them sick. In short, human society would be destroyed if everyone was non- judgmental.

The Apostle Paul repeatedly warned us not to let people deceive us (I Cor. 6:9–11; Gal. 5:19–21). If they are pagans, we should judge them so. If they claim to be Christians but disobey God's law, John tells us to judge them as "liars" (I John 2:4).

The loving thing to do is to judge people according to Scriptural standards. Yes, there will be opposition if you judge righteous judgments. Did not people oppose Jesus? But this opposition is hypocritical because they are judging you for judging! They are condemning you for condemning others! If they really believe that judging others is wrong, then how can they turn around and judge you? So, don't be intimidated by them. Boldly point out their hypocrisy. You have God's Word on your side (Rom. 8:31).

As you study this survival manual, you will be challenged and forced to think deeply about the ultimate questions of life. We will be as frank and as bold as the authors of Scriptures and the Lord Jesus Himself. Never be afraid of the truth. It can only bring you closer to the God who is the Origin of all truth.

CHAPTER ONE

Taking the First Steps

Venice, Italy (1981)

As you prepare to enter college, you need to think about WHY you are going to college. If you do not have clear goals that designate exactly what you want to accomplish at college, you will experience frustration and will end up wasting a lot of time and money. Remember,

If you aim at nothing,
you are bound to hit it.
If you fail to plan,
you plan to fail.

In the New Testament, we are told that we are to run the race that God has set before us (Heb. 12:1–2). And we should not think that it is enough just to make it to the end. We must run to *win*! We must strive for excellence in all that we do. This is how the Apostle Paul put it,

> Do you not know that in a race all the runners run, but only one gets the prize? Run in such a way as to get the prize. Everyone who competes in the games goes into strict training. They do it to get a crown that will not last; but we do it to get a crown that will last forever. Therefore I do not run like a man running aimlessly; I do not fight like a man beating the air. (I Cor. 9:24–26)

The Curse of Mediocrity

Since the Scriptures call us to strive to do the best we can in whatever we do, we must not fall into the curse of mediocrity. The curse of mediocrity would have us believe that the most important thing in life is to be a "balanced" person. Thus we should not work too hard at anything. We should do only what is required of us. We should not attempt to excel or to be superior in anything that we do. The absolute minimum should be the highest we go. In other words, we should only be "one of the guys," i.e., an "average" or "balanced" person.

The Chief End of Man

Mediocrity is condemned by such Scriptures as I Cor. 10:31 and Col. 3:23 where we are told that man exists to glorify God. Thus the glory of God is the goal of man's existence. We must excel to do the very best we can unto the glory of our Creator who is the Sovereign Lord of the universe.

Do you live unto the glory of God? The Apostle Paul said that whenever we do anything we should do it to God's glory. Thus we cannot be lazy, sloppy, or mediocre. We must strive to *do* the very best we can in order to *be* the best we can for the glory of God. Pause right now and say to yourself, "I exist for the glory of God."

This perspective is desperately needed today because far too many people think that God exists to make people happy. They view God as some kind of heavenly vending machine that exists for the pleasure of man. They demand that God provide them with whatever they want and then they get bitter if they do not get it. But God does not exist for man's happiness. Man exists for the glory of God.

The glory of God thus becomes the main motivation for excellence in academic studies. We do not want to bring shame on the name or cause of Christ by being sloppy or shoddy in our academic work. We want to bring glory to Christ and His Gospel. As Jesus taught us in Matt. 5:16,

> Let your light shine before men, that they may see your good deeds and glorify your Father in heaven.

The Apostle Paul also commands us in I Cor. 10:31,

> So whether you eat or drink or whatever you do, do it all for the glory of God.

Living for the glory of God means that instead of striving to do the absolute minimum to get by, we must strive to do the maximum to be the best that we can to the glory of God. If we have a class assignment that asks for a ten page paper, we will do fifteen pages. If we have a reading assignment of two books, we will read three or more books. Our motto will be, "Only the best for God." In other words, you have to *work* to glorify God. God is never glorified by laziness.

Diligence vs. Slothfulness

The book of Proverbs constantly tells us that diligence and hard work are the keys to success. Laziness leads to poverty and failure.

> Lazy hands make a man poor, but diligent hands bring wealth. (Pro. 10:4)

> Diligent hands will rule, but laziness ends in

8

slave labor. (Pro. 12:24)

Do you see a man skilled in his work? He will serve before kings; he will not serve before obscure men. (Pro. 22:29)

We must be diligent and hard working in all that we do. This means that we should not be lazy or slothful. We should excel to do the most and to be the best of which we are capable. Thus instead of viewing college as "party time," we should view college as a time for glorifying God. Instead of wasting time, we should be preparing to be successful in life.

Make no doubt about it. Academic success now will reap financial rewards in the future. Be not deceived on this point. If you are lazy and slothful while in college, you will probably be lazy and slothful when you get out of college. Proverbs tells us that only the diligent and hardworking will be rewarded by the fruits of their labor.

Losing Your Soul

Many students began their college experience with their Christian faith intact. But by the time of their senior year, many of them no longer attend church or even claim to be "saved." What happened to their commitment to Christ?

The vast majority of students lose their faith because they fall prey to the temptations of immorality and drugs. In the vast majority of cases there were no lofty ideals or motives behind their apostasy. Neither were there any great intellectual problems that caused them to abandon the Church. They left the faith because it stood in the way of their own personal pleasure.

In Jesus' "Parable of the Sower," only one out of the four professing Christians was really saved. The other three fell away because of a lack of interest, peer pressure, persecution, trials and the temptations of this world (see: Matt. 13:1–9).

The Warnings of Scripture

Because so many students lose their faith during their college experience, we would do well to pause and consider the causes of their apostasy. The Scriptures warn us in many places that there is the ever present danger of departing from the faith.

> Be self-controlled and alert. Your enemy the devil prowls around like a roaring lion looking for someone to devour. (I Pet. 5:8)

> Turn away from godless chatter and the opposing ideas of what is falsely called knowledge, which some have professed and in so doing have wandered from the faith. (I Tim. 6:20, 21)

> See to it that no one takes you captive through hollow and deceptive philosophy, which depends on human tradition and the basic principles of this world rather than on Christ. (Col. 2:8)

While the Scriptures repeatedly warn us that it is possible for someone who *professes* to be saved to fall away from the faith (Heb. 6:4–6), this is in contrast to someone who actually *possesses* true salvation. The Apostle John tells us that a true believer cannot fall away.

> They went out from us, but they did not really belong to us. For if they had belonged to us, they would have remained with us; but their going showed that none of them belonged to us. (I John 2:19)

Are You Real or Counterfeit?

It is very important that you make sure that you are a *real* Christian and not a counterfeit because there are many people today who think they are saved when in reality they have never personally known God. Jesus warned us of this possibility in Matt. 7:21–23.

Many people believe in Christ because they were raised in a Christian home and attended a Christian church. They "prayed" to "receive" Jesus and have run down countless aisles at church or camp meetings. Perhaps they were leaders in their youth group. But regardless of their experience in the church, once they got to college they soon abandoned their faith.

What should your attitude be as you enter college? Should you smugly assume that you are saved and that all is well? What did the Apostle Paul say in I Cor. 10:12?

> So, if you think you are standing firm, be careful that you don't fall!

If we take the Bible seriously, then we must examine ourselves to see if we are really in the faith.

> Examine yourselves to see whether you are in the faith; test yourselves. (II Cor. 13:5)

> Therefore, my brothers, be all the more eager to make your calling and election sure. For if you do these things, you will never fall. (II Pet. 1:10)

In the light of these Scriptures, it is clear that the most important priority in your life as you prepare to go to college is to make sure that you truly know the Lord Jesus Christ as your personal Lord and Savior.

How to Know If You Are Really Saved

In order for you to discern if you have had a true conversion experience, it is necessary to think through some of the biblical evidences and tests of regeneration. The entire book of First John is the fullest treatment of the assurance of salvation in the New Testament. In

I John 5:13 we are told, "I write these things to you who believe in the name of the Son of God so that you may know that you have eternal life."

Just as John gave us the theme for his entire Gospel in John 20:31, he also gave us the theme for his entire Epistle in I John in 5:13. Since John is dealing with the subject of how we can know if we are really saved, he lays out his material in a very logical and orderly manner.

An important distinction must be pointed out at this juncture. Salvation and assurance of salvation are NOT the same thing. Salvation has to do with justification that is by faith alone in Christ by grace alone. This is in contrast to assurance of salvation that has to do with sanctification, i.e., the Christian life.

Salvation deals with the issue of "being" while assurance deals with "well-being." Salvation determines whether you get to heaven while assurance determines how happy you are along the way. While obedience and works do not play a role in salvation, they do play a vital role in assurance of salvation. Your life must back up your lip when it comes to assurance of salvation.

Throughout the New Testament we are told that the proof of true salvation is obedience (John 8:12, 31; 14:15, 21–23; 15:14; I Cor. 6:9–11; II Cor. 5:17; Gal. 5:19–23). We do not have the right to say that we are saved if we are living in disobedience at the same time (I John 2:4). While the ground of our salvation is grace alone, the test of our assurance of salvation is obedience.

In his Epistle, the Apostle John constantly challenges our assurance by saying, "Hereby we know Him if...." He demands that we "prove" or "test" our assurance of salvation. This proof is obtained by self-examination. John calls upon us to examine our lives to see if God has truly given us a new heart.

I. Examine Your Faith

The first thing that John calls us to examine is our faith. John stresses that there are two distinct areas of faith that we must examine in order to see if we are truly the children of God.

A. The Content of Your Faith

First John tells us to examine the content of our faith. This means that what we believe about God, the Bible, Jesus Christ, salvation, sin, etc., is very important. If we do not believe in the historic Christian Faith, then we are not saved.

> This is how you can recognize the Spirit of God: Every spirit that acknowledges that Jesus Christ has come in the flesh is from God. (I John 4:2)

> If anyone acknowledges that Jesus is the Son of God, God lives in him and he in God. (I John 4:15)

> Everyone who believes that Jesus is the *Christ is born* of God. (I John 5:1)

As you enter college, you will meet people who openly deny that Jesus was the Christ. Marxist and atheistic professors will even claim that Jesus never existed and thus Jesus is a myth! Other people will claim that Jesus was only a humble Jewish rabbi, a moral teacher or a good example. Occultists will claim that all men are little christs and gods!

The issue of whether Jesus was *the* Christ is so important that the Apostle John said that anyone who denied it was a liar and an antichrist!

> Who is the liar? It is the man who denies that Jesus is the Christ. Such a man is the antichrist — he denies the Father and the Son. No one who denies the Son has the Father; whoever acknowledges the Son has the Father also. (I John 2:22, 23)

John warned us not to accept false prophets and their false

doctrines. We must test all religious claims and teachings according to Scripture.

> Dear friends, do not believe every spirit, but test the spirits to see whether they are from God, because many false prophets have gone out into the world … every spirit that does not acknowledge Jesus is not from God. This is the spirit of the antichrist, which you have heard is coming and even now is already in the world. (I John 4:1–3)

Sincerity Is Not Enough!

Do not be fooled by the rather stupid idea that it does not really matter what you believe as long as you are sincere. The Apostle John makes it absolutely clear that if someone does not believe in the Gospel, they are already under the just condemnation of God (John 3:18).

What can you say to people who are so foolish to think that sincerity is enough in religion? Point out to them that since sincerity is never enough anywhere else in life, why should it be enough in religion? Is sincerity enough in medicine, law, finances or politics? Ask them, "Do you really believe that it does not matter:

- What a doctor does as long as he is sincere?
- How a lawyer handles a case as long as he is sincere?
- How a financial manager handles money as long as he is sincere?
- What a politician does as long as he is sincere?
- If you got on a bus sincerely thinking you were on your way to New York City, when you actually got on a bus going to California, would your sincerity alter the

fact that you are going in the wrong direction?

Sincerity has nothing to do with the issue of Truth. Can't we be sincerely wrong?

Are All Religions True?

Since all religions contradict each other, either one religion is the true religion or none of them are true. They cannot all be true. But what do we say if we run across someone who says, "I have my truth and you have your truth. Truth is whatever you want it to be."

Point out to them that they are hypocrites because they do not really believe such nonsense. They cannot live what they believe. For example, if their bank took away all their money and said, "We have our truth that you never gave us any money, and you have your truth that you did," this person would be the first to say that truth is objective!

The Parent Trap

Another possible snare you must avoid at all costs is the blind faith of some parents. Now it is clear that Christian parents should desire that their children come to know and love the Lord Jesus early in life. This desire is one evidence that *they* are saved. A parent who claims to be saved but does not manifest any concern to see his children saved is no more saved than a stone.

While the desire to see your children saved is proper and necessary, some parents become so desperate to believe that their children are saved that they will grasp at anything. Even when their son or daughter openly denies the faith and engages in gross wickedness, they will still comfort themselves by saying, "Well, at least my son is saved. He may not act like it now but I know he is saved because he accepted Jesus when he was five years old. He doesn't go to church anymore and married an unbeliever but I still say he is saved."

Instead of facing the reality that their child is on his way to hell, some parents will cling to false hopes so they can sleep at night.

But instead of seeking their own psychological comfort, they should seek the conversion of their child by telling him the truth. Many sons and daughters have ended up in hell because their parents repeatedly told them that they were saved even while they were living in wickedness. Instead of helping their children, they damned them forever.

Salvation Is a Work of God

The basic problem is that we tend to forget that salvation is a work of God and not a work of man. We are not saved because we prayed but because *God* gave us a new heart. In such places as John 1:13; 3:3, 5 and Rom. 9:16, we are repeatedly told that God saves us by His power and not by our prayers.

Some people have a magical view of prayer in which if anyone, regardless of his age or understanding, prays certain words such as "Come into my heart, Lord Jesus," he is automatically saved! It never dawns on them that salvation is something the Lord does. Salvation is not worked by such magical incantations.

God is viewed as a vending machine that mechanically dispenses salvation the moment someone pushes the right button by saying the right words. Thus they get their children to ask Jesus into their heart and then they sit back and comfort themselves that their children are saved regardless if there is ever any evidence that God has truly done a work in their hearts.

The only way that we can know if God has saved our children is by their lifestyle. If they are saved, they have become new creatures in Christ and will show it by a change in their attitudes and actions (II Cor. 5:17). In other words, there will be clear evidence in their lives that God has worked true repentance and faith in their hearts. Thus they will:

- Thirst after the living God (Psa. 42:2).
- Hunger after righteousness (Matt. 5:6).
- Talk about the Lord and seek Christian fellowship (Mal. 3:16–18).

- Be fervent in prayer (Gal. 4:6).
- Be interested in, read, and enjoy Scripture (Psa. 1; 119:9, 11).
- Love the Law of God (Psa. 119:97).
- Go to church because they want to (Psa. 84).

If you are truly saved, you will show it by the way you live.

B. The Character of Your Faith

John not only tells us to examine the content of our faith but also the character or kind of faith we have. This is why in the Greek, John always uses the word "believe" in the present tense. He never refers to a date or a decision in the past as the basis of one's assurance of salvation.

Not once in the New Testament does anyone claim to be saved because they "made a decision" in the past. Rather we are told that assurance of salvation is always based on the present fact of personal trust in the Lord Jesus Christ.

> Everyone who [is believing right now] that Jesus is the Christ is born of God. (I John 5:1)

In John 3:16, John refers to faith in the present tense.

> For God so loved the world that He gave His only begotten Son, that whosoever [is believing right now] in him shall not perish but have eternal life.

When people apply for membership in a church, if the only question they are asked is "When were you saved?" a terrible mistake has been made. Where was such a question ever asked in Scripture? Far too many people base their assurance of salvation solely on some decision they made in the past when there is nothing presently in their lives to show that they love God!

17

Far too many churches are filled with unregenerate people whose unspiritual lives are excused by calling them "carnal Christians" or "nominal Christians." They only show up Sunday morning. They never volunteer for anything. They are not interested in studying the Bible. They don't witness at work or have private or family devotions. They are more concerned about the building than the ministry. They are pragmatists who consistently ignore or disobey Scripture. In short, there is no evidence in their lives that they are really saved.

Their "assurance" of salvation is based solely on some event in the past that has no bearing on the present. Such professions of faith are quite worthless, says James (James 2:14–26). While works do not save us, once we are saved, we will work for the Lord (Eph. 2:8–10). When someone wants to join a church, they should be asked, "What evidence do you see in your life right now that would lead you to believe that God has given you a new heart?"

This kind of question will reveal false confessions of faith and lead to true conversions. It will focus on the present spiritual state of people and deal with their present situation.

Questions to Ask Yourself

As you prepare to enter college or university, ask yourself:

- Am I really a Christian?
- Have I really been saved?
- Do I truly love and serve the Lord Jesus Christ?
- Do I have a personal relationship with Him?
- Do I live to bring glory to God?
- What evidence is there in my life that proves that I am saved?

Is it not better to search your soul *now* before you get to college, than to be overwhelmed by temptations once you get there? Many young people, like Judas, thought they were Christians. But, in the end, it was revealed that they had never truly been saved. You must search your soul to make sure that you know the Lord Jesus Christ as your own personal Savior. If you have never made that step of commitment on your own then you should do so now.

One of the reasons why we must examine ourselves to see if we are really saved is that childhood conversions seldom work out. Indeed, most of the young people who stop attending church after they reach the age of 18 had a childhood conversion in which they prayed to "receive" Jesus. But their conversion was psychological instead of spiritual.

The sad truth is that the vast majority of childhood conversions never pan out. Most churches experience a 75% or greater drop-out rate for their young people. While it is true that God can save a child, it is also true that we can get a child to pray to "receive" Bozo the Clown or Jesus with equal success. Beware of false assurance.

II. Examine Your Life

The Apostle John tells us to examine the way we live. He calls us to examine our lives in two ways.

A. Examine Your Heart: Your Attitudes

One of the clearest evidences of true conversion is a proper attitude toward God's Law. In I John 5:3 we are told that God's commandments are not grievous or burdensome. This means that the true child of God does not view God's Law as a straightjacket that keeps him from true happiness. Instead, a real Christian will view God's Law as containing the principles of success and true happiness in life.

> Do not let this Book of the Law depart from your mouth; meditate on it day and night, so that you may be careful to do everything written in it. Then you will be prosperous and successful. (Joshua 1:8)

In order to examine your own heart to see if you are truly saved, ask yourself the following questions:

- Do I love the Law of God or do I view it as

something that is keeping me from true happiness?
- Do I prize God's Law as principles of success or as a club to beat me down?
- Do I view the Law as a hindrance to what I really want to do?

One of the clearest evidences of salvation is when someone comes to *love* the Law of God with all of his heart. In Psalm 119:97, David reveals that the child of God *loves* the Law of the Lord. When someone is saved, God writes His Law in his heart (Jer. 31:33–34) and he will never depart from Him (Jer. 32:40). If your attitude toward the Law of God is negative then you must question whether or not God has ever given you a new heart.

The Apostle John not only tells us to examine our attitude to the Law of God, but he also calls upon us to examine the emotional focus of our lives (I John 2:9–11, 15–17).

Do we love what God loves and hate what God hates? If we love what God hates then we are the enemies of God (James 4:4). If we hate what God loves then we are not on God's side. We are to think God's thoughts after Him and to love what God loves and hate what God hates.

If someone is truly converted, he will love the people of God and seek out and enjoy Christian fellowship. He will love to talk about the Lord with those who know Him. This is how the righteous can be distinguished from the wicked according to Mal. 3:16–18. John also teaches this truth in the N.T.

> We know that we have passed from death to life, because we love our brothers. (I John 3:14)

> Dear friends, let us love one another, for love comes from God. Everyone who loves has been born of God and knows God. (I John 4:7)

On the other hand, if we hate what God loves and love the things of this world instead, then we know that the love of the Father is not in us.

> Do not love the world or anything in the world. If anyone loves the world, the love of the Father is not in him. For everything in the world — the cravings of sinful man, the lust of his eyes and the boasting of what he has and does — comes not from the Father but from the world. (I John 2:15, 16)

This means that we must ask ourselves some questions.

- Do I naturally gravitate toward other Christians or do I naturally hang out with non-Christians?
- Do I seek out the company of "spiritual" Christians or do I seek the company of "carnal" Christians?

It is a wise saying that, "Birds of a feather flock together." This means that who you choose to be your friends will indicate the true spiritual state of your heart. If you seek the company of non-Christians who are worldly in mind, attitude and actions, then you are probably not saved no matter how many times you have "prayed" or run down an aisle. The Apostle Paul warned us in I Cor. 15:33, "Be not deceived, evil company will corrupt good behavior."

During your high school experience, did you seek the company of those who loved the Lord or did you run with the non-Christian crowd? If you naturally gravitated to the company of non-Christians, you did so because you felt more comfortable around them. This is a good indication that you are not saved

B. Examine Your Life: Your Actions

Those who claim to love and know Christ and yet willfully disregard and disobey His Law do not give any evidence of true conversion.

"The man who says, 'I know him,' but does not do what he commands is a liar, and the truth is not in him." (I John 2:4)

Jesus explicitly taught that obedience to God's Law is the clearest evidence of true conversion.

"If you love me, you will keep my commandments." (John 14:23)

"If you abide in my word, then you are truly my disciples." (John 8:31)

The kind of obedience demanded in Scripture is *purposeful* obedience, not perfect obedience. While a true Christian sins in many ways every day (James 3:2), yet he continues daily to purpose in his heart not to sin against God's Law. Sin aggravates him and disturbs him. It is an unwelcomed guest. He yearns for holiness more than happiness.

The Apostle John was very wise in calling upon us to examine ourselves to see if we are truly saved. What if we were to gain the whole world but lose our immortal soul? Of what profit would there be if we deceive ourselves into thinking that we are saved when we are not saved?

Do not be deceived. The truth is never afraid of examination. The light is never afraid of exposure. If you are saved, all the self-examination in the world will not unsave you. If you are truly converted, you will not lose your salvation because you question it. Doubts have never damned anyone but false confidence has led millions into hell. If you are not converted and you do not examine yourself, then you will go on thinking you are saved when in reality you are still under the wrath of Almighty God.

What If You Fail the Test?

What if you have come to the conclusion that you do not have the evidences of true conversion as given by the Apostle John?

22

First of all, face reality. Don't try to evade or ignore the fact that your life does not have the evidences required by Scripture as manifesting true conversion. Don't try to run from the problem or cover it over with cheap shoddy prayers or quick decisions. Don't run down the nearest aisle and make some emotional demonstration in the attempt to delude yourself into yet another false conversion.

Second, tell your pastor that you doubt your salvation and that you want the real thing this time. Ask him to pray for you as you seek the Lord by yourself for the first time in your life.

It is important that you seek the Lord all by yourself because when you get to college your pastor and your parents will not be there to help you. You will have to stand up on your own two feet. You must know within yourself where you stand with God.

This perhaps is the most important turning point in your life. Jeremiah 29:13 says that if you seek the Lord with all of your heart you will certainly find him. In Rom. 10:13, the Apostle Paul says,

> Whoever shall call upon the name of the
> Lord shall be saved.

These precious promises point you toward the Lord Jesus Christ as the only one who can save you.

Perhaps the following prayer will help you in your commitment to Christ. Such a commitment could well be the turning point in your life as you prepare to enter college. The words are not magical. This is just an example of how to cry out to the Lord for salvation.

> "Lord Jesus, I confess to you and all of heaven that I am a sinner and that I cannot save myself. You have done everything that is needed for my salvation. I ask you to give me a new heart. Work salvation in me. Save me as I now submit to your Lordship over all of my life. Please make me your servant."

The issue of assurance of salvation involves submission to the

Lordship of Christ. Don't be deceived by those who peddle a cheap assurance in which you can have Jesus as Savior without bowing to Him as Lord (Rom. 10:9; Col. 2:6). You cannot cut the Lord Jesus Christ into pieces and accept only a part of Him.

The Lordship of Christ

After one is saved, the Lordship of Christ over all of life must be reaffirmed *daily*. This is why the Apostle Peter when writing to fellow Christians reminded them to renew Christ's Lordship in their hearts: "In your hearts set apart Christ as Lord." (I Pet. 3:15)

The Lordship of Christ means that you are willing to live for the glory of God and to demonstrate that God's will for your life is perfect, good and acceptable. Thus in Rom. 12:1, 2, the Apostle Paul tells us to present ourselves as a living sacrifice to God.

> Therefore, I urge you, brothers, in view of God's mercy, to offer your bodies as living sacrifices, holy and pleasing to God — which is your spiritual worship. Do not conform any longer to the pattern of this world, but be transformed by the renewing of your mind. Then you will be able to test and approve what God's will is — his good, pleasing and perfect will.

Have you made a definite commitment to serve God all the days of your life? Have you surrendered everything in your life to the Lordship of Christ? Have you made Christ the Lord of your life? Do you seek to serve Him in all you do? Do you seek His will for your life or do you seek to do only what you want?

The Lordship of Christ is not something that we once affirmed and then never bother with again. It is not to be viewed as some cheap decision that we made at an altar years ago. Since we face temptations to sin and to unbelief daily, we must reaffirm our commitment to the Lordship of Christ daily. This is why the Lord Jesus Christ emphasized that we must take up our cross and deny ourselves daily.

> If anyone would come after me, he must deny
> himself and take up his cross daily and follow
> me. (Luke 9:23–26)

Perhaps the following prayer will help you to reaffirm the Lordship of Christ in your life. This is not meant to be a once and for all experience or commitment to Christ. Neither should you view these words as magical. Merely saying these words will not do anything. But it is the God to whom you pray who can work true repentance and submission in your heart. This prayer is intended to be an example of the daily affirmation of the Lordship of Christ that should take place in the life of every true believer.

> "Lord Jesus, I love you because you first
> loved me. Just as you gave your life for me, I
> now give my life to you. I present my body
> as a living sacrifice to you that I may prove
> that your will is good and acceptable. I now
> reaffirm your Lordship over all of life."

Summary

The Bible calls upon Christians to bow before the Lordship of Christ. We cannot say, "Come in Savior but stay out Lord." We must put our trust and confidence in the Lord Jesus Christ for if the foundation be false, the house cannot stand. The first step toward Christian maturity is to discern where you stand in your relationship with God.

Questions for Discussion

1. What are my goals in life?
2. What role does God play in the decisions I make and the goals I set?
3. What conclusion must be drawn if God does not really make a difference in my life?
4. Do I live for the glory of God or only for my own

personal pleasure?

5. What evidence is there in my life that God has given me a new heart?

6. Do I hunger and thirst after righteousness or only after the things of this world?

7. Do I feel more comfortable among non-Christians or among Christians?

8. Do I desire to serve the Lord to the best of my ability or do I think only of personal pleasure, affluence, and popularity?

9. Do I view God, the Bible, the Church, and God's Law as hindrances or helps in my life?

10. Do I strive for excellence and success or do I settle for being mediocre?

11. Do I want to find, follow and finish God's will for my life or do I want to fulfill my own goals in life?

CHAPTER TWO

Knowing the God Who Made You

Bahamas, 1990

Have you ever asked yourself the question, "Why am I here?" One of the marks of maturity is that we begin to ask ourselves the ultimate questions of life. Have you ever wondered where you came from, why you are here, and where you are going? These questions focus on issues that are essential to an understanding of human existence. If you cannot answer them or your answer is wrong, you will not be able to live life to its fullest.

The secular humanists of the 21st Century ignore the great questions of life because they have finally come to the conclusion that there are no *secular* answers to such questions. They are quite aware of the *religious* answers that center on God as the Origin of Meaning. But they refuse to consider religion as a viable answer. Thus they do not want people to ask themselves questions concerning the origin, nature, purpose, or destiny of human life. Such questions invariably lead to God.

By coming to the conclusion that life is without meaning, the humanists have completely verified what Solomon wrote in the Book of Ecclesiastes thousands of years ago. In this book, Solomon points out that if one begins without God, life will have no meaning. Regardless if one considers wealth, knowledge, power, or respect among men, life without God is nothing but "vanity of vanities." I give an in-depth analysis of the Book of Ecclesiastes in *The Bible, Natural Law, and Natural Theology: Conflict or Compromise* (www.faithdefenders.com).

The book of Proverbs, in contrast to Ecclesiastes, teaches us that if one begins with God, life will have meaning and significance. The key to a fulfilling life of meaning, significance and dignity is the knowledge of God (Pro. 1:7).

Man was created to know and enjoy his Creator. This is why the Westminster Catechism states as its first point of teaching that the "end" or the purpose of man is "to glorify God and to enjoy Him forever."

Christians believe in a God-centered universe. In other words, the universe exists for the glory and pleasure of God (Rev. 4:11). This includes mankind. Thus we exist in order to bring glory to our Creator.

This is in stark opposition to a humanistic view of life in which man is the center of the universe. If a god or gods are allowed to exist, they exist only to serve man. Thus the happiness of man becomes the goal of life instead of the glory of God.

The Bible opens with the words, "In the beginning God," because God must always come first in all things. Thus the infinite God of Scripture is the Origin, Judge, and Basis of truth, justice, morals, meaning and beauty. If you begin with God you can have these things but if you begin with man you will end in chaos and confusion in which there is no truth.

The history of philosophy eloquently demonstrates that whenever we attempt to view man as the measure of all things, we always end up with skepticism and relativism. Because man is finite and sinful, he is not sufficient in and of himself to be the origin or judge of truth. Only the infinite God of Scripture can serve as the Origin of all things.

With this understanding, the knowledge of God becomes the chief purpose of life. Indeed, the apostle Paul tells us that he viewed everything else in life as nothing more than garbage when compared to the excellence of the knowledge of Christ (Phil. 3:8–10). In John 17:3, Jesus said that the knowledge of God is the central meaning of the eternal life offered to us in the Gospel.

If you are a real Christian, the smile and the frown of God is the most important thing in life. Because you know and love God, you will try to avoid those things that offend Him. You will seek to please Him in all that you do (II Cor. 5:9). You will no longer live unto yourself but unto Him who died and rose for you (II Cor. 5:15).

The knowledge of God not only concerns the heart but also the mind. Thus the Scriptures not only urge us to submit ourselves to God as His servants, but also to understand the nature and character of the God who made us. The first commandment found in the Decalogue has to do with obtaining a true and accurate understanding of the nature of God (Exo. 20:3).

False views of God lead to false views of the universe and man himself. Since we must begin with God, we must begin with a true and accurate understanding of the God who made us.

Theism comes in two forms: monotheism and polytheism.

Monotheism

Monotheism is the belief that there is only one God who exists apart from and independently of the existence of the material universe. God thus does not depend upon the approval or the belief of man for His existence. God is not the creation or projection of man's hopes or fears. His existence does not rely upon man's wishes or prayers. God truly exists in His own being or essence as a cognitive ego who says, "I am that I am."

In this sense, God is the Supreme Being who manifests the attributes of personhood. God thinks, plans, chooses and acts independent of the existence of the universe and the belief or approval of man. God is thus not to be viewed as an "it," but as a person.

God is the Supreme Being who created the universe. He is not to be identified as any kind of impersonal force or energy. He has all the attributes of personality and thinks and feels and acts as a true person.

Monotheism says there is only one true God who is the Creator and Sustainer of the universe. The three great monotheistic faiths are Judaism, Christianity and Islam. Within these three religions and their respective bibles, man is called upon to worship the one true God who is a true person. God is not an impersonal force and man does not participate in God's essence or being and man never becomes a God himself.

Polytheism

The second kind of theism is traditionally called polytheism. This is the belief in many gods. Polytheism can be viewed in terms of a rather primitive animism in which the gods or spirits inhabit everything from tree stumps to animals. Polytheism is also the basis for the ancient Greco-Roman gods such as Zeus and Hercules who supposedly lived on Mount Olympus. It is also the basis for popular Hinduism that claims to worship over three billion gods. It is embraced by southern Buddhism that leads to the worship of many gods.

Many modern-day cults such as Mormonism and the Worldwide Church of God teach the doctrine of polytheism in that they believe that they can become gods and thus there is more than one god.

The Scriptures are clear in teaching that there is only one true God by nature. There were no other gods before God. There are no other gods beside Him. And there will be no other gods after Him. He alone by nature is God. The following Scriptures clearly teach monotheism: Isa. 43:10–13; 44:6–8; 45:5–5, 14, 21–22; 46:9; I Cor. 8:4–6; 10:19–20; Gal. 4:8–9; I Tim. 2:5; 6:15–16.

As I demonstrated in great detail in my book, *Battle of the Gods*, polytheism cannot serve as a sufficient basis for truth, justice, morals or beauty because it cannot supply one single unifying principle for human society. The gods are immoral because they are involved in rape, murder, adultery, just as their human creators are involved in such things. There is constant conflict among the gods themselves. Some gods are good and some are evil. What is good for one god is evil to the next

Polytheism has never produced a sufficient basis for an absolute standard in truth, justice or morals. It cannot work because we must appeal to a higher standard or higher being by which we are able to distinguish a good god from an evil god. It is to this higher being that the monotheists point as being the true and everlasting God.

Atheism is the denial of theism. There are two kinds of atheism: religious and secular.

Religious Atheism

In religious atheism we find such systems as pantheism, which is the belief that the universe and God are, for all practical purposes, identical. Pantheism thus denies that God has His own separate existence apart from the existence of the universe. For the pantheist, the world is God and God is the world. Or, as it is sometimes stated, all is God and God is all. Thus pantheism is a subtle form of atheism in that it denies the existence of a God who stands apart from and independent from the existence of the universe. Pantheists believe that what is, is God.

Pantheism serves as the philosophic base of classical Hinduism, northern Buddhism, Zen Buddhism, Christian Science, Unity, the "mind" cults and the New Age Movement. In its Eastern or Western forms, God is often reduced to an impersonal "it" that forms the basis of the universe. God is referred to as the "force" or "energy" that makes up the world.

Pantheism has always had a difficult time with the problem of evil. Since God is all and all is God and God is good and thus all is good, there is no room for the existence of evil! Pantheism in its Eastern or Western forms always ends up denying the existence of evil. See my book, *Reincarnation and Christianity*, (www.faithdefenders.com).

Because Pantheism denies the existence of evil, it cannot recognize the existence of human suffering. Regardless if one is dealing with a Hindu guru or a New Ager, they will both tell you that there is no such thing as evil, thus there is no such thing as pain or sickness. It is all in the mind. In order for there to be no such thing as pain, there is no such thing as a physical body. Thus they deny the existence of the material world in order to escape the problems of evil and human suffering. One such example would be "holistic medicine" in which the human mind is said to create sickness or health.

Secular Atheism

Secular atheism manifests itself in various philosophical and political systems based on the concept of materialism that is the belief that reality is limited to that which has a physical nature. If something cannot be weighed and measured, it is not capable of sensory knowledge and cannot really exist. Thus God, the soul or the mind do not exist because they are supposedly of an immaterial nature.

Pantheists and materialists represent two extremes. While pantheists deny the existence of matter and affirm the existence of the mind, materialists deny the existence of the mind and affirm the existence of matter! They reduce reality to either matter or mind.

Materialism cannot provide a sufficient basis for truth, justice, morals, meaning or beauty. It is thoroughly committed to an amoral universe in which there are no standards of righteousness, truth, or justice. As I documented in *Death and the Afterlife*, materialism always ends in relativism and skepticism.

It was in this sense that materialism functioned as the basis of Nazism and now functions as the basis of Marxism and Western secular humanism. Human beings are viewed only as a random collection of molecules and have no intrinsic worth, significance or meaning. We must remember that both the Third Reich and the USSR created a vast system of concentration camps where human life had no value.

One great example of materialism is B. F. Skinner's book *Beyond Freedom and Dignity*. In this book, Skinner teaches that man should be viewed simply as an animal or a machine. Thus man does not have more dignity, worth or significance than a vacuum cleaner, a stone or a dog.

Materialism is philosophically absurd for it would have us believe that:

- everything came from nothing,

- order came from chaos,

- harmony came from discord,

- life came from non-life,

- reason came from the non-rational,

- personality came from the non-personal,

- morality came from the non-moral.

Materialism attempts to reduce all of life to the level of a stone or a tree stump. It cannot explain life as it is. It carries within itself the seeds of its own destruction when it says there is no such thing as an idea or a thought. If all "ideas" are simply chemical secretions of the brain, then materialism itself is only a secretion of the brain and is not to be viewed as being any more "true" than any other secretion of the brain. Any philosophic view, such as materialism, that refutes itself, must be viewed with pity as well as disgust.

How to Talk With an Atheist

There are several different kinds of atheists. The kind of atheist that one traditionally runs into on a college or university campus is rather dogmatic and claims, "There is no God." This kind of atheist is emphatic in that he *knows* that God does not exist.

This atheist can be dealt with quickly. The only person who can say with confidence that there has never been and never will be a deity of any shape, size, gender or description in the universe is God Himself. In other words, the atheist would have to become God in order for him to say emphatically that there is no God!

To say that there is no God means that you must have been everywhere at the same time throughout all of the past, present and future and can now state that you did not find any deity of any shape, size or description. In addition to being omnipresent, you would have to be omniscient or all-knowing. And, in order to be omniscient and omnipresent, you would have to be omnipotent. Thus the atheist in order to deny the existence of God would have to become God!

Another kind of atheist is what is traditionally called an "agnostic." There are two kinds of agnostics: ordinary and ornery.

An ordinary agnostic says, "I really don't know if God exists or not. If you can show me enough evidence of His existence I will accept the fact that He exists."

An ornery agnostic says, "I don't know if God exists. You don't know if God exists. Nobody can know if God exists."

When someone says, "God is unknowable" or "God cannot be known," they are giving a self-refuting statement. The only way that someone could say that God's existence is unknowable is that he knows everything about God. Thus the claim that God is unknowable is irrational.

It is also irrational when agnostics assume that if they do not know if God exists, then no one else can know. The attributes of a part cannot be attributed to the whole. Just because they are ignorant of God does not logically imply that everyone else is ignorant.

The typical logical Fallacies used by atheists and agnostics are examined in my book, *The New Atheism and the Erosion of Freedom*. Every student should have a copy of this book before heading off to college.

The ornery agnostic is actually a covert atheist who has been forced by smart theists to admit that traditional atheism is a philosophic absurdity. The attempt to prove a universal negative, namely that God does not exist, is a hopeless and fruitless task. This is why some atheists pretend to be agnostics.

It is interesting to note that the word "agnostic" comes from the Greek word that means ignorant or ignoramus. Most ornery agnostics are quite dogmatic about what they know even though the term that they use to describe themselves — agnostic — means that they do not know anything at all! A true agnostic cannot decide ahead of time what is or is not knowable.

An agnostic is someone who claims that he is open to the existence of God if God's existence can be demonstrated to him in ways that he finds acceptable. The key to this kind of mentality is that all proofs must be "acceptable" to him. Thus whenever you give him a sound evidence for the existence of God based upon human reason or experience, he can get out of it by simply stating that it is not "acceptable" to him. This is why you can chase such agnostics from argument to argument never finding anything that stops them for one moment. They rationalize any evidence that is presented to them.

One example of this kind of procedure is the attempt to deny the historicity of Jesus of Nazareth. Some modern agnostics make the claim that there is no evidence whatsoever that Jesus ever existed.

When one examines their arguments against the traditional evidence for the existence of Christ, one is left with the impression that no historical person's existence would be acceptable if the same standards were applied to them as are applied to Jesus. In this sense, one would have to deny the existence of Caesar Augustus or Abraham Lincoln as well as Jesus of Nazareth.

What we discover is that there is a double standard in operation. Some agnostics apply to the theistic proofs or the existence of Jesus standards of rationality or historicity that they are not willing to apply to any other subject or individual. This at once reveals that most of the arguments given by agnostics, skeptics and free thinkers against the existence of God, inspiration of the Bible and the historicity of Christ are actually based upon logical Fallacies such as "special pleading." When they have to justify their arguments against Christianity, agnostics reveal that they do not have any arguments at all.

Summary

Christianity begins with the biblical assumption of the existence of a God who is the Creator and Sustainer of the universe. The infinite/personal Triune God of the Bible provides the only sufficient basis for truth, justice, morals, meaning and beauty. Only by beginning with the God of the Bible can man have any dignity, worth and significance.

A wonderful window of opportunity has opened for Christian students on secular campuses because humanistic philosophers have finally concluded that there can be no absolutes of any kind. Without absolutes there can be no morality, meaning or purpose to life. Thus they have nothing to offer students but skepticism and relativism. On the other hand, the only ones on campus who have a message of hope are the Christians. They alone stand for absolutes in truth and morals. They alone have meaning, dignity, worth and significance. Now is the time for them to be bold with the Gospel.

Questions for Discussion

1. Please explain the two basic kinds of theism.
2. In what way does monotheism provide an absolute standard for truth, morals, justice and beauty?
3. Can polytheism provide a sufficient base for truth, morals, justice or beauty?
4. What is animism?
5. How many gods are worshipped in India?
6. How is Mormonism related to Hinduism?
7. In what two forms does atheism manifest itself?
8. How is pantheism a subtle form of atheism?
9. How is Christian Science related to Hinduism?
10. Can you name any of the popular science of mind cults?
11. Can any religion based on pantheism cope with the twin problems of the existence of evil and human suffering?
12. Can the philosophy of materialism generate any truth or morals?
13. How would you answer someone who said, "I know that God does not exist"?
14. Why does materialism always lead to totalitarianism in forms of government?
15. If you begin with man instead of God, will you end in total despair and meaninglessness? Why is this?
16. If you begin with God, will you end with truth, morals, justice, beauty, significance and meaning? Why is this?

CHAPTER THREE

Know Thyself

The Trevi Fountain, Rome, Italy (1981)

What is your self-image? Do you view yourself as being limited or unlimited? Do you have an infinite potential to be whatever you want to be? Do you view yourself as being on the same level as a dog or a god?

The issue of a proper self-image is not only essential to an understanding of the nature of man in general but also essential to living a successful life. If you have a very poor self-image, this will cripple your attempt to be successful at anything you do. On the other hand, if you have an overrated self-image, this will produce frustration and perfectionism in that you will attempt to be and do things for which you are not equipped. This is why the apostle Paul urged us not to have too high or too low a view of ourselves (Rom. 12:3).

The Scriptures address the question "What is man?" in such places as Psalms 8:3–9.

> When I consider your heavens, the work of your fingers, the moon and the stars, which you have set in place, what is man that you are mindful of him, the son of man that you care for him? You made him a little lower than the heavenly beings and crowned him with glory and honor. You made him ruler over the works of your hands; you put everything under his feet: all flocks and herds, and the beasts of the field, the birds of the air, and the fish of the sea, all that swim the paths of the seas. O Lord, our Lord, how majestic is your name in all the earth!

Throughout the history of philosophy, mankind has struggled with the issue of a proper self-image. Those who struggled with the issue without the aid of the Holy Scriptures invariably developed either too low or too high a view of man that always led to the loss of any dignity, worth, significance or meaning for human life.

Not only does our view of the nature of man affect our own self-image, but it also directly affects the way we look at economics, politics and society in general.

The Christian View of Reality:
God-Angels-Man-Animals-Things

In the Christian worldview, we begin with God for this is where the Bible begins (Gen. 1:1). God is placed first because He is the Creator and Sustainer of all things. The second category has to do with those beings that we generally call angels or spirits that God created to carry out His work. This class of beings encompasses all angels, good and bad.

The third category is that of man. Man is not God or even a part of God. Neither is man an angel. While the 19th Century romantic idea that people become angels when they die is the foundation of the *Book of Mormon*, the Bible knows nothing of such a concept.

Just as man is not to be confused with God or angels, neither is man to be viewed as an animal or a thing. While animals are creatures of God, they do not have an immortal soul. They were not made in the image of God like man.

The Christian worldview also makes a distinction between animals and things. We must not treat animals as if they were only rocks or machines. This is why in such places as Pro.12:10, we are told, "A righteous man cares for the needs of his animal, but the kindest acts of the wicked are cruel."

In the Christian system, man is placed above animals and things because as God's image bearer he was made the prophet, priest and king over all the earth. This is why he is called to take dominion over it.

> Then God said, "Let us make man in our image, in our likeness, and let them rule over the fish of the sea and the birds of the air, over the livestock, over all the earth, and over all the creatures that move along the ground." (Gen. 1:26)

In the Biblical view, mankind stands uniquely outside of nature. Man is not just one cog among many in the cosmic machine. He was given stewardship over the world. He has the unique responsibility of developing the world around him to its fullest potential to the glory of the God who made him.

The Humanistic View of Reality

In the non-Christian worldview, we find a downward process that ultimately reduces everything to the category of "things." Once you deny the existence of the God revealed in Scriptures, there is no rational basis to believe in the existence of angels. Once you have done away with angelic beings, there is no reason to speak of "man" as if he were unique.

Since it is man's relationship to God as His image bearer that gives man dignity and meaning, once God is gone, man is reduced to being an animal. There is nothing to separate man from animal. Human beings can be viewed as cattle that can be bred, slaughtered and processed at will.

Lest someone think that this is not possible, let us remember that it has already been done. The Nazis' concentration camps used human hair to make cloth; human flesh to make soap; human skin to make pocketbooks, lamp shades, belts and wallets; and human bones to make fertilizer.

The Communists in Russia, China, Vietnam, Cambodia, Cuba, etc., do the same things in principle with their slave labor camps. They have already slaughtered over 150 million people in the 20th Century. Human life is always cheap in non-Christian cultures.

But once you have reduced everything to animal life there is no reason to make a distinction between animals and objects such as rocks. Thus man can be treated as if he had no more significance than a tree stump!

This is the exact position of such totalitarian views as Marxism. Man is viewed as a commodity that either benefits or detracts from the state. People may be murdered at will because they have no more significance than dogs or cats. This is why the Russians starved to death over 5 million Ukrainians, the Cambodian Communists murdered over one half of the population of their country, and the Ethiopian Communists starved to death over half of their people.

The Marxists have murdered millions of people without any sense of guilt because to them people are only *things* and thus they do not have any intrinsic worth, significance, meaning, dignity or freedom.

If you view yourself as being only an animal, you will live and die as an animal. If you view yourself as only a machine, you will live and die as a machine. But if you view yourself as uniquely created to bear God's image and as being called upon to take dominion of this world for the glory of God, then you will live life to its fullest because you will have dignity, worth, significance, meaning and freedom.

Let us examine some of the false views of man that have generated defective self-images that cripple people and limit them from reaching the potential that God planned.

Too Low a View of Man

In those views that have too low a view of man, man is reduced to the level of an animal, a machine or a thing. This has great significance for such things as human rights and civil rights.

At one time, humanistic scientists and politicians decreed that black people were animals and should not be viewed or treated as human beings with dignity, worth or freedom. The Supreme Court at that time in a famous case backed up these humanists by ruling that the Negro was only an animal and hence a "thing" that can be purchased, sold or bartered at will.

What modern humanists failed to mention to their students is that they now believe that all people regardless of race are only animals. Thus no one has an immortal soul and there are really no "human rights" in opposition to "animal rights." This is why totalitarian forms of government arise in which people are viewed and treated as "slaves of the state," i.e. animals There are no intrinsic, civil or human rights because man is only an animal. Man as *man* doesn't have any more "rights" than a groundhog.

In some cases, certain animals have more "rights" than man! We are living in a time when it is a crime to destroy the egg of an eagle or to kill a baby seal but unborn human children can be slaughtered at will! While animal rights activists protest against the use of animals in medical experiments, they suggest using human beings instead! Man is now lower than the animals!

The only basis for human rights or civil rights as expressed in the American founding articles is that there is a supreme Creator who endowed man with certain inalienable rights. These rights are given to man from his Creator and not from the state. The state cannot take away what God has given. Thus man is viewed as having dignity, worth, significance, freedom and meaning because of the existence of the God who made him.

Not only is the dignity of man dependent upon the Judeo-Christian concept of a Creator who invests man with certain inalienable rights, but also the unity of mankind itself is based upon the Biblical model of Adam and Eve being the original parents of the entire human race.

Some evolutionists taught that the different races developed from different primate ancestries and hence are not developed from a single pair (ex. Spencer, Pendell, etc.). Christians believe that all of mankind ultimately came from Adam and Eve. The unity of mankind depends on racial solidarity and a common ancestry. Once you reject the Adam and Eve model of the book of Genesis, you have opened the door for racism.

Some modern evolutionists have tried to escape the theory of multiple origins of the races by taking a leap of faith that all people descended from one male/female primate couple in Africa. They understand that the "Adam and Eve" model is necessary to have any dignity or freedom for humanity. They have borrowed the model from Scripture.

One example of humanistic-based racism was the Nazis' glorification of the Aryan race. They believed that the Aryan race was the superior race that would ultimately produce the "superman." In the light of this commitment to racism, the Germans sought to purify the genetic basis of the Aryan stock by murdering countless millions of Jews, gypsies and other minority racial groups.

It is no surprise to find leaders connected with Planned Parenthood and professors in leading Ivy League colleges and universities who openly teach racism. They have gone on record as teaching that certain racial groups such as blacks be sterilized to prevent them from genetically reproducing their own kind. It is argued that if man is only an animal, then the state should have the right to weed out inferior individuals and entire races.

Another subtle form of racism that has been produced by the idea that man is only an animal, is that childbearing should be controlled by the state and the state should limit reproduction to those who meet various IQ tests or other qualifications.

Man is viewed as an animal that needs to be controlled in order to breed out undesirable qualities. This is the hidden agenda of such books as Skinner's *Beyond Freedom and Dignity*, or Orwell's *1984*.

Once you come to the position that man is only an animal kicked up by a meaningless chance-controlled evolutionary process that is not going anywhere for there is no predetermined plan or goal, you can accept such things as:

abortion:	the murder of unborn children for the sake of convenience or pleasure.
infanticide:	the murder of small children who are in the way of one's pursuit of personal pleasure.
mercy killing:	the murder of handicapped or terminally ill patients for economic reasons.
euthanasia:	the murder of the elderly in order to seize their properties and possessions.

The view that man is only an animal leads to the loss of dignity, worth, significance, meaning and freedom for humanity. Once you come to the conclusion that God is dead, you are driven to the conclusion that man is dead as well.

Too High a View of Man

In opposition to the low view of man that is taught by secular humanists, there are those who are involved in religious forms of humanism that teach a view of man that is too high.

Instead of man being reduced to the level of a dog, they elevate man to the level of a god. They have eaten the forbidden fruit of Genesis 3, which is the great lie that man can become a god.

Man is elevated to godhood by investing him with the attributes and powers that belong only to the Creator of the universe. Just as God created the universe by speaking it into being, man is said to be able to speak his own world into being as well.

Man's potential and power are said to be infinite. He is said to participate in the being and essence of God or to have flowed out of God and is in the process of flowing back into God. It is claimed that man's powers are infinite and absolute. Man can be and do whatever he wants to be or do.

This absurd view of man was taught by the Hindus for thousands of years. It was introduced into the West during the latter part of the 19th Century and has been popularized by all the Hindu gurus that have come to the West seeking their fortunes. One look at the filth, poverty and ignorance of Eastern countries reveals what such a false view of man produces in the lives of those who believe it.

The idea that man is a god is also taught by those involved in the New Age movement. One actress went so far as to claim to be God on national TV! Others speak of the "infinite" potential of every human being. They would have us believe that we are sick only because we think we are sick. We can be healthy, wealthy or wise if we only will it or wish it into being.

This is also the basis of the present fad of parapsychology and ESP experimentation. It is believed that man has "hidden" powers and that he can develop them through ESP. It is hoped that through parapsychology people will be able to develop their infinite potential as little gods to create and control the world around them.

One form of this new godism is what is popularly called "positive thinking." Norman Vincent Peale, the father of positive thinking, has revealed in his autobiography that he derived some of his concepts from such "mind" cults as Unity, Theosophy, Science of the mind, Christian Science, etc.

In each of these cults, man is viewed as being the creator of his own world. In other words, man is his own god and is not in need of God's grace or revelation. Man is self- sufficient and can create his own world through his own inherent powers.

Even some "Christian" groups have fallen into this form of godism. They would have us believe that we can be whatever we want to be and do whatever we want to do if we simply claim it, name it, pray it, or speak it into being. Instead of attributing Creation to the power of God, they claim that God had to tap into the power of "faith" to do it. In other words, God didn't create anything at all. It was the power of "faith" that created the world. Faith is viewed as the omnipotent power that all of us can utilize to create our own worlds. Thus God is pushed out of the universe and is no longer needed for "by faith" we can get whatever we want without Him.

The Biblical View of Man

The Biblical worldview interprets all of life in terms of three basic ideas:

1. The Creation of the universe out of nothing.
2. The radical Fall of man into sin and judgment.
3. The Redemption accomplished by Christ.

In Christian philosophy, we refer to these three principles as Creation, Fall and Redemption. They are the basis of all Christian thinking. This is why they are introduced at the very beginning of the Bible in Genesis 1–3. The rest of Scripture is a development and application of these three concepts to all of life. Just like a three legged stool, remove one of these principles and Christianity falls.

A Scriptural self-image begins with an application of Creation, Fall and Redemption to the nature of man.

Creation

First, in terms of Creation, man is not to be viewed as an animal or machine but as a unique creature created in the image of God. As such man is to be viewed as something wonderful and not as junk.

Man has been invested by his Creator with certain inalienable rights that no one, not even the state, should violate. Man is a free moral agent who has not been programmed deterministically by anything in the world around him. This means that man is responsible for his actions and will be held accountable on the Day of Judgment for how he lived his life.

When you look in a mirror you can say to yourself, "I have been created in the image of God and I have worth, significance, meaning and dignity. I have freedom to develop my potential according to the glory of God and to take dominion of the world around me."

The Fall

In terms of the Fall, when we look in the mirror we see ourselves as sinners who have rebelled against the God who made us.

Man was given the choice of either obeying or rebelling against God. In Genesis 3, man followed the advice of Satan and rebelled against God and plunged the entire human race into guilt and depravity.

This means that we are sinners by nature and sin comes quite naturally to us (Rom. 5:12–19).

The radical nature of the Fall explains the darker side of man's nature. How can such wonderful creatures, beautifully constructed by God with such great potential, do such horrible things? Where does human evil come from? Why do men do the evil they do?

When you look at a mirror you can say to yourself, "I am a sinner in need of God's grace and forgiveness. I have broken God's laws and deliberately transgressed His commandments. I will one day stand before God on the Judgment Day to give an account of every thought, word and deed."

Redemption

The third concept by which the Scriptures interpret all of life is the concept of Redemption. As I demonstrated in my book, *Studies in the Atonement*, God did not leave man in the state of sin, guilt, misery and condemnation. Instead, He sent His Son to do a work of redemption by which not only man but also the world will be redeemed from the evil consequences of the Fall (John 3:16; Rom. 8:19–22).

Salvation or redemption is not to be viewed in terms of absorption or annihilation. When God saves an individual, that person will not be absorbed into God's essence or being. As redeemed individuals we will exist for all eternity.

The atonement is the payment of the price demanded by Justice in order to set us free from the just condemnation of our sins. Christ Jesus has done all that is necessary for our salvation. Our responsibility is simply to receive His wonderful work of salvation (John 1:12). Thus salvation is by the grace of God and it is not based on human merit, performance or work (Eph. 2:8, 9).

Not only is the soul of man redeemed so that after death he can live in the presence of God in heaven, but his body will be redeemed at the Resurrection (1 Thess. 5:23). Thus man and his world are to be redeemed and purified by the Creator through the saving work of Jesus Christ.

God's plan of salvation gives us the solution to the problem of evil. Evil is going to be assessed and brought to judgment one day and then quarantined in a place called hell where it can never again affect the rest of the universe. All of the evil consequences of sin will be eradicated by God's work of redemption. Mankind and his world will be purified from all the effects of Adam's Fall into sin.

The work of Christ is thus the final answer to the problem of evil. Evil will be dealt with either by redemption or judgment. Christ has triumphed over sin and will one day bring the universe back into its original harmony and beauty (Col. 1:18–20).

If you are a Christian, when you look in the mirror, you can say to yourself, "I am a child of God through faith in the atoning work of Jesus Christ. I have been saved by grace alone, through faith alone, through Christ alone. He is my Savior and my God. I now trust in Him for all things and live only to please Him."

The biblical position on man involves three foundational concepts: We are wonderfully created in the image of God, terribly marred and twisted by the Fall and marvelously redeemed by the atonement of Christ. Any anthropology that does not take into account the threefold state of man in terms of Creation, Fall and Redemption is not a Christian or biblical perspective.

The threefold biblical view of man in which he is viewed as an image bearer, a sinner and a saint provides us with a sufficient basis not only to develop a proper self-image but also to develop a free society.

The authors of the American Constitution believed that man was a sinner and thus he needed a system of checks and balances for government to work. They believed that power corrupts and that absolute power corrupts absolutely. Therefore no branch of the government is to gain the supremacy over the other branches of the government. By its system of checks and balances, totalitarianism and tyranny can be prevented in this great land.

Capitalism and the free market system developed out of the Christian view of man. A planned economy has always led to utter disaster. Countries that have gone into Marxism cannot even feed themselves. Without the free economies of the West, these countries would have gone down in ruin years ago.

The only hope of humanity is to return to the Christian view of man and to the principles of form and freedom, dignity and worth that have been generated by the Christian system. The only alternative is totalitarianism that treats man only as a thing and ultimately means no truth, morals, justice, dignity, worth, significance, meaning, freedom or unity, abortion, infanticide, mercy killing, suicide, euthanasia, racism, genetic engineering, statism, socialism, Marxism, Fascism, totalitarianism and the death of a culture.

Summary

The healthiest self-image is the one derived from Scripture because it describes man as he really is. Thus there is no contradiction between what we experience in life and what we find in the Bible. Man and his world are understandable only if we look at them from the perspective of Creation, Fall and Redemption. Any other world view is doomed to fail.

Questions for Discussion

1. Is it possible to have too low or too high a view of man?
2. How will a wrong view of man affect your self-image?
3. Does a proper self-image have anything to do with success in life?
4. As a Christian, where should you obtain your self-image?
5. If you view man as being only an animal, what consequences will result in society?
6. On what concept is abortion, infanticide, mercy killing and euthanasia based?
7. How would you answer someone who said that abortion, infanticide, mercy killing, euthanasia, genetic engineering and racism were perfectly proper because man was only an animal?
8. Have you encountered individuals who believed that man is a god or can become a god or is a part of god? What would you say to them?
9. The idea of human autonomy is that man is self-sufficient and is not in need of God's grace or revelation. Thus man can

discover truth, morals, justice and beauty without God's word. Is this really possible?

10. Ethical relativism is the idea that there are no absolute standards for truth, justice, morals or beauty but each person is to develop his own standards. Can such a view lead to a just and orderly society or will it result in anarchy?

11. What are the implications of man being created in the image of God?

12. From whom do our "inalienable rights" come? Is it correct to say that the Constitution gives us rights or that it only recognizes those rights we already have from the Creator?

13. What significance does the radical Fall into sin have for mankind in general and man's political structure for government in particular?

14. Is God interested only in the saving of the soul or does salvation include the body and the world?

15. How will Jesus Christ solve the problem of evil?

CHAPTER FOUR

Getting the Essentials Down

The Milan Cathedral, Milan, Italy (1981)

Going to college for many young people means that for the first time in their life they must deal with a world that is quite hostile to Christianity without the support of their family, friends, or church. They enter a time of testing in which it will be revealed if they are really saved.

One of the most important aspects of spiritual survival on a college campus is to keep in mind the essentials of the Christian life. The first signs of apostasy or falling away from the Lord are always found in the abandonment of the essentials of the Christian life.

We have seen it far too often. Within a semester or two, many professing Christian students stop reading the Bible, praying, going to church, attending Christian campus groups or witnessing. By their senior year they either openly deny the Gospel or try to deceive their parents by attending church when they are home on the holidays. How can they walk away from the claims of the Gospel?

The key is to realize that their religion was something *external* to them. Their profession of salvation was the result of the external influences of a Christian home and church. Because there was no true Christianity in their hearts, once the external pressures of home and church were removed, they reverted to their natural pagan state. As soon as they were in a situation where they did not *have* to go to church, they stopped going.

But what if we go to a Christian college? Will this solve the problem? What often surprises students is that they can lose their faith at a Christian college as quickly as they can lose their faith at a state university or college. Why is this true?

Campus life gives students the opportunity to reveal what is really in their heart of hearts. If they love the things of the world and they view college time as "party time," they will party regardless if they are at a Christian or secular college. They will be involved in immorality and drugs regardless if they are attending an evangelical or state school. What is in their hearts will ultimately come out (Mark 7:21–23).

Going to a Christian college does not guarantee that you will keep the faith because the temptations to sin will be there. While the Christian atmosphere will put a damper on open wickedness, you can still find it if you look hard enough. You must not make the mistake of thinking that the external environment of a Christian college will automatically keep you from apostasy.

As a professing Christian, you should desire to retain your faith during your college years. Your parents and your pastor are also concerned that you survive all the spiritual tests, trials and temptations that one faces on a college campus. Only a fool would not seriously consider the possibility of apostasy. Surveys have clearly demonstrated that almost 75% of freshmen who profess to be Christians abandon Christianity by their senior year. Make sure that your faith is a true saving faith. You need to possess salvation as well as profess it. If you are truly converted you will endure unto the end (Matt. 24:13).

The warnings of the New Testament concerning the possibility of apostasy should be taken at face value. Apostasy concerns the Falling away of *professing* Christians from their belief and obedience to the Scriptures. All theological systems recognize that *professing* Christians can fall away. This happens far too often during their college years.

We can claim to be saved only as long as we are living and believing according to Scripture. If we deny the doctrines of the Gospel or disobey God's law, we do not have the right to call ourselves "Christians."

"By this gospel you are saved, *if* you hold firmly to the word I preached to you. Otherwise, you have believed in vain." (I Cor. 15:2)

"But now he has reconciled you by Christ's physical body through death, *if* you continue in your faith, established and firm, not moved from the hope held out in the gospel." (Col. 1:22–23)

"But Christ is faithful as a son over God's house. And we are his house, *if* we hold on to our courage and the hope of which we boast." (Heb. 3:6)

"See to it, brothers, that none of you has a sinful, unbelieving heart that turns away from the living God…We have come to share in Christ *if* we hold firmly till the end the confidence we had at first." (Heb. 3:12, 14)

"The one who says, 'I have come to know Him,' and does not keep His commandments, is a *liar*, and the truth is not in him." (I John 2:4)

All professing Christians must take care that they do not "fall from grace" (Gal. 5:4). There were people in Christ's own day who claimed to be His disciples and yet they turned away from Him (John 6:66). Did not Jesus reveal that some of His disciples were not really saved but were in reality the "children of the devil" (John 8:31–47)? There were many people who at one point had made a profession of faith and then they departed from the Church never to return (I John 2:19).

We should all be concerned about our salvation. Is it real or a sham? How can you survive college with your Christianity intact? This is a very reasonable and rational question. These are the kinds of questions that you must ask yourself in order to prepare yourself for all the trials and temptations you will face in life.

What is the most important thing you can do to survive the spiritual temptations and trials of college life? You must persevere in the private and public means of grace.

What do we mean when we speak of the "means of grace"? The "means of grace" simply refer to those activities that help us to grow in the Christian life. Such things as daily Bible reading, praying, church attendance and Christian fellowship have always been the mainstays of the Christian life.

If we abandon the private and public means of grace, we no longer have any Biblical warrant to claim that we are Christians. It is thus absolutely essential that we continue to do those things that build up our faith and strengthen our submission to the Lordship of Christ (Col. 2:6–8)

1. Daily Bible Reading

The reading of the Bible is essential for the Christian life. In Acts 20:32, we are told that the Word of God is the "word of grace" that will enable us to grow.

We will never be able to develop Christian character if we are not reading about Christ in the Scriptures. This is why in such passages as Psalm 1 or Psalm 119, the reading of Scripture is seen as the primary influence on developing godliness in the life. It is the reading and meditation on Scripture that brings success and prosperity in the Christian life (Josh.1:8).

The reading of the Bible is essential for the "renewing of the mind" (Rom. 12:2). We need to understand God, the world, ourselves and the issues of life. This is why the apostle Paul stated that the purpose of Scripture is to equip the child of God so that he is ready to handle anything that comes his way (2 Tim. 3:16–17).

One of the most important aspects of the reading of Scripture is that it must be done *daily*. This can be most effectively done by assigning yourself a chapter in the book of Proverbs that corresponds to the day of the month. For example, on the 5th day of the month, read the 5th chapter of Proverbs. This means that you will be reading through the book of Proverbs every month.

We emphasize the reading of Proverbs because it was specifically written for young people to teach them wisdom and understanding. Wisdom is the ability to look at issues from God's perspective as given in Scripture. Understanding is the application of God's wisdom to a specific problem.

Proverbs helps you to identify certain kinds of people that you should avoid at all costs: fools, sluggards, scoffers, scoundrels, skeptics, con-men, and immoral people. Proverbs equips young people to escape temptation and sin by utilizing the principles of successful living found in God's Word. Everyone should read and apply Proverbs to life every day.

In addition to reading a chapter of Proverbs every day, it would be helpful to read one other chapter of Scripture. It is important to alternate between reading a chapter from the New Testament and a chapter from the Old Testament. In this way you balance the Law and Gospel, the old covenant and the new covenant.

In addition to a daily reading of Scripture, you should be doing detailed studies in the Scriptures. It can be a doctrine or a principle of the Christian life. You can do this in a Bible study group or you can do this by yourself. But the important thing is that you are meditating on Biblical truth.

Although college life can be very exciting and full of activities, it is important that you retain a portion of time for yourself. This is the time that you set aside for the development of your own spiritual and intellectual life. Take dominion of your life and set apart a specific time in which you will devote yourself to the reading of Scripture. Make notes as you read. Write papers on various subjects.

In other words, use the mind that God gave you to search the Scriptures daily (Acts 17:11).

2. Prayer

As you read the Scriptures, you find an emphasis on prayer. We are given such examples as Enoch who "walked with God" (Gen. 5:22). What does it mean to "walk with God"?

Walking with God means that you are living a life in which whenever your mind is free from its responsibilities, it naturally and immediately flies to the presence of God like a homing pigeon. It means that whenever you are faced with a trial or temptation you immediately go to prayer and ask God for wisdom and grace. In this way, you fulfill the Biblical command that we "should always pray and not give up" (Lk. 18:1). Your goal as a Christian is to walk with God every day.

In addition to developing a prayerful attitude, you need to set apart specific times in which you will devote yourself to prayer. You need to pray for the family that you have left behind and for your home church. You need to pray about your friends. You need to pray about class assignments, upcoming tests, opportunities of ministry and opportunities of witnessing to the faculty and fellow students.

It has been almost a hundred years since a "Theology of Prayer" was taught in our schools and practiced in our churches. A prayer-less Christianity is a power-less Christianity. See my little book, *A Theology of Prayer*, if you desire to know what the Bible teaches about prayer.

A true Christian always complains that he does not have enough time to pray and that there are too many things to pray about. A "Christian" student who does not pray because he cannot think of anything to pray about is probably not saved. A prayer-less person is a Christ-less person.

Once God has given someone a new heart, he will instinctively pray to the God who saved him. This is how Ananias was assured that Saul of Tarsus was truly converted. God told Ananias, "Behold, he prayeth!" (Acts 9:11).

3. Christian Books

In addition to reading your Bible and to praying, your years at college provide you with the opportunity to develop a solid Christian perspective on all the academic subjects you are studying. Regardless if you are at a state university or a Christian college, you have a God-given responsibility to discover what the Bible says about history, psychology, physics, science, economics, political science, math, comparative religion, etc.

For the most part, you will never be assigned books that will give you the Christian position. Even on Christian campuses you will usually be given the same secular textbooks used in state universities. This is regrettable but true because most Christian colleges have never developed a distinctively Christian perspective on the subjects they teach. It is assumed that it is "Christian" education because the teacher utters a prayer before he teaches. A Christian college should teach every subject from a biblical perspective. This is rarely the case.

Even though this means that you will have to read more books than are assigned to you by your professor, it will pay off in the long run. Instead of filling your mind with false ideas and concepts that you must shed as fast as you can in order to retain your faith, your years at college will provide you with the opportunity of developing a Christian perspective on all of life. A special bibliography is given at the end of this book that will provide you with some solid Christian books to read.

In addition to reading Christian perspective books such as written by Francis Schaeffer, it would be good if you read Christian books that deal with growth in the Christian life, evangelism, biblical studies, theology and philosophy. You should also read good biographies that set before you examples of godly men and women who affected their generation in a real way.

In short, you need to read, read and read. Then you must think, think and think again if you are going to succeed and excel to greatness. You must understand what Christianity is all about and how it applies to all of life. Since non-Christian professors will not give you this understanding, you will have to get it yourself.

4. Church Attendance

In terms of the public means of grace, the first sign of apostasy is when a professing Christian stops attending church while at college.

All kinds of rationalizations are given. But a rationalization is only a lie stuffed into the skin of an excuse and served up as the truth.

Some students claim that they stopped going to church because they need their sleep Sunday morning. Other students point to exams or papers that are due on Monday and argue that Sunday must be a day of study and preparation. Some students do not attend church because there is not a church "good" enough for them. Whatever the rationalization, these students gradually come to the habit of never attending church while they are away at college. They have fallen away from the Faith.

In the New Testament we are taught that church attendance is not optional for Christians.

> Let us not give up meeting together, as some are
> in the habit of doing, but let us encourage one
> another — and all the more as you see the Day
> approaching. (Heb. 10:25)

The Scriptures view those who stop attending church as being apostates, i.e., no longer Christians (I John 2:19). A true child of God will seek out the fellowship of the saints (Mal. 3:16–18). The New Testament knows nothing of a churchless Christian any more than it knows of a prayerless Christian.

How does one go about choosing a church to attend? If you are away from your home church, the first step is to ask your pastor if he knows of a church he can recommend to you. Perhaps your parents have a friend in the area who attends a good church.

If you have to find a church on your own, there are several things that you should be looking for in the churches you try. Any church that fails the following tests should be avoided.

1. Is there a commitment to the supremacy of Scripture? Is the full inspiration and inerrancy of Scripture clearly taught by this church? Does the pastor believe that the Scriptures alone are to decide all issues of doctrine and life?

2. Does this church clearly teach that salvation is based solely on the unmerited grace of God? Is salvation by grace alone, through faith alone, in Christ alone? Any church that does not

openly teach that the sovereign grace of God is the sole foundation of salvation is not a true Christian church.

3. Does this church discipline its membership? If a member of the congregation falls into sin, is this person dealt with lovingly but firmly according to the biblical principles?

4. Does this church have a proper view of baptism and the Lord's Supper? Do they view these things as means by which we can be saved or as magical ceremonies? Any church that views baptism or the Lord's Supper in a superstitious way or as being a magical ceremony that saves or sanctifies is not a true Christian church.

5. Does this church practice the biblical principle of "Body Life"? Body Life means that the church is committed to the priesthood of every believer. This means that the church is not a one man show staged by a super pastor. Do the members of this congregation seek to minister to each other according to the gifts that God has given to them? Is there an emphasis upon the ministry that God has given to all the members of the church?

6. Is this church involved in dynamic and biblical worship? Are its services God-centered or man-centered? Do people attend church to be entertained or to worship God? Is there the awareness of the presence of God that draws you to His throne?

7. Are the members of this church actively involved in personal evangelism? Is the church as a whole interested in missions? Is there an emphasis upon winning people to Christ?

8. Does this church have a social conscience? Is the Lordship of Christ applied to all of life?

9. Is this church involved in applying the Bible to such subjects as politics, war, economics, abortion, mercy killing or euthanasia? Is this church opposed to secular humanism? Are they ministering to the poor and needy?

10. Does this church put slanderers and gossip mongers under church discipline? The #1 sin in Evangelical circles are the slander and gossip websites, blogs, YouTube videos, and Facebook accounts that slander pastors, missionaries, and Christian leaders. Dr. Jay Adams and many other well-known

Christian scholars have called for church discipline on gossip mongers. See my book, *A Bible Handbook on Slander and Gossip* (www.faithdefenders.com), for the documentation.

While these ten signs will not be found in perfection in any church, any sound gospel church will manifest these things to some degree. Such a church will deepen your faith in the Lord Jesus Christ, strengthen your love toward the brethren and encourage your hope in the Scriptures as God's absolute and final authority.

5. Christian Activities on Campus

God never intended for you to go it alone on the college campus. You will need the fellowship of other Christians on campus. If there isn't a Christian group already in existence, then you should start one. Begin a Bible study in your dorm.

One of the benefits of starting a new being involved with Christian groups on campus is that they can watch over your soul. If you begin to slip in your Christian life, they will exhort you and lead you back to repentance.

It is also helpful to know other Christians majoring in the same subjects that you are studying. Some of them may have already done research on a Christian perspective on your major and will be happy to share with you the principles of God's Word concerning that academic subject. There is no reason for you to "reinvent the wheel." Older and more experienced Christians will be able to refer you to books that give the Christian perspective on important topics.

6. Campus Activities

One of the mistakes that many students make is to be defensive when they go to college. They feel threatened and attacked on all sides and therefore withdraw into a shell. This defeatist attitude is in violation of God's call to take dominion and rule over all of life (Gen.1:28).

Instead of being on the defensive, Christian students should be on the offensive. Since they have everything going for them, they should not be burdened with an inferiority complex. They have a God who is greater than the gods of the heathen and who provides truth, meaning, justice, morals, worth, dignity and beauty.

In contrast, the humanists are utterly bankrupt when it comes to any subject requiring truth, justice or morals. They are the ones who should be put to shame today as they admit that they have nothing to offer mankind.

Christians have the high ground in life. Thus they should take dominion over all campus activities that are available to them. They should not sit on the sidelines of life under the mistaken notion that doing nothing is true spirituality. They must be involved in those activities that can form a base to mold the thinking of the student body such as campus newspapers, clubs, sports, theatre, etc.

This means that Christian students must view themselves as radical rebels for Christ. Instead of rebelling against Christianity as the humanists do, Christian students should be rebelling against humanism. It does not matter if the humanism that they rebel against is found in a Christian college or a state university. Humanism is humanism regardless if it is taught by a professing Christian or by someone who is openly anti-Christian.

One caution must be given. Being a rebel for Christ does not mean that we should be obnoxious, arrogant or disrespectful to those over us. We are referring to an intellectual rebellion in which you refuse to accept humanistic teaching. You can be respectful and disagree with your professors at the same time.

Taking dominion means that you will attempt insofar as your abilities allow to take over those aspects of campus life that can influence your school for Christ. For example, Christians should be actively involved in all the media expressions of their school. They should get on the school newspaper or work their way into the university television or radio station. Once they have worked their way into the structure then they can begin to give a distinctively Christian perspective on relevant issues such as drugs, AIDS, sex, abortion, etc.

What if the humanists say that Christians should not be allowed to speak out? Point out that the Constitution gives you the freedom of speech and the freedom of the press just like anyone else. Threaten to take them to court if they violate the Civil Rights Amendment by discrimination against you on the basis of creed. Do not take it lying down.

Those with artistic abilities should take dominion of the cultural activities on campus. If you are an artist, seek to dominate art shows, art committees or art clubs. If you have musical ability, get involved in musicals or the campus orchestra. If you have a dramatic flair, be involved in plays or the production of campus skits.

One way to influence students is to write a play that ridicules humanism and its policy of death, such as abortion or euthanasia. Do what you can to take dominion of the entertainment to be produced and staged at the university.

One great way to influence your college or university is to arrange for a showing of Francis Schaeffer's film series such as *How Then Shall We Live?* Arrange for the entire student body to see it. Have your philosophy or ethics class view it.

Be involved in political action and get on the student government. Win the highest office you can. Don't be intimidated or afraid but aggressively seek to take dominion of the student government. In one college, a dedicated group of Christian students took over the student organization and then were able to influence the entire student body.

Join those campus clubs related to your major or to some hobby that you have. Or start your own club. Regardless of what the club is, be it a French or philosophy club, not only attend but seek to take dominion over it for Christ.

Why do so many students think that the "Christian" thing to do is to do nothing? Why do they let the humanists bully them? Why are they so passive? Why don't they demand their civil rights to speak out on issues? Why do they allow the humanists to ridicule God and the Bible openly in class? They are paralyzed by the false idea that they are not to be involved in the "world." They are so afraid of the world that they never try to clean it up!

We have a responsibility according to Scripture to apply the Lordship of Christ to all of life (2 Cor. 10:5). Therefore, Christian students must be at the forefront of all fights for truth, justice, morals and beauty.

For example, Christian students should be involved in actively supporting the human rights of the unborn, the sick and the elderly. These human rights are inalienable because they have been given by the Creator. Christian students should be involved in pro-life demonstrations and activities. They should actively support the showing of such films as *Silent Scream* or Francis Schaeffer's *Whatever Happened to the Human Race?*

Christians should be the most dedicated activists on earth. This is the Biblical ideal for every Christian. The Apostles won the reputation that they "were the men who turned the world upside down" (Acts 17:6). Indeed, wherever the early Christians went, riots and demonstrations were soon to follow. The greatest enemies to Christianity are those who preach, "Peace at any price," "Don't make any waves" and "Go with the flow."

Some Christian students are afraid that if they stand up for Christ, they will not be "popular." If they apply the Lordship of Christ to all of life and openly fight for Christianity, their professors and fellow students may not "like" them. What these popularity seekers do not understand is that Jesus placed a curse on any one who lives for popularity. In Lk. 6:26, Jesus said, "Woe to you when all men speak well of you, for that is how their fathers treated the false prophets."

If you are ashamed of Jesus Christ and will not acknowledge His Lordship in the presence of men, then neither will He acknowledge you on the Day of Judgment (Matt. 10:32, 33). Christians have received their marching orders from Jesus Christ (Matt. 28:18–20). They are under authority to aggressively go into the world and take dominion (Elk. 14:23).

Does this mean that every Christian student is also a missionary? Of course it does! You are either a missionary or a mission field. You are either a rebel for Christ or a rebel against Christ. You are either gathering with Christ or you are scattering against Christ. You cannot be neutral. If you are not actively for Christ, then you are against Him.

There is no neutrality with Jesus. Either you are for Him all the way, or not at all. He is either Lord of all or not Lord at all. Jesus said, "He who is not with me is against me, and he who does not gather with me scatters." (Matt. 12:30)

All of these things may seem to be very radical to some students because they have a soft Christianity. But now is the time to develop a tough Christianity that takes God and His Word seriously. Only a tough Christianity can survive and triumph in the secular world.

Even though you may have never seriously considered the biblical truth that we are to be "over comers" (I John 5:4, 5), it is nevertheless true that God has called us to take dominion over this world (Gen. 1:26–28).

If the Christians of the last two generations had fought to win their world for Christ, we would not be in the terrible fix we find ourselves in today. We must not allow evil to overcome good but use the good to overcome evil (Rom. 12:21).

Summary

Will you commit yourself to be a rebel for Christ? Will you take that step of faith and determine within yourself that you are going to apply the Lordship of Christ to all of life? Are you prepared to pay any price for your allegiance to Jesus Christ? Are you going to obey God's command to take dominion? Perhaps the following prayer will help to seal your dedication to become an over comer.

> "Lord Jesus, I acknowledge your Lordship over all of life. I ask that you will give me the wisdom and the humility to apply Your Lordship to every issue. Give me zeal and boldness to proclaim your Word. Give me the grace I need to be an overcomer."

Questions for Discussion

1. What are the essentials of the Christian life?
2. How important are prayer and Bible reading to a Christian? Is it possible to be a "prayerless" Christian?

3. Is church attendance optional or necessary for a valid profession of faith? Can someone be a "churchless" Christian?

4. How important is it to find good Christian books on the subjects you are studying?

5. Should you get involved with Christian groups on campus? Is someone really a Christian if he avoids any contact with Christians?

6. Should you seek to take dominion of the school where you are studying? Should you be defensive or offensive?

7. Should you be involved in cultural or media events on campus?

8. Should you give the Biblical perspective on issues even if the humanists don't like it?

9. Should you seek to take over the student government for Christ?

10. Do you bear any social responsibility to the community in which you live?

11. What can you do about the millions of children who are brutally murdered in the name   of abortion and mercy killing?

12. Should you be actively involved in demonstrations that support civil rights such as "pro- life" marches?

CHAPTER FIVE

The Christian Worldview

Monument to Victor Emmanuel II, Rome, Italy (1981)

Victor was King of Sardinia and victor over the Austrian army in Lombardy. He became the symbol for a united Italy. Victor and Garibaldi defeated the papal army in 1861 and the Kingdom of Italy was proclaimed with Victor Immanuel II as king.

While you may not be planning to take a course in philosophy while at college, you will actually be studying philosophy in every single class you take. Every professor will be teaching his subject from the perspective of a certain identifiable worldview. This means that regardless if you are taking courses in mathematics, nursing, art, psychology, history, social studies or political science, you are in reality being taught somebody's philosophic worldview.

What is a worldview? When we speak of a "worldview," we are talking about the way we interpret all of life. We all try to understand ourselves, the world around us and all the interpersonal relationships that are involved. A worldview has to do with the assumptions and the presuppositions that structure our understanding of the universe. Our values and priorities arise out of our worldview.

Perhaps one illustration will help at this point. If you put on a pair of pink-tinted glasses, everything you see will be tinted pink. This does not mean that the piece of white paper is actually pink but that it appears pink to you because of the glasses you are wearing. The same can be said of the person who is wearing green-tinted sunglasses. Everything they see around them is tinted green. Your worldview can color your perception of the world.

The Christian looks at the world through the glasses of the Bible. These glasses are not tinted but clear and enable the believer to see life as it really is. Humanists have a warped view of reality because they see life through tinted glasses. Their worldview keeps them from seeing the world as it really is.

In the Christian worldview, man was created by God. Thus when a Christian looks at a man he sees an image-bearer of God who has intrinsic significance, worth and meaning. In humanistic worldviews, man is a product of meaningless evolution. Thus, when a humanist looks at the same man he only sees an animal that has no intrinsic significance, worth or meaning. It does not matter what issue is being discussed, the Christian and the humanist will always have radically different interpretations.

Everyone Is a Philosopher

Even though you may never have thought of yourself as a philosopher, you already have a worldview. You may have picked up your worldview much like a dog picks up fleas. In other words, you have picked up ideas here and there without any regard for consistency, unity or coherence.

Your present worldview is probably the result of the influence of your parents, church, friends and school teachers. Perhaps you are the kind of person that has been deeply influenced by books and movies. Regardless of how or where you got your worldview, it is time for you to reflect not only on what you believe but also why you believe it.

How We Get Our World Views

There are three basic ways that a person develops a worldview. In the first instance, the person simply accepts the worldview that has been taught him. The teaching may be theism from Christian parents or atheism from humanistic parents. Thus while some people believe in God because they were taught to believe in God, others do not believe in God because they were taught not to believe in God. In both cases, the reasons as to why they believe what they believe are never reflected upon. This person, regardless of whether he is a theist or an atheist, is living an unexamined life.

In the second instance, there are those who have decided to take what has been called a "leap in the dark." That is, they choose to believe or not to believe simply on the basis of what they feel or want.

This is indicative of those who have imbibed the bitter waters of existentialism that says there is no meaning, truth or absolutes in the universe. Thus it does not really matter what you believe as long as it makes you feel happy and comfortable.

In other words, something is true if you believe it. Truth in this sense has been totally relativized. It no longer has any objective meaning whatsoever. What is true to you may not be true to me and may not be true to others but it is, nevertheless, true because you believe it. Thus, it does not really matter what world view you adopt. You pay your nickel and take your choice because no one has *the* truth.

Some Christians have unknowingly fallen into this existential trap. They assume that Christianity is true because they believe it. They were taught Christianity in their home and in their church and they have always believed it. Therefore, they assume that it is true. They do not believe in Christianity because it is true; it is true because they believe it.

In the third instance, someone may adopt a world view because they believe that it is true in an objective and absolute sense. That is, after weighing all the evidences, arguments and implications of different worldviews, they have decided to adopt that worldview that in their mind is really the truth.

They are not concerned if they like this truth or if it makes them feel happy. They are not concerned whether anyone else likes it or accepts it. They will believe something if it is true. If it is not true, they will not believe it regardless of any other considerations.

The Christian Way

Biblical Christianity falls into this third category. The kind of faith spoken of in Scripture is not to be interpreted in an existential sense, i.e. a "leap in the dark." Instead He says, "Come now, and let us reason together, says the Lord." (Isa. 1:18). The word "reason" in the Hebrew means that God wants to talk with you about your sin and how to solve the problems it has created in your life.

In the book of Acts, we find that the Apostle Paul gave arguments from Scripture to demonstrate that Jesus was the Messiah (Acts 19:8). When he dealt with Greek philosophers, he boldly proclaimed monotheism (Acts 17:16–33). Nowhere did he ask people to take a mindless "leap in the dark" and believe in Jesus because it felt good.

We are asked to believe in the resurrection of Christ because, "He showed himself to these men and gave many convincing proofs that he was alive." (Acts 1:3)

People were not asked to believe in the resurrection of Christ simply "by blind faith." The resurrection of Christ was to be accepted because the revealed evidence for it was so over- whelming that it was not rationally possible to deny it. Thus, Luke in Acts 1:3–4 and Paul in I Cor. 15 give the biblical arguments that demonstrate the truthfulness of Christ's resurrection. We are asked to believe that Christ actually arose from the dead because Special Revelation and the physical evidence demonstrate that His resurrection actually happened in real space-time history.

This rugged attitude toward truth is exemplified and honored in Acts 17:10–12.

"As soon as it was night, the brothers sent Paul and Silas away to Berea. On arriving there, they went to the Jewish synagogue. Now the Bereans were of more noble character than the Thessalonians, for they received the message with great eagerness and examined the Scriptures every day to see if what Paul said was true. Many of the Jews believed, as did also a number of prominent Greek women and many Greek men."

In the passage above, the Bereans were praised because they did not simply accept what Paul had to say on the basis of an existential "leap in the dark." Instead, they searched the Scriptures to see if what Paul was saying was really true according to Divine Revelation. Once they were convinced by the biblical evidence Paul gave that Jesus was indeed the Messiah, they believed in Him. Their faith was based upon the truth and not vice versa.

Where the Confusion Comes In

Some Christian students have been deceived on this point. They have been taught by religious existentialists that one accepts Christ solely on the basis of "blind faith."

These students were encouraged not to ask questions. They were told that if you look too closely at the Bible, you would discover that there is no evidence to support it. Thus, Christianity is something that one accepts pietistically solely on the basis of a "leap in the dark" kind of faith. This attitude has driven many intellectuals from the Church.

Biblically based Christians do not accept existentialism in its secular or religious forms because they know that it is self-refuting. When someone tells you, "There are no absolutes," they want you to accept that statement as an absolute! When they tell you, "There is no truth," they want you to accept that statement as the truth! When they say, "Everything is relative," they want you to accept that statement as an absolute! The moment they make such statements they have refuted themselves.

When Thomas demanded proof of the resurrection of Christ, he was not rebuked because he wanted to know if the resurrection really happened. Christ physically demonstrated to him that He had in fact been bodily raised from the dead.

> "Now Thomas (called Didymus), one of the Twelve, was not with the disciples when Jesus came. When the other disciples told him that they had seen the Lord, he declared, 'Unless I see the nail marks in his hands and put my finger where the nails were, and put my hand into his side, I will not believe it.' "A week later his disciples were in the house again, and Thomas was with them. Though the doors were locked, Jesus came and stood among them and said, 'Peace be with you!' Then he said to Thomas, 'Put your finger here; see my hands. Reach out your hand and put it into my side. Stop doubting and believe.' "Thomas said to him, 'My Lord and my God!' " (John 20:24–28)

Philosophy and science actually depend on the Bible for their validity and are based upon the unalterable character of the God who cannot lie (Heb. 6:18). Whenever the Scriptures have been investigated, they have always been vindicated. Christianity should be accepted because it is true.

The Importance of the Bible

The Christian worldview is based upon the Bible as the inspired Word of God, not on human reason, experience, feelings or faith. When we look into the Bible we find that the authors of Scripture never appeal to human reason, experience or emotion as being the origin, basis, or judge of truth, morals, justice or beauty. The Bible does not point us to man as if man is capable of discovering truth apart from God. It always points us to God as the

Origin of Meaning. Man is the receiver of truth and not its creator. See my book, *The Bible, Natural Law, and Natural Theology, Conflict or Compromise?*, for an in-depth discussion of this point.

This is why the Bible begins with God and not with man. It begins at the very beginning and goes right through to the end. All of space-time history is covered in the 66 books of the Bible. From the Creation of the world to the End of the world all of history is mapped out by the Word of God.

In the first book of the Bible, Genesis, in the very first three chapters of that first book, we find the three foundational presuppositions by which all of life is to be interpreted.

The Three Foundational Truths

1. Thematically, everything else in Scripture is a development of these three concepts.
2. Exegetically, these three concepts serve as the glasses through which we understand and interpret all of life.
3. When Jesus dealt with the subject of marriage and divorce, He interpreted it in the light of Creation-Fall-Redemption (Matt. 19:1–6).
4. Paul always used Creation-Fall-Redemption as the motif by which all of life could be interpreted.
   a. The male and female roles in the home and in the church (I Cor. 11:3–12; I Tim. 2:12–14).
   b. Whether certain foods are to be viewed as intrinsically "evil" and should be avoided by Christians (I Tim. 4:1–5).
   c. Why the world is in a state of chaos and decay and how the world will one day be returned to perfection (Rom. 8:18–23).

To understand anything from the Christian perspective requires that the subject be looked at from the standpoint of Creation-Fall-Redemption. The failure to take these biblical themes seriously renders any attempt to construct a Christian worldview impossible.

I. The Creation

In Gen. 1, we discover that the universe is not eternal. It has a distinct beginning. The only eternal being is God Himself. He has always existed as the eternal "I AM."

God did not create the universe out of any pre-existing materials. He spoke the worlds into existence (Heb. 11:3). By an act of His divine will He brought the universe "out of nothing."

Neither is the universe to be viewed as being made out of the being of God. The universe was not made of any aspect of God's essence or nature. It has its own separate existence apart from the existence of God. Its existence, or being, is qualitatively distinct from the existence of the Creator.

Whereas the universe is finite, temporal and dependent, God is infinite, eternal and independent. The universe relies upon God for its very existence (Col. 1:16–17). God relies on no one and on nothing for His own existence. He is eternal.

From the biblical concept of Creation we learn the following things:

1. The world was created out of nothing.
   This means that all concepts that involve the eternity of matter or energy are false. There is no such thing as eternal hydrogen molecules. The universe is not in a state of oscillation in which it expands and contracts eternally.
2. The creation is distinct from the Creator.
   There are two different kinds of existence or being. This means that all concepts of monism, that involves the idea that reality exists only of one kind of being and existence, are erroneous. Pantheism, pan-entheism and pan-everythingism are false concepts.
3. The material universe exists.
   This means that any philosophy or religion that denies the existence of material reality must be rejected. Be it Buddhism or Christian Science, any denial of physical reality must be rejected. All forms of spiritualism, that reduces reality to immaterial things such as the mind or cosmic energy, are wrong.

4. The spiritual universe exists.

God created not only the material universe but immaterial beings such as angels and immaterial things such as the human soul or spirit. This means that materialism that reduces all of reality to material objects must be rejected by Christians.

5. After God created the universe that has both matter and spirit, He declared that it was "very good" (Gen. 1:31).

This means that the material world is not to be viewed as evil. The human body is not to be viewed as evil or any of its functions or purposes. Thus, the Christian rejects all philosophic or religious worldviews that entail the evilness of matter or of the human body.

6. The universe was not created by accident. God has His own plans for the universe and for history itself. Thus, we read in such places as Eph. 1:11, "The plan of Him who works out everything in conformity with the purpose of His will." everything in life has purpose and meaning from the very beginning (Pro. 16:4; Ecc.3:1). This stands in contradiction of those views of the universe that would see life as a gamble based on blind luck and contingency. They would view life as having no meaning or purpose. This the Christian cannot accept.

7. The universe does not begin with the impersonal but with the personal because it begins with the personal Creator.

Man is not in contradiction of his own existence. His personality is reflective of the personal Creator who made him. This means that all humanistic views that reduce man to the level of an animal or a machine must be viewed as erroneous.

8. Because man was created in the image of God, we must view man as a unique creature who stands outside of the rest of the Creation.

Indeed, God placed man over the earth to rule as His vice-regent (Gen. 1:26–29). Man stands outside of the cosmic machine. Any world view that traps man in "nature" is false. Man stands outside of nature as its prophet, priest and king. He is not an animal or a machine but the unique image bearer of God.

9. We can speak of the unity and dignity of mankind only because all of humanity ultimately came from Adam and Eve.

The different races are simply genetic variations on the descendants of Adam and Eve. The unity and dignity of man depend upon the Adam and Eve model of creation. We can speak of "mankind" because we all came from Adam and Eve. This is in stark contrast to some humanistic ideas of evolution that view each race of man as evolving from different primates. If this is true, then one race could claim to be superior over the other races. Slavery could be justified because there is no such thing as "mankind."

10. Because man is God's image bearer, he is a responsible moral agent who will be held accountable by God for his thoughts, words and deeds on the Day of Judgment at the end of the world.

While animals are not viewed in the Bible as responsible moral agents because they do not have immortal souls, man is viewed in this way. This means that all views of man that negate his being responsible for his own actions must be rejected. The Christian view does not accept any chemical, environmental, societal or economical determinism. Man is not the victim of his circumstances. He will be held accountable for what he does.

II. The Fall

The Bible tells us that at the very beginning of human history man fell into a state of sin and guilt. The radical Fall of man is viewed by the biblical authors as being a real event in space-time history (Rom. 5:12ff; 1 Cor. 15:21ff). It is never viewed as a myth. It was an actual event that you could have witnessed with your own eyes.

The original sin was not sex. It was rebellion against God and His Law. Man attempted to become his own god (Gen. 3:5). Self-deification is one way in which man tries to be autonomous, i.e., independent from God. This is always the goal of apostate thought. Indeed, the history of philosophy is nothing more than man's attempt to escape God and His Law.

In his temptation, Satan told man three lies:

1. You can be whatever you want to be.

   This lie denies that man is a finite being and is thus limited by his finite nature. Just as man is not a bird and thus he cannot flap his arms and fly away, neither is he autonomous. We can be only what God has made us to be.

2. You can know whatever you want to know.

   This denies that man's understanding is finite. But man and his thoughts are finite and, hence, cannot obtain an infinite comprehension of anything. We can know only what God has made us capable of knowing.

3. You can do whatever you want to do.

   In this lie man is told that he can be his own law-giver. He does not have to obey God's Law but he can make up his own laws. Unbelief comes from man's rebellion against God and His Law.

The biblical account of man's radical Fall into sin gives us a key to understanding life. The world that now exists is not to be viewed as "normal." This means that death is not normal. Sin is not normal. Evil is not normal. Man is now subnormal. His problem is not his humanity but his depravity. Man's problem is not that he is finite but that he is a sinner by nature (Eph. 2:1–3).

The old saying, "To err is human but to forgive is divine," is built on the humanistic assumption that man's problem is his humanity. But this is not true. Adam and Eve were created righteous in the beginning. They were human and sinless at the same time. Jesus Christ was a real human being but He was also sinless. After the Resurrection, believers will be sinless. "Humanness" does not automatically mean sinfulness.

Once you equate "humanness" with sinfulness, you arrive at the basis of the liberal denial of the inspiration of Scripture. They usually argue in this way: "Since 'to err is human,' and the Bible was written by humans, this means that the Bible has to have errors. The errors and contradictions in the Bible only prove its humanness."

This argument fails to take into account man's original righteousness, his subsequent fall into sin and guilt and the sinlessness of Jesus Christ (2 Cor. 5:21). The Living Word and the Written Word are both errorless and sinless. Man's problems are fundamentally *moral* in nature and not physical, environmental or social.

III. Redemption

According to Scripture, God did not leave man in a state of sin and guilt. As we demonstrated in *Studies in the Atonement*, the triune God of Father, Son and Holy Spirit worked together to provide a salvation for sinners.

God the Father planned salvation from eternity past (Eph. 1:4). God the Son entered history and died on the cross for the sins of His people (1 Cor. 15:3, 4). And God the Holy Spirit takes what Christ accomplished according to the plan of the Father and applies it to the people of God (Eph. 4:30): "We are chosen by the Father, purchased by the Son, sealed by the Spirit, blessed God Three in One."

God's wondrous plan of Redemption began in eternity past and secures eternity future for His people. Jesus Christ has entered history and through His life, death and resurrection has created a new humanity that will one day enjoy a new earth that has been returned to its original paradise condition (2 Pet. 3:11–13).

Summary

The biblical worldview of Creation-Fall-Redemption supplies us with the only way of understanding reality as it really is. If we do not accept the biblical worldview, we will never find truth, justice, morals or beauty.

Questions for Discussion

1. What is a worldview?
2. Where did you get your worldview?
3. Have you ever thought about why you believe what you believe?
4. Is something true simply because you believe it?
5. Is Christianity a "leap into the dark" or are there good evidences

that back up the Bible and its claims?

6. What is existentialism?
7. What are the three foundational concepts of the Bible?
8. What ten facts arise from Creation-Fall-Redemption?
9. If we do not start with the biblical worldview, is it possible to understand life?
10. What logical implications does the theory of evolution have on the subject of racism?

CHAPTER SIX

Five Great Facts

Tower of Pisa, Italy (1981)

There are five great facts of reality that must be explained by any worldview. The degree to which a worldview recognizes and gives satisfying answers to these five facts determines its validity.

Fact #1: *The existence of the universe.*
The fact of the existence of the universe of men and things cannot be ignored. While it can be denied, it cannot be escaped. The same Hindu who denies the reality of the material universe must eat and drink like everyone else. While he may deny that his material body exists, he cannot escape the reality of having to clothe and feed it. In other words, he cannot live what he believes! A worldview must recognize and explain why the universe exists rather than not existing.

Fact #2: *The form of the universe.*

The universe that confronts us is not formless or lawless. It is not a willy-nilly universe where each of us experiences his own private reality. If a Jew, a Christian, a Muslim, a Hindu, an atheist, and a Buddhist jump off the same cliff, they will all die because the universe that exists is one in which there is a law of gravity that does not care what you may or may not believe. Someone may claim that the universe is devoid of law but they still have to obey the laws. They cannot live what they believe. A worldview must recognize and explain why the form of the universe is what it is rather than being formless.

Fact #3: *The uniqueness of man.*

Man cannot be reduced to a rock or to an animal. His desire to find truth, justice, morals, meaning and beauty immediately sets him apart from the rest of creation. He is unique in so many ways. He is a cognitive ego who can say, "I am." He can make and appreciate art. He cannot escape giving moral judgments. The "mannishness" of man is something that cannot be ignored or escaped. A worldview must recognize and explain why man is unique.

Fact #4: *The failure of humanism.*

Humanists have tried for thousands of years to explain man and the world around him on the sole basis of reason, emotions and experience. But the reality that confronts us all is that rationalism, mysticism and empiricism have never been able to generate a sufficient basis for truth, justice, morals, meaning or beauty. After all is said and done, when man attempts to "go it alone," he fails to get anywhere.

What has humanistic thought produced after thousands of years? It has produced *Skepticism* that denies that there are any truths to find, *Relativism* that denies there are any morals by which you can judge right from wrong, and *Existentialism* that denies that life has any meaning at all. As a worldview humanism has failed to recognize or explain the existence and form of the universe, the uniqueness of man, and its own failure.

One illustration of how humanism has failed would be its attempt to find meaning without God. As I pointed out in my book, *Battle of the*

Gods, the Greek philosopher Plato tried to find meaning for the things around him by stating that the meaning of something was not to be found "down here," but was to be found "up there" in the World of Ideas. Thus while a thing did not have meaning in and of itself, the idea of the thing is what has meaning.

If you pointed to a dog, Plato would say that the dog in front of you did not have any meaning in and of itself. But the idea of "dogness" is what gives meaning to the dog in front of you. The dog had meaning only because there was the idea of dogness in the World of Ideas.

When Aristotle came along he saw that Plato had not really given any "meaning" to the dog but he had simply duplicated him in the World of Ideas. In other words, the idea of dogness also needed to have "meaning." To shuffle the dog from this world "down here" to another world "up there" did not solve anything.

Aristotle thought he could solve the problem by dumping the concept of a "World of Ideas." Instead, he taught that meaning could be found "in" the thing itself. It is possible to abstract or discern the "essence" or "meaning" that exists in objects. Thus as you examine the dog, you will find that the object has its own intrinsic meaning and all you have to do is to abstract the essence or meaning of it. Meaning is not "up there" but "down here."

Although other variations to Aristotle's themes have been developed during the Middle Ages, particularly by Thomas Aquinas, when we arrive at the Renaissance and, in particular, the so-called "Age of Enlightenment," we arrive at the correspondence theory of meaning.

This theory stated that objects have meaning within themselves if there is a corresponding meaning in the mind of man. Thus meaning is "out there" in the object and "in here" in the mind of man.

One such philosopher who taught this was Leibniz. He stated that the meaning must be in the mind as well as in the object and when the two meanings contact, knowledge takes place.

The next stage of development in humanistic thinking was Emmanuel Kant. He is so important that the history of philosophy is divided into pre-Kantian and post-Kantian philosophy.

Kant's claim to fame was to deny that there was any meaning in Plato's World of Ideas, in Aristotle's thing in itself, or in the correspondence between the mind and the object as in Leibniz. Instead, Kant proposed that all meaning is to be found in the mind of man. This means that objects or the thing in itself has no meaning except what the human mind projects on to it.

Kant's epistemology involves the ability of the human mind to project order and meaning onto life through the categories of the mind. Thus meaning was not "up there," "down here," or "out there" but only "in here" in the mind of man! The humanists were running out of options.

Humanistic philosophy was now ready to shift from essentialism, which had assumed that objects had an "essence" or "meaning," to existentialism, which stated that things exist without having any "essence" or "meaning."

If meaning was not to be found in Plato's World of Ideas, Aristotle's essence and form, in Leibniz's correspondence theory, or in Kant's categories of the mind, the existentialists such as Sartre concluded that meaning cannot be found anywhere. Nothing including man has any real meaning. Meaning was not "up there," "down here," "out there," or "in here." It was nowhere.

Sartre went further than to simply deny the existence of meaning. He pointed out that a particular must have an infinite reference point in order to have any meaning whatsoever. This infinite reference point could only be found in the infinite God of the Scriptures. Happily, toward the end of his life, Sartre abandoned existentialism and returned to belief in God as the only hope of man.

This is the modern humanistic problem. God is no longer acceptable to modern humanists. In this sense, God is dead to them. Since they cannot accept God, they find themselves without a sufficient basis for meaning, hope, significance, love, truth, morals or justice.

Once we reject the God, who is the infinite reference point and thus is the Origin of Meaning, then we must reject everything that flows from that God such as the dignity and worth of man and that life has any significance or meaning. In other words, if God is dead then man is dead. And if man is dead then truth, justice, morality and beauty are likewise dead.

The present philosophy of death and despair that grips the

secular campus is self-refuting. When a humanist says, "There is no meaning," the statement is self-refuting because he wants you to grasp the *meaning* of this statement. When he says, "There is no truth," he wants you to accept that statement as *true*! He is cutting his own throat when he makes such stupid statements.

A worldview must explain why humanism has failed to find a sufficient basis for truth, justice, morality, meaning and beauty.

Fact #5: *The superiority of the Christian worldview.*

The Bible gives us a satisfying explanation of the existence and form of the universe, the uniqueness of man and the failure of humanism. When man attempts to understand the world without God's special revelation given in Scripture he always ends in foolishness (1 Cor.1:20–25; Rom. 1:21–23). Only the Bible gives us a sufficient basis for truth, justice, morals, meaning and beauty.

Summary

Man has failed to escape the necessity of divine Revelation. He cannot know anything as it really is if he does not begin with God as He has revealed Himself in the Bible.

The God who has revealed Himself in Scripture is the infinite reference point that supplies us with the absolutes we need to distinguish reality from fantasy, truth from falsehood, justice from injustice, good from evil, right from wrong and ugliness from beauty.

Questions for Discussion

1. What five great facts have to be explained?
2. Humanism has led to skepticism and relativism. What do these words mean?
3. How has humanistic philosophy tried to find meaning?
4. What is the only way for man to have meaning and significance?
5. How is the Christian worldview better than humanism?

CHAPTER SEVEN

An Evangelical Appraisal of Aristotle

Bust of Aristotle (384 BC – 322 BC) by Lysippus (c. 330 BC)

Introduction

Evangelical Christians have historically held fast to the principle of Sola Scriptura as defined by the Protestant Reformers. The truth about God, man, sin and salvation has been revealed in the Bible alone. The self-revelation of God in Scripture is thus the final court of appeal in all matters of faith and practice. To "go beyond what is Written" leads to conceit and pride (1 Cor. 4:6).

While Roman Catholics base their theology on a combination of the Bible and pagan philosophers, particularly Aristotle, the Reformers were men of the Book. They knew that Romans 1 and 2 teach that natural theology is useless because sinful man suppresses any truth he might have derived from the creation around him or looking within himself. Man shuts his eyes and plugs his ears and then wonders why he does not see the light or hear the music of God's existence and attributes. Thus, sinful man naturally goes into idolatry as Paul illustrates in Romans.

Catholic Natural Law and Natural Theology replace the Bible with human reason. But what is "rational" to one person is ridiculous to another. "Common Sense" is relative to both culture and time. The words "nature" or "natural" are meaningless because no one can define them. See my book, *The Bible, Natural Law, and Natural Theology: Conflict or Compromise?*, for the documentation (www.faithdefenders.com).

In contrast, Evangelicals follow the same path as the Early Church Fathers who denounced Greek philosophers (such as Plato and Aristotle) as demon-possessed. They boldly proclaimed that Christ and Jerusalem had nothing to do with Baal and Athens. As I demonstrated in the book, *Battle of the Gods*, the early Christians had nothing but contempt for pagan theology and philosophy. I give an in-depth discussion of this fact in my book, *Is Eastern Orthodoxy Christian?* (www.faithdefenders.com.).

The Early Church was Jewish in origin and reflected the orthodox Jewish hostility toward heathen religions. One will search in vain to find a single prophet of God in the Old Testament who showed any appreciation for heathen religions or philosophies. The Gentiles and their religions were all condemned as idolatrous and demonic in worship (Deut. 32:17; Psa. 106:36-37). The apostles followed the prophets and thus repeated the same condemnation (1 Cor. 10:20; Gal. 4:8; Rev. 9:20).

What about the Lord Jesus? Surely He must have said something to indicate that God appreciated all the pagan philosophers. Alas, Jesus was just as exclusive as the prophets before Him and the apostles after

Him. His words to the Samaritan woman, "Salvation is from the Jews" (John 4:22), clearly mean that salvation is not from the Greeks, Romans, Indians, Chinese, Africans, Europeans, as well as the Samaritans. Jesus' words in John 14:6: "I am the way, the truth, and the life. No one comes to the Father but through me," forever doom all the ecumenical delusions of such apostates as Peter Kreeft.

While modern Romanists, Protestant liberals, Witches, and New Agers join in an ecumenical frenzy of exalting pagan philosophy, Evangelicals exalt the Word of God. They know that we are saved by grace alone, through faith alone, in Christ alone, according to the Bible alone.

With these few introductory words, the following statement represents the historic Evangelical position:

> Since no one seeks after the God who is there, all natural religions have their origin in man's suppression of and rebellion against divine revelation. Greek philosophy is just as apostate as Hinduism, Buddhism, Islam or Animism. The gods of the Greek philosophers were demonic in origin and idolatrous in nature. The Greek philosophers never found the true God. Their natural theology sprang from their worship of "Nature" instead of the Creator, who is blessed forever. Their foolish hearts were darkened as they gave themselves up to vain speculations and immoral practices. Their so-called "proofs" for the existence of their false deities do not lead to the one true God of Scripture. Since they do not speak according to the Law and the prophets, they have no light.

The Pagan Philosopher Aristotle

What then shall we say about Aristotle (387-322 B.C.)? He is rightly called, "The High Priest of Empiricism" (John Gates, *Adventures in the History of Philosophy: An Introduction From a Christian Viewpoint*, Zondervan, 1961, p. 27).

Any standard reference work on the history of philosophy, secular or Christian, will document that Aristotle believed that all knowledge comes to us via the five senses. This automatically excludes any and all forms of supernaturalism, Christianity included.

Not only is his epistemology anti-Christian, Aristotle's views on all other subjects are just as pernicious. His metaphysical dichotomy of "form/essence" produced the heresy of the secular/sacred dichotomy that kept papist priests in power for centuries. The idea that the form of something need not correspond to its essence, not only renders knowledge impossible, but it provided the philosophic framework in which the blasphemy of the popish error of transubstantiation in the Mass developed. His ethical relativism was based on a pleasure/pain sliding scale that has no room for the Ten Commandments.

Humanistic "evangelical" philosophers pretend that Aristotle believed in the one true God found in the Bible. But anyone who actually reads the works of Aristotle knows that he was a polytheist. Among the gods and goddesses he worshiped, Aristotle paid homage to a supreme deity whom he defined as "thought thinking itself."

How anyone can confuse the Triune God of Scripture with an abstract principle of "thought thinking itself" is beyond us. Aristotle's supreme deity thinks only on itself. How one can reconcile this god with the God revealed in John 3:16 remains a mystery.

Conclusion

Any Christian who is under the delusion that we can find the basis of Christian theology and philosophy in the works of Socrates, Plato, Aristotle or pagan philosophy in general, is either ignorant or deceptive. No philosopher ever found the true God by human reason, experience, feelings or faith. There is no other foundation for truth, justice, morals, meaning and beauty than Jesus Christ!

Questions for Discussion

1. What did the Apostle Paul say about the world's attempt to understand God? 1 Cor.1:20-25

2. What did the Jews think about the pagan philosophers of their day? Did the prophets quote them as the basis of what people should believe or how people should live? Or, did they say, "Thus says the LORD!"

3. What did Jesus and the Apostles do with the Greek philosophers of their day? Did they quote them as their authority for their doctrines?

4. Was divine Revelation or human reason the basis of truth, justice, morals, meaning, and beauty?

CHAPTER EIGHT

The Failure of Natural Theology

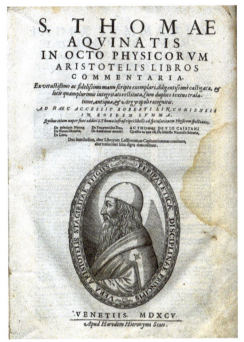

Super Physicam Aristotelis (1595).

Thomas Aquinas (1225-74 A.D.) was an adherent to Aristotle, but towards the end of his life he renounced his philosophical work and refused to write anything else on natural theology. Aquinas declared, "all my work is like straw!" Aquinas might have become a born again/born from above Christian at the end of his life (justification by grace alone, through faith alone, in Christ alone, apart from works).

Ideas have the potential of affecting generations after generations after it has been expressed. This is known as the "ripple effect." When we throw a stone into undisturbed water it creates ripples on the surface. The stone immediately sinks to the bottom, but the ripples continue long after.

Sometimes the ripples can be good and sometimes bad. The life of Adolf Hitler, for instance, caused evil ripple effects that are still with us to this day and will continue until the end of history. The life of Charles H. Spurgeon caused good ripple effects and they too will continue until the end of history.

The ripple effects of Mother England included those thinkers of the halls of British academia. Thus you must examine why and how Natural Theology influenced the rest of British and American history.

British Natural Theologians, such as William Paley, abandoned the Reformation doctrine of *Sola Scriptura* (i.e. Scripture alone is the final authority on doctrine and morals). As a reaction to this apostasy, the Puritans wrote the Westminster Confession of Faith that reaffirmed *Sola Scriptura*.

In the political realm, the Puritans also overthrew the neo-Catholic King Charles I and cut off his head. The Puritan politician Oliver Cromwell ushered the nation into a period of righteousness and political stability. Cromwell stripped the King of England of his so-called "divine right of rule" and made Parliament the ruling body. This has rightly been called "The Puritan Age."

After Cromwell died, the neo-Catholic King Charles II regained the power of government and the Puritans were now persecuted both religiously and politically. As a direct result of the ascendency of Charles II, the Roman Catholic doctrine of Natural Theology, which was based on Aristotle's doctrine of human autonomy, replaced the Westminster Confession of Faith. In the end, *Sola Rationé* replaced *Sola Scriptura*.

The neo-Catholic Protestant Natural Theologians believed that it was possible to develop a purely "natural" (i.e. secular) explanation of the world apart from and independent of God and the Bible. This opened the door to hundreds of anti-Christian philosophers who claimed that they had developed a purely "rational," "natural," and "secular" explanation of the world. "God" was no longer needed to have truth, justice, morals, meaning or beauty. Man was the measure of all things, including God.

It was thus Natural Theology that created the intellectual climate that made it possible for the rise of godless (i.e. secular) natural explanations of the world that either ignored or openly denied the Bible. Such anti-Christian philosophies as Deism, Darwinianism, Socialism, Communism, and Nazism are all based on Natural Theology.

The rationale for Natural Theology rests on two claims:

1. Natural Theology can prove the existence of God, the nature of God, the attributes of God, the way to God, our responsibility before God, etc., on the sole basis of human reason, experience, feelings, or faith.
2. Natural Theology can solve the problem of evil on the sole basis of human reason, experience, feelings, or faith.

Has Natural Theology Failed or Succeeded?

What about the existence and nature of God? Did the Natural Theologians succeed in finding an argument based on reason alone that proved the existence of God? No. In the end, they utterly failed to accomplish their goal.

Some might object at this point and ask, "What about the famous five-fold proofs for God's existence? Don't they work?" The answer is a resounding, "No." The five traditional proofs for !the existence of God came from Thomas Aquinas, who stole them from Muslim philosophers such as al-Ghazali and Averroes, who stole them from Aristotle, who tried to prove the existence of "thought thinking itself." Today many ignorant Evangelical apologists foolishly use them.

These so-called "rational" proofs of God's existence are a complete bust. They do not prove the existence of the triune God of the Bible - who is personal and infinite in His Being and attributes. The arguments fall short of proving what they start out to prove. Any argument that leads to a lesser god, goddess, or gods, is not the God of the Bible. If you claim you want to find Jesus, but end up with Shiva and Kali, the argument is invalid. The following illustration may be helpful to understand this point.

If you took a taxi to the airport but it dropped you off five miles from the airport, would you pay the fare? No. He did not take you where you said you wanted to go. In the same way, the arguments used by Natural apologists fall short of proving the existence of the God of the Bible. A few honest modern apologists admit this. See my book (*The Bible, Natural Law and Natural Theology*) for the documentation. They admit that all they can prove is the possible existence of a vague finite deity of some kind floating around somewhere. But most pretend that the God of the Bible can be found at the end of the yellow brick road they are building one argument at a time. But the wizard at the end of the road is a fraud.

If you begin with man, you will end with man. If you choose a godless methodology in pursuit of the truth, you will end up without God and without the truth. The attempt to find God without God was doomed from the beginning.

The Classical Theistic Arguments

While I give a detailed refutation of Thomas' five arguments in my book, *The Bible, Natural Law, and Natural Theology*, I will give a brief summary of why the arguments do not work.

1.   The "Ontological Argument"

Is it possible to imagine or think of a perfect Being? Yes. Then to have the idea of a perfect Being necessarily means that Being must exist, otherwise you would not be able to conceive it in your mind. And this perfect Being must be God. Therefore God exists.

There are so many problems with this argument it is hard to know where to begin. For example, the word "perfect" poses tremendous problems. "Perfect" does not necessarily mean "immutable," as the Greeks assumed. A rose can be "perfect" today and rotten by the end of the week. One rose can be more "perfect" than another. The Bible uses the word "perfect" to describe Job (Job 1:1). Does this mean that Job is God?

The word "existence" poses a lot of problems as well. Thus it is never defined. When you say "existence," are you talking about some kind of existence that you've never experienced, that does not exist in the universe? Or is it some unknown "X" that nobody knows anything about?

What about the monster under the bed? Children believe in his existence because they can conceive of him under their bed. Just because we can conceive of something does not mean that it actually exists.

2.   The "Teleological Argument"

Also known as the "Cause-and-Effect Argument," it is based upon the idea that every object in the world must be either a cause or its effect. For example, the cue-stick (the cause) hits the cue ball and makes it roll across the table (the effect).

It sounds like a simple explanation. But what if the cue ball hits another ball and that ball hits a third ball and bounces off the side of the table and then hits the ball that just hit it? The second cause is also an effect. Things can be both a cause and an effect at the same time. If a ball bounces back and hits the ball that first hit it, then it is the cause of the effect of the cause that affected it!

The problem with this line of reasoning is that a cause need be only a little bigger or stronger than the effect it produces. On what grounds can we suddenly leap from finite effects to an Infinite Cause? Even if we imagine the entire universe as one huge effect and seek for a cause to explain it, since the universe is finite, then all we need to explain it is a finite cause slightly bigger than the finite universe it produced.

The most you can get from a finite effect is a finite cause. How then can you go from finite effects to an infinite Cause, material effects to a non-material Cause; chaotic effects to harmonious Cause; many effects to one cause? The most you can come up with is the possibility of multiple finite causes for the finite effects in the universe. Thus it is no surprise that the Greeks believed in multiple finite gods and goddesses (i.e. causes). This does not prove the existence of the God of the Bible.

3.   Arguments Based Upon Design

The problem with this argument is that all the "designs" we find in "nature" are finite, material, and non-divine. Thus the most you can get from this argument is a finite designer or designers who is/are finite, material, and non-divine. Maybe a UFO of really smart aliens seeded life on this planet and have been guiding human evolution all along.

4.   Arguments Based Upon Personal Experience

Just because you have "experienced" God in your life, this does not automatically mean that God exists. There are millions of Muslims, Hindus, Mormons, witches, etc. who claim the same thing for their religion. Your personal experience can only confirm it, not prove it.

5.   Psychological and Sociological Arguments

Is something true just because it makes you feel happy or it gives you inner peace? A lie can make people happy and give them false security and peace. This is not the right way to "prove" that Christianity is true.

What then?

While the Book of Ecclesiastes teaches us that if we begin with man, we will end with nothing but meaninglessness, the Book of Proverbs teaches us that if we begin with God, then we will end with dignity and worth. Thus if we begin with God, we can have truth, justice, morals, meaning, and beauty. If we begin with man, we will fall into the dark hole of meaninglessness.

Conclusion

Well-meaning Christians with the greatest of motives have

attempted to defend Christianity with the lousiest arguments possible. This has not helped the Gospel one iota. By adopting humanistic Natural Theology as their basis, in the end, they destroyed what they wanted to defend. No argument is always better than a bad argument.

Questions for Discussion

1. If you begin only with yourself, apart from and independent of God and His Word, can you find your own way to God through your own reason, experience, feelings or faith?
2. Why does the Bible never refer to something called "Reason" and never uses the word "rational?"
3. If you begin without God, can you have truth, justice, morals, meaning or beauty?
4. Why did Natural Law and Natural Theology fall into the abyss of the unrelated?

CHAPTER NINE

A Biblical Philosophy of Science

**Sir Isaac Newton (1642 – 1727) by Sir Godfrey Kneller (1689)
& Albert Einstein (1921) by Ferdinand Schmutzer**

Introduction

The rationale, basis, function, and nature of "science" is something that natural philosophers and theologians have staked out as the sole domain of human reason and experience and thus we do not need any information from Special Revelation, i.e. the Bible. But, must we "put away our Bibles" when it comes to science? Are science and the Bible like oil and water, i.e. you cannot mix the two? Humanists assume this to be true. But, is this really true?

Lots of Questions

There are many questions about "science" that have to be answered before we can evaluate the different views of science that are in the world today.

- What is the origin, nature, means, methods, and purpose of science?
- Can it explain everything, most things, a few things or nothing?
- Does it have any limits or can it do and be everything?
- Does science deal with absolute truth or are its theories relative to the surrounding culture and times?
- What are its foundational faith-based principles, presuppositions, and assumptions?
- What kind of faith is it based upon? Arbitrary faith, blind faith, cultural faith, etc.?
- Why did science come into existence?
- How, where, when, and through whom did the idea of science arise?
- Does the universe really need an explanation?
- If so, what kind of explanation?
- Is a rational, empirical or mystical interpretation the right one?
- Is the universe actually explainable? In its entirety? Or are there things in the universe that are mysteries, i.e. not explainable in nature?
- Or is the universe chance-driven and thus not explainable in nature?
- Is science actually a psychological phenomenon? Is it the projection of man's futile attempt to deal with his fear and insecurity by projecting order and purpose onto a meaningless and chaotic universe?
- Or is the universe orderly in and of itself?
- Does everything in the universe have a purpose, function, and place?
- If the universe is meaningless and purposeless in nature because it is the result of a random combination of chance plus

time plus energy plus matter, on what grounds do we think that it is capable of explanation?

- Is history guided by irrational forces?
- Why does man assume he can explain the world around him?
- How can we justify the existence and enterprise of science?
- Is science actually religious in nature?
- How and in what ways?
- Why have the hard sciences fallen on such hard times today?

These kinds of questions are the focus of the philosophy of science. Humanists usually disguise their philosophy of science by pretending that science is factual. But, don't be deceived. What secular humanists call "science" is actually 99% a mixture of philosophy and religion.

When someone says, "I believe in science," he actually means that he believes in a religion called *scientism*.[1] The following dialogue has taken place many times in a university setting. The unbeliever has rejected the Bible and the gospel because he "believes in science."

Unbeliever: I don't believe in God. I believe in science.

Christian: What is this "science" in which you believe?

Unbeliever: What do you mean?

Christian: Where can I find this "science?" Does it have a physical address or an email address? What is the telephone number for science? Where is its headquarters? Who is the head of it? Does it pay taxes? Does it have a mission statement or manifesto?

Unbeliever: Science does not have a physical address or an email or a website. By "science" I mean what we know by observation and experimentation.

Christian: So, you admit that "science" does not exist *per se*. The word "science" is a symbol for what some people, some of the time, in some cultures, believe about the world. The word "science" is what current religious and philosophic ideas are dominant in a society. Each society creates its own science.[2]

Unbeliever: But "science" is based on objective facts. It is objective and neutral.

Christian: That's what some people have said some of the time. But, one man's science is another man's superstition. Western "science" simply means Western cultural consensus. If 51% of people who call themselves "scientists" vote for an idea, is it "science" or politics? Scientific theories change all the time. Larry Laudan has documented how Western science has radically changed its view of reality over thirty times.[3]

Unbeliever: But science is not just mob rule! It is not consensus, but fact. Christian: Have you read Kuhn's work?[4]

Unbeliever: What are you talking about? Science is an agreed upon body of knowledge supported by observation and experimentation. Christian: Your definition of science is just one *belief* among a vast number of different philosophies of science. It is called "realism" and was invented by the philosophy of Logical Positivism. Many scientists today hold to other views of science such as anti-realism. Unbeliever: Are you saying that "science" is relative to its cultural context?

Christian: You got it! Does the sun revolve around the earth or does the earth revolve around the sun? Science first taught one and then the other. Is the world flat? At one time science taught that it was. Do atoms really exist or is the atom paradigm only a convenient fiction? Newton's science taught that an object's mass does not depend upon its velocity, while Einstein's science taught the opposite.

Scientists evangelize each other and try to convert each other to their position. Young scientists are told that they have to believe in what passes as "scientific orthodoxy" at the time. Take the global warming theory. If a scientist refused to convert to this faith-based theory, he was punished in various ways, such as being fired from his job or by losing his government funding.

Unbeliever: I thought science was based on inductive reasoning. Christian: The so-called "scientific method" of inductive reasoning is laden with a *priori* ideas that are gratuitously accepted. If you do not accept those presuppositions, then all the induction is no more than circular reasoning.[5]

Unbeliever: If this is true then all hope for truth and meaning is lost! Christian: If you mean that if we start with *man* as the Origin and measure of truth, then, yes, all is meaningless.[6] But I have good news for you. If we begin with the God of the Bible as the Origin and Measure of all things, including truth, justice, morals, meaning, and beauty, then we can have all those things. Humanistic science is sinful man's attempt to explain the world without God. It can't be done. Biblical science begins with God and then explains the world in terms of its relation to Him. Unless we start with "In the beginning God created the heavens and the earth," all is meaningless.

A brief review of ancient Greek philosophy would be helpful to understand the roots of humanistic ideas about science.

PART ONE

ANCIENT GREEK PHILOSPHY

The philosophers of Greece supposedly based their ideas on human reason and experience, and they prided themselves on being "rational" in all things. From the very beginning of recorded history, the word "rational" referred to what psychologically "felt" right to the majority of people in a given culture. To the Greeks, the idea that the world was a flat plane "felt" rational. The idea that the world was a round sphere would have been deemed "irrational" in that day.

Science at one time taught that the sun revolved around the earth; that astrology could predict the future; the spontaneous creation of life; that disease was healed by bleeding the patient; light is unaffected by gravity; etc., etc. Thus what is "rational" is relative to the dominant social beliefs at that time.

The Duckbilled Platypus

The duckbilled platypus is a good example of the psychology of rationality. When the first explorers of Australia returned to Europe, they reported the existence of a weird animal that had the bill of a duck, webbed feet, fur, laid eggs, and suckled its young. The rationalistic scientists of Europe pronounced it a fraud and that such a creature could not "rationally" exist. They considered it a sick joke.

Then explorers returned to Australia and brought back the skins of the animal as proof.

But the same scientists declared the skins of the platypus to be a clumsy fraud created by sewing together body parts from different animals. It was stated in universities across Europe that it was not "rational" that such a creature could exist. The real is the rational and the rational is the real. If something is "unthinkable," then it does not exist.

The explorers had to bring a live duckbilled platypus back to Europe, and only when the scientists were forced to watch it swimming around did they grudgingly admit it must be real. The "irrational" was the real, and rationality once again showed one of its weaknesses as a philosophy.

Greek Rationality

Besides the invention of the psychological term "rational," other philosophical ideas developed by Greek philosophy are still with us today. Zeller, one of the more astute humanists of our day, states in his standard work on the pre-Socratic philosophers,

> From Greek Philosophy, however, the whole of European philosophy has descended. For the ideas that the Romans express in their philosophic literature were not original, but were taken from the Greeks, clothed in the Latin language and passed on to the medieval and modern world.[7]

Most modern philosophers, such as Alfred North Whitehead, have admitted their indebtedness to Greek philosophy. On numerous occasions Whitehead proudly proclaimed that "philosophy only repeats Plato!" He assumed that the closer we get to Greek philosophy and the farther we depart from Christianity, the better off we will be philosophically and morally.[8]

Greek Philosophy and Secular Humanism

Greek philosophy is also important because it represents secular humanism in full bloom. The Greeks attempted to explain the existence and form of the universe and the uniqueness of man solely on the basis of human reason, intuition, experience, and faith. They developed their philosophies from themselves, by themselves, and upon themselves without any reliance on divine revelation. Again, Zeller comments,

> It was the Greeks who won for man freedom and independence of philosophic thought, who proclaimed the autonomy of reason.[9]

Zeller goes on to define what he meant when he said "freedom" and "independence." He meant "freedom" and "independence" *from* God. It did not matter if one is considering the being, attributes, sovereignty, salvation, works, law, or revelation of God, man must be "free" of God or he is not "really" and "truly" free.

First, as Zeller states, the Greek philosopher was free "to live life as he pleased" because he was "free" from "ethics founded on religious authority."[10] This has always been the great goal of man since his Fall into sin and rebellion in the Garden. Man must be "free" to be his own lawgiver and judge. God and His Law must go if man is to be free.

Second, the Greek philosopher was free "to behave as he pleased" because he was "free" from "a religion based on revelation."[11] If man is to be a truth-maker, law-maker, and god- maker, he cannot be limited by the Bible or any other divine revelation. Truth, justice, morals, meaning, and beauty must be decided by what man thinks or feels about it. The concept of a God who reveals absolute truth or morals is clearly repugnant to Zeller.

Religion, philosophy, and science by human reason alone (not by Revelation) were the basis of Greek thought and are still the basis of all apostate thought. "Freedom" to apostate man always means freedom *from* the God who made him. If man is not free in this absolute sense, he is not "truly" free.

Human Autonomy

When Zeller spoke of "the autonomy of reason," he meant that the Greeks did not think that they were dependent on the gods or God for their existence, knowledge, or ethics. They assumed that they could "go it alone" without God because they were "autonomous," i.e. independent *from* God. They did not need God or His grace or revelation.

The philosophic doctrine of human autonomy is the very soul and substance of all humanistic thought. But, can man really "go it alone" by relying solely on his own finite and corrupt reason, intuition, and experience? Is truth or morality possible if man begins by rejecting God and His revelation and relying only on himself?

When the Rubber Meets the Road

Let us examine the Greek philosophies to see if they were able to produce anything of lasting worth. After all, if man's reason, intuition, and experience are really sufficient, then surely the Greek thinkers would have come up with a philosophy that was both believable and livable. But, if after thousands of years in which humanistic thinkers have had all the time and resources needed to produce something, they have in reality produced nothing — then evidently man's reason, intuition, and experience are not really self-sufficient or autonomous after all.

After all the exaggerated claims about human reason, intuition, and experience, if man fails to "go it alone," then this calls for a radical change in the way that truth, justice, morals, and beauty can be discovered and known.

To trace Greek philosophy from the pre-Socratic period to Aristotle requires us to examine their development of the four main divisions of philosophy:

1. *Metaphysics*: The science of being. What really exists? What is "reality"? What lies behind or beneath reality?
2. *Epistemology*: The science of Knowledge. Can we know what exists? How can we know it? Is it possible to "know" anything?
3. *Ethics*: The science of Morals. What is "good" and "evil?" Can we discern good from evil? How do we do this? Are there moral absolutes or is everything relative?
4. *Aesthetics*: The science of Beauty. What are "beauty" and "ugliness?" Are there absolute standards by which we can discern and judge whether something is "beautiful"? How can we discover them?

Metaphysics
The Pre-Socratics

With the appearance of a slave-based society, a leisure class appeared in Greek society. People had the freedom and time to sit around and try to figure out final answers to the ultimate questions of life. Where did we come from? How did we get here? Why are we here? What are we to do? Where are we going?

Thales is considered to be the earliest of the Greek philosophers. The main question that Thales addressed was, "What is ultimate reality?" i.e. "Of what is it composed or made?"

Thales assumed many things that he never questioned. They were faith-based assumptions that he did not question or prove. His philosophy grew out of and rested upon these assumptions. For example, he gratuitously assumed that ultimate "reality" was "One," not "Many." This is the doctrine of Monism, which states that there is no *qualitative* distinction between gods, men, animals or things. All is One and One is All. They are all part of "what is." They are all "One."

This is in stark contrast to the Biblical idea that God is distinct qualitatively and quantitatively from the universe. The Biblical doctrine of Creation means that God and the creation are two totally different things. They are *not* "One." We are not a part of God or one with God or an emanation from God. While the Greeks, Hindus, Buddhists, and all monists believe that "All is One," the Bible teaches that "All is Two."

Since Thales assumed that everything was eventually and ultimately "One," he wanted to know the identity and nature of this "One" thing that composed all of reality. This "One" made up the existence of the world. Thales also gratuitously assumed that whatever this "One" thing was:

1. It was a material substance,
2. It could be perceived by the five senses of man.
3. It was as eternal as the world of space and time.

Earth, Air, Fire, Water

In other words, the "One" substance, which made up everything, was something man could touch, taste, see, feel, or hear. Thales chose WATER as the "One" ultimate eternal substance that made up all of reality. Ultimate reality was "One" and this "One" was WATER.

After Thales asked what is the identity and nature of the "One" basis of reality, other philosophers put forth their own answers. At first, they assumed along with Thales that this "One" was a material substance perceivable by the five senses.

Heraclitus chose FIRE as ultimate reality. Anaximenes proposed that AIR was the "One." Empedocles and Aristotle topped them all by stating that reality was composed of a combination of EARTH, AIR, FIRE, and WATER!

If you are tempted to think that these philosophers were just plain stupid, you must realize that their idea that EARTH, AIR, FIRE, and WATER made up reality is still with us today. The psychological theory that there are four basic personality types (sanguine, phlegmatic, choleric, melancholic) is a modern version of the Greek idea of EARTH, AIR, FIRE, and WATER!

Idealism

Once the Greek philosophers had exhausted all the material substances open to sense perception that they thought were qualified to be the "One," some of them decided that it was "rational" to believe that the "One" must be a material substance that was *not* perceivable by the senses. This "substance" lay "behind" or "beneath" earth, air, fire, and water. Although it could not be seen, touched, heard, tasted, or smelled, it existed anyway.

Anaximander was first to propose this step toward abstract idealism. He stated that "APEIRON" underlay all of reality. It is difficult to translate this word, but it seems to refer to a material substance lying behind or below all things as a "ground of being."

Pythagoras was the philosopher who took the next step. He believed that a material substance could not be the "One" of reality, regardless of whether it could be perceived by the senses or not. Reality was actually something abstract. It was a "Number."

This step in philosophy opened the door to Idealism, which believes that "ideas" or "numbers" are more real than material substances. This led to the classic contrast between "mind" and "matter" in Greek thought.

The Greek philosophers finally came to the conclusion that the "One" that made up ultimate reality was *not* a material substance open to sense perception. It was an "idea" or a "number" that could be perceived only by the mind apart from the senses.

One or Many?

This led philosophers to consider further questions concerning the "One" that supposedly made up reality. Was this "One" one or many in *quality* or *number*? Was this "One" at *rest* in an *unmovable* and *static* sense or was it in *constant flux* or *motion*?

Democrates put forth the idea that reality was "One" in quality but "many" in number, while Empedocles stated that the "One" was many in quality but one in number! Parmenides felt that reality was "One" in both quality and number. The "One" was ultimate. All else was illusion. This idea is the basis of such eastern religions as Hinduism.

Monism and Pluralism

Thus from the Greeks came the conflict between the monists and pluralists. Yet, they both assumed that reality was "One" and that it was eternal. No real distinction lay between things in this life. They all existed as part of "One" world, and man could discover the nature of the "One" by reason alone.

Being or Becoming?

Another conflict that arose centered in the debate between Parmenides and Heraclitus.

Becoming?

Heraclitus championed the position that there is no "being," but all is "becoming" in a dynamic process of constant change. "No one steps in the same river twice" was Heraclitus' slogan. Everything was in flux. Thus absolute knowledge of truth or morals was impossible because everything is constantly changing. What seems "permanent" is illusory. Nothing is fixed, perfect or immutable, not even the gods.

Heraclitus never realized that he had only succeeded in refuting himself. If "Nothing is true in an eternal immutable sense" is true, than Heraclitus' ideas are not true either! If he is wrong, then he is wrong. If he is right, then he is wrong. Either way, he is wrong!

Parmenides taught that there is no "becoming," but that all is "being." Thus everything is static, fixed, and immutable in the sense of immovable. His disciple Zeno tried to demonstrate by several famous paradoxes such as an arrow in flight that motion is an illusion. What is "real" is permanent. Change and movement are illusory.

The pre-Socratic period ended in a classic stalemate between Heraclitus' "becoming" and Parmenides' "being." They could not solve the contradictions between the two.

Plato

Plato was the first philosopher to attempt a synthesis between the two systems of Parmenides and Heraclitus. He began by assuming by faith that ultimate reality was "One," that it was eternal, and that man could discover its identity on the basis of his reason alone.

The Platonic solution was to place "being" on top of "becoming" like a sandwich. Plato's "World of Ideas" with its "Idea of the Good" took on all the attributes of Parmenides' being. It was eternal, static, immutable, and transcendent. Heraclitus' world of flux became the "World of Matter" that Plato defined as "non-being." It had all the attributes of Heraclitus' "becoming."

But, merely laying Being (Mind) on top of Becoming (Matter) did not bring them into contact with each other. No knowledge of this world was possible as long as "matter" and "mind" remained isolated from each other.

In order to overcome this problem, Plato invented the concept of a finite god who exists between the World of Ideas and the World of Matter. This "Demiurge" was not omnipotent, omniscient or sovereign. The Demiurge molded formless matter according to the patterns he saw in the World of Ideas without any idea of what he was making or what the future of it would be. Thus Plato's god was not infinite in knowledge or power. He did not exist prior to or independent of reality. He was a finite part of a finite world. As such, he could not know the future of what he made.

But, even with a Demiurge, Plato never solved the problem that what was knowable and what was real belonged only to the World of Ideas. The World of Matter remained unknowable and only reflected the ideas or patterns that molded it.

The Platonic system only satisfied philosophers for a brief time. Skeptics eventually took over Plato's Academy and ended up teaching that no true knowledge of anything was possible. Thus no absolute morals were possible. This is the logical conclusion of all philosophic systems that begin with the assumption of human autonomy. When man begins only with himself, from himself, and by himself, he will always end in skepticism and relativism.

Aristotle

Even though he had been a disciple of Plato, Aristotle saw that Plato had not really solved the problems of meaning and knowledge. As a matter of fact, he had merely relocated them. For example, instead of explaining the meaning of the chair in front of him, Plato pointed up to the idea of "chair-ness," which supposedly resided in the "World of Ideas." But, merely shuffling the chair from "here" to "there" hardly constitutes an explanation!

In his Metaphysics, Aristotle put forth fourteen arguments that refuted Plato's system. Plato was too idealistic and rationalistic in that he did not explain matter, he merely defined it away! Rearranging Parmenides' "being" and Heraclitus' "becoming" into a dichotomy did not resolve anything. But, like all the philosophers before him, Aristotle assumed Monism and human autonomy. Instead of Plato's dual world, Aristotle had one world composed of a mixture of "form and matter," "mind and matter" or "essence and matter."

"Matter" was pure potential and "mind" was pure actuality. There was an Ultimate Cause unto which all things were being attracted. This produced the motion involved in moving from potential to actual. In this way, Aristotle hoped to blend together Parmenides' "being" with Plato's "mind" and Heraclitus' "becoming" with Plato's "matter."

Aristotle rejected the idea of "atoms" making up matter that had been developed by earlier Greek philosophers. Most modern followers of Aristotle accept the idea of atoms even though Aristotle rejected it as absurd.

The fatal flaw in Aristotle's reasoning was that the "form" of something did not have to be consistent with its "essence." Thus, the knowledge of particulars becomes impossible. Only universals were knowable in the last analysis. Once again no knowledge of this world was really possible.

Aristotle believed in many finite gods who were neither omniscient nor omnipotent and were only a part of the process of potentiality becoming actuality. These gods did not know the future. Since Aristotle's gods could only know universals, they could not know particulars. They were incapable of knowing you or your future.

Epistemology

The Pre-Socratics

The early philosophers were empiricists, and restricted knowledge to what was perceivable by the five senses. When this went nowhere, they turned to rationalism that relied only on ideas in the mind. Further refinements such as idealism, materialism, realism, etc. flowed out of the basic conflict between Parmenides and Heraclitus.

The radical problem was that they all assumed that man could "go it alone," i.e. he is autonomous. The doctrine of human autonomy doomed all their philosophies to ultimate relativism and skepticism.

Plato

Since Plato was a rationalist, he did not believe that all knowledge came from the senses. Man actually already knew everything because he had pre-existed his birth in the World of Ideas. He had "Fallen" into a physical body. This Fall was a bad thing because it made man forget all he knew. But, as man *reasoned*, he could "remember" or "recollect" the ideas that existed in the "World of Ideas." While the Demiurge god was not omniscient, Plato felt that man was!

Aristotle

Aristotle championed empiricism against the rationalism of Plato. But, like Plato, he still assumed monism and human autonomy. In his theory of knowledge, Aristotle taught that we can "abstract" or "grasp" the "essence" or meaning of an object logically. Thus Aristotle placed knowledge not in things "as they are" but in their "essence." Matter (i.e. form) was still unknowable. Aristotle's system as well as Plato's was eventually abandoned. Skepticism and relativism triumphed once again.

Ethics

The Pre-Socratics

Not having any authority higher than their own finite reason, the pre-Socratic philosophers could not generate any ethical absolutes that were infinite or universal. But, this did not stop them from *calling* their ideas universal, intuitive, and self-evident.

The fact that the philosophers had *conflicting* ideas did not seem to bother them. But, how can two contradictory ideas, that were mutually exclusive, be universal, intuitive, and self-evident at the same time? If one idea is "universal, intuitive, and self-evident," then how could the opposite idea also be "universal, intuitive, and self-evident?" Due to this "Law of Non-Contradiction" they cannot both be all of those things.

Universal, Intuitive, Self-evident

One way to solve the problem that your ideas were not really "universal, intuitive, and self-evident" even when you pretended they were, was to claim that your ideas were "universal, intuitive, and self-evident" among men who were rational, cultured, and of good will. Your ideas were "universal, intuitive, and self-evident" among those people who were superior in intellect or class, who agreed with you! Anyone who thought differently did not really count as they were obviously inferior to you. In this way you could exclude women, children, non-whites, and third world "savages."

They based their ideas on the consensus of their society. No one else matters to them. Whenever you hear or read philosophers claiming that their ideas are "universal, intuitive, and self-evident," they are guilty of racism, classism, and snobbery. They are also hypocritical since they ignore contradictions between themselves of their same class.

Plato

Socrates and Plato tried to create absolutes on the basis of their own subjective and personal conceptions of the "idea" of the "Good." Everything that conformed to their idea of "Good" was good. Anything that contradicted their idea of the "good" was "evil." How convenient!

The main problem with this line of reasoning was this question: How could Plato or Socrates prove that their subjective, personal, culturally-limited, and finite idea of what was "good" was better than someone else's idea of what is "good?" To Socrates, homosexuality was both natural and good. We tend to excuse this side of Socrates because it reflected the consensus of Greek society at that time.

In the end, Socrates never refuted Thrasymachus's argument that "Might Makes Right." Socrates' and Plato's own finiteness relativized any absolutes they tried to make.

Aristotle

Aristotle abandoned Plato's attempt to generate absolutes by an arbitrary concept of "the idea" of "the Good." In its place he taught that ethics was a sliding scale of pleasure and pain and not an issue of absolutes. What was "good" would be attracted to the Ultimate Cause to which all things were moving. But, this attempt to have "relative" and "mutable" morals failed.

Aesthetics

To the Greek philosophers, ideal perfection was the standard of beauty. Imperfection was ugliness. This is why they painted and sculpted perfect bodies for the gods, man, and animals, set in the background of a perfect nature. For example, the nude male body was pictured in its ideal form without imperfections of any kind because it was, in their mind, the pinnacle of ideal perfection. It was not until much later that the female body was likewise judged perfect ideal beauty.

The dogma of human autonomy ultimately led humanists to the idea that, "Beauty is in the eye of the beholder." Since man was the measure of all things, this includes both beauty and ugliness. In the end, this idea leads to the destruction of any hope of objective standards of beauty and ugliness. One man's beauty was another man's ugliness.

Summary

In the end, each philosopher was contradicted by the philosophers who followed him. Nothing was permanently established as certain or absolute. The Greeks failed to produce a philosophy or worldview that was *believable* or *livable*, i.e. they could not live what they believed.

We should not be surprised by this fact. Humanistic thought always fails in the end because its foundational commitment to human autonomy renders it incapable of success. When finite man starts only with his own reason, feelings or experience, he will always end in skepticism (no knowledge is possible) and relativism (no morals are possible). After all the exaggerated claims of man's independence from divine revelation, when the "rubber met the road," human reason, intuition, and experience led man down a blind alley.

PART TWO

Humanistic Science

The history of humanistic science has always followed the history of Natural Philosophy. As the philosophic worldview of society changed, science changed along with it. In this sense, humanistic science is a "tag along" because it always follows the ever-changing wind of philosophic fads. Like a chameleon that changes its color to match the color of its background, science has changed and adapted to whatever dominant worldview is in vogue at the time. It is thus relative, not absolute.

The Golden Age of Greece

Humanistic "science" was first developed by the Pre-Socratic philosophers who assumed the validity of the pagan dogma of human autonomy, i.e. "man is the measure of all things." They assumed that man was the Origin of truth, justice, morals, meaning, and beauty; that man could understand the universe by reason alone, apart from and independent of any special revelation from God.

At the beginning, some Greek philosophers such as Heraclitus believed that their observation of "Nature" was the way to obtain knowledge of the world around them. Hence, the word "science" originally meant "knowledge from observation."

These early philosophers believed that if something could not be experienced by the five senses, it did not exist. This position was later revived in modern times under the name "empiricism" and the Vienna School of Positivism. Scientism and realism are modern expressions of this ancient theory.

Monism

Another mega-shift took place in Greece around the same time. In addition to human autonomy, the Greeks now adopted the religious doctrine of Monism, borrowed from Orphic mysticism, which taught, "All is One." The "Many" diversities around us do not really exist even if that is what our eyes told us. All is ONE, not four.

Note: Monism is the basis of Eastern religions such as Hinduism and Buddhism. This is why modern science has returned full circle to its roots in Eastern mysticism.

Once Monism became an article of faith in Western philosophy, everything could be viewed as being a "uni-verse," i.e. unity out of diversity. A "uni-versity" is supposed to bring all knowledge together in one grand theory. Since humanism begins with man instead of God, it has not and, indeed, cannot generate a grand theory that encompasses all things. This is why modern universities teach there is no truth to discover, no morals to live by, no justice to implement, and no meaning to life.

The Theory of Atoms

In contrast to drifting off into idealistic non-material "Being," philosophers such as Leucippus, Democritus, and Epicurus believed that the universe was composed of very small material "atoms." They were the material "stuff" that made up all four elements.

"Atoms" were invisible and thus could not be observed by the five senses. They could not be defined and their existence was accepted by faith alone. Although they could not be seen or felt, "atoms," whatever they were, were said to be the basic building block of the universe. They were a paradigm or model of what reality was as expressed on a piece of paper. The diagram of an atom reflected what was out there in the world although no one had ever seen or touched an atom.

These "atoms" were little particles of matter like very small marbles or beads. Each atom was an exact replica of the universe complete with a central sun called a nucleus and planets rotating around it called electrons and neutrons. Each micro atom was only a miniature version of the macro universe! This model was neat and tidy and felt "rational."

The religion of Atomism was later rejected by Aristotle, but resurrected in the 17th century and is still taught in most high school science classes to this day. When your high school teacher showed you a plastic model of an atom, did he or she tell you that it was only one scientific "model" among many? It is actually a religious myth from ancient Greece.

Quantum Mechanics

When college students take their first class in quantum mechanics, they discover that "atoms" do not really exit. They are only a "model" or picture of what philosophers in the past imagined lay "beneath" the visible universe. No one had ever seen any little atomic micro-universes. No nuclei, electrons or protons were observed.

Instead of little pieces or particles of matter, like tiny pebbles, ultimate reality was now defined in terms of "sub- atomic" elements composed of magnetic energy fields.

By this time your head should be reeling with the realization that what you thought in high school was "science" was oversimplification, poor models, and even ancient religious dogma. In defense of the atom theory, realists point out that the theory led to the development of the atom bomb and nuclear power. Thus the theory *worked*.

Some people assume that something is true if it works. But anti-realists rightly point out that the atom idea is only one possible explanation for such things. After all, we can go to the moon using Newton's physics or Einstein's physics. While they contradict each other, we can make it to the moon using either one of them.

Realists argue that while it is true that no one has ever seen atoms, they have left "tracks" in cloud chambers.[12] But there are other scientists who can explain these so-called "tracks" without using the theory of atoms.

Plato's Academy

When Plato set up his famous Academy, over the door was written that only those who knew geometry could enter. He was referring to the "plane" geometry invented by some Greek scientists and philosophers who believed that the uni-verse was a flat plane with four corners. They had no concept of a round earth or uni-verse.

Astrology

This is why the astrologers such as Ptolemy assumed that whatever stars he saw over him in the Greek night sky would the same ones that everyone one else saw. The idea that people could be living on the other side of a round planet and thus see a different night sky with different stars in view never occurred to him.

Ptolemy is the father of modern astrology. He assumed that you were born under a certain astrological sign on a specific date because everyone is living on the same flat plane. Your "sign" assumes you were born in Greece! Since I have dealt at length with astrology elsewhere, I refer you to that resource.[13]

Ptolemy was also the father of "plane" geometry, which taught that sides of a triangle are never parallel and parallel lines never intersect. These ideas are the theorems, i.e. faith commitments, of plane geometry. All calculations are based upon such ideas.

SMSG's Universe

When I was a tenth grade high school student, I was selected by Yale University to become part of its Student Mathematics Study Group (SMSG). Edward Begle introduced us to Einstein's round earth and a bubble universe in which sides of a triangle are ultimately parallel and all parallel lines ultimately intersect. Given the curvature of the surface of the earth, every line is actually bent as it follows the curvature of the planet. It is actually impossible to draw a straight line!

Imagine a large soap bubble floating in the air in front of you. As you move your head from side to side, you see little flashes of light sparking on its surface. Now take away the soap film that made up the bubble's skin but leave behind the sparkles of light. All you now see is a sphere of dancing sparkles of light that is expanding outward as you watch it. That was the universe according to SMSG!

Modern Math

We also learned that modern mathematics no longer assumes the validity of ancient Greek ideas of mathematics. Most people do not understand that the Greeks developed a "base ten" mathematical model because they had ten fingers! But, what happens if we move over to a different base? For example, if we adopt a base two model instead of a base ten numeric system, one plus one now equals one-zero instead of two!

Another new approach we learned is that mathematical equations cannot "prove" anything because they are only *translations* from one language to another. Just because you can translate a sentence from the English language into a mathematical meta-language, this is no different than translating English into French or German. This is why I am unimpressed by natural theologians who think they have proven a theory because they can put it into the form of a mathematical equation. Big deal! They are only *translating* their theory, not proving it.

Aristotle

Aristotle was the first humanist philosopher who divided "science" into categories such as biology, zoology, physics, theology, etc. He followed the pre-Socratics in utilizing observation as his basic methodology to discover reality. He believed that earth, air, fire, and water were the four basic elements that made up the world.

Based on his observation that the sun rose in the East and set in the West, Aristotle taught geocentrism, i.e. the earth was the center of the universe and the sun, moon, and stars revolved around it. This became a scientific faith-dogma for over a thousand years. It could not be questioned.

Note: Since no one at that time had gone into outer space and looked back and saw the shape of the earth or its relationship to the planets, moon and sun, was a "geo" or "helio" view of earth the result of observation or were they both nothing more than mere speculation? They were both statements of what humanist man believed at that time.

Thomas Aquinas

When the official natural philosopher and theologian of the Roman Catholic Church, Thomas Aquinas, adopted the philosophy of Aristotle, geocentricism became part of Roman Church dogma. This explains why there was such a violent reaction when Copernicus and Galileo taught helio-centricism, i.e. the earth revolved around the sun. If the sun were indeed the center of the universe, this would threaten the very foundation of Aristotelian Natural Philosophy and Theology, and, by logical extension, the foundation of Catholic teaching.

The Copernican Revolution

The issue that faced Copernicus was not science versus religion but religion masquerading as science versus organized religion. Aristotelian science taught that the sun revolved around the earth. This was based on the observation that the sun rose and set. But Copernicus boldly stated that observation was not a guide to truth. The sun does not really rise or set. Your eyes are deceiving you.

It took a hundred years for the heliocentric model to triumph over Aristotle's geocentricism. But, after the work of Johannes Kepler, the battle was over. Science changed its worldview once again.

The Rise of Rationalism

Once modern science discarded observation, the way was open for speculations based solely on an abstract concept of human "Reason." Science was now following Rationalism, which had become the dominant worldview during the Renaissance. The real was the rational and the rational was whatever *felt real* to you.

Descartes' "reason" told him that invisible corpuscles made up the mechanistic world in which we lived. Spinoza drew up a mathematical model for the universe in which everything could be reduced to an equation. Rationalistic science reigned supreme. It supposedly dealt in absolutes deduced from self-evident, intuitive, universal truths.

Science was now viewed as a rational enterprise that could explain everything. Nothing was beyond its reach. "Miracles" were mysteries that science had not yet explained. Scientists were little gods in white coats running around pontificating on everything. Since they were objective and neutral in their work, their speculations and theories were accepted as "facts" regardless of the amount of empirical evidence to support them.

Note: Science now faced the conflict between induction and deduction. Some scientists arrogantly called induction "the" scientific method. This claim was first refuted by the philosopher David Hume and later by Karl Popper.[14]

Isaac Newton

Isaac Newton's worldview of the universe as a vast machine running according to immutable mechanical laws became dominant as it fit in with the rationalist dream that everything had a "rational" explanation. This is why Darwin's theory of evolution became an overnight success - even though there were no hard facts to support it. The "missing links" that he promised would show up, have never appeared!

Genetics renders Darwin's belief that acquired characteristics could be passed on to one's descendants not only obsolete but absurd. The "survival of the fittest" is a joke. While we smile at Darwin's claim that primate-man lost his tail by sitting on it, the theory of evolution still remains a religious dogma of scientism.

Empiricism Takes Over

When Empiricism dislodged Rationalism, science adapted to the change in worldview and became empirical in nature. If a word or statement could not be empirically verified or falsified in the laboratory, it was meaningless according to the Vienna School of Logical Positivism. Since such words as "God," "soul," or "angel" are not empirically verifiable, they were simply dismissed as meaningless. Religion was not refuted *per se*. It was simply defined out of existence.

Laboratory experiments became the rage until people caught on to the fact that scientists began with a theory in mind and then set up experiments that would validate it. When they did not get the results they expected, they tossed those results out and kept trying until they got what they wanted. For example, whenever an experiment demonstrates that the universe is actually only thousands of years old instead of billions of years, it is dismissed because it contradicts the dogma of the old earth. The test results that support a young earth are thrown into the trash.

Empiricism collapsed when its self-refuting nature became obvious. *It could not be empirically verified that things needed to be empirically verified!* Thus the principle of empiricism was itself meaningless according to its own foundational principle! Humanistic philosophers and scientists were once again adrift in the abyss of the unrelated.

This was the same problem with the principle of induction. *It itself could not be validated by induction! It depended on deductions drawn from a priori ideas such as the uniformity of nature, human autonomy, etc.*

Note: Any scientific theory that successfully refutes itself is doomed.

Einstein Rides to the Rescue

Albert Einstein's "theory of relativity" was another Copernican Revolution in the philosophy of science. His ideas forever changed the way we look at the world. He combined his love of music with his Talmudic heritage and blended them with the philosophy of Spinoza and ended up with a unified field of knowledge that he called "the theory of relativity." His view of the world was as dynamic as Newton's was mechanical.

The phrase "theory of relativity" is unfortunate because Einstein did not believe in moral or physical relativism. Einstein's scientific laws were as rigid, immutable, and absolute as Newton's. The speed of light in a vacuum is the same everywhere in the universe. There is no such thing as chance or free will because everything, including the thoughts and choices of man, are determined. His faith-based presuppositions were written in concrete.

One surprising element in Einstein's worldview that is not well-known is that he believed that science and religions were compatible. Max Jammer explains,

> Einstein never conceived of the relating between science and religion as an antithesis. On the contrary, he regarded science and religion as complementary to each other or rather as mutually depending on each other, a relating that he described by the metaphor quoted above, "Science without religion is lame, religion without science is blind."[15]

The reason why science and religion are compatible is that science itself springs from a priori religious ideas. Einstein stated,

> Speaking of the spirit that informs modern scientific investigations, I am of the opinion that all the finer speculations in the realm of science spring from a deep religious feeling, and that without such feeling they would not be fruitful. I also believe that, this kind of religiousness,

which makes itself felt today in scientific investigations, is the only creative religious activity of our time. The art of today can hardly be looked upon at all as expressive of our religious instincts.[16]

When faced with having to "prove" his belief that the speed of light in a vacuum is the same everywhere in the universe, Einstein retorted, "God does not play at dice." Jammer comments,

Einstein's persistent objection to the new quantum mechanics, on the grounds that "God does not play at dice," was, at least to some extent, religiously motivated.[17]

Where did he obtain his ideas of the unity of nature, the rationality of the universe, unrestricted determinism, and the denial of free will? All these concepts are faith-based religious dogmas he derived from Spinoza's pantheistic, philosophic religion.[18] Einstein declared his love of and dependence upon the religious and philosophic concepts of Spinoza on many occasions.

The Search for the Impossible

One great example of scientific religious dogma is what Jammer describes as Einstein's "indefatigable tenacity in searching for a unified field theory."[19] Like most past humanists, Einstein believed that man was the Origin of truth, justice, morals, meaning, and beauty. He really *believed* that someone, somewhere, somehow, some time would create a unified theory of knowledge that explained EVERYTHING.[20] He spent his entire life trying to produce a theory that encompassed all things.

While some humanists today have abandoned the search for a unified field of knowledge, it still resurfaces now and then and creates great excitement at the possibility. One example is the work of Stephen Hawking.[21] He created a world in his mind in which God *could not* exist. His rejection of God was not intellectual but emotional.

Quantum Mechanics

Einstein's unified field theory began to fall apart as Quantum mechanics attacked the basis of the theory of relativism by rejecting his doctrine of unrestricted determinism.[22]

Heisenberg demonstrated that Einstein's laws did not work when applied to sub-atomic elements. Heisenberg's famous "principle of indeterminacy" demonstrated that we could not know the position, speed, or direction of sub-atomic particles because the moment we tried to view or measure them, we alter their position, speed, and direction.

Stop and think for a moment. Humanists had always assumed that they could KNOW ultimate reality by observation and experimentation. But, if Heisenberg was right, then they CANNOT know reality, because the moment they try to observe it or experiment to know it, they alter it! Thus, the universe is ultimately *unknowable*.

Einstein realized that his Spinozian belief in unrestricted determinism was the foundation of his theory of relativity, and tried his best to refute Heisenberg. But, as Jammer correctly saw, "Einstein failed to disprove Heisenberg's indeterminacy relations."[23]

Einstein's worldview fell apart as his assured "laws" of science were no longer viewed as absolute or true. They were only sentences written on a piece of paper. Quantum Mechanics now rendered Einstein just as obsolete as Newton had done to Aristotle.

Constant Change

As we have pointed out, science tags along with contemporary religious philosophy and Natural Theology tags along with science, in that it always adopts whatever secular view of science is in vogue at the time.

- Medieval Roman Catholic Natural Theology based its arguments on the philosophy of Aristotle via Thomas Aquinas. Today many Catholic philosophers (and a few erstwhile

Protestant philosophers) still yearn for the "good old days" when Aquinas was the dominant worldview.[24]

- When Newton displaced Aquinas, Protestant Natural Theologians, particularly in Great Britain, shifted their theoretical base to Newtonian physics. The world was one vast machine like a watch. This is why there were so many arguments from the watch to the Watch Maker.
- When Einstein displaced Newton, Protestant Natural theologians, British ones taking the lead once again, simply switched their theoretical base over to his Theory of Relativity.
- When Quantum Mechanics displaced Einstein, a few Natural Theologians once against had to shift their theoretical base to a new mystical, Eastern worldview.

When you build your worldview on the shifting sand of popular opinion instead of upon the solid rock of Scripture, your views will change from day to day as you try to keep up with the ever-changing culture around you. Being "relevant" can be exhausting.

Time and Eternity

This is particularly true of Einstein's concept of the relationship between time and eternity. Roman Catholic theology traditionally based its understanding of time and eternity on Aquinas who had "Christianized" Aristotle's view. Most modern Catholic theologians have yet to move on in their worldview.

Since Neo-Protestant theologians are always trying to be "relevant," they have been faster to adopt whatever is in fashion at the time. But, they are usually twenty five years behind the secular world. By the time they adopt a new worldview, the world has already moved on to newer ideas.

With the advent of Einstein's physics, a shift took place in Natural Theology. Aquinas and Newton were "thrown under the bus" and Einstein was now enthroned.

Post-Modern "Christian" Theologians

This is the key to understanding the writings of such scholars as Whitehead, Hartshorne, Torrance, Annenberg, Boyd, Sanders, Rice, etc. They abandoned Newton and moved over to

Einstein's view of time and eternity. But, their dependence on the theory of relativity is a sign of spiritual weakness, not strength. They are violating the biblical command not to conform to this world (Rom. 12:1-2).

Evangelical theologians often fail to understand that Process Theology, Neo-Processianism, the Open View of God, etc. are nothing more than versions of Einstein's theories. The origins of such heresies are philosophic in origin and nature, not *biblical*. This is why you can cite Scripture after Scripture to them that clearly refute their heresies but they remain unmoved. Their faith-based doctrines are from Einstein, not God.

What is particularly absurd is that "evangelical" rationalists, such as J. P. Moreland and William Lane Craig, do not accept Einstein's doctrine of unrestricted determinism. They still cling to the old pagan Greek idol of "free will." Their attempt to deny the foundation of Einstein's unified field of knowledge (i.e. determinism), but, at the same time, adopt his view of time and eternity will not survive the test of time or consistency. [25] They will learn the bitter truth that you cannot have your cake and eat it too!

The Black Hole of Existentialism

After the demise of Rationalism and Empiricism, Existentialism took the philosophic world by storm. Man's attempt to build a unified field of knowledge of the universe was now abandoned as not only impossible, but delusional. The humanistic hope that man could be the Origin of truth, justice, morals, meaning, and beauty died. Everything became relative and subjective. There was no objective truth to believe, no morality to live by or beauty to admire. All was meaningless, including science.

Existentialism revealed that scientific objectivity and neutrality were illusions. Everything was relative, including math and logic. There were no absolutes or order behind the scenes, not even the so-called "laws" of science. The crisis was indeed great as the motivation for and the basis of humanistic science was now destroyed.

Relativism has always been the inner cancer eating away at the soul of humanism. If l am the Origin of truth and you are the Origin of truth, and yet we end up with contradictory "truths," either I am right and you are wrong or we are both wrong! We cannot both be right - unless truth is relative, i.e. there is no truth.

Public Indoctrination or Education?

In the 1960's the public school system aggressively taught existential relativism. All is meaningless and without significance. That generation was excited to learn there were no absolutes in the bedroom. Anything goes! If it feels good, do it! Make love, not war! Turn on, tune in, drop out!

The artists caught on quickly and modern anti-art soon became the norm. A crucifix in a jar of urine was viewed as art. The line between pornography and modesty was erased. In film, murder without guilt and sex without meaning was the new art.

Relativism then moved on to the factory. It did not make any real difference if you made a good car or a shoddy one. It is all relative in the end and without meaning. People no longer took pride in their work because it had lost all meaning. We should work to live, not live to work.

It then moved to politics. Political "science" died. Politicians could now say something, deny they said it, and later boast that they had said it. What they said was relative to the audience at hand.

Medicine was relativized and doctors were called upon to murder unborn and newly born babies, children with physical or mental defects, the mentally disturbed, and, finally, the elderly. They now became merchants of death.

The Last Idol to Fall

The last vestige of the old Newtonian worldview to succumb to the killer virus of relativism was science. Once humanists took relativism to its logical conclusion, science died. It no longer had any absolute value or meaning. Science was not good or evil. It just was.

This downward process is why students today are not interested in protesting wars or becoming chemists. It all means nothing. Personal peace and affluence are the only values today. We have finally arrived at the end of the yellow brick road of humanism and the Emerald city was only a mirage.

How Did We Destroy Ourselves?

How did we get in such a mess? By falling prey to the humanist dream that man, starting only from himself, by himself, with himself, could understand the world around him without special Revelation from God. Any progress the West made in scientific knowledge came from those early scientists who believed that the Bible was the basis for the existence and necessity of science.

Francis Schaeffer traced this line of despair and then challenged humanists to turn back to the Bible as the only basis of science.[26] In contrast, Natural Theologians, i.e. religious humanists, do not call secular humanists to turn to the Bible. Instead, they pick up the torch dropped by secular humanists and continue to dream the impossible dream that man is the Origin of truth, justice, morals, meaning, and beauty.

The Alternatives

Some scientists could not tolerate Existentialism and moved over to "new" worldviews and "new" epistemologies. Following the Beatles and the hippie drug culture of the 1960s, some scientists abandoned Western secular philosophy entirely and moved their theoretical base over to New Age forms of Hinduism and Buddhism. The findings of modern physicists, particularly in the field of quantum mechanics and Heisenberg's principle of indeterminacy, have raised serious doubts about the scientific validity of materialism's understanding of the nature of reality.[27]

Many young physicists have adopted Eastern idealism, which assumes reality to be "mind," and denies the existence of "matter!"

There is a growing fascination with Taoism or Buddhism that have become a popular religious framework for modern physics.[28]

Why? The sterile character of Western materialism has driven people into the seductive arms of Shiva. The pendulum has begun to swing from the extreme of materialism to the extreme of idealism.

Dr. Bernard Ramm foretold this shift toward idealism in modern physics in 1953. His prophetic words are worth considering:

> Both Nevius and Hocking believe that the current shift in physics from the older Newtonian physics to the new relativity and atomic physics is seriously damaging to the naturalistic program...If the contentions of such men as H. Weyl, A. Compton, J. Jeans, W. Carr, A. Eddington, and F. Northrop are correct, then it is conceivable that fifty years of science will see an abandonment of the naturalistic program by the scientists...The slight breeze in the direction of idealism may turn to prevailing winds. [29]

People familiar with modern physics know today Eastern idealism is fearless and aggressive.[30] Materialism is vulnerable, because it is beset by a simplistic and reductionistic methodology that renders it philosophically unacceptable.[31]

The Tao of Physics,[32] The Dancing Wu Li Masters,[33] Instant Physics,[34] and a host of other books have signaled the shift to Eastern philosophy. But, since Hinduism and Buddhism were not capable of developing a theoretical basis for science in the East, how could it provide a basis for science in the West? The attempt to find a basis for science in Eastern Mysticism will fail because the Eastern denial of material reality renders science delusional.

Second, those who did not move toward the East, went in the direction of Linguistic Analysis in which everything is reduced to semantics. They have concluded that a scientific "law" expresses someone's personal and subjective culturally-bound perception of what he or she thinks is reality. But, one person's reality is another person's fantasy. Thus, linguistics has not been able to generate an intellectual basis for science.

Summary

Humanistic science has tried every possible method to find an intellectual basis of and motivation for science. It has followed Western philosophy into the abyss of the unrelated. In the end it has Fallen into the black hole of Existentialism and lost any hope or meaning.

This gives the biblical Christian a window of opportunity to remind the heathen that God has made foolish the philosophy of this world (1 Cor. 1:20). It is by the Bible alone that science can have any meaning or significance. Let us now turn to the Biblical view of science.

PART II

The Bible and Science

The humanists have done a great snow job in obscuring the relationship between science and the Bible. They want you to believe that science is against the Bible and the Bible is against science. Thus there is a natural antagonism between religion and science. They claim that religion is based on faith while science is based on facts. They usually bring up the Scopes Monkey trial and then mock Christians as ignorant baboons.

First, the truth is that *humanistic* science and the Bible are enemies because humanism (i.e. *scientism*) is itself a *religion*. Since the Humanist Manifesto I and II both state that humanism is a *religion*, the underlying conflict is between the *religion* of humanism and the *religion* of the Bible. Don't let them bully you on this issue.

Second, humanists presuppose the classic Greek philosophic dichotomy in which reality is divided into a lower and upper level.

Upper	Lower
mind	matter
essence	form
grace	nature
freedom	nature
faith	reason
belief	knowledge
noumenal	phenomenal
religion	science
faith	facts
sacred	secular

By framing philosophic issues within these dichotomies, humanists have already rigged the issue. You must object to these dichotomies because they are a priori religious ideas that contradict the Bible. I simply refuse to be pigeonholed into these dichotomies.

Third, humanists like to pretend that they are neutral and objective and that their theories come from their observation of brute facts. In reality, they presuppose a host of unproven faith-assumptions such as human autonomy, ontological thinking, evolution, brute facts, Monism, etc., and these presuppositions control their perception and interpretation of the world. To ask proof for the so-called method of induction is "to cry for the moon" according to Frank Ramsey.[35]

Humanistic scientists begin with blind faith in certain presuppositions that they use to build their worldview. Their philosophy of science is derived from their worldview. Their so-called "scientific theories" are applications of their philosophy of science, which were derived from their worldview based entirely on faith assumptions. The following diagram may help. You move up from faith to scientific theories.

↑ false scientific theories

false philosophy of science

false philosophic worldview

false presuppositions

faith assumptions

Fourth, the development of science did not take place in the non-Christian pagan world because humanistic worldviews could not provide a sufficient theoretical basis of or motivation for science.

- The Greeks believed that the world came out of chaos, that chance and luck control it, and that it will one day fall back into chaos.
- Eastern humanists denied material reality.
- African and Meso-American cultures were based on mythological cosmologies that could not generate science.

The Biblical Philosophy of Science

As with all things, science must be understood in the context of Creation, Fall, and Redemption.

Science in the Light of Creation

First, the biblical doctrine of Creation gives us the only basis of and motivation for science. The Christian knows from his Bible that he can pick up a rock and ask, "What is the meaning of this rock? What is its purpose? What function does it have in the environment? How can I use it to benefit mankind? How can I glorify God through this rock?"

Humanism cannot answer any of these questions because it begins with the faith assumption that there is no Creator who made the rock with meaning and purpose. It cannot give us any reason why the rock should be used to benefit mankind. What if there is a rare slug that lives under that rock?

I know from the Bible that all things, including the rock, have objective meaning because it was given meaning by the Creator.

> YHWH has made everything with its own purpose in mind. (Pro. 16:4))

The Hebrew text is clear that,

> ...all is made by God for its purpose, i.e. a purpose premeditated by Him that the world of things and of events stands under the law of a plan, which has in God its ground and its end.[36]
>
> Everything in God's design has its own end and object and reason for being where it is and such as it is; everything exhibits his goodness and wisdom, and tends to his glory.[37]

God told Adam to pick up a rock, a plant, or an animal and try to understand its divine meaning and purpose. How can we use these things to benefit mankind and to glorify Him? Man was to use his capacity to reason within the context of Revelation, not outside of it or in opposition to it. Logic, like fire, is good in its place. But once logic, like fire, runs wild, it destroys all there is including itself.

The biblical worldview of Creation teaches us the following

points that provide the philosophic framework for the existence and value of science. These points were already discussed in previous chapters on Creation. In Genesis 1-3, the following doctrines are set forth.

- Man was created by God. Thus he did not evolve from lower animals.
- God made man unique in that he is the image bearer of God.
- No animal was created to bear God's image.
- Man has intrinsic dignity, worth, and significance because he is the image bearer of God.
- Man is more valuable and important than animals. Thus animals serve the existence and benefit of man as well as the glory of God.
- God commanded man to take dominion of the earth. Thus man has the responsibility to take dominion over the animals and the earth itself.
- God commanded man to name the animals and to take care of the garden, which means that science began in the Garden of Eden as a command of God to man.
- In naming the animals, man used observation and his mind to come up with names that reflected the nature of the animal named. The Hebrew concept of naming someone or something was significant (e.g. Gen. 17:5; 28:19). We must not confuse it with the modern practice of giving arbitrary and meaningless names.
- Since everything has a divine purpose

and a meaning, man is responsible to discover the purpose and meaning of everything.

- The basis of science is the Genesis Cultural Mandate to take dominion of the earth.
- Man has the responsibility to be a good steward of the planet because he will have to answer to God for what he did with it..

Second, in the Biblical worldview, science is man's Fallible attempt to understand the divine purpose and meaning of things, how to use that knowledge to take dominion over them, and then to use them for the glory of God and the benefit of mankind.

Third, science is limited to taking dominion over the earth. It cannot answer the following ultimate questions:

- Does the universe exist, or is it an illusion?
- Did the universe have a beginning?
- Will it have an end?
- How long did it take for the universe to come into existence?
- How old is the universe?
- Why does it exist as opposed to not existing?
- Why does the universe have a uniform structure capable of prediction?
- Is man to be viewed as separate from other life forms on the planet?
- Is man only an animal, or is man a "higher" form of life?
- Is man's existence and comfort more important than the existence and comfort of animals?
- Does man have intrinsic purpose,

meaning, significance, dignity, and worth?
- Is man more important than plants and animals?
- Does man have the right to alter his environment?
- Does man have the right to consume and control animals?
- Are there moral absolutes?
- Does man have an immortal soul?
- Is the soul conscious after death?
- Does it go to heaven or hell, or is it reincarnated into another body?

One example is light. Science cannot explain what it is. Some say it is composed of particles and others say it is composed of energy waves. They have each created tests that confirm their theory. According to the Bible, science should take dominion over electricity and use it for benefit of mankind and the glory of God.[38]

Fourth, the Bible reveals absolute answers to the questions above.

- The universe exists.
- It had a beginning.
- It will have an end.
- It took six days for God to bring the universe into existence.
- The universe is between six to ten thousand years old.
- It exists for the glory of God.
- The universe has a uniform structure capable of prediction.
- Man to be viewed as separate from all other life forms on the planet.
- Man is not an animal, but a "higher" form of life.
- Man's existence and comfort are more

important than the existence and comfort of animals.
- Man has intrinsic purpose, meaning, significance, dignity and worth.
- Man is more important than plants and animals.
- Man has the right to alter his environment.
- Man has the right to consume and control animals.
- Man has an immortal soul.
- Man is conscious after death.
- He ends up in hell or heaven.
- Reincarnation is not true.
- There are revealed moral absolutes.

Fifth, the Biblical worldview begins with God (Gen. 1:1) and everything is defined in terms of its relationship to that God, who is the measure of all things.

God

Miracles

Angels

Demons

Man

Morals

Meaning

Animals

Plants

Things

Sixth, the humanistic worldview begins by denying the

existence of the infinite/personal Creator revealed in the Bible. Once there is no God, there begins a downward spiral that reduces everything in the end to the level of meaningless "things." Once God is dead, man is dead; meaning is dead; everything is dead, including science.

No Meaning Means No Morals

This is why humanistic science cannot generate any values or morals. It has never been able to generate an "ought" from what "is." Because of this, humanism cannot distinguish between evil and good science. It cannot judge that inventing a bomb that will kill all life is evil or that inventing a cure for cancer is good. It is all one and the same.

Seventh, only Creation gives us two essential ideas that make science possible.

1. The universe is intrinsically intelligible, understandable; it can be organized, altered, and controlled because it was created by the infinite mind of a God of order, not confusion. The pagans always assumed that the universe was ultimately *mysterious* in nature and thus not really intelligible. It is a waste of time to try to figure things out because there is nothing to figure out.
2. Man was created by God with the mental capacity to understand, relate, alter, and control the world around him because he was created in the image of God.

What good would an intelligible universe be if the brain of man was not wired by the Creator to understand it? A universe not quite intelligible or a man not quite intelligent enough to understand it would be a bridge broken at either end.

Humanism is the bridge broken at both ends. This is why modern animal rights groups commit terrorism. They do not believe that "man" exists. We are only one species of primates that got in control of the world because we evolved a thumb. Man-ape does not have any rights that the other life forms on the planet do not share. Man-ape is not special with special rights over and above other animals. Given the history of man-ape, he should go extinct for the good of the world. If we have to kill millions of people to save one bald eagle, so be it. Human life is no more important or sacred than the toad squashed under the wheels of a truck on Route 66.

Science in the Light of the Fall

The implications of man's radical Fall into sin and guilt are important. The pre-lapsarian world of man and his environment were totally different from the post-lapsarian world in which we now live. The Bible records that God placed various curses upon the environment as part Adam's punishment (Gen. 3:17f; Rom. 8:20-22). Divine judgments such as the Flood, the destruction of Sodom, etc. were catastrophic in nature. Thus the humanistic dogma of uniformitarianism, which teaches that everything has always been the same, is erroneous.

Man was radically altered by the Fall. Every aspect of his thoughts and life was corrupted and polluted by sin. All of psychology and sociology is aberrant in nature and not normal because man is not normal. He is a fallen creature in rebellion against his Creator.

It is important to remember the Fall because Natural Theology and Natural Law presupposes that man's "mind" and "will" escaped totally or to a great extent the effects of the Fall. Man's "Reason" is still inerrant and his will is still "free"! These are the hidden assumptions upon which humanists view man as the measure of all things.

Science In the Light of Redemption

In the 1960's, Star Trek gave young people the hope that mankind would one day ultimately overcome nationalism and become a united earth under a one-world government. Man would cast off materialism and capitalism. This is why the crew were never seen being paid money or spending money. Everyone worked for the common good and their needs were met. No one was interested in getting rich.

Star Trek also pictured all religions, even alien ones such as Spock's, as equally valid. It did not matter what you believed as long it did not hurt anyone but yourself. But, did the humanists who created the TV series have any basis for their *utopian* hopes? None whatsoever! Given the history of mankind, there is no reason to believe that man can change himself or his environment for the better.

Utopian Dreams

Where did the producers of Star Trek get their *utopian* hopes? They borrowed them from the biblical doctrine of Redemption. The Bible *alone* gives us a sound basis for utopian hopes for human nature and the earth. Paradise was lost, but one day it will be regained! Man will be perfect in a perfect world once Messiah comes back.

When King Messiah returns to this world, human history as we know it will be brought to its preordained conclusion. The resurrection of the body and the Day of Judgment will encompass all of humanity (Matt. 25:31-46). The old earth will be purged by fire and a new earth with a new atmosphere will be created (2 Pet. 3:3-15). The elect will be recreated incapable of sin (1 John 3:2) and, as a result, there will be no pain, sickness, suffering, death or crime for all those things will have passed away (Rev. 21:4).

The Biblical View of Aesthetics

Most Christians understand that the Bible has much to say about ethics, but they seem unaware that it also has a lot to say about aesthetics. Prof. Caverno in his excellent article on beauty in *The International Standard Bible Encyclopedia* begins his discussion with this comment.

That the Bible is an ethical book is evident. Righteousness in all the relations of man as a moral being is the key to its inspiration, the guiding light to correct understanding of its utterance. But it is everywhere inspired and written in an atmosphere of aesthetics. Study will bring out this fact from Genesis to Revelation. The first pair make their appearance in a garden where grew "every tree that is pleasant to the sight" (Gen 2:9), and the last vision for the race is an abode in a city whose gates are of pearl and streets of gold (Rev 21:21). Such is the imagery that from beginning to end is pictured as the home of ethics--at first in its untried innocence and at last in its stalwart righteousness. The problem will be to observe the intermingling of these two elements--the beautiful and the good--in the whole Scripture range.[39]

The extensive vocabulary of Hebrew words for beauty found in the Old Testament is astounding. God is described as "beautiful" (Psa. 27:4). Thus His House of Worship was filled with works of art "for the glory of God and for beauty's sake." (Exo. 28:2, 40; 2 Chron.3:6).

The word "beauty" was used by Solomon more than any other writer. He described the husband and wife in the Song of Songs as calling each other "beautiful" at least fifteen times. This is one of the keys to a happy marriage.

We are also warned that physical beauty will not last, but will fade away with time (Pro. 31:30). Thus your relationship to your mate must not be based upon external beauty but upon the inner beauty of a godly character (1 Peter 3:1-6).

Beautiful jewelry, clothing, crowns, buildings, etc., are described as "beautiful" (ex. Isa. 3:18). There is nothing wrong with surrounding yourself with beauty.

After several years of studying this issue, the following is a brief summary of the biblical view of aesthetics.[40]

Aesthetics in the Light of Creation

The biblical account of Creation supplies us with the only valid basis for a proper understanding of the Origin, existence, function, and explanation of beauty and the art that expresses it. Thus art is not a meaningless fluke of a meaningless chance-driven evolutionary process. It is a reflection of the image of God in man.

Man's aesthetic being is patterned after God's aesthetic being. Animals and machines do not produce or appreciate art. But man, as God's image-bearer, is both an art-maker and an art-appreciator. Art is part of human existence from the very beginning because it is based on the Creator-creature relationship.

Man as image-bearer was given a Creation Mandate in Genesis 1:28–30. Man's art was intended to be a vital part of his obedience to this Mandate. Humanism tries vainly to provide a mandate for art or science.

After the work of Creation was finished, God looked over all He had made and pronounced it " טוֹב," i.e. the creation was *beautiful* as well as perfect. The intrinsic goodness of the Creation means that no art medium is intrinsically evil. No combination of sounds, forms, colors or textures is intrinsically evil.

This is why Christian artists must take their stand against the idea that matter (ex. the human body) is intrinsically evil. There is no biblical reason to put diapers or leaves on nude statutes! No combination of tones or colors is intrinsically evil or demonic.

Christian art should reflect the original Creation in all of its beauty, form, harmony and goodness. For example, David composed musical compositions that celebrated Creation by using the mediums of poetry, song, and instrumental music (Ps. 8; 19; 89; 100, etc.). Franz Joseph Haydn's *Creation* is another good example of an artistic display of the beauty of the original creation.

The biblical doctrine of Creation supplies us with the only valid basis upon which to explain the origin, existence, function and diversification of color. The theory of evolution can never explain why a black cow eats green grass and produces white milk.

The Bible reveals that color is here in all of its diversification simply because God likes color. Beauty is thus ultimately in the eye of *the Beholder*—the Creator God. He is the original artist who is the aesthetic pattern for man who was created in God's image.

When we look at the world of color and form that God created (such as a beautiful sunset), we must confess that God is the great

Painter. When we examine the shape of the mountains, the different forms of animal and plant life, and the human body, we know that God is the great Sculptor.

When we read in Scripture that in heaven God surrounds Himself with angelic and human choirs; that angelic choirs sang their heavenly music at Creation and the birth of Christ; that the stars sing for joy; that God made musical instruments in heaven to be played continuously before Him; that God commanded man to worship Him through music, we know that He is the great Musician (Rev. 5:8; 14:1–3; Luke 2:13, 14; Job 38:7; Ps. 30:4;33:3).

Ideal Geometric Form

One interesting feature of biblical aesthetics is the geometric form that symbolized perfection. While the Greeks thought that the circle represented perfection and the Egyptians thought that the pyramid form was perfection, the Bible always pictured perfection in terms of a rectangle.

The Ark, the Tabernacle, the Temple, the Heavenly Jerusalem, the rebuilt temple of Ezekiel, etc., were all rectangles, not circles or pyramids. God revealed rectangle blueprints to Noah, Moses, and Ezekiel. Since He is the Great Architect, what is the significance of the rectangle as opposed to the circle or pyramid?

When we examine the literary forms within Scripture, we find beautiful poetry, prayer, prose, praise and proclamation. Thus we must confess that God is the great Poet and Writer.

Art is not for art's sake. It exists for God's glory for He is here and is not silent. The little bird singing in the forest, where and when no human ear can hear it, is still beautiful because God hears it. The desert flower, where and when no human eye can see it, is still beautiful because God sees it.

Aesthetics in the Light of the Fall

The radical Fall of man into sin and guilt supplies us with the only valid basis to understand the origin and existence of ugliness, evil, pain, suffering, chaos, war, pain, sorrow, and death. What is now is not what originally was.

Since the Fall polluted every aspect of man's being, the aesthetic aspect of the image of God in man was corrupted by sin. Man's aesthetic abilities are now used against God instead of for God. Thus we find the rise of apostate art that finds its climax in idolatry where the art object is worshiped as God. Idolatry reveals that man now worships the creature instead of the Creator (Rom. 1:18–25).

Biblical art should reflect the ugliness of man that sin has caused. It should reveal the misery, agony, and pain of sin, death, and hell. It should point to the ultimate despair of a life without God. It should portray the horror of hopeless sinners in the past who were the recipients of the great judgments of God against sin. The Flood or the destruction of Sodom should be depicted by art.

Art should supply the mediums through which the people of God can express their own despair, conviction of sin, confusion, pain, discouragement, etc. We need "songs in the night," songs when loved ones die, songs of confession of sin. The Psalms supply us with many examples of this kind of art (Psa. 51, etc.)

The Christian artist should aesthetically surpass the pessimistic existentialist artist when it comes to portraying the despair, ugliness and hopelessness of sin. The doctrine of total depravity as taught in such places as Rom. 3:9-19 is more realistic and frightening than anything the humanists can come up with. We need aesthetically to confront man with the ugliness and horror of his rebellion against God and with the reality of divine judgment against sin.

Aesthetics in the Light of Redemption

The biblical doctrine of Redemption gives us the only basis for artistic portrayals of truth, justice, meaning, morals, and beauty. We should reclaim every square inch of this world for Christ. Every thought and talent is to be redeemed unto God's glory for all of life is to be lived for Him (I Cor. 10:31; II Cor. 10:5). All of culture is to be conquered for Christ. Even though sin makes it impossible to attain total perfection in this life, Christians are given the Spirit of God to execute this Mandate as much as possible in all of culture.

It is from the Bible we get the idea that the good will ultimately triumph over evil; that justice will be established and injustice punished. Christians know from the Bible that they "will live happily ever after" through the merits of the person and work of Messiah.

When Jesus returns and creates a new earth, the Elect will fulfill the original Creation Mandate given to Adam. Our wildest dreams cannot comprehend the wondrous art, science, and philosophy that shall be produced by the glorified saints in the eternal state.

Redemption supplies us with the only valid basis for Christians going into the arts. It is through grace alone and Christ alone that we escape apostate art such as the veneration of idols and icons.[41] Redeemed sinners respond aesthetically to God because the image of God is renewed within them (Eph. 4:24; 5:18, 19)..

The arts should be viewed as:

- Obedience to the Creation Mandate (Gen. 1:28).
- Obedience to the Mission Mandate (Matt. 28:19, 20).
- The stewardship of God-given talents (Matt. 25:14–30).
- Worship, praise, rest, recreation, prayer, and confession (ex. Psa. 19; 23; 51; 90; 100).
- The edification of the saints.
- The evangelism of sinners.

Christian art should at times reflect the great moments in the history of redemption, the thanks, prayer, and praise of redeemed sinners, and the saints' desire for sinners to be saved. Again, many of David's Psalms are artistic expressions of thankfulness to God for salvation (Ps. 103, etc.). Christian art should portray the following:

- God exists and has communicated to man.
- There is hope, love, meaning, truth, etc.
- The beauty and dignity of Christ.
- There is order behind the chaos of life. God is still in control.

- The beauty that will be in the new creation.
- That good will ultimately triumph over evil.
- That the righteous will be vindicated and the wicked punished.

Christian artists engaged in evangelism should attempt to push sinners to despair in order to drive them to Christ. We should reveal both the ugliness of sin and the beauty of salvation. In this sense every artist is an evangelist to a lost, sick, and dying world, for every Christian is scripturally called upon to evangelize his world for Christ (Matt. 28:19-20). This means that the Christian artist should view himself or herself as a prophet, priest and king to the people of God.

- As a prophet, he should protect the people of God from idolatry.
- As a priest, he should lead people to worship of God alone through the arts.
- As a king, he should provide for the aesthetic needs of the people of God and protect them from apostate art that leads to idolatry.

Perhaps it would be helpful to see that art has various functions. The following describes some of these functions. A given piece of art may have one, some, or all of these functions:

- "Cool" art: art aimed at creating a distinct mood, impression or emotion on those exposed to the art. *Example*: Psalm 150.
- "Hot" art: art aimed at communicating truth to the intellect. This can be called "message art." *Example*: Psalm 1 and Proverbs.
- "Reflective" art: art that expresses and reflects the mood and emotional state of the artist. *Example*: Psalm 51.
- "Aesthetic" art: art aimed purely at the aesthetic sense of man. It is "beautiful" without being cool, hot or reflective. It is for entertainment

purposes. This is art for beauty's sake. *Example*: the art work in the tabernacle and temple (Exod. 25; II Chron. 3:6).

- "Enrichment" art, i.e. the "hidden art" of daily life: flower arrangements, table settings, attention to the selection of color of different foods, etc. This is art in which every home should be involved.

Closing Questions on Aesthetics

1. *Is it proper to distinguish between secular and religious art?* Answer: Yes/No. Yes, if you mean the distinction between art that portrays a biblical or "religious" event or scene and art that has a non-religious subject as its focus. There is a difference between a picture showing Noah's Flood and one showing a country picnic. No, if you mean that only religious art is "Christian art." Christian art is not restricted to events in biblical history, for the entire world is God's world (Ps. 24). Also, all art is "religious" in the sense of being either apostate or God-glorifying or somewhere in between. There is no "secular" art in the sense of "neutral" art.

2. *Can a Christian artist create art to entertain people?* Answer: We are to glorify God and to *enjoy* Him forever. Entertainment and recreation are legitimate creature necessities and, therefore, legitimate fields of work for the Christian. Those who are negative and suspicious of entertainment reveal a hidden strain of Platonic thinking.

3. *Should we judge a work of art on the basis of the life style of the artist?* Answer: No, just as we can take a crooked stick and draw a straight line, even so wicked men and women can produce

beautiful art.

4. *Can a Christian artist create "cool," reflective, or aesthetic art or must he restrict himself to portraying and conveying the gospel through "hot" art?* Answer: The Christian is not restricted to any one particular function or form of art. A still life painting of a bowl of fruit is just as "Christian" as a painting of the crucifixion if it is done for God's glory. The artist is not restricted to "hot" art.

5. *Is "good" art determined on the basis of the intent of the artist or on the amount of biblical truth it conveys?* Answer: The quality of a work of art is not determined solely on the basis of the intent of the artist or the clarity of its message. A Christian artist can produce poor art even though he did it for God's glory and tried to convey the gospel.

6. *How do we judge the quality of art?* Answer: By such aesthetic standards as:

   a. Technical excellence: Does the artist have the technical ability to do superior work in his medium of choice?

   b. Validity of style and medium: Is the medium the appropriate one to the style?

   c. Intellectual content: Is the artist's worldview clearly expressed in the art?

   d. The integration of content and vehicle: Are the two united in making one statement?

   e. The difference between art and pornography. The portrayal of the nude body is art when done to glorify God in His creation of the human body. Pornography is the portrayal of the nude body to stimulate sexual lust and immorality.

Conclusion

Many humanists today believe that "science" is a curse that has brought us Global Warming, nuclear energy, and other environmental disasters. We should all go back to living in a grass hut; walking around looking for vegetables and fruits to eat; living without electricity or cars.

The Bible alone gives us the only theoretical foundation for science and the arts. It alone provides us with a reason why they should exist and why we should do them. Humanism cannot provide us with any rationale or motivation for either one.

To God alone belongs all the glory!
Great things He has done.

Questions for Discussion

1. How has this chapter changed your view of science?
2. If you reject God and the Bible, is there any basis for science?
3. Can science be good or evil?
4. Relativism has destroyed science today. What evidence have you personally heard or seen that confirms that "science" today is more philosophical than factual?
5. Has "science" always been absolute and immutable or is it relative to culture, time, and situation?
6. What is the difference between science and scientism?
7. How does this material in this chapter disprove the different theories of evolution?

CHAPTER TEN

Creation Ex Nihilo

**Garden of Eden with the fall of man (Genesis 3:4) by Peter Paul
Rubens & Jan Brueghel the Elder (circa 1615)**

The Apostles' Creed begins with the first foundational concept of the biblical worldview when it identifies God as "Maker of heaven and earth." The Creed is not only right, but brilliant. It begins with the doctrine of Creation ex nihilo because Creation not only defines the nature of God, the world, and man but it also explains God's relationship to the world and to man. Indeed, everything that exists must be understood through the biblical idea of Creation ex nihilo. Trees are a good example.

How Humanists View Trees

When a humanist looks at a tree, he sees a chance-produced evolutionary tree to which man gives relative meaning because he thinks he is the Origin of truth, justice, morals, meaning, and beauty.

Humanists assume that meaning, like beauty, is in the eye of the beholder, i.e. man, because they believe that man is the measure of all things. Thus trees, like everything else, have no intrinsic meaning, worth or significance.

Because human autonomy always collapses into relativism, each man is free to define things according to his own subjective and personal prejudices, formed and influenced by his environment and upbringing. Thus a tree in and of itself is actually quite meaningless.

You can worship the tree or chop it into firewood. It doesn't really matter. The tree is a fluke, i.e. an accident, spawned out of a chance-driven meaningless evolutionary process with no rhyme or reason.

We must remember that evolution is not progressing or regressing; it is not going up or down; it is not moving toward anything, but it lurches through time according to chaotic luck and chance. This is why species become extinct.

This means that Humanism can never provide a sufficient basis for environmentalism. Nothing has absolute value or meaning. Everything is relative. In the end, man can either destroy the world or save it – either way it does not mean anything.

How a Christian Views Trees

When a Christian looks at a tree, he sees a Creator-produced tree that God has given absolute meaning because He is the Origin of truth, justice, morals, meaning, and beauty. Meaning, like beauty, is in the eye of the Beholder, God. He is the measure of all things, including trees. Thus trees have intrinsic meaning and worth.

The difference between the theist and the humanist could not be greater. For example, a typical humanist professor might ask his students, "If a tree Falls to the ground in a forest, when there is no one around to hear it fall, does it make a sound? If a flower blooms and man is the Measure of all things, then the tree makes no sound and the flower is not beautiful. If man is absent, meaning is absent as well.

The theist has an entirely different view. Since God is Omnipresent, He hears the tree fall to the ground and He sees the desert flower bloom. This is why David could play his harp and sing when he was alone. He knew that YHWH was listening (Psa. 55:17).

The Owner

Who owns the trees? Humanists believe that no one really owns the trees *per se*. Those inclined toward socialism would assert that trees belong to the state. But the state "owns" trees only by the power of the gun. Since man is the measure of all things, trees can be used by man.

Theists point out that since God created the trees, He is the Owner. This is why the Bible refers to them as "the trees of YHWH" (Psa. 104: 16). Trees exist to glorify the God who created them (Psa. 96:12; 148:9-13).

> The earth is Yahweh's, and everything it
> contains, the world, and those who dwell in
> it. (Psalm 24:1)

God, not man, is the Creator and Owner of all things – including trees. Thus He is the only one who has the right to determine their meaning and how they are to be treated. In the early chapters of Genesis, God tells man how to treat trees.

> Then Yahweh Elohim took the man and
> put him into the Garden of Eden to
> cultivate it and protect it. (Gen. 2:15)

The two words לְעָבְדָהּ (cultivate) and וּלְשָׁמְרָהּ (protect) summarize the original Creation Mandate that God gave to man in the Garden of Eden. Since the first word is used in Scripture to refer to *herding* domesticating animals as well as *cultivating* vegetation (ex. Deut. 15:19), the word "cultivate" is not a good translation. It should be translated "manage."

Adam's naming the animals was part of this original Creation Mandate (Gen. 2:19). In Hebrew thought, the act of naming the animals meant that he took dominion over them.

The second word usually meant "to protect" or "to guard." It is used for tending sheep in Gen. 30:31. These two Hebrew words must be taken together as a literary unit. Together they indicate that God gave man the stewardship to protect, guard, cultivate, shepherd, and manage the Garden of Eden. This involved physical labor as well as intellectual activity.

We have to remember that the word "Garden" means that Adam and Eve were placed in a protected animal and plant preserve surrounded by high walls. Fausset defines "garden" as,

> an enclosure in the suburbs, fenced with a hedge or wall (Isa. 5:5; Prov. 24:31), planted with flowers, shrubs, and trees, guarded (from whence comes "garden").[42]

God planted the Garden with an orchard of nut trees and fruit trees for man's food and then placed harmless domesticated animals in it for man's companionship. *The International Standard Bible Encyclopedia* comments:

> The Arabic jannah (diminutive, jannainah), Like the Hebrew Heb: gannah, literally, "a covered or hidden place," denotes in the mind of the dweller in the East something more than the ordinary garden. Gardens in Biblical times, such as are Frequently referred to in Semitic literature, were usually walled enclosures, as the name indicates (Lam 2:6 the American Revised Version, margin), in which there were paths winding in and out among shade and fruit trees, canals of running water, fountains, sweet-smelling herbs, aromatic blossoms and convenient arbors in which to sit and enjoy the effect. These gardens are mentioned in Gen 2 and 3; 13:10; Song 4:12-16; Eccl 2:5,6; Ezek 28:13; 31:8,9; 36:35; Joel 2:3. Ancient Babylonian, Assyrian and Egyptian

records show the fondness of the rulers of these countries for gardens laid out on a grand scale and planted with the rarest trees and plants. The drawings made by the ancients of their gardens leave no doubt about their general features and their correspondence with Biblical gardens.[43]

Too often Christians assume that the Garden of Eden encompassed the entire planet and that man had to deal with dangerous animals and dinosaurs. The reason why Moses used the word "Garden" was to point out that man was placed in a protected zoological park surrounded by walls on all sides.

This explains how man was able to name the animals in a few hours. If Adam had to name *all* the animals, fish, and insects on the planet, including all the ones in the oceans, it would have taken *many, many* years! Since Eve was not created until *after* he finished naming the animals, he would have been so old that he could not have procreated the human race!

Once Adam finished naming all the animals in the Garden, it became apparent to him that he, unlike the animals, was alone, i.e. without a mate. Once he realized this, Eve was created to be his mate.

All of this happened in the course of a single Creation day because Adam named the animals only in the Garden, not all the animals outside of it. The animals in the Garden were domesticated barnyard animals such as chickens, cows and dogs. T Rex, the tigers, lions, bears, etc. were outside the walls of the Garden.

The Basis of True Environmentalism

God commands man to take dominion over the planet by exercising stewardship over the Garden, including the trees. On the Day of Judgment, man will be judged by God concerning his stewardship of the planet and its natural resources. The mismanagement of the planet and the abuse of its resources is a violation of the divine Creation Mandate and will result in divine judgment.

As Francis Schaeffer pointed out in his insightful book, Pollution and the Death of Man, the only sufficient basis for environmentalism is the biblical doctrine of Creation ex nihilo. The humanist, regardless of whether he is Eastern or Western in worldview, has no mandate to protect, take care or rule over nature. There is no basis for human accountability except within the biblical worldview.

Who Says What?

God tells man which trees he may eat from and which trees he is forbidden to eat from. Since God owned all the trees, He had the right to dictate to man what to do and not to do with His trees. But, under the influence of the first Natural theologian, Satan, man chose to give his own meaning to the trees and to decide which trees he can eat from. He rejected the Divine Revelation of the meaning of the tree of knowledge and substituted Satan's meaning in its place.

God warned man that if he ate of the tree of the knowledge of good and evil, he would die. But Satan convinced man that the tree was not a threat of death but a promise of life; it was not the end but the beginning; it meant his deification, not his destruction.

The Fall of man revolved around the issue of who is the Origin of truth, justice, morals, meaning, and beauty:

God or Man?
Revelation or reason?
Revelation or experience?
Revelation or feelings?
Revelation or faith?

This is why the first sin was broken down into different components.

When the woman saw,
(*She had adopted Satan's worldview*)
the tree was good for food,
(*lust of the flesh*)

and that it was a delight to the eyes,
(*lust of the eye*)
and that the tree was desirable to make one
wise,
(*pride of life*)
she took from its fruit and ate;
(*open rebellion*)
and she gave also to her husband with her,
(*tempting others to sin*)
and he ate.
(*Adam joined her in rebellion*)

(Genesis 3:6)

Dr. Carl F. Henry, one of the most important and influential Evangelical thinkers of the 20th century, pointed out that the original sin was not the physical act of eating the forbidden fruit but the intellectual shift from a theistic view of life revealed by God to a humanist view of life derived from human reason through the deceit of Satan.

> The arch-liar begins by calling into question the truth of God's word. He skillfully leads the woman to question the goodness of God. Such questioning is mistrust and doubt, the opposite of faith. The very moment the woman began to mistrust God the Fall took place; the act of taking forbidden fruit was merely evidence that the Fall had occurred. The woman apparently used the same approach upon Adam when "she gave some to her husband, and he ate."[44]

This is why conversion begins with God opening the mind or heart of man to understand the biblical worldview.

And a certain woman named Lydia, from the

city of Thyatira, a seller of purple fabrics, a worshiper of God, was listening; and <u>the Lord opened her heart</u> to respond to the things spoken by Paul. (Acts 16:14)

καί τις γυνὴ ὀνόματι Λυδία, πορφυρόπωλις πόλεως Θυατείρων σεβομένη τὸν θεόν, ἤκουεν, <u>ἧς ὁ κύριος διήνοιξεν τὴν καρδίαν</u> προσέχειν τοῖς λαλουμένοις ὑπὸ τοῦ Παύλου.

It is also interesting to note that while sin entered the world through a tree, salvation entered the world through another tree (Gal. 3:13; 1 Pet. 2:24). God has a great sense of humor!

In the Beginning

The very first concept that God wants you to understand when you open the Bible is that the space/time universe is not eternal, but had a Beginning. We translate the first two verses of Genesis as follows in order to emphasize its dynamic character.

When the Beginning began,
Out of nothing,
God created the heavens and the earth,
And the earth was devoid of life and a desert,
And darkness covered the surface of the sea,
And the Spirit of God was brooding over
the surface of the waters.

בְּרֵאשִׁית

בָּרָא

אֱלֹהִים אֵת הַשָּׁמַיִם וְאֵת הָאָרֶץ:

וְהָאָרֶץ הָיְתָה תֹהוּ וָבֹהוּ

וְחֹשֶׁךְ עַל־פְּנֵי תְהוֹם

וְרוּחַ אֱלֹהִים מְרַחֶפֶת

עַל־פְּנֵי הַמָּיִם:

We must remember that the punctuation found in our English Bibles is not part of the Hebrew text, but is a modern interpretation, not a translation.

The Hebrew text has a series of vav [וַ] consecutives that reveal that verses one and two are actually one sentence in terms of the grammar of the Hebrew syntax, not two sentences as found in the KJV. The description of the earth as it came forth from the hand of the Creator is given by three vav consecutives.

And (וַ) the earth was devoid of life and a desert,

And (וַ) darkness covered the surface of the sea,

And (וַ) the Spirit of God was brooding over the surface of the waters.

The KJV made the mistake of putting a period at the end of verse one, thus giving the false impression that verse one was a title. Because of this error, verse one was cut loose or separated from the verses that followed. This is the root error of such obnoxious doctrines as the "gap theory" and all the vain attempts by "theistic" evolutionists to insert billions of years between Gen. 1:1 and 1:2. As Keil and Delitzsch pointed out,

> Heaven and earth have not existed from all eternity, but had a beginning; nor did they arise by emanation from an absolute substance, but were created by God. This sentence, which stands at the head of the records of revelation, is not a mere heading, nor a summary of the history of the Creation, but a declaration of the primeval act of God, by which the universe was called into being. That this verse is not a heading merely, is evident from the fact that the following account of the course of the Creation commences with וַ (and), which connects the different acts of the Creation

with the fact expressed in ver. 1, as the primary foundation upon which they rest.[45]

All pagan thought is built on the assumption that the space/time universe is eternal.

> What is
> Has always been,
> And shall always be
> What it is.

It does not matter if you look to the East or to the West, the eternity of the space/time universe is the foundational concept of all Natural philosophies and religions, and it forms and shapes all their other concepts. Mathew Henry, the most famous of all English preachers, commented on Gen. 1:1,

> The foundation of all religion being laid in our relation to God as our Creator, it was fit that the book of divine revelations that was intended to be the guide, support, and rule, of religion in the world, should begin, as it does, with a plain and full account of the Creation of the world—in answer to that first enquiry of a good conscience, "Where is God my Maker?" (Job 35:10). Concerning this the pagan philosophers wretchedly blundered, and became vain in their imaginations, some asserting the world's eternity and self-existence, others ascribing it to a fortuitous concourse of atoms: thus "the world by wisdom knew not God," but took a great deal of pains to lose him.[46]

Rationalism, empiricism, mysticism, and fideism never produced or discovered the doctrine of Creation *ex nihilo*. It never crossed the mind of any pagan philosopher or religious sage that the space/time universe was created out of nothing by an infinite and personal God.

This is why the biblical concept of Creation *ex nihilo* is maligned and hated by both secular and religious humanists. The famous German commentator, Peter Lange, comments,

> By faith we understand that the world was made (prepared) by the word of God, so that the things that are seen were not made of things that do appear. The record of Creation is therefore a record of the very first act of faith, and then the very first act of revelation, which, as such, lies at the foundation of all the following, and in its result reproduces itself in the region of faith, from the beginning on to the end of days. It is the monotheistic Christian creative word, the special watchword of the pure believing view of the world. *Ex ungue leonem.* The first leaf of scripture goes at a single step across the great abyss of materialism into which the entire heathen view of the world has Fallen, and which no philosophic system has known how to avoid, until perfected by this. **Pantheism** here meets its refutation in the word of the eternal personal God of Creation, who established the world by his almighty word; **abstract theism**, in the production of the world out of the living word of God; **dualism**, in the doctrine that God has created matter itself; **naturalism**, in the clear evidence of this positive divine foundation of the world, in the origin of every new step in nature. With the pure idea of God, we win at the same place with the pure idea of the world, and with the pure idea if Creation, the pure idea of nature.[47]

Humanists are always offended when you tell them that God created the world. Lange goes on to state,

The Pantheist often takes offense here, because the record speaks of an eternally present God, and, in opposition to his view, of a temporal world which the eternal God has called into being through his word; **the dualist** stumbles at the assumption that even matter itself, the original substance of the world, has sprung from the creative power of God; **the deist**, on the contrary, finds in the assumption that God, after the day's works were completed, had then rested, a childish dream, which ignores the idea of omnipotence; **the naturalist** believes that with the co-working of omnipotence from moment to moment the idea of the natural orderly development of things is destroyed; philosophy generally thinks that it is here dealing with a myth, which is arranged partly through its orthodox positiveness, and partly through its sensuous pictures or images; the modern skeptical natural philosopher makes it a matter of ridicule that the sun, moon, and stars should first be formed in the fourth creative day, and indeed that the whole universe is viewed as rendering a service to this little world; that the heavenly light should have existed before the heavenly lights, but especially that the original world should have arisen only 6000 years ago, and that its present form, for which millions of years are requisite, should have been attained in the brief period of six ordinary days. But the opponents who differ most widely agree in this, that it is fabulous, that the Bible should make an entirely new report of pre-historical things, with the most perfect assurance. [48]

In his classic commentary on Genesis, H. C. Leupold surveys all the ancient cosmologies and demonstrated that none of them taught the concept of Creation ex nihilo. [49]

This poses a tremendous problem for those professing Christians who believe in Natural Theology and Natural Law instead of revealed truth. All the Greek philosophers, such as Aristotle, believed that the world was eternal.

Aquinas usually followed Aristotle. But even he could see that Aristotle's eternal world contradicted Scripture. This was a problem also for the Muslim philosophers who likewise followed Aristotle.

To solve this problem, Muslim philosophers set up a false dichotomy between faith and reason. Their "reason" told them that the world was eternal, but their "faith" told them it was created. They could accept both "truths" at the same time if they assumed a false dichotomy between "reason and faith."

They argued that knowledge came only from human reason. Faith did not give man any knowledge per se, but referred to the disposition of the heart or emotions. It is a humanistic trap in which the only option you are given is, which aspect of man should be absolutized into the Origin. You could choose man's reason, experience, feelings or faith. God had nothing to do with the issue.

Many professing "Christians" today have adopted humanism as the basis of their worldview. They often claim that evolution is a "fact" of reason while Creation is a statement of "faith." They "know" evolution is true, while they "believe" in Creation.

They foolishly think that they can have their cake and eat it too! While they like to think of themselves as smarter than other people, they are, according to God, quite stupid (Jer. 10:8, 14, 21). They know neither the power of God nor the Scriptures (Mat. 22:29).

It is either one way or the other. Either the Bible is true or it isn't. Either one of the various conflicting theories of evolution is true or it is false. There is no middle ground.

Dear Reader, you must make up your mind about who will you believe: Moses or Marx; Jesus or Socrates; Paul or Plato; the Bible or the philosophers; David or Darwin. Your eternal destiny hangs on your choice. Choose wisely.

Out of Nothing

When we read the Hebrew text of Gen 1-2, what do we find? First, the word בָּרָא "created" in Gen. 1:1, means that the universe was created by God without using any pre- existing eternal materials whatsoever. The universe was not even made out of God's being. The world is not divine, but created; it is finite, not infinite; temporal, not eternal; particular, not universal; dependent being, not independent being.

Liberals in the 19th and the early part of the 20th century tried to twist בָּרָא into meaning that God only formed or molded pre-existing materials. They were guilty of trying to reduce the God of the Bible to Plato's Demiurge! But their assertion was not based on sound linguistic principles of Hebrew grammar. It was actually philosophic in nature. Why?

Humanists always assume that the Jews had to borrow (i.e. steal) their ideas from the surrounding pagan religions. Since no ancient pagan religion or philosophy taught Creation ex nihilo, how could the Jews teach something that was totally unique and out of step with the surrounding religions?

If they admitted that the Jews had a unique idea of Creation ex nihilo, this might lead to the abhorrent idea that their religion was actually revealed by their God as they claimed. This couldn't be tolerated!

This is why liberals are both deceitful and foolish when they claim that the Genesis Creation account was "borrowed" from the Babylonian Gilgamesh or another ancient pagan mythology. The Gilgamesh poem and other pagan mythologies all teach an eternal universe! They do not teach Creation ex nihilo.

The average professor of religion usually delights in telling his Christians students, "The Bible got its ideas of Creation from older pagan stories such as the Gilgamesh myth. Thus the Bible is not the Word of God."

The Christian student should be trained how to deal with such nonsense by asking the question: "Are you saying that the Gilgamesh poem or some other ancient pagan mythology spoke of Creation ex nihilo? Are you prepared to stake your academic credentials on it? The truth is that no ancient religion ever taught Creation ex nihilo. They all believed that the world was eternal."

Second, the tenses of the Hebrew verbs used in the Genesis account of Creation describe God's acts of Creation as taking place at once, i.e. instantaneously. They were not slowly done over a long period of time and the process was not a long drawn out affair.

An analysis of the tenses of the Hebrew verbs used in Genesis chapter one, reveals that Creation was a fast, instantaneous, series of divine fiats. Three illustrations are sufficient to establish this grammatical fact.

> Then God said [וַיֹּאמֶר], "Let there be light"; and there was light [וַיְהִי־אוֹר]. (Gen. 1:3)

> Then God said [וַיֹּאמֶר], "Let the waters below the heavens be gathered [יִקָּווּ] into one place, and let the dry land appear [וְתֵרָאֶה]"; and it was so [וַיְהִי־כֵן]. (Gen. 1:9)

> Then God said [וַיֹּאמֶר], "Let the earth sprout [תַּדְשֵׁא] sprouts, plants yielding seed, *and* fruit trees bearing fruit after their kind, with seed in them, on the earth"; and it was so [כֵּן־וַיְהִי]. (Gen. 1:11)

The Hebrew grammar refutes the liberal interpretation that sees billions of years transpiring in Genesis one. The verbs are dynamic and instantaneous in nature. God commanded and it came into existence at once.

The pernicious theory of theistic evolution requires billions or millions of years between God's divine command and the event taking place. But this is not grammatically possible.

God created the world by speaking it into being. In Psa. 33:9 we read,

> For He spoke-
> כִּי הוּא אָמַר
> and it was done;
> וַיֶּהִי
> He commanded-
> הוּא־צִוָּה

162

and it stood fast.

וַיַּעֲמֹד

Notice the tenses of the verbs.

אָמַר qal perfect

וַיְהִי qal imperfect

הוּא־צִוָּה piel perfect

וַיַּעֲמֹד qal imperfect

The Hebrew text pictures God's creative acts as instantaneous in nature, not drawn out and protracted over billions of years. Nowhere in Scripture is it ever taught that Creation took billions or even millions of years. Thus the "old earth" people are fideists in that they make blind leaps of faith to believe that evolutionists are more reliable than the inspired authors of the Bible.

The only example of man's creative word has to do with legal declarations. When a judge pronounces you "guilty" or "innocent," his words render you instantaneously guilty or innocent before the law.

When a Justice of the Peace pronounces a man/woman, man/man or female/female couple "husband and wife," their marriage is legally created merely by his speaking the words. In the same way, God spoke the universe into existence by speaking it into existence!

The "old earth" theory of Creation is championed by humanistic Christians who want to accommodate the heathen idea of evolution. But it is simply not biblical. The billions of years required by the heresy of evolution cannot be reconciled with the dynamic tenses of the Hebrew verbs used in Genesis.

God commanded, "Let there be light,"
and instantaneously "there was light!"

God commanded,
"Let the earth sprout sprouts,"
and instantaneously it happened.
There is simply no way that you can squeeze billions of years

out of these texts. In the end, they must choose between God and man. Oh that they, like the Apostle Paul, would proclaim, let God be true even if it means that all men are liars! (Rom. 3:4)

Third, Adam and Eve were both instantaneously created. God did not take an ape and transform him into Adam. The text says, "man became a living being" (יְהִי הָאָדָם לְנֶפֶשׁ חַיָּה), not "a living being became man." Any theory that entails the existence of pre-Adamic humanoids that became man is a very serious heresy. It should be rebuked as such.

Fourth, the days of Genesis were literal 24 hour days. It is so amusing to see humanists dancing around the six days of Creation, trying desperately to magically transform each day into billions of years.

I once debated an "Evangelical" theologian on the "days" of Genesis. I took a different approach by asking, "Since we are dealing with a biblical text, the first issue to debate is hermeneutics. A biblical text must be interpreted in the light of its cultural context as well as its literary context. A text taken out of context becomes a pretext for false teaching. Do you agree with the hermeneutical principle that the context rules the interpretation?"

The "Christian" evolutionist was not prepared to discuss the hermeneutical principles that he had to follow when attempting to interpret the days of Genesis. But I would not let him off the hook until he promised to submit to the historical grammatical hermeneutic that all Bible-believing Christians utilize when interpreting Scripture. Once this was established, I then asked him,

> "The second issue we need to debate is the hermeneutical principle that we must not read back into the Bible modern concepts that could not, in principle, be found in biblical times because those ideas did not exist at that time. For example, if you tried to convince me that the authors of the Bible ate "Kentucky Fried Chicken," you would be wasting your breath. Do you agree that the attempt to insert modern ideas into

ancient biblical texts is a false hermeneutic?" I could tell he did not like where we were going, but I made him admit that it would be wrong to take modern ideas and insert them into the Bible.

My next point was his "Waterloo."

"The most important aspect of this debate is *the history of numbers and mathematics.* According to what you have written on the "days" of Genesis, your position is that Moses and the people of his day understood that the "days" of Genesis represented billions of years and not literal twenty four days? Yes? Ok. Then it is crucial to your position that the abstract mathematical concept of "billion" be present in the culture of the age in which Genesis was written."

The evolutionist could see that I had just placed a hood over his head, a noose around his neck, and my hand was on the lever of the trapdoor under his feet. Of course, I pulled the lever and let him swing in the breeze. I pointed out:

I have in front of me various histories of numbers and mathematics.[50] The abstract concept of "billions" of years is a Western European idea of recent origin and was not known in biblical times. The authors of Scripture, such as Moses, knew only concrete numbers and the very idea of "millions" or "billions" of years or anything else for that matters was simply not possible in that time frame. What we call "Arabic numbers" (1,2,3, etc.) were unknown to the authors of the Bible. If you asked Abraham,

"What does 2+2 equal?" he would not have a clue what you were talking about. The authors of the Bible used concrete items to correspond to things. For example, the number of stones in a bag corresponded to how many sheep were in their flock. The highest Hebrew word with numeric value was ten thousand. The ancient Egyptians, Babylonians, Assyrians, etc., did not have any abstract numbers either. How were amounts of items recorded in Scripture? They wrote out the words that indicated the amounts in view. For example, they wrote out the three words "one hundred thousand" because "100,000" did not exist at that time. I submit that it was impossible for Moses and his readers, in their cultural context, to teach or even to understand the modern abstract mathematical concept of "billion" that is essential to your view.

The debate began to fall apart at that point, as he did not want to discuss the history of mathematics. Instead, he tried to change the subject to modern Western European interpretations of Genesis such as the framework theory. Of course, I dismissed all modern interpretations as logically and hermeneutically irrelevant to the issue of what Moses and his readers understood the "days" of Creation meant. It was at this point that he made an astounding admission: "Ok. But what if I admitted that Moses and his readers understood the days of Creation to mean 24 hour days? It doesn't matter. They were ignorant and were in error. They also believed that the world was flat and had four corners. Surely you don't defend them on this issue, do you?"

Now the truth finally came out. After claiming all along that he was a fellow "Evangelical" theologian who believed in the full inspiration of the Bible, he revealed that he was actually an apostate liberal masquerading as an Evangelical. He had thrown off his sheep skin and now we could all see that he was a vicious wolf!

In my reply, I pointed out that his response was a flat denial of the inerrancy of Scripture. If the authors of Scripture wrote things that were in fact not true, who was the pope to tell us which verses to believe and which verses to ignore?

He went on to assert that the Hebrew word "yom" could mean an indefinite number of years. When I pointed out that when the word "yom" was modified by a number, for example, "*first* day, *second* day, etc.," it always meant a literal day. He responded that in Hosea 6:2 yom was modified by a numeral, but it clearly did not mean a literal day. But, when I pressed him, he admitted that he had not bothered to look up the Hebrew text. But I had already done so and found that he was 100% in error. The passage is as follows.

> He will revive us after two days;
> יְחַיֵּנוּ מִיֹּמָיִם
> He will raise us up on the third day
> בַּיּוֹם הַשְּׁלִישִׁי יְקִמֵנוּ
> That we may live before Him.
> וְנִחְיֶה לְפָנָיו:

In the first occurrence of "yom," it is a simple dual absolute and it is *not* modified by a numeral. The English word "two" was added by the translator and is *not* in the Hebrew text *per se*. In the next occurrence of "yom," it is indeed modified by the numeral "third" (הַשְּׁלִישִׁי) as in "third day." But the question still remains whether the word "yom" modified by a numeral in this passage refers to a literal 24 hour day or an indefinite period of time.

Under the inspiration of the Holy Spirit, the apostle Paul in 1 Cor. 15:4 interpreted Hosea 6:2 as prophesying the resurrection of Messiah "on the third day" after His death.

> For I delivered to you as of first importance what I also received, that Messiah died for our sins according to the Scriptures, and that He was buried, and that He was *raised on the third day according to the Scriptures.*

If the professor would have bothered to read the Hebrew text on Hosea or exegete 1 Cor. 15:4, he would have seen that Hosea was prophesying about the *literal* three 24 hour days between the death and resurrection of the Messiah. Jesus had promised that on the "third day" after his death He would be resurrected.

> From that time Jesus Christ began to show His disciples that He must go to Jerusalem, and suffer many things from the elders and chief priests and scribes, and be killed, and be raised up on the third day. (Matt. 16:21)

Matthew Henry pointed out that,

> Hosea 6:2 seems to have a further reference to the resurrection of Jesus Christ; and the time limited is expressed by *two days* and the *third day*, that it may be a type and figure of Christ's rising the third day, which he is said to do *according to the scriptures*, according to this scripture; for all the prophets testified of *the sufferings of Christ and the glory that should follow*.[51]
> By Old Testament predictions. He died for our sins, according to the scriptures; he was buried, and rose from the dead, according to the scriptures, according to the scripture-prophecies, and scripture-types. Such prophecies as Ps. 16:10; Isa. 53:4-6; Dan. 9:26, 27; Hos. 6:2... Note: It is a great confirmation of our faith of the gospel to see how it corresponds with ancient types and prophecies.[52]

The classic commentaries agree:

> The burial was a single act; the Resurrection is permanent and eternal in its issues. According to the Scriptures (Ps. 16:10; Isa. 53:10; Hos. 6:2; Jonah 2:10; comp. Matt. 12:40; 16:4; Acts 2:31; 13:34).[53]

It is impossible for the Christian to read this text and not wonder if it foreshadows Christ's resurrection on the third day. Wolff attempts to eliminate the idea of resurrection here, which he casts in a pagan light, and asserts that this text only describes recovery from illness. The language Hosea employs, however, renders this view impossible. Besides that, recovery after a two-day illness, as opposed to two days in the grave, is hardly significant. The New Testament does not explicitly cite this verse, but 1 Cor. 15:4 asserts that Christ arose on the third day "in accordance with the Scriptures," and no other text speaks of the third day in the fashion that Hos. 6:2 does. It is clear that in its original context this passage describes the restoration of Israel, the people of God; and for many interpreters this is proof enough that the resurrection of Christ is not in view here. Such interpretation, however, understands messianic prophecy too narrowly as simple, direct predictions by the prophets of what the Messiah would do. In fact, the prophets almost never prophesied in that manner. Instead, they couched prophecy in typological patterns in which the works of God proceed along identifiable themes. Furthermore, Christ in his life and ministry embodied Israel or recapitulated the sojourn of Israel. Thus, for example, Christ's forty days in the wilderness paralleled Israel's forty years of wandering, and his giving of his Torah on a mountain (Matt 5–7) paralleled the Sinai experience.[54]

I have waited over forty years for those who believe that the days of Genesis refer to billions of years to show me just one clear verse in the original text where yom modified by a numeral meant anything other than a literal 24 hour day. Hosea 6:2 is the only text they tried to twist, but it actually proves our position.

Since this is not a book on the days of Genesis *per se*, we will leave the issue at this point. Enough has been said to establish that any attempt to insert modern abstract ideas of billions of years into the Genesis Creation account is hermeneutically fallacious.

Two last points that need to be understood. First, God created a *mature* universe that was instantaneously *complete* and *whole*, He created a chicken, not an egg, trees with rings, sun light between earth and the sun, a man and a woman, not little babies, etc.

What does this mean? Humanists can invent all the dating methods they want that show a universe billions of billions of billions of years old because their *faith assumption* is that the universe began by chance with a Big Bang billions of years ago and the infant universe over many billions of years slowly evolved to where we are today. But the age of the universe and the earth are only apparent age. The fact that God created an entire universe COMPLETE and MATURE by speaking them into being falsifies all dating methods that assume that billions of years are necessary because there is no Creator God.

Christians do not have to run around disproving this or that dating methodology that humanists are using at the moment to "prove" that the universe is billions of years old. All such dating methods are erroneous in principle because they are based upon false assumptions.

The Chicken or the Egg Riddle?

A few evolutionists try to avoid the mature universe argument by asserting that if God created a mature universe, i.e. a mature chicken and not an egg, this would make God a liar. The chicken would look like it had been alive for many months the second God spoke it into being by divine fiat.

There are several problems with this silly argument. First, it is based upon a riddle the humanists cannot solve on the basis of their faith assumptions. If you ask an evolutionist where did the chicken come from, he will say that it came from an egg. But where did the egg come from? It came from a chicken. They end up with an infinite regression of eggs and chickens or they assert there was a first chicken that came from a non-chicken. Don't bother to ask for hard evidence of the leap from non-chicken to chicken.

Another problem is that humanists are ethical relativists who do not believe that lying is intrinsically wrong or evil. If you press them, they will even admit that lying is "OK" in many situations. On what grounds then do they claim that creating the first chicken and not the egg is a lie? They have no universal standards of right and wrong and thus cannot sit in judgment of God.

Again, it cannot be a "lie" because God told us in His word that He created a mature chicken first, not an egg. Since He told us He spoke a fully formed mature universe into being, how is it lying? It would only be a "lie" if he said that He did not create a mature earth.

Second, sin and death existed before Adam fell into sin. Satan sinned and brought evil to this world before the Fall. Vegetation died as man and animals ate it. Adam was raking dead leaves and taking care of the Garden. Animals were eating animals as well as plants. The teeth of carnivorous animals were created by God for biting, shredding, and devouring flesh, not weeds. I go into greater detail on this fact in my book, *The Bible, Natural Law, and Natural Theology: Conflict or Compromise?*.

Conclusion

One last word is needed. Should we make the length of Creation days of Genesis a test of salvation? Of course not! There are many true Christians today who have never studied the issue and naively follow their humanistic pastors and teachers on this point. They don't know any better.

Our evangelical colleges, seminaries, and universities today are dominated by ignorant professors who are incapable of exegeting the original text of Scripture. They are now controlled by Boards who are only interested in studying "market driven" techniques for hyper-church growth. "Buildings, numbers, and money" are the new "holy trinity" of the church growth movement, not Hebrew, Greek, and Latin. The bottom line is not knowledge but sales.

The ignorant professor I debated is just one example of thousands of teachers who are leading their students astray. He did not even bother to check the Hebrew text because he was philosophically committed to a humanistic view of God, the world, man, and the long days of Creation. It really did not make any difference to him what the Bible actually taught. His mind was already made up before he picked up his Bible.

True Christians can and do disagree over the days of Genesis. But, if someone honestly believes that Moses was in *error* in his understanding of the days of Genesis, that is a serious issue. Anyone who denies the inerrancy of Scripture is not a fellow Christian. He is a "false brother" who is preaching a "false gospel" and is under the divine anathema of Gal. 1:8.

The biblical doctrine of Creation is the first pillar of divine revelation. Everything in life must be interpreted and understood in its light. No philosophy or theology deserves to be called "Christian" if it does not begin where the Bible begins.

Questions for Discussion

1. The "gap theory" teaches that there are billions of years between verses one and two in Gen. 1:1-2. Thus we can throw into that "gap" such things as dinosaurs, cave men, etc. Given the grammar of the Hebrew text of Gen. 1:1-3 (which is actually one sentence in the Hebrew text), is the gap theory based on ignorance of Hebrew?
2. Those who believe in "Bible Numerics" often claim that Gen. 1:1 is divisible by seven. What if verses one through three are one sentence in the Hebrew?
3. Did God create the universe out of His own being so we are part of God?
4. Were the acts of creation recorded in Genesis 1 instantaneous in action?
5. Was the Garden of Eden the entire planet or an enclosed park?
6. Was Adam mortal or immortal at his creation?
7. Did evil, sin and death exist outside of the Garden before Adam was created?

CHAPTER ELEVEN

Christianity and Culture

**Major General Comte Jean de Rochambeau,
Lafayette Park, Washington, D.C. (09/22/07)**

There are ten basic principles that reveal why humanism is now the dominant force in the United States. These ten principles must be grasped by Christians in order for them to understand why humanism has gained the upper hand.

1.   A person's beliefs, values and morals will always be reflected in the way that person lives. His life style will reflect his beliefs. This law of life is taught in the Scriptures in such places as Pro. 23:7 and Matt. 12:33–37. Those who believe that they are only animals will

generally live like one. Those who believe that they are the children of God and are called upon by God to take dominion over the earth will live in accordance with that idea.

2.   The Scriptures command us to judge people on the basis of how they live. When Jesus said in Matt. 7:1, "Judge not lest you be judged," He was referring to the hypocrisy of the Pharisees who condemned people for doing certain sins that they themselves were actually doing (Matt. 7:5). When Jesus was speaking to His own disciples He told them to "judge righteous judgment" (John 7:24). We are called upon in Scripture to identify and to reject false prophets (Deut. 18:21, 22; Matt. 7:15–23). Paul warns us concerning those who would claim to be Christians but their lifestyle refutes that claim (Gal. 5:19–21). John tells us to identify people who live in disobedience to God's Word as "liars" if they claim to be Christians (I John 2:4).

3.   The culture of a nation reflects the lifestyle of those who are involved in the culture-forming process. The philosophers, artists, teachers, politicians, lawyers, judges, doctors, wealthy people, the clergy, media people, etc., will lead a nation either into wickedness or righteousness. The cutting edge of a culture always sets the standard for morality and justice. This cutting edge is generally composed of the professional people of that society. Their influence far exceeds their numbers.

4.   We have the biblical responsibility to judge a culture on the basis of its laws because these laws are simply codified lifestyles. It was on this basis that the Egyptian, Canaanite and Philistine cultures were judged worthy of destruction. Paul could condemn the Cretan culture as decadent (Tit. 1:10–13). We can condemn such modern cultures as Hitler's Third Reich or the former Soviet Union. The concept of cultural relativism in which all cultures are to be viewed as good is condemned by Scripture. The people who usually teach the idea of cultural relativism are hypocrites because they also teach

that Western or American culture is decadent and evil. They never seem to realize the contradiction between the two ideas. If all cultures are good, then how can they condemn American culture? How can they condemn Christian missionaries for spreading their culture in the Third World? Isn't their culture good?

5. Pre-Christian, Greek, and Roman pagan cultures codified laws supporting abortion, infanticide, child abuse, rape, suicide, incest, murder for entertainment, etc., because these things were a part of their lifestyle.

6. When enough Christians became involved in the culture forming process of the Roman Empire, they became the cutting edge of that culture. Their beliefs, values and morals led them to repeal pagan laws and to legislate biblical laws. Thus the state ended up forbidding the very things that the previous pagan culture had honored.

7. Western history, in term of its culture, was basically Christian because its laws reflected the beliefs, values and morals of the Scriptures. Even to this day, there are many laws still on the books that reflect biblical morality. Those people who say, "You cannot legislate morality," are absurd. Every law ever legislated was instituting somebody's morality.

8. Christians in the United States during the 1920's fell into a pietistic focus on one's personal devotion to Christ that led them to abandon the culture-forming process. It was assumed that it would be unspiritual for Christians to be involved in law, medicine, education, entertainment, government, art, etc. Their only concern was "soul winning." This led them to abandon any attempt to influence their society for the good. This extreme separationism was in clear violation of Paul's explicit statements in I Cor. 5:9–13.

9. Because Christians abandoned the culture-forming process, a vacuum was created in the United States and the humanists moved into this vacuum. Instead of there being Christian lawyers, judges, politicians, teachers, artists,

etc., Christians were only involved in evangelism or missions. The idea of "full time Christian service" meant only the clergy or missionary profession. The vacuum created by the retreat of the Christians was filled by the humanists. Since they were now in control of the government, public education and the media, they have begun to reinstate the laws that reflect their pagan lifestyle. This is why the laws are changing on such issues as abortion, infanticide, mercy killing, etc. Modern humanists are putting into law what they believe. The historic understanding of the Constitution and the Bill of Rights is now being overthrown. Modern humanists do not believe in the historic meaning of the freedom of religion. If the humanists have their way, the freedom of religion will be limited to believing what you want but not the freedom to practice it! As we document in *The New Atheism and the Erosion of Freedom*, modern humanists do not believe that Christians have the "freedom" to teach their religion to their children, witness, pass out tracts or show any public signs of religion. The only "freedom" they will allow is freedom from religion. Modern laws that legalize such things as abortion come from humanists who are legislating their view of morality. They are legalizing their pagan lifestyle while trying to criminalize Christian education, church camps and orphanages, personal evangelism, Christian TV and radio programs, etc. Their understanding of religious freedom is the same as found in the former Soviet Union! (21st century Russia is promoting Christianity.)

10. The only hope for Western culture is for Christians once again to take over the culture-forming process. Then when they are in control, to repeal the pagan laws and to reinstitute Christian laws. If they do not do this, modern pagans will soon be in a position to begin the same kind of persecution against the Church that their forefathers in the Roman Empire had done to the Christians earlier. Since it took a full generation for Christians to lose control of the

culture, it will probably take another generation to win it back. So, do not be fooled by those who look for easy answers and a "quick fix." It won't work! If God does not send us another mighty Reformation, Western culture will die.

Summary

Those of you who are students will have to be the generation that takes over our culture by becoming politicians, media people, artists, lawyers and judges. The survival of Western civilization falls on your shoulders. Only you can gain control of our culture and once again institute biblical laws that make up a just and orderly society.

Coat of Arms for the Russian Federation

Note: 21st century Russia under the leadership of President Vladimir V. Putin (United Russia party: 2000 to 2008 & 05/07/2012 - present), an honorable man, to their credit, is paying families (a father and mother) to have children. Russia also condemns abortion and homosexuality and it is illegal to teach homosexuality or any other sinful lifestyles to students. In contrast, the school system in the United States promotes unbiblical events such as the "Day of Silence," which is used to legitimize homosexuality, bisexuality and transgenderism under the guise of tolerance. (The Gay, Lesbian, Straight Education Network (GLSEN) promotes the "Day of Silence" as their annual day of action in the month of April at U.S. high schools across the nation.)

A quote from an article entitled "In Which Direction is Vladimir Putin Taking Russia?" by Dr. Peter Hammond (Director of *Frontline Fellowship* located at https://www.frontline.org.za/):

> I ministered throughout Eastern Europe in the 1980s before the Iron Curtain collapsed and on numerous Missions since. I have many Russian and Ukrainian friends. Russian Christians have expressed their shock to me at how America has become the new evil empire. Xavier Lerma of Pravda in Moscow has written that Ronald Reagan was right to call the Soviet Union "The Evil Empire". But now the United States has become The Evil Empire: promoting abortion and privileges for perverts, with an aggressive pro-homosexual marriage agenda, bullying African governments to legalise abortion and perversion and sending generous aid to radical Middle-Eastern governments which severely persecute the Christian church.

We pray that Russia will continue to be guided by the Bible and fear God.

Questions for Discussion

1. How is a culture formed?
2. How did our culture become so pagan?
3. Who allowed the humanists to take over?
4. What is the "cutting edge" of a culture?
5. Where do laws come from?
6. Can you legislate morality or immorality?

CHAPTER TWELVE

Humanism and Human Life

The White House in Washington, D.C. (09/22/07)

Humanism teaches that man is the result of a chance-governed evolutionary process in a closed system wherein God or any act of God is excluded in principle. God is not so much refuted as He is defined out of existence. Since there is no infinite reference point that could possibly give meaning or significance to any particular, human life has no intrinsic value, dignity, freedom or meaning.

While human life or animal life in general has no intrinsic value or dignity, it can have "acquired worth" in terms of its utility or function. When a person's utilitarian worth is over so far as society is concerned, that person no longer has any "right to life."

The "privilege of life" can be withdrawn by the state at will.

Because human life has no intrinsic worth, it is perfectly proper, if deemed for purposes of utility, to abort unborn babies, murder babies already born, to put to death those who are sick, handicapped, disabled or old.

The following points are usually argued by humanists to demonstrate that it is perfectly proper to do away with human beings if it is deemed "useful" to society.

1. Economic considerations may lead to the termination of "useless" lives. This "useless" person may be the child of a welfare mother. It is cheaper to kill that child than to give additional financial aid for the care and raising of that child. Thus it is no wonder that the primary object of the abortion clinic is the killing of black babies rather than giving black women the support they need to raise a family in dignity.

2. People who are "miserable" may be terminated. The argument is usually given that this person has in their future a "miserable life" due to the fact that they are handicapped or that they may possibly experience pain in the future. What this argument really means is that those around them will feel "miserable" when they have to care for or look at the individual. Thus physical deformity as well as disability is usually looked upon as viable grounds for abortion or mercy killing.

3. Children who are "unwanted" can be killed. This killing may take place before they are born (that is abortion) or after they are born (that is infanticide). Pagan judges have upheld both forms of murder. Under Chairman Mao and his fellow Communist Party leaders, the ultimate evil took place. They feasted on soup containing human fetuses harvested from abortion clinics and hospitals. The fetus soup was even proclaimed a "Spring Tonic!"[55] Bring this up the next time someone says it does not make any difference if you believe that people are just animals. Are *they* ready to eat their babies? If not, they are hypocrites.

4. Inconvenient pregnancies can be terminated at will. Human life has no intrinsic worth and if this child will be inconvenient because it will interfere with your career or personal pleasure, then it is perfectly proper to kill that baby.
5. The "right to life" is not absolute. There are no inalienable rights given by a divine Creator to anyone because there is no God. Rights are given by the state and can be withdrawn by the state at will.
6. Over-population necessitates the killing of worthless human beings. This means that the unwanted, the handicapped, the terminally ill, or the elderly should be encouraged to take their own life or they should be forced into suicide clinics where their life will be forcibly taken from them. Death pills or suicide pills should be made available to anyone who wishes to take his life.
7. In the future there will be food and fuel shortages that mean that the state will have to "liquidate" unnecessary "assets," i.e., people.
8. The few (i.e., the poor, the sick and the elderly) should be willing to sacrifice for the many (i.e., the wealthy, healthy and young). They should be willing to go to suicide clinics so the rest of us can enjoy life.
9. If someone wants to die, doctors should be willing to perform this task. Physicians should become doctors of death as they did in the Third Reich.
10. People who can no longer make any contribution to society are to be viewed as "parasites" and since they do not produce any goods or services, they should be "terminated." This is what communist countries have practiced for years. Life is cheap where there is no God.

Summary

Without God, human life loses all dignity and worth. Man is reduced to an animal and is treated as such.

Questions for Discussion

1. What do you think of the argument that if a baby is not wanted and he would be inconvenient, it is all right to kill that baby?
2. Should your grandparents be put to death because they are old?
3. If someone asks to die, is it all right to kill them?
4. Have you ever felt you wanted to die? What if some doctor decided to kill you at that time? Would it be all right?
5. Your brother is mentally retarded and lives at home with you. What would you do if the government decided he should be terminated?
6. You have been told that you are not allowed to have children because your IQ is not high enough. How would you respond?
7. Should governments force abortions on people?

CHAPTER THIRTEEN

Christianity and Human Life

Snake River Canyon in Twin Falls, Idaho (07/12/09)

Man was created in the image of God. Thus every human being from the moment of conception to death has intrinsic worth and inalienable rights. The intrinsic worth and dignity of man is immutable and cannot be affected by a lack of "acquired worth" or "economic considerations." The utility of a person has no bearing whatsoever on the issue of the worth of man as the image bearer of God.

The sanctity of human life is clearly taught in Scripture. The killing of human beings because they are in the way of personal pleasure or affluence is murder. Only the God who gave life has the right to order the death of anyone. This is why Christians believe in capital punishment and are against abortion at the same time. While God has ordered capital punishment in certain cases (Gen. 9:6), He has condemned the killing of the innocent (Exo. 20:13).

The Sanctity of Life Declaration

1. Genetic experimentation on fertilized human eggs is morally wrong and should be illegal because the destruction of such eggs is the killing of human life. Some techniques used to overcome infertility are immoral and should be made illegal. When fertilized human eggs are washed down the sink, this is the murder of innocent human beings.

2. It is morally wrong and should be illegal to experiment on the human DNA code to predetermine the race, sex or physical characteristics of human beings. Human beings should not be genetically programmed or "bred" as is done with cattle. We have already seen how Hitler's dream of breeding a "super-race" ended.

3. Abortion is morally wrong and should be made illegal except where the life of the mother is threatened. Even though the case where the life of a mother is threatened is exceedingly rare, yet the biblical principle would be to preserve the life of the mother as opposed to the life of the child.

4. All acts of infanticide in which babies are murdered either through active or passive means are immoral and should be made illegal regardless of what economic or other considerations are made. Active means of infanticide include choking the child to death, stabbing the child in the heart or poisoning the child. Passive usually means placing the child in a closet or in a container and allowing the child to die slowly and excruciatingly through starvation and dehydration. Some have cried for days before they died a horrible death. If someone killed a dog this way, it would be viewed as a crime. How then can human babies be killed this way without criminal charges? Have we come to the place where to kill a dog is more heinous than the murder of

precious little babies?

5. All so-called "mercy killing" is morally wrong and should remain illegal. It is nothing more than murder regardless if it is done through passive or active means.

6. Active or passive euthanasia is morally wrong and should be made illegal. To encourage the elderly to commit suicide is to aid and abet murder.

7. Medical care should not involve age limits or "useful life" standards. To deny medical care to someone because they are no longer viewed as being "useful" is nothing but murder.

8. Suicide should not be legalized. Suicide clinics or "death pills" should not be forced on or offered to the elderly.

9. The state should not have any "final solution" for "undesirables." This is exactly what Hitler did to Jews, gypsies and other ethnic and racial groups that they deemed as "undesirables."

10. There should be no program of "liquidation" of those who think or teach differently than the state. The Gulags of the Soviet Union and the gas chambers of the Nazis both resulted in death for anyone who thought or taught differently than state policy. This is immoral and should remain illegal.

Summary

The end result of humanism is death while Christianity brings life and light through the Gospel. Humanism brings man down to the level of an animal while Christianity lifts him up to be the image bearer of God. Christians are the only ones on campus who promote life. The humanists are the merchants of death.

Questions for Discussion

1. How do humanists view human life?
2. How do Christians view human life?
3. What do you think about abortion, infanticide, mercy killing and euthanasia?
4. Explain: "Christians believe in life."
5. What will happen to our culture if Christians do not regain control?
6. Is genetic engineering moral?
7. What countries have put a humanistic view of man into practice?

CHAPTER FOURTEEN

Do Not Be Deceived

Rome, Italy (The Ruins) – 1981

We know that it is difficult for young people to accept the fact that there are religious groups that knowingly use lies and deception to convert people. It can come as quite a shock to some people that not all religious people are sincere and that some religions are no more than glorified con games run to make the leaders rich.

The typical Christian student was raised in a sincere religious home, attended a church that was honest and went through a Christian school system that valued truth and morals. Then he comes to a college where he meets new religions. He naturally assumes that they must be as sincere as were his parents and pastor. But this is a deadly mistake.

Most of the cultic groups that are recruiting students on today's campus only want three things out of their recruits: their money, their mind and body. In order to get these things, they will lie, cheat, and steal. They will use sex and drugs. They will use the same brainwashing techniques used by the Communists. A congressional subcommittee found that some cults put people under hypnotic control and that they will kill people if the need arises.

All of this means that religion is not the innocent game that most people think it is. People have died as a result of such cults as Christian Science, Jehovah's Witnesses, the People's Temple, Hare Krishnas, Black Muslims and many others. If you fail to heed the warning of Jesus, you might lose your life as well as your immortal soul.

Just because some group, church or organization says it is "Christian" does not mean that it is Christian. Just because someone tells you that he believes in "God" or "Jesus" does not mean that he believes in the same God or Jesus you do.

You probably will meet some people who say, "All religions are the same because they all worship the same God under different names. So, it does not really matter what religion you believe as long as it makes you happy."

Such statements are totally irrational. Logically speaking, since all religions contradict each other, either one of them is true and the others false or they are all false. They cannot all be true.

Words can have different meanings. Such words as God, Christ, Jesus and salvation are redefined by the cults and given a meaning that is anti-Christian. For example, when a Christian uses the word "God" he is referring to the only true God of Father, Son and Holy Spirit who is infinite in His nature and thus eternal, omnipresent, omniscient, omnipotent and sovereign. But when a Mormon uses the word "God" he is referring to one of many finite gods who were men and women at one time and have now become deities. Obviously there is no relationship between the Christian concept of God and Mormon theology. See the *Battle of the Gods* for further details.

When people ask you, "Is Christianity the one true religion?" Sweetly tell them, "Yes! And thank God it is or there would be no salvation." They will often argue that your belief is wrong because "Truth is whatever we want it to be." Point out to them that they are being hypocritical at this point for they are claiming that their view is "true" and yours is "wrong!"

It never fails to amaze us when people say that all religions are true but then turn right around and say that Christianity is wrong! They cannot have their cake and eat it too!

The same kind hypocrisy is found in people who argue, "It is not right to push your views on others." They will even condemn you for witnessing to them. The only problem is that *they* are trying to push their views on you! Do not let them get away with it.

All religions do not worship the same God. Obviously, it would be totally irrational to claim that monotheism is the same as polytheism. The same can be said of the Eastern cults such as Hinduism or Zen Buddhism that would define the entire universe as God. Pantheism cannot be reconciled with the personal God of the Bible.

Some humanists will challenge you by asking, "But what about the heathen? Do you mean to tell me that they are going to hell just because they never heard of your Jesus?" There is no reason for Christians to feel intimidated by this issue. Did Jesus say that He was the ONLY way, the truth, the life and that no one can come to the Father except through Him (John 14:6)? He was either telling the truth or He was lying. Which was it? Did Peter say that Jesus is the ONLY way under heaven to be saved (Acts 4:12)? Was he lying? Can anyone deny that Paul taught that the gospel is the ONLY way of salvation (Rom. 10:9–15)?

All religions claim to be the true religion. A Muslim is a Muslim because he thinks it is the true religion. So, why pick on Christians as if they are the only ones who claim to have the truth. Even the humanists think they're right!

Get the Facts Straight

To answer the heathens' questions we must get our facts straight.

1. No one goes to hell because he did not hear the gospel. People go to hell because they are sinners who have rebelled against God's

Law (Rom. 1:18–32; 2:12–16).

2. No one goes to hell because he rejected the gospel. We were perishing in our sins and under God's condemnation before we ever heard it (1 Cor. 1:18; John 3:36).

3. All of humanity is in a state of sin and guilt and is under the wrath of God (Rom. 3:23). God does not owe salvation to anyone (Rom. 4:1–5). He would be perfectly just if He let everyone go to hell for their sins. It is only by His grace and mercy that anyone is saved.

4. The religions of the world are not the result of man's search for God but man's running from God (Rom. 3:11). People made up false gods and false religions to escape from the Creator (Rom. 1:18–25). Their worship does not go to God but to the demons (1 Cor. 10:20). All the nations that forgot God will be thrown into hell (Psa. 9:17).

One nice way to reply to the question "What about the heathen?" is to ask,

> "Well, what about *you*? Are not *you* one heathen who has heard! I don't think you are really concerned about the heathen. For example, how much money have you given to missions lately? Your question is just your way of trying to escape from your responsibility to repent and to believe the gospel."

But what do you say to people who claim to be Christians but who say that it is not nice to "put down" other religions? They are disregarding Scripture. Jesus did not hesitate to "put down" false religions. He was not afraid to offend religious leaders by telling them that they were not only wrong but hypocrites (Matt. 23). They have to make up their minds if they really want to be Christians. If they do, then they must follow Christ.

God commands us to demolish all the arguments raised against Him (2 Cor. 10:4, 5). We are to give logical answers when challenged (1 Pet. 3:15). We must defend the faith (Jude 3). Could anything be clearer?

Now, we are not talking about quarreling and shouting or being argumentative. The servant of the Lord must not get involved in such stupid things (2 Tim. 2:24). Both Jesus (Matt. 7:6) and Solomon (Pro. 26:4) warn us not to argue with fools. But we are to be patient and to teach people the truth praying that God will give them repentance (2 Tim. 2:25–26)

Summary

Christians are commanded in Scripture to defend the cause of God and truth. The world needs to hear an authoritative gospel. There can be no compromise with sin or false teaching. We are not called to be wimps but bold soldiers engaged in a spiritual warfare with the powers of darkness (Eph. 6:10–18).

Questions for Discussion

1. Are all religions the same? How would you respond to someone who believes that they are?
2. Do all religions worship the same God just under different names?
3. What is the difference between monotheism, polytheism, and pantheism?
4. Did Jesus tell the truth when He said that He was the ONLY way to God?
5. What is the best way to answer the heathen question?
6. Did pagan religions come from man's search for God?
7. How are people hypocritical when they condemn Christians for condemning other religions?
8. Does God expect us to defend the Gospel?

CHAPTER FIFTEEN

Hermeneutics
How to interpret the Bible for all it's worth.

Papyrus 46 is one of the oldest extant New Testament manuscripts in Greek written on Papyrus (175 – 225 A.D.).

Section One

The Nature of Exegesis

The English word "exegesis" is a transliteration from the Greek word ἐξήγησις. We got the word "excavate" from the same Greek word. It means to interpret a literary unit by digging out of the words the syntax, the context of the passage, and the original meaning in the mind of the author who wrote the text. The theological term was developed from John 1:18, where Jesus Christ is described as the "exegesis" of the Father.

We are always amused by liberal theologians who claim that it is impossible in principle to discover the original meaning of the authors of the Bible. We always respond by asking,

> Do you expect your students to understand the original meaning you had in mind when you wrote your book? Do you not test them to see if they have exegeted your book correctly? Do you allow your students to make up whatever had meaning to them? No. Let's be honest. You expect your readers to discover the original meaning you had in mind when you wrote your book. How then do you deny this fact to the authors of Scriptures?

Obviously, when liberals claim that it is impossible to discover the original meaning of the Bible, they do not want you to apply their rule to their writings!

Deconstructionism and Postmodernism

We have had some good belly laughs at a recent modern attempt to deny that it is possible to discover the objective meaning of biblical texts. Deconstructionists argue that the interpreter must subjectively "enter into" the meaning of the text. But as soon as you begin to deconstruct deconstructionism and treat their books as they treat the Bible, they are the first to cry foul. They fully expect you to understand the objective and original meaning in the texts they have written! *Any literary principle that if valid would render itself meaningless is nonsense.*

The Nature of Eisegesis

The English word "eisegesis" is a transliteration from the Greek.

The prefix "eis", which means "*into*", is in contrast to the prefix "ex," which means "*out of.*" Eisegesis means to insert a meaning into the words and syntax of the text that is foreign to the original meaning in the mind of the author of that text. When we read modern ideas or scientific models back into the text of Scripture, we are guilty of eisegesis.

For example, I have heard many preachers interpret the word "nature" in I Cor. 11:14 as a reference to "natural law." But the concept of "natural law" that forms the basis of their interpretation did not appear in human history until Sir Isaac Newton! Obviously, the Apostle had never heard of Newton or his concept of "natural law." It is sheer eisegesis to insert the Newtonian world and life view into the Bible.

Widespread Problem

One of the greatest problems we face today is that most pastors and Christians abuse the Bible by using constant eisegesis. There is little concern today to discover the original meaning of the text. The so-called "inductive" Bible study has deceived many naïve people to think that what the text "means to them" is what the text means. They do not understand that when you relate a text to your personal life, this is application, not interpretation.

The exegesis of a text gives you the objective meaning of the passage and has nothing to do with you or your circumstances. But when you take the meaning and relate it to your personal life, this is *application.*

The interpretation of Scripture is objective because it is based on the grammar, syntax, literary context, and cultural context of the passage in question. The application of a passage is subjective and personal.

Theological Distinctions

There is another pitfall in biblical interpretation that has produced a great deal of confusion. I am referring to the problem of "theological distinctions." They are clichés or nifty phrases that arise in Church history as a byproduct of the process of doctrinal formulation. Theological distinctions can be good or bad. They can clarify Scripture or blind us to it. Perhaps an illustration will help us at this point.

As a ship sails through the sea, barnacles slowly attach themselves to the hull of the ship. These barnacles pose a threat to the ship's survival. Thus a ship has to be put into dry dock and the barnacles knocked off. If they are not removed, the ship will eventually sink under their weight.

As the Church sails through human history, theological distinctions, like barnacles, gradually attach themselves to theology and philosophy. They have to be knocked off from time to time, or the Church will sink under their weight. This was what the Reformation was all about.

Spiritual Gifts

One clear illustration of how the problem of modern theological distinctions can color one's interpretation of Scripture is the issue of spiritual gifts. The anti-gift theologians interpret I Cor. 12-14 with such a *priori* distinctions as "permanent vs temporary gifts," "natural vs supernatural gifts," "sign miracles vs power miracles," etc. Then they arbitrarily run through the gifts listed by Paul and pronounce one gift "permanent" and the next one "temporary." They seem oblivious to the fact that Paul could not have understood spiritual gifts in terms of such modern distinctions. The anti-gift crowd is clearly guilty of gross eisegesis.

The Law of God

Another clear example of how theological distinctions can get in the way of exegesis is when we fall into the trap the dividing the law of God into the three categories of "civil, ceremonial, and moral" laws. These theological distinctions arose in medieval Catholic theology and, unfortunately, were retained by Protestant scholasticism and ended up in various Protestant creeds. It is thus not surprising that most Christians today assume them to be true and use them to interpret the Bible.

While the theological distinctions of "civil, ceremonial, and moral" enable some people to define what they believe about the law of God, the authors of Scripture never heard of, much less believed in, these distinctions. This fact, however, does not stop most Christian philosophers and theologians from reading these theological distinctions back into biblical texts, making exegesis impossible. Any attempt to read these distinctions back into Scripture is nothing more than gross eisegesis.

This problem is apparent when we examine commentaries on the Book of Galatians. The commentators run through the book assuming that νόμος in this or that verse is "moral" or "ceremonial" or "civil" law. The entire process is so arbitrary that when νόμος appears more than once in the same sentence, it is interpreted as "moral" in one instance and "ceremonial" in the other!

Galatians 3:13 is a good example of this error. It states that the Messiah "redeemed us from the curse of the law." Now, did Jesus redeem us from the curse of the civil, ceremonial or moral law, or did He redeem us from the curse of "the law" in its entirety? If Jesus only redeemed us from the curse of the ceremonial law, then we still have to bear the curse of the civil and moral law! If that is the case, we are all doomed to an eternal hell. See my book, *How the Old and New Testaments Relate to Each Other*, for an extended discussion of the many problems with the traditional threefold division of the law.

We will never understand the New Testament concept of "law" by taking medieval ideas and inserting them into the text. Since we have discussed this issue elsewhere, it is sufficient to illustrate how theological distinctions can hinder our understanding of Scripture.

Principles of Approach

The following principles of approach should be observed:

- First, we must first admit to ourselves that we have unconsciously adopted many theological distinctions that do not arise out of the text of Scripture. We pick up these ideas like dogs pick up fleas – Here, there and everywhere. If we do not become epistemologically self-conscious of these distinctions, they will so color our interpretation of Scripture that we end up being guilty of eisegesis.

- Second, once we have identified the hidden theological distinctions that clutter our minds, then we must judge whether they are:

valid or false,   *helpful or harmful,*
vague or clear,   *necessary or unnecessary,*
useful or useless,   *exegetical or creedal*

Not all distinctions are harmful and some can be helpful if they truly arise out of solid exegesis.

- Third, beware of taking modern doctrines and trying to read them back into the Bible. For example, the doctrine of "Middle Knowledge" was invented by a Jesuit priest named Luis de Molina. He developed it as a way to attack the biblical gospel that we are saved by grace alone, through faith alone, in Christ alone. His doctrine was so radical that even the Catholic Church almost condemned it as heresy! But, sadly, several popular "evangelical" apologists have swallowed it hook, line, and sinker!

All scholars, Catholic and Protestant, acknowledge that Molina invented a radically new doctrine that had never been taught by any Jewish Rabbi, church father or theologian. Since the doctrine of "Middle Knowledge" did not come into existence until the Counter-Reformation period, it cannot, in principle, be found in the Bible, because it was written thousands of years before Molina was born.

Smart Molinists do not appeal to the Bible, but depend entirely on philosophical arguments. But the not-so-smart Molinists find a verse here or there in the Bible that they think they can twist to teach Middle Knowledge. Their "biblical" arguments are nothing more than fanciful eisegesis. Since Molinism is not part of "the faith once and for all delivered to the saints" (Jude 3), it cannot in principle be found in the Bible.

Conclusion

Although theological distinctions can become so widely accepted that they become part of the vocabulary of orthodoxy, we must not unconsciously impose such distinctions upon Scripture. We must not take modern ideas and pretend that they can be found in the Bible.

Section Two

Basic Definitions

The importance of rightly interpreting Scripture cannot be underestimated. If the people of God do not know how to read the Bible, false teachers will easily deceive them (Acts 20:28-32).

I.   **What is Hermeneutics?**
      Hermeneutics is the science of the (1.) discovery, (2.) understanding, and (3.) use of those linguistic and literary principles and rules of interpretation that should be followed when interpreting the Bible or any other ancient literature.

II.   **What Are the Foundational Concepts of Hermeneutics?**
      A. The bible is literature. It is not music or paintings. It is composed of ancient Jewish scrolls.
      B. Since the Bible is *literature*, it should be interpreted the same way any other ancient literature is interpreted. No special methods of interpretation should be followed.

III. **What is Exegesis?**
      A. Exegesis is the application of hermeneutics to a particular text of Scripture to discern the ideas that the author was conveying to his readers by his choice of words and the syntax of his sentences.

EXEGESIS -	Superstructure (application)
HERMENEUTICS -	Foundation (principles)

    B. Exegesis is the opposite of eisegesis, which is the reading into a text your own ideas with little or no concern for what the author was saying.

IV. **Why Bother with Hermeneutics?**

    A. The Bible comes to us as literature: prose, poetry, historical narrative, apocalyptic literature, letters, dialogue, theological treatise, biography, etc.

    B. Hermeneutics is the study of the valid ways in which we interpret any piece of literature.

        1. We must observe vocabulary, grammar and syntax.

        2. We must observe literary units such as context (paragraph, chapter, book, and place in the canon).

        3. We must seek to discern the historical and cultural context of the situation of the author.

V. **There Are Right Ways and Wrong Ways to Interpret the Bible.**

    A. The Right Way:

        1. II Tim. 2:15:

        "Be diligent to present yourself approved to God as a workman who does not need to be ashamed, <u>handling accurately</u> the word of truth."

σπούδασον σεαυτὸν δόκιμον παραστῆσαι τῷ θεῷ ἐργάτην ἀνεπαίσχυντον ὀρθοτομοῦντ σπούδασον σεαυτὸν δόκιμον παραστῆσαι τῷ θεῷ ἐργάτην ἀνεπαίσχυντον ὀρθοτομοῦντα τὸν λόγον τῆς ἀληθείας

The Greek word ὀρθοτομοῦντα translated "<u>handling accurately</u>" is in a present active participle (imperative sense) masculine 2nd person singular from the verb ὀρθοτομέω, to use or interpret correctly. It is found only once in the New Testament. A.T. Robertson comments:

"**Handling aright** (*orthotomounta*). Present active participle of *orthotomeo*, late and rare compound (orthotomos), cutting straight, *orthos* and *temno*), here only in the N.T. It occurs in Prs3:6;11:5 for making straight paths (*hodous*) with which compare Heb. 12:13 and "the Way" in Acts 9:2. Theodoret explains it to mean ploughing a straight furrow. Parry argues that the metaphor is the stone mason cutting the stones straight since *temno* and *orthos* are so used. Since Paul was a tent maker and knew how to cut straight the rough camel-hair cloth, why not let that be the metaphor? Certainly plenty of exegesis is crooked enough (crazy-quilt patterns) to call for careful cutting to set it straight."

B. The Wrong Way:
    1. Matt. 22:29:
       "But Jesus answered and said to them, 'You are mistaken, <u>not understanding the Scriptures</u>, or the power of God.'"
       Jesus rebuked the Sadducees because they did not have a valid interpretation of Scripture. This led them to false doctrine.

       Ἀποκριθεὶς δὲ ὁ Ἰησοῦς εἶπεν αὐτοῖς· Πλανᾶσθε <u>μὴ εἰδότες</u> τὰς γραφὰς μηδὲ τὴν δύναμιν τοῦ θεοῦ·

Πλανᾶσθε is a perfect active participle nominative masculine 2nd person plural from πλανάω . μὴ is the word for "not." Jesus rebuked the Sadducees because they did not have a valid interpretation of Scripture. This led them to false doctrine.

2. II Pet. 3:16:
   "As also in all his letters, speaking in them of these things, in which are some things hard to understand, which untaught and unstable <u>distort</u>, as they do also the rest of the Scriptures, to their own destruction."

   ¹⁶ ὡς καὶ ἐν πάσαις ἐπιστολαῖς λαλῶν ἐν αὐταῖς περὶ τούτων, ἐν αἷς ἐστιν δυσνόητά τινα, ἃ οἱ ἀμαθεῖς καὶ ἀστήρικτοι στρεβλοῦσιν ὡς καὶ τὰς λοιπὰς γραφὰς πρὸς τὴν ἰδίαν αὐτῶν ἀπώλειαν.

   "Distort" is a present active indicative 3rd person plural from στρεβλόω, to distort, twist.

3. Other wrong ways:
   a. Partial quotation: "There is no God" (Psa. 14:1).
   b. Not observing who said it: "You shall be as God" (Gen. 3:5).
   c. Stringing together unrelated proof texts (Matt. 23:37 cf. Lk. 19:41)
   d. Taking a verse out of context: (John 15:1-6).
4. Allowing tradition to influence your interpretation of Scripture: (Mk. 7:1-13; Phil. 2:10).
5. A mystical approach, where you let the Bible fall open at random and pick a verse by "chance."
6. A cultic or occultic interpretation that comes from God, angels, spirits, ascended masters, aliens on UFOs, the dead, etc.
7. Misquoting a verse (Mat. 23:37; Phil 2:10-11).
8. Deliberate mistranslation of verses. ex. The New World Translation (JW), The Jewish Publications translation, the Anchor Bible, The Promise, The Living Bible, RSV, etc.
9. Not noticing to whom the verse is directed (Heb. 6:1-10).

VI. **How Should We Interpret the Bible?**

It is erroneous to say, "The Bible can be interpreted any way you want." Except for a few difficult places, if the principles of hermeneutics are consistently followed, there will be only *one valid* interpretation of a text.

We should interpret the Bible by following *objective rules*. By "objective" I mean that our reason, feelings, faith or experience should not enter into the meaning of a text. Thus the meaning comes from the grammar and syntax of the text. The text reveals the meaning the author intended to convey to his readers when he wrote it. Note: If this is true, then why are there so many denominations? The reason why there are conflicting interpretations is that people allow religious traditions, personal prejudices, racism, pagan philosophy, and denominational biases to influence their interpretation of Scripture. Some people approach the Bible determined to make it say what they want it to say. They run through the Bible looking for proof texts to support their pet doctrine.

VII. **Where Should We Obtain our Hermeneutical Principles?**

A. The foundational principle of approach:

The same basic linguistic and literary rules which we use when interpreting any historic or contemporary literature should be utilized when reading the Bible. Since the Bible does not contain any unique literary forms, our hermeneutics should not be unique only to Scripture.

B. The science of hermeneutics reveals the basic error of liberal and neo-orthodox hermeneutics. They have developed hermeneutical principles that cannot be applied to any historic or contemporary literature. They then apply these special hermeneutics to the Bible to discredit it. The so-called "New Hermeneutics" are nothing more than another way that liberals twist the Scriptures to their own eternal damnation.

    1. The J.E.P.D Higher Critical Theory cannot be applied to Homer, Plato, Shakespeare or contemporary works.

    2. A computer analysis of vocabulary cannot be applied to literature in general.

C. This basic principle also reveals the error of Medieval or Roman Catholic hermeneutics. It was taught that a text had three meanings:

    1. A literal meaning that ignorant and uneducated people could discern.

    2. A moral meaning that educated and cultured people could discern.

    3. A spiritual meaning that only the clergy could discern.

D. This basic principle also reveals the fallacy of cultic and occultic hermeneutics. Each cultic or occultic leader or group gives an "inner" or "secret" meaning which is not discernible from the text. Their interpretation ignores grammar, syntax, context, etc. ex. Christian Science, The Church of Bible Understanding, The Watchtower, The Metaphysical Bible Dictionary, SDA, etc.

E. The fact that the Bible was written in everyday language for normal people dispels all "secret" and "mystical" interpretations. A "plain" Bible written for "plain" people needs a "plain" interpretation. There are no "secret keys" to interpreting the Bible because it does not come to us as a locked book waiting for some special mystical interpreter to arrive on the scene.

F. This is why the "Bible Codes" fad is a fraud. It came from the occultic teachings of the Kabala, and attempts to find hidden meanings beneath the plain meaning of Scripture.

VIII. **How Should We Approach the Bible?**

A. In an attitude of Worship: Isaiah 66:1-2, Psa. 119:97; Psa. 138:2;John 1:1-2
   1. Spirit of dependence: Psa. 119:18, 24; I Cor. 2:11-12; Lk. 24:25-32.
   2. Spirit of submission: John 7:17; Psa. 119:4, 5, 11; Heb. 11:6.
B. It involves our Whole Being:
   1. Mind – Call to believe: Jn. 20:31; Acts. 17:10-12.
   2. Will – Call to obey: Rev. 2:5; Psa. 119:33-35; Matt. 7:24.
   3. Emotions – Call to feel: Phil. 3:1; Jn. 15:11-12.

IX.   **Who is Qualified to Interpret the Bible?**

The Basic Qualifications of the Interpreters of Scripture:

A. We must have a heart regenerated by the Holy Spirit (John 3:3-5). Why?
   The natural man cannot understand the things of God (I Cor. 2:11-14; Rom. 3:11).
   1. The sinful nature of man renders him incapable of understanding the truth (Rom. 3:10-11; 8: 3-9).
   2. Man's love of darkness rather than light renders him unwilling to understand the truth (John 3:19-21; John 5:40).
   3. Man's allegiance to Satan and to sin renders him rebellious against understanding the truth (John 8:43-47).
B. We need a mind illuminated by the Holy Spirit. ex. Paul's prayers on behalf of the saints (Eph. 1:17).
C. We must have an impartial and seeking spirit. We must come to the Bible totally convinced that we want nothing but the truth. Some use the Bible to prove their pet ideas or to defend their denominational doctrines. We should come realizing that the truth:
   (1) Liberates (John 8:32)
   (2) Sanctifies (John 17:17)
   (3) Enables us to worship God (John 4:23-24).

D. We must have a humble spirit. Why?
   1. God resists the proud (James 4:6)
   2. God reveals truth to the humble (Matt. 11:25)
   3. Man knows so little (I Cor. 8:2; 13:9-12)
E. We must have a praying heart (Psa. 119:18, 34, 73, 125, 144 and 169).
F. We must have a pious motive (Psa. 119: 34, 73; Col. 1:9-12).

X. **Basic Principles of Interpretation**
   A. The Absolute Inspiration of the Scriptures.
      The Christian doctrine: the verbal, plenary, inspiration of the infallible, inerrant Bible, which is the Written Word of God.
      1. **"VERBAL:"** Every single letter and word of Scripture as put down in the original autographs was inspired of God (Matt. 5:18; 22:32).
      2. **"PLENARY:"** All of the Bible, in all of its parts, is equally inspired. No part is more inspired than the other parts. The 66 books comprising the Old and New Testaments are all equally inspired (Matt. 5:17-18; II Tim. 3:16).
      3. **"INSPIRATION:"** God sovereignly prepared the authors of Scripture from birth in all things. He stirred them up to write. He guided them so they wrote down the very words of God. God's sovereign control of the authors did not remove the characteristics and personalities of the authors, but such things were ordered by God to be a better vehicle of expression.
      4. **"INFALLIBLE:"** In principle, the Bible is infallible, i.e., incapable of error or mistake. Why? God cannot lie (Titus 1:2), and the Bible is His Word; therefore, the Bible cannot be a lie (John 17:17).
      5. **"INERRANT:"** The Bible is without error in all it affirms as true, including matters of science, geography, miracles, history, etc.

6. **"Bible:"** The books in the Protestant Bible. There are no "lost" books. The Apocrypha is not inspired.

7. **"WORD OF GOD:"** The Word of God expressed in human words by human authors under the direct control of the Holy Spirit (2 Pet. 1:20-21).

B. The unity of the Bible.

Although it was written by over 40 different authors from many different walks of life over a period of 2000 years with no collaboration between authors, the Bible is a harmonious unit. It contains no contradictions. The N.T. does not contradict the O.T.. Paul does not contradict Jesus or James. All the teachings of the Bible dovetail into one another. The Bible presents one, consistent, cohesive, coherent view of truth throughout all its parts. Liberals say that the Old Testament and the New Testament contradict each other and even present different gods. This comes from ignorance, both spiritual and scriptural. The following chart reveals how the New Testament completes the Old Testament.

OLD TESTAMENT	NEW TESTAMENT
Unexplained Ceremonies	Ceremonies Explained
Unfulfilled Prophecies	Prophecies Fulfilled
Unsatisfied Longings	Longings Satisfied
Incomplete Destiny	Destiny Completed

Some liberal theologians have claimed that Jesus contradicted the O.T. in His "Sermon on the Mount:"

"Look at Matthew 5 where Christ contradicts the Old Testament and throws out the "eye for eye and tooth for tooth" doctrine of the primitive and uncivilized Jews who believed in a bloody and savage tribal war-god named Jehovah. In its place, Jesus teaches the Fatherhood of God, the brotherhood of man, pacifism and other teachings shared by all the great religious leaders of all religions."

But the Liberals misinterpret Matthew 5 completely:

1. Christ came to fulfill, not to contradict or destroy (Matt. 5:17-19).*
2. Christ was contradicting the rabbinic interpretation of the Torah, which had externalized it.

- He did not say "As it is written...."
- He did not quote Scriptures but the Rabbis (Matt. 5:21, 27, 33, 38, 43).
- He was establishing a "New" Covenant with greater laws.

C. Diversity of clearness
   While all Scripture is equally inspired, it is not equally clear (II Pet. 3:16).
Thus we must interpret the:
   1. Unclear in the light of the clear.
   2. Difficult in the light of simple. ex. John 14:28 must be interpreted in light of John 1:1, 18; 5:18, 23; 20:28.

*Note: Legalists also twist Matt. 5:17-19 to bring people back into bondage with the *Old/Mosaic Covenant* such as Sabbath keeping, food laws, women cannot teach or hold an office (see I Cor. 5:11 & I Timothy 13:5-9), etc. However, even under the *Old/Mosaic Covenant* there were women Prophetesses (Miriam (Exodus 15:20-21), Huldah (2 Kings 22:14), Noadiah (Nehemiah 6:14), Isaiah's wife (Isaiah 8:3) and Judges/Leaders (Deborah; Judges 4:4-5)). The New Testament has Anna & The daughters of Philip as examples of Prophetesses under the *New Covenant* (Luke 2:36 & Acts 21:9) and Presbutidas (women elders that "teach the women"; see Titus 2:3-5) and Deaconesses (who were women; see Romans 16:1). Yes, men are still the "head of the household" (this is a different sphere – the family; see Ephesians 5:22-24). The Bible tells us "do not be under the beggarly elements" of the Old/Mosaic Covenant (Heb. 10:1). For example, Matt. 5:17-19 is not referring to <u>individual laws</u>, but the <u>Scriptures</u>. Christ was establishing a *New Covenant*, not the *Old/Mosaic Covenant* polished—there are 4 Covenants in the Old Testament (the *Noahic Covenant*, the *Abrahamic Covenant* (the land promise is part of the Abrahamic Covenant), the *Mosaic Covenant* (David & Solomon are personal applications of the Mosaic Covenant), and the *New Covenant*); only the *Mosaic Covenant* was defective and obsolete. The other Covenants are still valid. The (4th) *New Covenant* is everlasting. (See my book entitled *How the Old & New Testaments Relate to Each Other*.)

Section Three

I. Basic Method of Interpretation

 A. The example of Christ and the Apostles: They dogmatically appealed to the Scriptures as the sole source of their authoritative teaching (Matt. 4:3-10 cf. I Cor. 15:3-4).

 B. The method used by Christ and the Apostles in their interpretation of Scripture should be our method (I John 2:6).

 C. The writers of Scripture treated the text of Scripture in terms of grammar and syntax.

  1. ex. Galatians 3:16-17: The difference between singular and plural nouns.

  2. ex. Matthew 22:32: The difference between present and past tense.

 D. The writers of Scripture treat the text of Scripture as being a reliable historical account from which they can draw doctrinal conclusions. ex. Romans 4:9-12: Two doctrines are drawn from the historical fact that Abraham was justified before he was circumcised.

  1. Justification is by faith alone, apart from works.

  2. Gentiles are now included in Abraham's Covenant.

E. The writers of Scripture treat the text of Scripture as being a reliable historical account from which they can draw ethical and moral imperatives and prohibitions.
1. I Corinthians 10:1-12
2. I Timothy 5:19
3. Matthew 12:1-8

F. Why did Christ and the Apostles treat the Scriptures the way they did? They had a primary assumption concerning the nature and use of the Bible (II Tim. 3:16-17).
1. All Scripture:
   a. Is inspired
   b. Its purpose is to perfect and to protect the elect.
   c. Its method or use:
      (1) Doctrine – Theology and Philosophy
      (2) Reproof
      (3) Corrections
      (4) Training in righteousness

II. The Canon of Scripture

A. The canon was not a product of human invention or ingenuity, but it everywhere manifests itself to be the product of Divine design.

B. Justification of the canon of Old Testament and New Testament:
1. The historical roots of the canon end in mystery.
2. The arrangement is not according to chance, size, chronology, date of composition or authorship.
3. The arrangement is according to subject matter. See diagrams #1 and #2.
4. The arrangement manifests a Divine hand.

C. The significance of canonical observations in studying a book of the Bible:
   We can find a clue as to the theme of a book and its importance in the whole counsel of God by observing where it is placed in the canon. (See my book *The Bible: Intelligent Design or Chance?*)

III. How to Study a Book of the Bible
Seek to answer these basic introductory questions:

A. What is its place in the canon?

B. Who wrote it?

C. What were the circumstances of the author?

D. To whom was the book written?

E. What do we know about them and their relationship to the author?

F. What is the tone and theme of the book?

G. What is the outline of the book?

IV. **How To Study a Verse**

Basic questions to ask yourself:

A. Who spoke or wrote it?

B. To whom was it spoken or written?

C. What is the context?

D. Are there any parallel passages?

E. Is it an Old Testament quotation or allusion?

F. Is there a clearer or fuller passage which explains this verse?

G. Is this a passage of full mention?

H. Are there any historical observations which throw light on the verse?

I. What is the grammatical significance of the verse?

V. **How to Do a Word Study**

Basic principles:

A. Identify all the places in the Bible where the word occurs. There are books and computer software that do this.

B. Be careful to observe the principle of progressive revelation. The meaning of a biblical word changed as God revealed more truth. For example, what "soul" meant in Genesis is not set in stone. It developed and deepened in meaning as revelation progressed.

C. Check the Greek/Hebrew dictionaries for the basic meaning.

D. If there are different meanings to the word, classify them into groups. Make a chart to show the different meanings.

E. The context of the passage in view determines the meaning of the word. Do not assume that the lexicon definition fits the verse you are studying.

F. Check the classic commentaries to make sure you are not coming up with a nutty interpretation. (Pro. 11:14).

VI. **Special Principles**

A. Analogy of faith (Rom. 12:6): Any interpretation of any particular verse in the Bible must not contradict, but be in harmony with the teaching of the whole of Scripture.

B. A simple positive implies a negative and a simple negative implies a positive (Psa. 40:9, 10; Eph. 4:25, 28).

C. Rhetorical questions are expressed for emphasis sake (Matt. 6:27; 16:26; 22:42; John 5:44; Rom. 9:14).

D. Do not absolutize general statements and promises (Pro. 17:6; 18:22; 23:1, 2)

E. Observe non-literal language (Matt. 15:11; 16:6, 7; John 4:32, 33).

1. Metaphor: John 6:35; 15:1

2. Ironical language: I Cor. 4:8

3. Hyperbole – exaggeration for emphasis sake: Josh. 11:4; Judges 7:12; John 21:25

F. Observe the significance to types. Various people, places, actions and things in the Old Testament were instituted by God for the express purpose of prefiguring the person and work of Jesus in the New Testament (John 1:29; Heb. 12:22).

G. Seek out the passage of full mention. There is usually one central passage in which a particular doctrine is expounded. All other scattered references should be interpreted in the light of the passage where it is discussed in full. ex. Isa. 40 (the transcendence of God); John 3 (regeneration); Matt. 24-25 (the return of Christ); I Cor. 15 (the resurrections), etc.

H. Do not forget to remember that divine revelation was progressive in nature (Heb. 1:1-2). This means that the N.T. interprets the O.T.. The N.T. has the priority over the O.T.

I. Principles for interpreting parables:

1. Parables are not be regarded or used as a proof of truth but only as an illustration of truth.

2. As illustrations, they never expressed the whole truth but only part of the truth.

3. They emphasize one major lesson or truth: the details are only part of the study, i.e., "filler" and, as such, cannot be viewed as teaching anything significant.
4. They are always in subjection to doctrinal passages.
5. The context determines the scope or purpose and the point of the parable (Lk. 15:2).
6. The best interpretation is the one that Christ or the Apostles supply.

Conclusion

The Bible is the revelation of the mind and heart of God. It is our responsibility not to corrupt (2 Cor. 2:17) or adulterate (2 Cor. 4:2) the Word of God.

Appendix

Verse Abuse – Introduction

The importance of rightly interpreting Scripture cannot be underestimated. If the people of God do not know how to interpret the Bible accurately, false teachers can easily deceive them.

Traditions have always been a problem for the people of God. Like barnacles, they slowly grow on the hull of the ship of the Church, and must be removed or the ship will sink. It is a hard, dirty, painful, and smelly job. But someone has to do it!

A. Jesus faced this problem in His own day. Matt. 15:1-20 cf. Mk 7:1-23
   1. Man-made traditions that come from outside of scripture.
   2. False interpretations of Scripture that render the Word ineffective.
B. Evangelicals rightly condemn Roman Catholicism, Greek Orthodoxy, the cults and the occult for having traditions that

contradict or nullify Scripture. These traditions are so serious in nature that they deny the Gospel.

C. But we evangelicals have also been blinded at times by our own vain traditions. While these "evangelical" traditions are not so serious in nature as to damn us, they do keep us from understanding the Bible correctly and can make the Christian life difficult. They obscure the truth of Scripture and rob us of many precious blessings.

D. There are three ways we can mishandle Scripture:

1. **Misquotation**: A Tradition of not quoting the words of a verse accurately.

   Examples:
   Matt. 23:37
   Eph. 2:8
   Phil. 2:9-11
   2 Pet. 3:9

2. **Mistranslation**:

   Examples:
   Matt. 16:19
   Matt. 28:19
   John 3:3-5
   1 Cor. 4:6

3. **Misinterpretation**:

   Examples:
   Gen. 3:16
   Matt. 5:9
   Matt. 7:1-5 (cf. John 7:24)
   Matt. 18:20
   Matt. 23:37
   Lk. 15:11-32

Old Testament –Diagram No. 1

History			Experience		Prophecy	
Basic Law	Pre-Exile History	Post-Exile History	Inner Life	Basic Prophecy	Pre-Exile Prophets	Post-Exile Prophets
5	9	3	5	5	9	3

New Testament – Diagram No. 2

History	Doctrine	Doctrine	Experience
Historic Foundation	Church Epistles	Pastoral Epistles	General Epistles
5	9	4	9

Questions for Discussion

1. Can we interpret the Bible any way we want or are there objective rules of grammar and syntax that must be followed?
2. Are all interpretations of the Bible equal (i.e. subjective and relative)?
3. What is the difference between the "interpretation" and the "application" of a biblical passage?
4. Are all interpretations of the Bible nothing more than personal opinion and prejudice?
5. The New Testament tells the members of a congregation to submit to the teaching and discipline of the elders (or pastor) of the church (Heb. 13:7, 17). Yet, people today think that their interpretation of Scripture is equal to the elders (pastors). Thus they disrespect their pastors and rebel against the doctrine of the church. What is the root cause of this modern rebellion? Is relativism the root problem?

CHAPTER SIXTEEN

How to Know if the Bible Is God's Word?

The Prophet Isaiah (c.740 - 681 BC) by
Michelangelo (1512)

No other book besides the Bible has over 2,000 prophecies that have been fulfilled such as Daniel 2:39-43 (four kingdoms in Nebuchadnezzar's dream: *Babylon, Medo-Persia, Greek and the Roman empire*; see chart of "Daniel's Outline of World History" below); Nah. 1:10, 3:7, 15, Zeph. 2:13-14 (Nineveh), Ezek. 26 (Tyre) and Isaiah 13:1-22 (Babylon) and Isaiah 44:28; 45:1; and 45:13 (Cyrus); Peter W. Stoner (1888 – 1980), who was a professor of Mathematics & Astronomy at Pasadena City & Westmont College, in <u>Science Speaks</u> (Online Edition, Revision Nov. 2005, Revised & HTML formatted by Don W. Stoner <http://sciencespeaks.dstoner.net/>) considers 48 distinct prophecies about Yeshua/Christ and states that to find any one man to fulfill all 48 prophecies to be 1 in 10^{157}. The estimated number of electrons in the universe is around 1 in 10^{79}--

Yeshua/Christ did not fulfill those 48 prophecies by accident or chance.

Introduction

Our presentation of "Why I Believe the Bible Is God's Word" begins with the internal foundation of our faith and then slowly builds the whole picture.

I. The Inner Witness of the Holy Spirit (Lk. 24:32; John 16:13-14)

Our assurance that the Bible is God's Word begins with an inner conviction that what we are reading is God's Word. The Bible authenticates itself as you read it with an open mind and heart. This is the work of the Holy Spirit who bears witness to the Word. This subjective witness is not sufficient in and of itself to "prove" the inspiration of the Bible. Yet, without it, the Bible would never be received as inspired. It is something that the Bible tells us will happen if we read it. This is the position of historic Christianity.

The Westminster Confession of Faith

Our full persuasion and assurance of the infallible truth and divine authority thereof, is from the inward work of the Holy Spirit, bearing witness by and with the word in our hearts." (I, V)

The Westminster Larger Catechism

Q. 4 How doth it appear that the Scriptures are the Word of God?

A. "The Spirit of God, bearing witness by and with the Scriptures in the heart of man is alone able to persuade it that they are the very Word of God."

A.A. Hodge, The Confession of Faith (pp. 36-37): "The highest and most influential faith in the truth and authority of the Scriptures is the direct work of the Holy Spirit in our hearts. The Holy Spirit opens the blinded eyes and gives due sensibility to the diseased heart; and thus assurance comes with the evidence of spiritual experience."

II. Lest someone think that "feelings" are the only basis for accepting Scripture, we must go on to set forth the evidences that confirm this faith. Historic Christianity goes on to state the evidential confirmation of faith.

A.A. Hodge, The Confession of Faith, p. 37: "When first regenerated, he first begins to set Scripture to the test of experience; and the more he advances, the more he proves them true and the more he discovers of their limitless breadth and fullness, and of their evidently designed adaption to all human wants under all conditions."

The Evidences

DANIEL'S OUTLINE OF WORLD HISTORY		
	DANIEL 2	DANIEL 7
	HEAD OF GOLD BABYLON (B.C. 605 - 539)	LION
	BREAST OF SILVER MEDO-PERSIA (B.C. 539 - 331)	BEAR
	THIGHS OF BRASS GREECE (B.C. 331-168)	LEOPARD
	LEGS OF IRON ROME (B.C. 168 - 476 A.D.) FEET OF IRON AND CLAY ROME (A.D. 476 - TODAY)	BEAST
MOUNTAIN FILLING EARTH	KINGDOM OF CHRIST	KINGDOM GIVEN TO THE SAINTS

I. The Scriptures claim to be the inspired Word of God. While this does not in and of itself "prove" the Bible to be God's Word, without this claim, there is no reason to view the Bible as God's Word. Its claim to inspiration is what we would expect to find if it is God's Word. What do we mean when we say that the Bible is inspired? Theologians refer to the doctrine of the verbal, plenary inspiration of the infallible and inerrant Word of God.

    A. **"Verbal":** every letter and word in the original manuscript.
       1. Matt. 5:18; cf. Matt. 22:31-32
       2. I Cor. 2:13
    B. **"Plenary":** all 66 books of the Bible.
       1. O.T." Matt. 5:17; cf. 2 Tim. 3:16
       2. N.T.: 2 Pet. 3:15-16; 2 Tim. 3:16; I Cor. 14:37
    C. **"Infallible":** without error in all matters of faith and morals.
    D. **"Inerrant":** without error in all that is says about anything including "scientific" matters.
       1. Num. 23:19; cf. Heb. 6:18
       2. John 10:35
       3. John 17:17

Note: This is not "arguing in a circle" because the Bible is not one book. The Bible is a library of 66 books written by more than 40 authors over several thousand years. To quote one book to document another is the soul and substance of all scientific research.

With the Bible we have an experiment over a period of several thousand years. The data from such documentary evidence cannot be swept aside by a wave of a hand. This is in opposition to the "Bibles" of other religions such as the Koran or the Book of Mormon. They are one book with no historic documents to substantiate them.

II. Personal Experience Confirms It.
    A. Conversion experiences confirm it. (Convinced-

Convicted-Converted)
B. The Christian life confirms it.
1. Everything that happens is exactly what the Bible said would happen.
2. We can live what we believe and believe what we live.
3. The Bible is constantly validated by all the facts at my disposal.
C. Witnessing experiences confirm it.

Non-Christians react and believe exactly the way the Bible said they would.

Example: When an arrogant atheist in New York City demanded to know how I knew that the Bible was true, I responded by telling her that she proved the Bible to be true every time she opened her mouth! She was shocked and asked. "How is this true?" I asked her, "Do you fear God?" She said, "No." "Well, then you just proved that Rom. 3:18 is true. Is the Gospel foolishness to you?" "Yes!" "Well, you just proved that 1 Cor. 1:18 is true. Do you want your own way instead of living according to God's way?" "I don't want God's way. I will do as I please." "Well, you just proved that Isa. 53:6 is true. Every time you open your mouth you confirm the Bible by saying what it said you would say. Thank you for making me a stronger Christian."

III. Scientific Facts Support It.
A. We are talking about hard "facts" and not scientific theories.
1. All the hard "facts" so far validated support the teachings of the Bible. No "facts" disprove the Bible.
B. Archaeology proves much of Scripture to be true.
1. Sir William Ramsey's conversion and his vindicating of Luke's and Acts' historicity.
2. Verifying fulfilled prophecies: Tyre (Ezk. 26-27).
3. Resolving apparent contradictions
4. Clarifying biblical words

IV. The Bible teaches a completely satisfying philosophy and way of Life.

Conclusion

There is more than enough evidence on every hand from every department of human experience and knowledge to demonstrate that Christianity is true. The light is shining and the music is playing but the non-Christian shuts his eyes and plugs his ears and then pretends that there is neither light nor sound.

Questions for Discussion

1. Why do you believe in the Bible?
2. Is something true because we believe it or should we believe something only if it is true?
3. Would the Bible be true even if no one believed in it?
4. Discuss the following statement and explain why it is erroneous: "I believe in the Bible because it makes me feel happy and gives me a lot of peace."

CHAPTER SEVENTEEN

The Inerrancy of Scripture

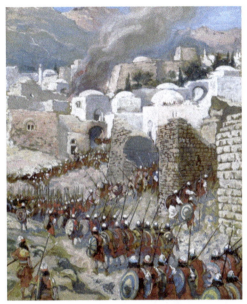

The Taking of Jericho (approx. date 1400 BC) by
James Jacques Joseph Tissot (French, 1836 – 1902).

During time of Yeshua's/Christ's incarnation, there
were two settlements—the original Jewish Jericho
and a Gentile Jericho set up by the Romans two
miles from the Jewish Jericho.

Introduction

Would you call someone "reliable" who:

- Was frequently mistaken on what he
  believed and said?
- Contradicted himself many times?

- Deliberately and knowingly lied to you on many occasions?
- Made up stories whenever it suited him?
- Would you continue to trust his word after being deceived by him again and again? I don't think so! Yet, this is what liberal theologians ask us to do with the Bible! They claim:
- The authors of the Bible were often mistaken in what they believed and wrote.
- They frequently contradicted themselves and other biblical writers.
- They deliberately and knowingly tried to deceive people into thinking that their books were written by such famous men as Moses, Daniel, Matthew, Paul, etc.
- They made up details of the birth, life, sermons, miracles, death and resurrection of Jesus.
- They fabricated a new theology around their fabricated Christ and created a new religion called Christianity, which Jesus would have never recognized.

I.   The Reliability of Scripture

When Christian theologians use such words as "infallibility" and "inerrancy," they are simply saying that the Bible is reliable in everything it records. Thus you can count on the Bible because it is true, factual, real and historical. The Bible is:

- A reliable record of the experience and beliefs of the biblical authors. Illustration: In the book of Romans, we have a reliable record of what the Apostle Paul experienced and believed.
- A reliable record of the beliefs and experiences of other people.
  Illustration: The beliefs and practices of the

Pharisees are described in the Gospels (Mark 7:3-4).
- A reliable record of the lies and false ideas of men and demons.
Illustration: Gen. 3:4; Job 42:7
- A reliable record of the good things that people do.
Illustration: Dorcas (Acts 9:3-39)
- A reliable record of the evil things that people do.
Illustration: The rape of Dinah (Gen. 34:1-2)
- A reliable record of the historical events—natural and supernatural—which surrounded the rise and progress of the people of God.
Illustration: The Creation, the Fall, the Flood, the Tower, the Patriarchs, the Exodus, the rise, fall and return of Israel, the life of Christ, and the expansion of the early church into Europe.
- A reliable record of biblical authorship.
Illustration: Isaiah, Daniel, Matthew, etc.
- A reliable record of what God revealed to the authors of Scripture. Illustration: Gal. 1:1, 11-12.
- A reliable record that does not contradict itself.
Illustration: 2 Pet. 2:20-21.
- A reliable record of what we must believe to be saved and how to live the Christian life. Illustration: Acts 4; 12; Rom. 12:1-2.

II. Common questions about inerrancy
- "Should we interpret the Bible literally?" Answer: No. The Bible contains many different kinds of literature: history, poetry, prophecy, doctrine and ethics. Figurative language is frequently used.
- "If it is in the Bible, is it true?" Answer: No. The Bible is a reliable record of the lies and false ideas of men and demons as well as a record of the truth. A verse must be interpreted in the light of its context.
Illustration: Ecclesiastes.
- "If it is in the Bible, is it good?" Answer: No. The Bible records many evil things, which it condemns.

Illustration: Rape, cannibalism, murder, etc.

- "Is the Bible a textbook on history, science, mathematics, biology, etc.?" Answer: No. The writing of textbooks was not the intent of the authors of the Bible. But whenever they do touch on such areas, they are reliable.

- "Can we judge the Bible by today's literary standards?" Answer: No. Each book of the Bible must be judged by the literary standards of the age in which it was written. Illustration: Paul's name at the beginning of his letters. Moses' use of the third person.

- "Are the Gospels biographies of Christ?" Answer: No. The modern idea of writing a chronologically structured "biography" was unknown in the first century. It was not the intent of the gospel writers to write a "biography" of Jesus in the modern sense. Each gospel writer selected certain things from the life of Christ to illustrate a particular theme that he wanted to convey to a specific audience he had in mind. He would arrange these things in a way to highlight his message, thus they did not try to give a precise chronology of the words or actions of Christ. For example, Matthew groups together all the kingdom parables in chapter 13 regardless of when they were given. He structured his gospel account to certain themes—not chronology.

Book	Theme	Audience
Matthew:	What did Jesus say?	The Jews
Mark:	What did Jesus do?	The Romans
Luke:	Who followed Jesus?	The Greeks
John:	Who was Jesus?	The Christians

- "If two or more accounts of the same incident are different in any way, are they contradictory?" Answer: No. Differing accounts can be supplementary and not contradictory. Liberals assume that if two or more accounts "differ" in any details, they automatically are "contradictory." But this is a common logical fallacy.

- When two or more accounts of the same incident are given by different individuals, they will always "differ" in some details. But these "differences" only supplement each other and once they are put together, they give us the whole picture. Different accounts by different people will usually differ for the following reasons:

  1. The accounts are given from different viewpoints. Example: Four people see an accident from four different corners.
  2. People are emphasizing different things. Example: Political, society and gossip reporters' accounts of a Washington party.
  3. When one account is written after the others and it adds new information that was not available before, this is not contradictory but supplementary.
  4. The intent of a person must be recognized.
     - If he did not intend to put things in a chronological order, but to group things thematically, he cannot be faulted.
     - If he did not intend to give a literal word for word quotation but to summarize a sermon in his own words, or to paraphrase a statement in order to emphasize its meaning, he cannot be faulted.
     - If he did not intend to give an exact numerical count, but to round things off to the nearest whole number, he cannot be faulted.
     - If he did not intend to use literal language, but to use figurative language in a description of something, he cannot be faulted.
  5. The audience must also be taken into account. We do not speak to a child in the same way we speak to an adult. What we say in a court is

more formal than a casual conversation with a friend. When one audience is Jewish and another is Gentile, different terminology may be used given the different backgrounds.

6. Leaving out those details that do not fit in with your theme is perfectly normal. Example: A black history course that only describes black inventors is not erroneous because it omits any reference to white inventors.

7. When one account mentions one person while another account mentions more than one, there is no logical contradiction if the first account does not say "only" one person was present. The author is simply emphasizing the presence of one person without denying the presence of others.

8. Objection: "But how about when Matthew says that two blind men were healed while Mark and Luke say that only one was healed?" Answer: It must be pointed out that you added the word "only" to the accounts. This is a point of logic that must be emphasized. Neither Mark nor Luke said that "only" one blind man was healed. They just tell the story of the one man whose name was known as Bartimaeus. Matthew mentions in passing that there was a second blind man healed. They supplement each other. There is no logical contradiction.

9. Objection: "Mark 10:46 says that his healing took place as Jesus approached Jericho, while Matthew 20:30 says that it took place as He was leaving Jericho. You can't be approaching and leaving a city at the same time. Isn't this a clear contradiction?" Answer: No. Archaeology has discovered that when the Romans tried to set up a base in Jericho, the Jews rioted so much that the Romans went down the road about two miles

and set up their own settlement, which they also called Jericho. Thus, the word "Jericho" in New Testament times referred to two settlements: one Jewish and one Gentile. The merchants and beggars would gather between the two settlements to catch the traffic going either way. In this light, it is clear that the healing took place after Jesus had left the Jewish Jericho but before He got to the Gentile Jericho. In other words, it took place between the Jewish and Gentile sections of Jericho. Since Matthew was writing to the Jews, he referred to the Jewish section of Jericho. And, since Mark was writing to the Gentiles, he referred to the Gentile section of Jericho, thus, there is no contradiction.

10. Objection: "But the New Testament authors frequently misquote the Old Testament. Is this not a clear contradiction?" Answer: No. The modern literary practice of giving an exact quotation of someone's words was not practiced in the first century. The biblical authors, like the rabbis, would paraphrase (i.e. put into their own words) an O.T. text in order to emphasize its meaning. They had just as much right to paraphrase the Bible as we do today.

11. Objection: "But what if the wording of what Jesus or someone else said is different from one gospel to the other?" Answer: The authors of Scripture plainly stated that they did not record the full text of what Jesus or others said (John 21:24-25). They usually summarized in their own words what people said. They did not usually quote verbatim. (Illustration: Matt. 5-7; Acts 2)

12. Objection: "But what about all the numbers and names that contradict each other in 1 and 2 Kings and 1 and 2 Chronicles?" Answer: Divine

inspiration only covers the authors of Scripture and what they originally wrote—not all the copyists since that time. Logically speaking, the existence of simple copyist errors in numbers and names cannot negate the inspiration of the original text.

13. Objection: "What if something or someone in the Bible is not mentioned in extra-biblical literature? Is this a contradiction?" Answer: It is illogical to say that something or someone mentioned in the Bible did not exist because we do not have extra-biblical confirmation. Archaeology has a nasty habit of crushing those kinds of arguments. Example: No writing in Moses' day; no Hittites, etc. Some liberals claim that the town of Nazareth mentioned in the New Testament did not exist at that time because the Talmud and Josephus did not mention it. They are wrong for several reasons.

- This is a logical fallacy because it is an argument from silence. Did the Talmud and Josephus mention every town in Israel? No.
- They are evidently ignorant of the "Nazareth stone," which archaeologists found in 1878, which must be dated A.D. 45-54. The stone proves that Nazareth existed at that time.
- While the Talmud does not use the noun "Nazareth," it does use the adjective "Notzri" as in "Jesus ha-Notzri." The word "Notzri" comes from the word Nazareth.

Conclusion

The Bible is reliable in all it records because its authors were sovereignly guided in what they wrote by God himself, and thus infallible and inerrant. You can trust the Bible.

Questions for Discussion

1. The Bible records murder, rape, theft, lying, and even cannibalism. Does this mean God approves of such things?
2. The Bible records "the good, the bad, and the ugly" of man's history including man's inhumanity to man.
3. Should we judge ancient literature such as the Bible by modern standards?
4. Should we accept what the Bible asserts as true or can we pick and choose what we want to accept in the Bible?
5. Should you believe what the Bible teaches or what philosophers or scientists teach?

CHAPTER EIGHTEEN

The Gnostic Gospels

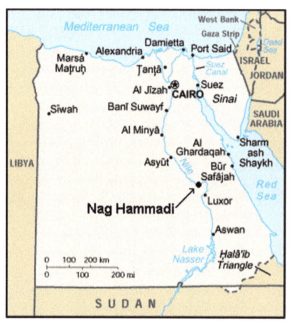

The site of discovery (1945), Nag Hammadi in map of Egypt

Introduction

It has become quite popular on college campuses for atheistic professors to attack Christianity by stating that Gnosticism was the "original" Christianity. Thus, the Christian student today has to have a basic understanding of Gnosticism in order to defend the faith (Jude 3).

I. The Early Christian Church rejected various fake gospels produced by a Greek mystery religion called Gnosticism that attempted to absorb Christianity. The Apostle Paul attacked Gnosticism directly in Colossians while John attacked it in I and II John and Revelation. Every subsequent Church Father and council attacked the Gnostics. At no point did the Christian Church accept Gnosticism.

2. The Gnostics denied the existence of the Biblical personal/infinite God, monotheism, the Trinity and that Jesus was human and divine. They even denied that He was Christ! Jesus, to them, was simply a link in the chain of Being. They also denied Jesus died for our sins and His bodily resurrection. The Gnostics rejected the Old Testament and New Testament and drew upon Eastern ideas such as Reincarnation and pantheism.

3. While the New Testament began within ten to fifteen years of the death of Jesus (AD. 33) and we have a fragment of Mark that must be dated AD 50 and a fragment of Luke that has to be dated AD 57, the vast majority of the Gnostic gospels were not written until late into the third and fourth centuries.

4. The Gnostics had a stronghold in Egypt and some fourth century manuscripts have been found in Nag Hammadi. These false gospels contained historical and literary blunders that reveal that they were not written in the first century. Their literary style is drastically different from the New Testament and they exalt absurd stories of Jesus' childhood such as:

    (a) Jesus would make clay birds and change them into real ones.

    (b) While playing hide and seek, Jesus searched for some children in a particular house into which they had run. When He came to the door and asked the mother if there were any children inside she said, "No, only kids." Outraged, Jesus turned all of the children into goats.

    (c) Jesus had a twin brother.

    (d) Jesus had sexual involvement with various women.

5. In John 2:11, the Apostle John stated that the first miracle Jesus did was turning the water into wine at the wedding of Cana. The Gnostic materials, which are filled with absurd miracles of the child Jesus, cannot be viewed

as valid in the light of John 2:11.

6. Certain newspaper writers sensationalized the finding of the Gnostic gospels as they did the finding of the Dead Sea Scrolls. Once scholars had a chance to translate these works nothing new was discovered that was not already known from the writings of the early Church Fathers. The Early Church never said or pretended that these fake gospels did not exist. The Church never hid anything from anybody. They showed that these were spurious works.

7. While the New Testament is organically linked to the Old Testament, the Gnostic works reject the existence of God, the creation of the world out of nothing, the goodness of matter and flesh, the necessity of a substitutionary blood atonement, etc. Whereas Christianity is an extension of Old Testament Judaism, Gnosticism is an extension of Eastern religions such as Buddhism.

8. No Biblical scholar today feels that there is any significance to the Gnostic works beyond that of historical curiosity as to what this mystery religion believed. Since none of them were written in the first century and they did not appear until several hundred years after Christ, they are worthless as a guide to Jesus' life. The first century New Testament, written by the Apostles who were eye-witnesses and friends of Jesus Christ, is logically and historically a superior guide to the life and teaching of Jesus.

9. Christianity triumphed over Gnosticism because of the superiority of the Biblical Gospel. While such writers as Pagels try to

prove that Christianity triumphed because of its political structure, this is a very superficial position. We must ask on what basis did the early Fathers have political authority in the Church? The historic Christian won out because it was in harmony with the Old Testament and New Testament and descended from the Apostles and other eye-witnesses. It was rooted in the historical bodily resurrection of Jesus Christ as a real space-time event that was verified by over 500 eye-witnesses. Gnosticism was built on myth and subjectionism.

10. Modern forms of Gnosticism attempt to discount the New Testament and appeal to the Nag Hammadi texts as "Lost Bibles". This is historically and theologically absurd. The attempt to identify Gnosticism as a part of Early Christianity is doomed to failure once it is understood that Gnosticism existed before Christianity appeared and that it tried to absorb all the religions it encountered. It was clearly denounced as "Anti-Christ" by the Apostles and Church Fathers. It never represented Biblical or Historic Christianity. Since the Gnostic "gospels" attack the New Testament, it is obvious that the New Testament existed before them.

11. There is but one eternal personal infinite God who created the world out of nothing. This God eternally existed in three centers of consciousness or personality that the New Testament identifies as the Father, the Son and the Holy Spirit. This Triune God has done all that is necessary for man's forgiveness and salvation. Jesus Christ was incarnate as a real man and died a real death. He was bodily raised from the dead, having paid off all the punishment that God's Law demands. Christ's death makes Karmic reincarnation unnecessary. Jesus has paid it all. Our responsibility is to repent of our sin and to accept Jesus Christ as the Lord of all of life

Conclusion

Gnosticism was never a part of Christianity. It was always viewed as a pagan religion. The so-called Gnostic "Gospels" are obvious frauds.

CHAPTER NINETEEN

How We Got Our Bible

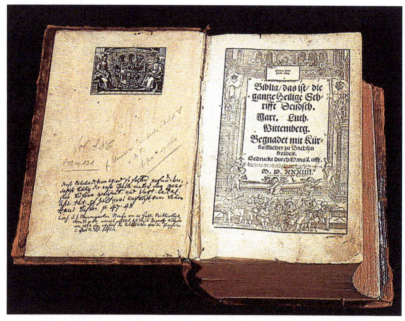

The Bible translated into German by Martin Luther (1534)

Because of the modern attacks on the integrity of the text of the Old and New Testaments, Christians should have a basic understanding of the historical process that began with the original manuscripts and ends with the Bible in the English language.

1. The Original Manuscripts
    A. These refer to the actual animal skins or papyri that the authors of the various books of the Bible used.
    B. Theologians refer to the original manuscripts when they speak of the

infallible, inerrant, verbal, plenary inspiration of the Bible. These original manuscripts were perfect because the authors were inspired of God.

C. As far as we know, all the original manuscripts have been lost.

1. Some have argued that these original manuscripts still exist because: (1) Would God inspire them and then lose them? (2) God's sovereignty guaranteed their preservation. (3) Do not such verses as Psalm 119:89; Isa. 40:8; Matt. 5:17-18; John 10:34 prove that these inspired manuscripts would be preserved for us?

2. The only problem with the above arguments is that there are no original manuscripts that exist today. All these arguments mean nothing if you cannot produce an original manuscript.

3. There is a good reason why God would purposely see to the destruction of these original manuscripts: to prevent us from worshiping them as idols. Remember what happened to the brazen serpent pole that Moses made? It was destroyed because it had become an idol (2 Kings 18:1-4). The idolatrous heart of man would have enshrined the originals long ago.

4. The importance of these manuscripts lies in what was written on them and not the manuscripts themselves. Through textual criticism we are

about 99 percent sure of what was written on these originals.

II. The Copies of the Original Manuscripts

    A. While the originals were perfect because the authors were inspired, we must state that no copy is perfect because no copyist was inspired. While there are no errors in the originals, there are errors in the copies.

    B. The errors in the copies are generally easily detected and are the result of honest mistakes such as:

        1. Wrong division of letters. Early copies do not have any word divisions.

        Example: "GODISNOWHERE."

        How should we divide the words in this sentence?

    God is now here.

    God is no where.

III. Mistakes during dictation. Some words are pronounced the same but are spelled differently.

    Example #1: Rom. 5:1: ομεν or ωμεν?

    Example #2: English: blue or blew?

    A. Skipping lines because a word begins or ends several sentences.

            KAI.....
Skipped → KAI.....
            DIA.....

            KAI.....
Skipped → DAI.....
            KIA.....

IV. Dropping a word. Example: The "wicked KJV Bible," which dropped the word "not" out of the seventh commandment.

V.   Misinterpreting a copyist's comment as being part of the text. Example: 1 John

VI.   There are deliberate insertions or deletions in some copies. Example: 1 John 5:7

VII.   Old Testament Manuscripts
  A.   Only 1,700 exist.
  B.   Nearly all are quite late and date from the Middle Ages (A.D. 1000).
  C.   The Jews were very meticulous in their copying of the manuscripts.
    1.   Only the scribes were allowed to do this as an occupation.
    2.   They counted words and destroyed any defective manuscripts, etc.
  D.   The accuracy of the Masoretic text has been verified by a comparison between the Dead Sea Scroll of Isaiah with the Masoretic text of Isaiah. After 1,200 years of copying and recopying, only 13 errors happened. These were simply errors like the switching of letters.
  E.   When we have a conflict, we can compare the Dead Sea Scrolls, the Septuagint, the Masoretic text and other versions. The only controversy in O.T. textual criticism are questions about the priority of the Masoretic text or the Septuagint. The N.T. quotations of the Septuagint in passages where the Hebrew is different are problematic to this day.

VIII.   New Testament Manuscripts
  a.   There are 5,000 Greek manuscripts, 8,000 Latin and 1,000 ancient versions of the N.T. or parts of the N.T.
  b.   Nearly all are quite late and date from the Middle Ages (A.D. 1000).
  c.   The N.T. copyists were not meticulous.
    i.   Lay people did the copying.
    ii.   No strict rules were followed.
  d.   More than 200,000 variant readings have resulted

from the "lay" copying. Out of them all, only about 50 readings are problematic and all of them would fit on one page. The other mistakes are obvious and are easily corrected.

e. When in doubt about a text, we have a wealth of resources to consult.

    i. Greek manuscripts (skins, papyri)

    ii. Latin manuscripts

    iii. Ancient versions

    iv. Early Fathers

    v. Early Heretics

f. How do we decide which variant reading is correct?

    i. Are the majority of manuscripts always right? Not necessarily. What if the majority are copies of a poor ancestral manuscript? And they are the majority because they were geographically, politically, culturally or ecclesiastically favored? A simple majority may be wrong in manuscripts as well as in politics.

    ii. Is the oldest manuscript always right? Not necessarily. There are too few of them to compare. What do we do when they disagree? Could an early manuscript come from a poor ancestral copy?

    iii. Do we exalt one particular manuscript as being perfect? We should not. There is not a perfect one around. This is an easy way out and appeals only to those who want a "simple" and quick answer. Example: Lamsda and the Peshitta (Fifth Century)

    iv. We should take all the evidence into account and make an eclectic choice.

       1. Internal evidence: the literary context, the author's vocabulary and style, parallel passages, etc.

       2. External evidence: papyri, uncials,

Fathers, ancient versions, minuscules, Latin, etc.

g. Constructed Greek texts of the New Testament

    i.   A Catholic Cardinal, Ximenes, decided to put out a Greek text of the N.T. that he would construct by examining several Greek manuscripts and making a compromise text.

    ii. When the humanist scholar Erasmus heard of the Cardinal's plans, he rushed into print a constructed Greek text of his own. He only took six to 10 months to produce this text! He used only six very late and quite poor manuscripts. His four editions are filled with a multitude of corrections. Since none of his manuscripts had the last of Rev. 22, he translated the ending from the Latin into the Greek. Although none of his manuscripts had 1 John 5:7, he put it into his later editions because of the Pope's dogmatism. His work is marked by hastiness and a multitude of mistakes, some of which he tried to correct with each new edition.

    iii. Robert Stephanus (1546) put out his own text. It was basically Erasmus' text. He continued the tradition of putting such verses as 1 John 5:7 into the text. He was the first to separate the text into chapters and verses.

    iv. The Elzevirs put out a text in 1633. In their second edition they claimed that their text was "the text received by all." It has been called the Textus Receptus since that time.

    v.   Bengel (1687-1752) was "the father of textual criticism." He taught that the manuscripts should be "weighed" instead of just being counted.

    vi. The period from 1831-1881 was filled with a host of men who spent their lifetime studying the manuscripts. Much progress was made by

Lachmann, Tischendorf, Tregelles, Alford, etc.

vii.   The climax was reached by Westcott and Hort (1825). They did the following:

1. Designated "families" in manuscripts
2. Proclaimed the superiority of the Vaticanus manuscript and the Neutral Family
3. Codified the general rules for textual criticism
4. Dismissed the Textus Receptus as unimportant and mistaken
5. Became the position on the N.T. for the next 50 years

viii. A radical reaction rose up to defend the Textus Receptus. Such scholars as Burgon refuted the exaltation of the Vaticanus and the superiority of the Neutral Family. Others went to the extreme of exalting the Textus Receptus and the Byzantine family.

ix.   These two positions took the same approach but violently disagreed with the end result.

Position	Westcott & Hort	Scrivener
One Family	Neutral	Byzantine
One Text	Vaticanus	Textus Receptus

Both assumed that we needed one family and one text to act as the ultimate standard to decide all variant readings. Both positions have gradually given way to a more balanced approach.

x.   The present eclectic position:

1. No one family, text or manuscript is to be viewed as perfect.

      2. All the internal and external evidence should be consulted.

      3. There will be a few readings where we will never know for sure with 100 percent certainty.

      4. Variant readings should be rated in terms of degrees of certainty.

      A- B-C-D

IX. The English Bible

  a. Various partial translations were made by such men as Bede (A.D. 674-735).

  b. Wycliffe's Bible (A.D. 1382) was the first complete translation. It was translated from the Latin, not from the Hebrew or Greek. Tyndale's Bible (1534) was the first printed English Bible. Although it was incomplete, he went from the Hebrew and Greek.

  d. Coverdale's Bible (1535) was the first complete printed English Bible.

  e. The Geneva Bible (1560) was translated by the Calvinist Reformers in exile in Geneva. It was the Bible of the Puritans and Pilgrims. It contained Calvin's notes on various verses. It was the Bible of the English people for almost 100 years.

  f. The King James Version (1611).

      i. One of England's most wicked kings, King James, had a particular hatred of the Geneva Bible because of its Calvinistic footnotes. He disliked the Puritans and supported the Anglo-Catholic religion instead.

      ii. At the Hampton Court, 1604, the King was presented with a Puritan petition that the Geneva Bible become the Bible of the English Church. He chose to have a new translation issued that would not have the Calvinism of the Geneva Bible in it.

iii. The Puritans did not appreciate the new translation but continued to use the Geneva Bible. One of the reasons the Pilgrims left England was to get away from the KJV and to freely use the Geneva Bible. The Geneva Bible was the Bible of early Colonial America.

g. Ultimately the KJV became the most widely used Bible by English speaking people. Its beauty has never been surpassed.

X. Major revisions began to appear as the study of the manuscripts uncovered the mistakes that Erasmus and other early scholars had made. The KJV was based basically on Erasmus via Stephanus' Greek text and not on the Textus Receptus. The KJV was translated in 1611 and the Textus Receptus did not come out until 1633. The Textus Receptus and the text of Stephanus disagree in 287 places. They are not the same text.

Conclusion

To decide which translation you should use, the following things should be taken into account:

1. Faithfulness to the Hebrew and Greek.
2. Clarity in vocabulary and sentence structure.
3. Readability, i.e., it can be read without labor or difficulty.
4. Beauty in style.
5. Purpose of reading it: casual, study, etc.

CHAPTER TWENTY

Signs of a Cult

Great Salt Lake, Utah (2014)

One hundred years ago there were only around a dozen cults with two or three thousand followers. Today there are over 5000 cults operating in the United States alone. A new cult is incorporated every day of the week. No one individual is capable of keeping track of them all.

There has been a cultic explosion in which 60 to 80 million people in the United States are involved in the cults or occult to some degree. And most of these groups focus on converting college students!

Part of Christian maturity is discerning between truth and error (Heb. 5:12–14). This particularly concerns the ability to spot a false prophet (Matt. 7:15–23).

Even if someone says that he believes in the gospel of Jesus and the Holy Spirit, you cannot assume that what he means by such terms is what you mean by such terms. He may have totally different definition of who Jesus was and what the gospel is all about. What "Jesus" does he believe in? The Jesus of the Jehovah's Witnesses whom they claim was only an angel named Michael? The Jesus of the Unitarians who was only a Jewish rabbi? Or, was Jesus God the Son, second person of the Holy Trinity? Paul warns us that,

> I am afraid that just as Eve was deceived by the serpent's cunning, your minds may somehow be led astray from your sincere and pure devotion to Christ. For if someone comes to you and preaches another Jesus other than the Jesus we preached, or if you receive another spirit from the one you received, or another gospel from the one you accepted, you put up with it easily enough. (II Cor. 11:3, 4)

The apostle Paul had to deal with false prophets in his own day. They were trying to teach Christian people "another gospel," which was not the true Gospel of Christ. The "Jesus" they preached was not the true Jesus. The "spirit" that animated them was not the Holy Spirit as they claimed but the spirit of antichrist. This is what he said about them:

> But even if we or an angel from heaven should preach a gospel other than the one we preached to you, let him be eternally condemned! As we have already said, so now I say again: If anybody is preaching to you a gospel other than what you accepted, let him be eternally condemned! (Gal. 1:8, 9)

Paul's Christianity was strong and virile and not wishy-washy. We need to be bold with the truth. It does not matter if someone claims an angel or God Himself appeared and revealed to them a new gospel. Let them be condemned as heretics! Throughout the centuries, false prophets have always come to deceive and confuse the people of God (Deut.18:21, 22). The Scriptures tell us that we must not be ignorant of Satan's devices (2 Cor. 2:11).

In Jude 3, Christians are called upon to defend the Faith. This text also says that the Faith was once and for all delivered unto the saints in the First Century within the pages of the New Testament. This means that the Christian is not to expect or accept any further revelation of doctrines or morals in the future. Thus, the *Book of Mormon* or any other supposed additional revelation that challenges the sole authority of Scripture must be rejected. If a doctrine is not a part of the original historic faith of the Christian Church, it is to be rejected.

What Is a Cult?

These considerations help us to define the word "cult." What is a cult? *A religion whose leadership is viewed as having equal or greater authority than the Bible and who claims to be Christian while denying the historic doctrines of Biblical Christianity.*

The two key issues in the above definition are religious authority and theology. The authority structure of a cult always rests on an infallible leadership who is viewed as being either God's representative or prophet on earth or as God or Christ Himself. Thus the members of the cult must give absolute submission to the authority of the cult leadership. Every aspect of life must be placed in total obedience to the cult. You may not question or challenge the teachings or rulings of the leadership. There is total control of the mind as well as the body in cultic structures.

There are some "Christian" cults operating on campuses today that while they do not deny the fundamental doctrines of the gospel, they are a cult because of their authority structure.

Beware of any group that is against thinking, asking questions, reading books or doing research. When a group emphasizes absolute submission to the leadership, it is cultic in structure.

Most cults deny the theology of Biblical and historic Christianity. The following doctrines are usually the most frequently denied truths.

Fifteen Signs of a Cult

1. *The Personhood of God*

Most New Age, Eastern or "science of the mind" cults teach that God is an impersonal force or energy. They are not accountable to a personal God who will one day judge them. It is fruitless to pray for there is no personal God who can hear and answer your prayers. Pantheism is a form of atheism because it denies the biblical God who exists apart from and independent of the universe.

2. *The Trinity*

Most cults deny the doctrine that God eternally exists in the three Persons: the Father, the Son and the Holy Spirit. They either deny that the Son and the Holy Spirit are God or they teach that the Father and the Holy Spirit are only different modes or masks worn by the Son of God who alone is God.

3. *The Virgin Birth*

The cults usually deny that Mary was a virgin when she conceived Jesus. They deny it despite the clear teaching of the Bible in Isa. 7:14; Matt. 1:21–25 and Lk. 1:26–35.

4. *Jesus is the Christ*

All of the New Age, Eastern and "science of the mind" cults believe that the "Christ" is an idea or an ideal that exists in everyone. In this sense, Jesus was only "a" Christ and not THE Christ. Jesus became a Christ at his baptism and ceased to be Christ at his death. There have been many different Christs and you are a Christ too. This is flatly contradicted by the apostle John in I John 2:22.

5. *The bodily resurrection of Christ*

Just as the deity of Christ is rejected by most cults, His bodily resurrection from the dead is also denied. Either His body dissolved into gases as was taught by the early Jehovah's Witnesses or He went on to be reincarnated in other human beings as taught by New Age cults.

6. *The literal return of Christ*

Christians believe that Jesus Christ is going to return to this world with great power and glory and that this return will be personal, bodily and literal. Cultic groups that teach anything concerning the second coming of Christ usually state that the coming was invisible and has already taken place as with the Jehovah's Witnesses. They claim that Jesus returned in 1914. Others claim that Jesus has returned in the person of some present cultic leader as in the New Age Movement.

7. *The atonement of Christ*

The cults always reject the atoning work of Christ in which He dies for the sins of His people and does all that is necessary for their eternal salvation. They speak of atonement only in terms of Jesus being an example of self-giving love. In the science of mind cults, "at-one-ment" means that we are to be absorbed back into the impersonal force of the universe in the classic Hindu sense of Nirvana. Reincarnation is a flat denial of the atonement in that we have to pay off our own karma in some future life.

8. *Justification by grace alone through faith alone in Christ alone*

In all cultic structures salvation is based on works. You have to work exceedingly hard at earning your salvation whatever it may be. You may have to go door to door selling magazines, books, flowers or candy in order to fulfill your obligation to the cult. You may have to work day and night in order to deliver your own soul. Baptism is usually made a part of salvation. Eph. 2:8, 9 demonstrates the vanity of trying to work for your salvation.

9. *The authority of Scripture*

One of the most important elements in any cultic structure is that the leadership of the cult has more authority than Scripture itself. Thus the cult member is not under the authority of God or His Word but under the authority of the cult leadership. This is usually hidden from outsiders. They will claim that they believe in the authority of the Bible in order to get you into their meetings. But once you are there, you will discover that the Bible has authority only so far as it agrees with the teachings of the cult.

10. *The new birth*

The cults redefine the new birth as having reference to the resurrection as with Armstrong's Worldwide Church of God or reincarnation as with Edgar Casey. They do not accept the teaching of Jesus that we must be born by God's Spirit in order to enter God's kingdom.

11. *Election and Predestination*

The cults have a special hatred of the doctrines of sovereign grace or Calvinism. In all my many years of researching thousands of cults, I never found a single cult that believed in Calvinism! They all denied that salvation was planned by the Father in eternity, purchased by the Son in history, and applied by the Spirit in the present, blessed God Three in One. The cults believe in "free will" and that man, not God, determines the future. See my book, Studies in the Atonement, for the details (www.faithdefenders.com).

12. *God's knowledge of the future.*

Most cults deny that God knows and controls the future. Mormons, Jehovah's Witnesses, and the Open View of God cults all deny the omniscience of God. If someone denies that God knows and controls the future, he is not a Christian in the biblical sense of the word.

13. *Heaven or hell at death*

The cults deny that there is conscious life after death in which the wicked suffer punishment and the righteousness experience bliss in heaven with Christ. They either teach the idea that one is totally unconscious after death or they teach reincarnation in which your soul immediately goes into another infant to start a human life all over again. Christians believe that they go to heaven at death to be with Christ while the wicked go to hell. For a modern defense of the Christian position, see *Death and the Afterlife.*

14. *The Resurrection and Judgment Day*

Many of the cults deny the bodily resurrection of all men at the Day of Judgment. They do not like the idea that they are going to be held accountable by God for how they lived.

15. *The eternal state of the wicked and righteous*

One way to identify someone who is involved in cultic teaching or who is a member of a cultic group is to ask him if he believes in eternal conscious punishment. If he does not believe that the wicked go "into eternal punishment" (Matt. 25:46), then you are dealing with someone who is probably a member of some cultic group. The same with the eternal blessings of the righteous. We are not going to be continuously recycled like old beer cans. We will dwell with the Lord Jesus on a new earth.

How to Handle Them

What is the most effective way of dealing with cultists? The first thing you must avoid is arguing over peripheral issues. Do not waste your time arguing with Jehovah's Witnesses over saluting the flag or blood transfusions. Do not argue with Mormons about polygamy, baptism for the dead or temples. Do not argue with the followers of Armstrong as to whether or not we should eat lobster. Do not bother arguing with a Moonie as to whether or not Moon's recent time in jail was valid.

The only issue that must be dealt with when confronted by a cultist is the issue of religious authority. As long as this cult member is resting on the absolute and infallible authority of the cult leadership, there is nothing you will ever be able to say or show him that will in any way affect him. You can show him Bible verses and give him theological arguments until you are blue in the face and he will ignore everything you say. You must destroy the religious authority of the cult leadership.

The most effective way of dealing with the authority of cultic leaders is to use the principle stated in Deut. 18:21, 22.

> You may say to yourselves, 'How can we know when a message has not been spoken by the Lord?' If what a prophet proclaims in the name of the Lord does not take place or come true, that is a message the Lord has not spoken. That prophet has spoken presumptuously. Do not be afraid of him.

In the above passage, God's Word tells us that we can identify a false prophet when his predictions concerning the future fail to materialize. You will also notice that it only takes one false prophecy to identify a false prophet. No amount of rationalizing can avoid the inevitable logic of the passage: If someone is God's prophet then his predictions will not fail. If someone's predictions fail then he or she is not God's prophet.

The denial of the consequence is always valid in logic. This approach immediately cuts through all extraneous issues and goes to the central and foundational problem between the Christian and the cults. The Christian looks to God's Word as being the final authority in all matters of faith, life and practice. The cultist looks to the cult leadership as providing him with his doctrine and guidance. The conflict is irreconcilable.

Conclusion

Just because someone says that he is a Christian does not mean that he is really a Christian. We must not be so gullible as to accept religious groups on face value. They must define their terms before we can accept them as fellow Christians.

Questions for Discussion

1. What is a cult?
2. How does Deut. 18:21–22 help us refute cult leaders?
3. What are the signs of a cult?
4. What is the key issue when dealing with cultists?
5. If someone says that he believes in Jesus, how are you to respond?
6. You are asked to go to a Bible study on campus. What questions should you ask before you go?
7. A campus group invites you to a free weekend retreat at a ranch; should you go?

CHAPTER TWENTY-ONE

Some Popular Cults

Feast of Tabernacles (1991) celebration by the Worldwide Church of God (renamed Grace Communion International on 04/03/09) in Pasadena, CA. Herbert W. Armstrong, founder of the Worldwide Church of God, was considered a cult leader because of his false gospel, heretical doctrines, false prophecies and his false claim that his organization was the only true church and he was God's apostle (Herbert W. Armstrong was a false apostle & prophet—see Gal. 1:8, 2 Pet. 2:1-3, Deut. 18:22 & Ezek. 13:1-23). After Armstrong's death in 1986, Joseph W. Tkach (03/16/1927 - 09/23/1995) was appointed successor to Armstrong as President and Pastor General in 1986 and he changed the organization from a cult to orthodox evangelical Christianity and thus renounced Armstrong's heretical doctrines.

Perhaps you are wondering why the subject of the cults or the occult would be included in this manual. The reason is quite simple. As a college student you will be asked to join several different cultic groups during your college career. It does not matter if it happens to be the Moonies or the

Hare Krishnas, you will be confronted with cult members who will try to recruit you to their group.

It was for this reason Jesus gave a warning nearly 2000 years ago that His followers must be prepared to encounter religious deception. False christs and false prophets will try to deceive the people of God.

> Watch out that no one deceives you. Many false prophets will appear and deceive many people. At that time if anyone says to you, 'Look, here is the Christ!' or, 'There he is!' do not believe it. For false Christs and false prophets will appear and perform great signs and miracles to deceive even the elect — if that were possible. See, I have told you ahead of time. So if anyone tells you, 'There he is, out in the desert,' do not go out; or, 'Here he is, in the inner rooms,' do not believe it. For as the lightning comes from the east and flashes to the west, so will be the coming of the Son of Man. (Matt. 24:4, 23–27)

The following material will introduce you to some of the popular cultic groups and will give you the ammunition you need to deal with them quickly and effectively. Keep to the issue of religious authority. Do not deal with peripheral issues. Deal only with the question: Is this leadership a false prophet or a true prophet?

These brief overviews are not intended to teach the history or theology of the cult in question. We are only seeking to give you a brief answer that can be remembered and utilized easily. For further study consult the bibliography. "Be prepared" should be your motto.

Jehovah's Witnesses

The Jehovah's Witness cult is based upon the religious authority of its leadership who has repeatedly claimed down through the years to be God's prophet on earth and that their doctrines are revealed to them by angels. See my book, *How to answer A Jehovah's Witnesses*, for the documentation (www.faithdefenders.com).

In terms of predicting dates, the Watchtower Society has been 100% consistent in that every time they have predicted the future, the prediction failed! They have consistently failed the test of Deut. 18:21, 22.

The Jehovah's Witnesses originally taught that the "last days" began in 1799, Jesus returned invisibly in 1874 and the end of the world would take place in 1914. When 1914 came and went without Armageddon, they reprinted the same books and inserted the date 1915. When 1915 didn't work out, they reprinted the books with 1916 as the new date.

It was in 1916 that their founder, Charles Russell, died and the new president, Rutherford, took over. He immediately pointed to 1918 as the new date for the end of the world. But when 1918 proved to be another false prophecy, he published a book entitled, *Millions Now Living Will Never Die*, in which it was stated that 1925 would be the end of the world.

When 1925 did not materialize as expected, they tried to prop up the hopes of Jehovah's Witnesses by building a mansion in San Diego called Beth Sarim where Abraham, Isaac and Jacob would live after their bodily resurrection perhaps in 1929 or thereafter. Needless to say, they never showed up. So, Rutherford moved into the mansion.

In the 1930's they dropped the 1874 date as the invisible return of Christ and substituted 1914 in its place. Most Jehovah's Witnesses do not know that the Society switched Christ's return from 1874 to 1914.

In recent times, 1975 stands out as the clearest example of the Watchtower's attempt to predict the end of the world. In Watchtower books, magazines and taped sermons, 1975 was predicted to be the end of the world. Jehovah's Witnesses were encouraged to cash in their life insurance policies, sell their homes and quit their jobs in order to be involved in full time work for the Watchtower society.

When 1975 did not see the end of the world, 27% of the Jehovah's Witnesses left the organization. Since that time, Jehovah's Witnesses have now been instructed by the leadership to deny that the Society ever said anything about 1975.

One of the difficulties in dealing with the Jehovah's Witnesses is that in their book, *Aid to Bible Understanding*, the Watchtower defines a lie as not telling the truth to someone who deserves it. Anyone who opposes the Watchtower does not deserve the truth and, hence, may be lied to freely.

This explains why Jehovah's Witnesses who know that 1975 was predicted to be the end of the world, will say that the Watchtower never said anything about the date 1975. They have been told to lie to anyone who brings up all the false prophecies of the Society.

This is where the documents come in handy. Instead of allowing the burden of proof to be upon you, you must place the burden of proof on the Jehovah's Witness to demonstrate that their prophecies came true. If they cannot show how these predictions came true, then the Watchtower is a false prophet. The documents are presented in my book *How to Answer a Jehovah's Witness*.

Jehovah's Witnesses have also now been instructed to say that the Watchtower has never claimed to be a prophet. Ask them to obtain for you a copy of the April 1, 1972 Watchtower magazine in which there is an article entitled "And They Shall Know That a Prophet Was Among Them." In this article, the Watchtower claims to be God's prophet.

Some Jehovah's Witnesses will admit under pressure that the Watchtower has predicted the end of the world many times. But they dismiss this on the grounds that "everyone makes mistakes." Point out to them that while everyone makes mistakes, not everyone claims to be God's prophet on earth! A false prophecy is not the same thing as a mistake. Do you claim that you get your doctrines directly from angels?

If you stick to the issue of the false prophecies of the Watchtower, you will have success in winning Jehovah's Witnesses to Christ. In one survey we took of ex-Jehovah's Witnesses who are now Christians, we found that in the vast majority of cases, they became Christians as a result of seeing that the Watchtower was a false prophet.

Mormonism

There are over one hundred different Mormon denominations that all claim to be the "true Mormon church." But, unless you live in the Midwest, you will probably only encounter missionaries of the Church of Jesus Christ of Latter Day Saints (LDS) that has its headquarters in Salt Lake City, Utah.

Regardless if you are dealing with the Latter Day Saints or one of the other Mormon churches, all of them have one thing in common. They all claim that Joseph Smith was God's prophet and that his doctrines are to be received as coming directly from God. See my book, *How to answer A Mormon,* for the documentation (www.faithdefenders.com).

The claims of Smith are so fantastic that there are only four possible logical responses we can have about him.

1. He was a prophet of God.
2. He was crazy.
3. He was a liar.
4. He was a crazy liar.

If he were a prophet of God, then we should all become Mormons. But since there are over a hundred competing Mormon denominations all claiming to be the "true" church of Smith, this might be difficult. If he were crazy, he should have been locked up and his followers are to be pitied. If he deceived people in order to obtain money, sex and power, then he should be exposed as a fraud. If was a crazy liar, who wants to follow him?

How can we know which of these four opinions we should take of Joseph Smith? Deut. 18:21, 22 tells us to test the predictions of Joseph Smith. As a matter of record, Smith gave many prophecies concerning the future. If these prophecies did not come to pass, he was a false prophet.

Even though the prophetic test found in Deut. 18 seems quite reasonable and straightforward, Mormons have been told by their leaders to evade this test. In order to prove that Joseph Smith was a prophet, they are instructed to argue in a circle and base everything on a "burning witness" in the heart.

In their circular argument, Mormons will say, "Joseph Smith was a prophet of God because God spoke to him." But if you ask them how do they know that God spoke to Joseph Smith, they reply, "God spoke to Joseph Smith because he was a prophet of God!"

Just as a dog chasing his tail or someone rowing with only one oar never seems to get anywhere, the circular argument that Joseph Smith was a prophet because God spoke to him and God spoke to him because he was a prophet will never go anywhere either.

Subjective feelings or "a burning witness in the heart" is the next argument that Mormons are encouraged to give. Mormons have memorized and will repeat something like this,

> I know that Joseph Smith is a prophet of God and the Book of Mormon is the Word of God because I got on my knees and I asked God to give me a burning witness in my heart if these things were so. I now bear you my testimony that I have a burning witness in my heart that Joseph Smith was indeed the prophet of God and the Book of Mormon is the Word of God.

What the Mormon fails to recognize is that the members of any major religious group would state that their "heart" tells them that they are right. But feelings do not prove anything. One way to drive this home is to respond to the Mormon immediately after he has borne his testimony by saying,

> And I bear you my testimony that I have a burning witness in my heart that Joseph Smith was a false prophet and the Book of Mormon is a fraud.

Once you have refuted the Mormon's attempt to use circular reasoning and subjective feelings, you have cleared the way to deal with the prophecies and predictions of Joseph Smith.

Joseph Smith's False Prophecies

Joseph Smith made over sixty false prophecies. The following prophecies are particularly useful in dealing with Mormons. The documentation for these and other false prophecies can be found in my book, *How to Answer a Mormon.* (www.faithdefenders.com)

1. In 1835, Joseph Smith clearly taught that Jesus Christ would return and the end of the world would happen around 1891 or 1892. That he predicted the end of the world is clear from the documentation found in such church literature as the History of the Church, Vol. 2. pg. 182. It is also found in the diaries and sermons that were written during this same time period. For example, in the journal of Oliver Boardman Hamington, vol. 2. pgs. 128–129, we read,

> On the 14th of February, 1835, Joseph Smith said that God had revealed to him the coming of Christ would be within 56 years which being added to 1835 shows that before 1891 and the 14th of February the Savior of the world would make his appearance again upon the earth and the winding up scene take place.

The documentation that reveals that Joseph Smith predicted the end of the world is so clear that Mormons try to "stonewall" the situation. But just keep hammering home the fact that Smith predicted the end of the world and it did not happen. Thus he was a false prophet.

2. Joseph Smith prophesied that people live on the moon who are 6 feet in height, live to be 1000 years old, and dress like Quakers. If there are no 1000-year-old, 6 ft. Quakers on the moon, Joseph Smith was not a prophet of God.

Once again, the documentation for the prophecy of Joseph Smith concerning men on the moon is so full and clear that Mormons have to pretend that it does not exist. But in official church literature published during the early history of the Mormon church we find such statements as,

> As far back as 1837, I know that he [Joseph Smith] said the moon was inhabited by men and women the same as this earth, and they lived to a greater age than we do —that they live generally to near the age of 1000 years. He described the men as averaging near 6 ft. in height, and dressing quite uniformly in something near the Quaker style. In my patriarchal blessing, given by the father Joseph the Prophet, in Kirkland, 1837, I was told that I should preach the Gospel before I was eleven years of age and that I should preach the Gospel to the inhabitants upon the islands of the sea, and to the inhabitants of the moon, even the planet you can now behold with your eyes.

(*Young Woman's Journal,* 1892, pgs., 263–264)

Brigham Young taught that people lived on the sun as well as the moon! In *The Journal of Discourses*, Vol. 13, pg. 271, Young states,

> Who can tell us of the inhabitants of this little planet that shines of an evening, called the moon? When you inquire about the inhabitants of that sphere you find that the most learned are as ignorant in regard to them as the most ignorant of their fellows. So it is in regard to the inhabitants of the sun. Do you think it is inhabited? I rather think it is. Do you think there is any life there? No question about it: it was not made in vain.

Not only did Joseph Smith say that there were 6 ft, 1000-year-old Quakers living on the moon, but Brigham Young added that there were people living on the sun!

3. On August 6, 1836, Joseph Smith prophesied that he was going to go to Salem, Massachusetts and that he would return with enough

money to pay all the debts of his followers and with a large group of converts.

This prophecy is recorded in the Mormon scriptures such as *Doctrine and Covenants*, chapter 111, verses 2, 4 and 5. This prophecy completely failed. Smith returned with his saddle bags empty and only a small group of converts. It is no wonder that contemporary diaries record Mormons who left the church because they saw that Joseph Smith was a false prophet.

These are some of the clear false prophecies made by Joseph Smith that are recorded in official Mormon literature or in the early writings of the Mormon church. These false prophecies must be taken at face value and evaluated according to Deut. 18:21–22. Even one of the presidents of the Latter Day Saints Church has stated,

> If God has not spoken, if the angel of God has not appeared to Joseph Smith, and if these things are not true of which we speak, then the whole thing is an imposture from beginning to end. There is no halfway house, no middle path about the matter; it is either one thing or the other.(*Journal of Discourses*, Vol. 21, pg. 165)

Another Mormon president, Joseph Fielding Smith, added to this,

> Mormonism, as it is called, must stand or fall on the story of Joseph Smith. He was either a prophet of God, divinely called, properly appointed and commissioned, or he was one of the biggest frauds this world has ever seen. There is no middle ground. If Joseph Smith was a deceiver, who willfully attempted to mislead the people, then he should be exposed; his claim should be refuted, and his doctrine shown to be false. (*Doctrines of Salvation*, 1959, Vol. 1, pgs. 188–189)

Do not let your Mormon friends off the hook. If there are no 6 ft., 1000-year-old Quakers on the moon, if there are no people living on the sun and the end of the world did not take place in 1891, then Joseph Smith was a false prophet.

The Unification Church: The Moonies

In dealing with Moonies, always deal with the person of Moon himself. Do not argue over doctrine or politics. Concentrate on the authority of Moon.

The Unification Church is in a unique situation in that the leader, Mr. Moon, is not only a cult leader but also involved in the occult.

As a cultic leader, Moon's authority is above Scripture. He views himself as the "Second Lord of the advent." He claims to be the physical manifestation of the divine principle in human form. Moon's view of God is that of Eastern religions in which "God" is the yin and the yang, the positive and the negative, the male and the female principle of the universe. He views himself as the incarnation of this impersonal principle of opposites and thus as the true representative of God on earth.

His authority over his followers is absolute. He can marry them at will and dictate how many children they are to have. No one can contradict him or do other than what he says.

Moon is also into the occult as well as being an occultic leader. Moon is what is classically known as a "shaman." A shaman is someone who claims that they are able to control the spirit world and the forces of nature.

Moon claims to have been a spiritistic clairvoyant from his youth. He claims that he can see the spirits of the dead. He even claims that he entered the spirit world and there conquered the spirits of Jesus, Moses and Buddha. He has attended séances with such mediums as Arthur Ford.

In dealing with the Moonies you have two approaches. The first approach is to deal with Moon in terms of Deut. 18:21–22. Has moon made predictions concerning the future that have failed? Yes, he has.

He originally taught that the Lord of the Second Advent would be revealed in 1967. When this prophecy failed, 1980 through '81 or possibly '82 was picked as the time when the world would recognize him and his kingdom would begin. These prophecies obviously failed. He felt that he would receive not only worldwide recognition but acceptance.

In the midst of the Watergate scandal when the resignation of Richard Nixon was being called for, Moon prophesied that "God has chosen Richard Nixon to be President" (*San Francisco Chronicle*, January 19, 1974).

When confronted later with the fact that Nixon resigned, Moon prophesied that Nixon resigned because Communists had threatened to kill him if he did not resign,

> I am sure there is a Communistic power working behind the scenes. They came to threaten to kill him if he did not resign, and that's what compelled him to do so.
> (*San Francisco Chronicle,* December 10, 1975)

The second approach to dealing with Moonies is to point them to Deut. 18:9–12 where the Bible condemns all attempts to communicate with the dead. Thus séances and mediums in which you try to contact the spirits of the dead are condemned as an "abomination unto the Lord." This is what sorcery and witchcraft are all about.

Moon claims in his book, *The Divine Principle*, that he is in communication with the spirits of the dead. Not only did he teach that he was a medium and involved in mediumistic activities, but in his autobiography Arthur Ford reveals that Moon had a séance with him in which Moon sought to speak to the spirits of the dead. Moon wanted the spirit world to acknowledge him as Lord but they refused. Moon left quite disappointed.

The cultic and occultic activities and teachings of Mr. Moon forever disqualify him from being Lord of anything. He is not the successor to Jesus Christ or Moses for both of them were against sorcery and witchcraft.

One thing you will have to watch out for with the Moonies is their program of "heavenly deception," which involves their lying to get your money or to get you to an isolated spot where they can try to brainwash you. Moonies have been known to ask for donations for drug abuse programs, Christian youth groups, the homeless, the United Way, missions, churches and handicap programs while the money actually goes to uphold Moon's lavish lifestyle.

They will advertise free weekend seminars on pollution, international relations, anti- communist programs, and science. But when you get there, all they want to talk about is Moon! So, don't accept any "free" weekend seminars unless your pastor knows the group.

Seventh Day Adventists

The Seventh Day Adventist Church relies upon the authority of Ellen G. White, whom they view as God's prophet.

> Seventh Day Adventists hold that Ellen G. White performed the work of a true prophet during the 70 years of her public ministry. As Samuel was a prophet, as Jeremiah was a prophet, as John the Baptist, so we believe that Mrs. White was a prophet to the church of Christ today.
> (*The Advent Review and Herald,* 10–4-1928)

Ellen G. White viewed her writings as being as inspired as the writings of the apostle Paul or any other author of Scripture (*E.G. White Testimony,* Vol. 3, pg. 275; Vol. 5, pg. 661). She stated on one occasion,

> God was speaking through clay. In these letters which I write, in the testimonies I bear, I am presenting to you that which the Lord has presented to me. I do not write one article in the paper expressing merely my own ideas. They are what God has opened before in vision — the precious rays of light shining from the throne.

(Visions of Mrs. E. G. White Testimony, #31, pg. 63)

Just as we applied the test of prophecy to Charles Russell, The Watchtower, Joseph Smith and Moon, we must apply the same test to Ellen G. White. What does the record reveal?

Ellen G. White prophesied that Jesus Christ would return in 1843. She learned this date from William Miller and fully accepted it as valid *(Early Writings,* pg. 64, 1882 edition). She even stated in 1844.

> We heard the voice of God like many waters, which gave us the day and hour of Jesus' coming.
>
> *(A Word to the Little Flock,* pg. 14, 1847 edition)

When he 1843 date failed, she tried 1844. When that date failed to materialize she said confidently in 1845,

> It is well known that many were expecting the Lord to come at the 7th month, 1845, that Christ would then come we firmly believed. A few days before the time passed … Ellen was with one of the band at Carver, Mass., where she saw in a vision, that we should be disappointed.
>
> *(A Word to the Little Flock,* pg. 22, 1847 edition)

In 1849, she taught that,

> the time is almost finished, and what we have been 6 years learning they will have to learn in months.
>
> *(Early Writings,* pg. 57)

She was so confident that the Lord was going to return when she predicted that she stated to a group assembled to hear her,

> I was shown the company present at the

conference. Said the angel: Some food for
worms, some subjects of the seven last
plagues, some will be alive and remain upon
the earth to be translated at the coming of
Jesus.
(*Testimonies for the Church,* Vol. 1, pg. 131–132)

The record of those present at this prophecy conference has been
discovered and it is clear that all of them have since died.

The evidence has also revealed that she was a lying prophet in
that she plagiarized her books from the works of others. See Walter
Rea's book, *The White Lie.* This includes her so called "visions of
health" as well as her Bible studies. See Ronald Numbers' book,
Prophetess of Health. She was dishonest when she put her name on
other people's writings and claimed that they had come to her in a
vision from God.

Conclusion

The Christian must be alert to those cults that prey on college
students. Do not be intimidated by them but witness to them of the
saving grace of God and the freedom you have found in Christ.

Questions for Discussion

1. Did the Jehovah's Witnesses ever predict the end of the world?
2. How do Mormons use circular reasoning?
3. Can a subjective feeling prove anything?
4. What evidence is there to show that Joseph Smith was not a
   prophet of God?
5. What can you say to a Moonie?
6. What claims did Mrs. White make? Was she a true or false
   prophet?
7. Did she copy her books from the works of others?
8. Where did she get her "visions" of health?

CHAPTER TWENTY-TWO

The "Church of Christ" Churches

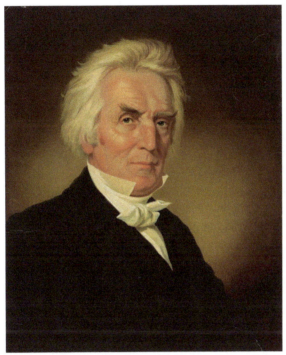

Alexander Campbell (son of Thomas Campbell),
founder of the Disciples of Christ, head-and-
shoulders portrait (02/28/1872).

Part One

THE RESTORATION MOVEMENT

The "Restoration" Movement began in the 19th Century under

the leadership of Thomas Campbell, Barton Stone, Walter Scott and Alexander Campbell (1788-1866). The importance of these "Restorers" was based on their claim that:

1. The Christian Church disappeared in the 1st Century. The "true" Gospel was lost at that time.

2. The Roman Catholic Church and all Protestant Churches are apostate organizations and are not to be viewed as "Christian" churches.

3. All the historic creeds and confessions are worthless and should be ignored.

4. God raised up Alexander Campbell to "restore" the "true" Gospel and to re-establish the Christian Church. He restored the pure "Apostolic" Church.

5. The Millennium was going to be ushered in during their lifetime by the "Restoration" Movement.

6. The "true" Gospel teaches that "baptism unto remission of sins" is essential for salvation. The "Restorers" spoke of this as "baptismal regeneration."

7. The "baptism" given by all other churches is not saving. You have to be re-baptized in accordance with the Campbellite doctrine of baptism to be saved.

8. Only Bible names should be used in the name of a church. It is wrong to use such names as Baptist, Catholic, Presbyterian, etc. Even though they first called themselves "Reformed Baptists," they later took up such names as "Disciples of Christ," "the Churches of Christ" and "The Christian Church."

9. Nothing should be allowed in the Church unless there is a "book, chapter and verse" for it. On this basis the "Reformers" were opposed to the use of musical instruments in worship, missionary societies, etc. This point has led to thousands of church fights and splits. The "Churches of Christ" split off from the "Disciples of Christ" over such issues and have never stopped splitting since that time.

10. Some Campbellite theologians have denied the omniscience of God by teaching that God does not know

the future. (For example see: The Gospel Plan of Salvation, by T.W. Brents published by the "Gospel Advocate" Company in Nashville, Tenn.)

Significant Dates in Campbellite History:

1809 Thomas Campbell censured by the Presbyterian Church for false teaching.

1809 Thomas Campbell writes "Declaration and Address" for the "The Christian Association of Washington." It functioned as a "creed" for the young movement.

1809 Alexander Campbell arrives in America and joins his father's association.

1811 The Association becomes an independent church after being rejected by the Presbyterians once again.

1812 The Campbells are re-baptized by a Baptist preacher at Buffalo Creek. This was fifteen years BEFORE Scott originated the doctrine of "baptism unto remission of sins."

1813 The Campbells join the Redstone Baptist Association.

1820 Alexander Campbell represents the Baptist Church in a debate with John Walker, a Presbyterian.

1823 August: The Redstone Baptist Association prepares to censure the Campbells for false doctrine but they resign and set up an independent Baptist Church.

1823 October: Alexander Campbell debates McCalla still claiming to represent Baptists. The Campbells now call themselves, "Reformed Baptists."

1827 Nov.: Walter Scott preaches "baptism unto remission of sins." William Amen was the first one "baptized unto remission of sins." Scott's followers call themselves the "Christians."

1832 Campbell's "Disciples of Christ" openly unite with Scott's "Christians."

1849 Controversy over missionary societies splits the "Restoration" Movement.

1860 Controversy over musical instruments splits the movement.

1906 The "Churches of Christ" listed as a separate denomination apart from the "Disciples of Christ" and the "Christian Church." The Campbellites popularize Scott's doctrine of "baptism unto remission of sins."

1920 Over a hundred controversies split the movement on such issues as musical instruments, head-coverings, communion cups, schools, orphanages, Sunday School, divorce, re-marriage, etc.

Part Two

The Origin Of The Major Cults: "The Church of Christ!"

I. Campbellism And Mormonism

The evidence is clear that Mormonism arose out of the Campbellite "Restoration" Movement is undeniable.

1. The leading figures in early Mormonism were originally preachers in Campbellite churches and many of them had personally worked with Alexander Campbell: Sidney Rigdon, Parley Pratt, Oliver Crowdery, Orson Hyde, Lyman Wight, Edward Partridge, John Corril, Isaac Morely, John Murdock, etc.

2. So many thousands of "Disciples of Christ" joined the Mormons that Alexander Campbell called Mormonism "Satan's counterfeit" of the Disciples of Christ

3. Joseph Smith was taught the "Restoration" concept and its peculiar doctrines by Sidney Rigdon. When Joseph Smith adopted most of the points of the "Restoration" Movement, he put himself as the "Restorer" of the Gospel and the Church in the place of Alexander Campbell:

   a. The Church and the "true" Gospel was lost in the 1st Century.

   b. All subsequent churches are apostate.

   c. Joseph Smith "restored" the Church and the Gospel.

   d. A church should use Bible names. The Mormons first called themselves the "Church of Christ." Most Mormon denominations still use such names.

   e. You must be baptized "unto remission of sins" by a

Mormon priest to be saved.

   f. Smith challenged Alexander Campbell to a public debate on the issue of who was the true "Restorer."

BIBLIOGRAPHY

1. Mormon Sources:
   History of the Church, (by Joseph Smith) vol. I:120- 125, 188. vol. II:268, 269n, 270.
   Journal Of Discourses,vol. II:17, 18; vol. XI:3.
   Joseph Smith: An American Prophet,(by John Evans) 211,214- 216.
2. Anti-Mormon Scholars:
   Shadow Or Reality, (by the Tanners) pp.66-68.
   Origin of Campbellism, (by J. Milburn)
3. Campbellite Sources:
   Memoirs of Alexander Campbell, vol. II:344-347

II. Campbellism And Christadelphianism

Dr. John Thomas, a prominent "Disciple of Christ" and personal friend of Alexander Campbell decided that if we should throw out the creeds and use only Bible names, then why should we believe in the Trinity? He went on to deny the deity of Christ, the personhood of the Spirit, the bodily resurrection of Christ, Christ's physical return to this world, the immortality of the soul. He taught "soul sleep" and denied the doctrine of Hell. He did not believe in a paid clergy but each member was viewed as a minister.

He was able to persuade many other "Disciples" to join him in establishing the "Christadelphians" or "Brethren in Christ." His movement was composed of Campbellite and Millerite churches.

BIBLIOGRAPHY

Cyclopedia of Biblical, Theological And Ecclesiastical Literature, (by McClintock and Strong), vol. XI: 937- 938.

III. Campbellism and Jehovah's Witnesses

Benjamin Wilson was a "Disciple of Christ" who followed Dr. Thomas into Christadelphianism. Although he never studied Greek, he published a Greek-English interlinear called *The Emphatic Diaglott*

It was Wilson who introduced Charles Taze Russell to those very doctrines that have become the central theology of the Jehovah's Witnesses. The Watchtower Society even published and used Wilson's interlinear for many years. Campbellism through Christadelphianism is the origin of the Jehovah's Witnesses.

BIBLIOGRAPHY

Cyclopedia Of Biblical, Theological And Ecclesiastical Literature, (By McClintock and Strong), vol. XI:937-938; vol. XII:868-869.

Apostles Of Denial, (Ed Gruss) pp. 14-16, 193-196.

Part Three

The Doctrinal Errors of Campbellism

While there are many doctrinal issues that divide the evangelical from the Campbellite, the greatest point of controversy is their view of baptism.

The Evangelical believes that salvation is by grace alone, through faith alone, in Christ alone. Human works such as baptism, church membership, etc., are not necessary for salvation. While obedience to God's Law has a role to play in assurance of salvation, it has no role to play in salvation. Baptism like circumcision is an outward rite that symbolizes an inner state. While both ceremonies symbolize regeneration, they do not accomplish it.

In opposition to Evangelical doctrine, Campbellite theology teaches "baptismal regeneration." It is claimed that water baptism by immersion of adults only unto remission of sins does not merely symbolize regeneration but it actually accomplishes it. Faith is not enough. Obedience to God's Law must also take place or salvation is not possible. Unless you are baptized in the exact way they dictate (immersion, adults only), for the exact purpose they have in mind (unto remission of sins), and by the right person (a Campbellite preacher) not only is your baptism invalid but you are not yet saved no matter how sincerely you believe in Jesus Christ as your Savior!

To add baptism to faith is nothing more than adding works to grace, which is impossible according to Rom. 11:6. The attempt to evade this by claiming that baptism is part of faith is not linguistically or grammatically possible. If obedience to God's commands such as baptism is what "faith" is, then why stop with baptism? What about all the other commands of God such as "love your wife?" A works-salvation can never say when enough works have been done!

The Reasons Why Baptism Is Not Essential For Salvation

1. If the Campbellite doctrine were true, then the Restorers were not saved men! Thomas Campbell, Alexander Campbell, Walter Scott and Barton Stone were never baptized "unto the remission of sin." While they repudiated their infant baptism when they were baptized by the Baptists, they never repudiated their Baptist baptism and re-baptized according to Campbellite baptism.

2. Jesus never baptized anyone. If baptism is essential for salvation, then Jesus never saved anyone.

3. Paul did not view baptism as part of the Gospel (I Cor. 1:14-17).

4. John's baptism did not save anyone even though it was "unto remission of sins" (Mk. 1:4 cf. Acts 19:1-5).

5. Since there is only one God, there is only one way of salvation (Rom 3:28-30). This means that whatever is necessary for salvation today was also necessary during O.T. times.

6. The Gospel of justification by faith alone apart from obedience to God's commands is taught in both O.T. and the N.T. (Rom 1:1-2)

   Abraham: before the Law (Rom. 4:1-5)

   David: after the Law (Rom. 4:6-8)

Habakkuk: in the Prophets (Rom. 1:17)

7. Baptism is the N.T. parallel of circumcision just as the Lord's Supper is the parallel of the Passover (Col. 2:11-12). Since circumcision was not essential for salvation, then neither is baptism.

8. Abraham was saved BEFORE he was circumcised in order to emphasize that salvation was by faith alone apart from obedience to God's commands and that the Gentiles would be saved by faith alone apart from obedience to any command such as baptism (Rom. 4:9-11, 16, 23-5:2).

9. Cornelius was saved and baptized by the Holy Spirit before he was baptized (Acts 10:44-48). This passage clearly refutes baptismal regeneration.

10. Baptismal regeneration:
   a.) makes salvation depend on the availability of water
   b.) makes salvation depend on the availability of a Campbellite preacher
   c.) confuses the symbol with the reality
   d.) makes faith and obedience the same thing
   e.) is based on a superstitious and magical view of baptism.

11. The thief on the cross was saved without baptism. The Campbellite argument that he was saved under the O.T. way of salvation is not possible seeing that Christ had already died on the cross and finished the atonement before the thief died. The thief belongs on the N.T. side of the cross and not on the O.T. side.

12. Campbellites claim that the word "unto" in Acts 2:38 (eis in the Greek) always means "in order to obtain" and is always "forward looking." In this way they make remission of sins follow the act of baptism in a cause and effect relationship. Baptism causes forgiveness of sins. The problem with this idea is that Greek scholars do not see this as the meaning of "eis." Liddell and Scott, Thayer, A.T. Robertson, Dana and Manty, Vine, etc... state that "eis" often used in the sense of "in reference to something already previously existing or accomplished." In this sense, baptism is done AFTER and BECAUSE of remission of sins. Once our sins are forgiven,

then you should be baptized. That the Greek scholars are correct is seen from the way"*eis*" is used in the N.T.:

1. Matt. 3:11 "baptism unto (eis) repentance"
   You get baptized because you have repented. You do not get baptized so you can obtain repentance. The order is, "repent and be baptized."
2. Matt 12:41: "they repented at (*eis*) the preaching of Jonah" Obviously, the preaching came first and then the people repented in response to that preaching.
3. Matt. 28:19: "Baptizing them in (*eis*) the name of the Father and of Son and of the Holy Ghost"
   The Triune God exists before one is baptized.
4. Mk. 1:9: "baptized of John in (*eis*) Jordon"
   Jesus did not come into possession of the Jordon River as He was baptized. The Jordon existed long before baptism was invented.
5. I Cor. 10:2: "baptized unto (*eis*) Moses"
   Moses existed before the "baptism" in the Red Sea. The people were not "baptized" in order to obtain Moses. Their "baptism" was in response to his leadership.

Conclusion

As long as the Campbellites teach that baptism is essential for salvation, they will be viewed as a cult by evangelical Christians. Salvation is by grace alone, through faith alone, apart from obedience to any of God's commands. Works are the evidence of salvation instead of the basis of it.

CHAPTER TWENTY-THREE

The Truth about Black Liberal Theology
— Its Racist Origins

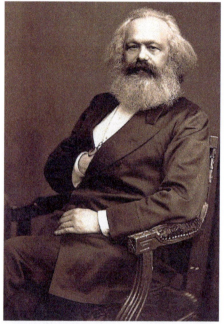

Karl Marx by John Jabez Edwin Mayall (08/25/1875)

The fundamental ideas of Black Liberal Theology did not come from black thinkers but from such white European thinkers as Hegel, Darwin, Marx, etc. It is Euro-centric in its ideology although it is Euro-phobic in its rhetoric. Black liberal theologians are in reality "Uncle Toms" still licking the boots of their white, Marxist masters at such bastions of white liberalism as Princeton, Yale, Harvard, etc.

Introduction

All racist theologies have the same basic core ideas and methodology. Thus it does not really matter if we are talking about the KKK, the Nation of Islam or Black Liberal Theology, their focus is always on skin and not sin; race and not grace; gossip and not gospel.

Racism is always focused on the outward instead of the inward because it cannot deal with the root problem of sin. Hatred and violence feed on bitterness and racist rage. Class envy does not help anyone in this life or in the next. Blaming others for one's own sin and guilt will not solve the problem. We must take responsibility for what we do in life instead of blaming "the man" for our failures and woe. This is why we need to break the shackle of black liberal theology that enslaves the black man and keeps him poor and angry. May God use this study to liberate black men and women from the lie of Black Liberal Theology.

I am aware that while the vast majority of Black Liberal Theologians are clearly guilty of believing in white liberalism and Neo-Marxist liberation theology, there are a few "conservative" writers who have fallen for some of their lies. Thus they will complain that not everything stated in this article applies to them. But as with any other movement, we must deal with the majority view and not with those few who are out of step with that majority.

I. The "Roots" of Black Liberal Theology.

"Black liberal theology" is another name for Marxist Liberation Theology that was created by white, middle-class, European, Marxist, liberal theologians to foster social change by manipulating the lower classes to violent revolution against democratic governments in order to establish a communist state. Thus Black Liberal Theology did not originate in Africa but in Europe.

The fundamental ideas of Black Liberal Theology did not come from black thinkers but from such white European thinkers as Hegel, Darwin, Marx, etc. It is Euro-centric in its ideology although it is Euro-phobic in its rhetoric. Black liberal theologians are in reality "Uncle

Toms" still licking the boots of their white, Marxist masters at such bastions of white liberalism as Princeton, Yale, Harvard, etc. They are the slaves of the white "master" Karl Marx.

II. The Goals Of Black Liberal Theology
Its goals are to turn religion into sociology, Christianity into a political agenda, Jesus into a black Marxist rebel, and the gospel into violent revolution. They are more interested in politics than preaching the gospel.

III. The Methodology of Black Liberal Theology
The main method employed by Liberal Theologians is to manipulate embittered young blacks by turning their feelings of inferiority, alienation, jealousy, hopelessness and self-hate, into racist rage against whites, Orientals and affluent blacks who are conveniently blamed for their lack of personal initiative to better their lot in life.

IV. The Main Philosophic Error of Black Liberal Theology
It is based upon the philosophic error of relativism in which "Jesus" is viewed as only a religious symbol that can be interpreted anyway they want. Thus it does not matter who and what the historical Jesus really was. They invented a black Marxist Jesus to lead the way to violent revolution because such a "Jesus" will serve their purpose. It is condemned in II Cor. 11:4 and Gal. 1:8-9.

V. The Racism Of Black Liberal Theology
While it is filled with racist statements against whites and Orientals, it is primarily a form of "black on black" racism. The following evidence demonstrates this to be true.

A. While it claims to give blacks a better self-image, they unwittingly encourage a poor self-image among blacks by defining "blackness" in such negative terms as "the poor," "the oppressed," and "niggers." Why do they always define the "black experience" in such negative terms? Why do they assume that all blacks live in the ghetto subsisting on welfare in the midst of crime and filth?

B. With its constant emphasis on God loves the poor, the oppressed, etc. it actually paralyzes and demoralizes blacks to accept a parasitic life- style dependent on the government dole instead of fostering self-reliance and entrepreneurship.

C. It seems to me that it feeds off of class envy and racist rage. Instead of spending their time blaming the white man for the black man's problems, they ought to be encouraging black men and women to become financially successful through hard work and self-reliance.

D. It often describes the black man as a helpless victim of forces and people beyond his control. But this negative stereotype often leads young black people to accept poverty, drugs, crime and filth as their unalterable fate.

E. Black Liberal Theology makes a great mistake when it assumes that poverty automatically means crime and filth. Just because you are poor does not mean you have a license to rob, rape, or murder others. The poor are for the most part good and honest people. Crime is crime regardless of who commits it. Poverty is no excuse for criminality.

F. It judges people on the basis of the color of their skin instead of the content of their character.

G. It gives the impression that the black man's problem is his skin instead of his sin.

H. Most of their books glorify rage, hatred and violence instead of faith, hope and love.

I. It preaches race instead of grace as the solution to problems.

J. It cries out for political liberation instead of spiritual salvation.

K. It thinks more of Marx than it does of Jesus.

L. It is more interested in black culture than in Jesus Christ.

VI. The Liberalism of Black Liberal Theology

It is not a fundamental, Bible-believing, Christ-honoring theology. It was created by white Marxist liberation theologians at white Marxist liberal seminaries and universities that are radically anti-Christian and anti-Bible.

A. Most of those involved in it do not believe in the Trinity, the deity of Christ, His virgin birth, sinless life, vicarious death, bodily resurrection, literal ascension or return to this world. They claim that all such doctrines are "Western."

B. Many of those who teach it openly deny the immortality of the soul, a conscious after- life in heaven or hell, the resurrection of the dead, the Last Judgment and the eternal conscious torment of the damned in hell. They usually say that hell is "being black on welfare in the ghetto." They attack those blacks who talk about heaven as a "pie in the sky by and by slave mentality."

C. It often denounces Christianity as racist and the "white man's religion." But then it turns around and claims that Jesus was black. If Jesus were a black man, then how can Christianity be the "white man's religion?"

D. Most of its writers deny the inspiration, inerrancy and authority of the Bible while at the same time using it to foster their racist agenda.

E. Many of its leaders teach the theory of evolution in which man evolved from an ape in Africa as if that theory can give dignity to blacks or to anyone else. The theory of evolution actually destroys all dignity and morals by reducing man to an animal.

VII. The Absurdity of Black Liberal Theology

It is so filled with self-contradiction and erroneous ideas that it is has no intellectual merit. For example, they define "blackness" and "whiteness" in the Marxist sense of class struggle. Thus they are not really talking about blackness as a race but as a class. WAKE UP! Read that last sentence again. Did you get it? Black liberal theology is really concerned with class struggle and not about black people per se. What is "black" and "white" according to their books?

Black = anyone regardless of race or color who is economically and politically oppressed by the upper classes.

White = anyone regardless of race or color who is guilty of oppressing the lower classes.

Walter McCray, to his shame, in his book, *The Black Presence in The Bible*, quotes with approval the definition of blackness given by his liberal slave master, Charles Copher. "Additionally, one may be defined as black regardless of color or race; all who suffer oppression…are classified as black". (p. 161, n.72.)

This irrational definition ends up with some white people being "black" and some black people being "white." According to their definition, a blond, blue- eyed, white Swede on drugs and welfare is "black" while the successful black man who owns his own company is "white." Other absurdities abound in their writings.

A. It claims that Adam and Eve were black. If this were true, then all men and women are "black" because they came from the first black parents. On what grounds then do they divide up mankind into black vs. white and black vs. yellow? Aren't we all "black" having come from the same original black DNA?

B. It claims that Noah, his wife and their three sons and wives were all blacks. Yet, they also claim that the blacks descended from Ham. And they run through the Bible looking for Hamite references to trace the history of the black race. How can this obvious contradiction be resolved?

C. As part of its Marxist ideology, they believe that history is as relative as morals. Thus they rewrite history to foster their own socio-political goals. This is why they do not hesitate to teach lies and to practice academic chicanery. The "truth" is not their concern. To manipulate young blacks into racist rage is always their real goal.

D. It claims that nearly every individual and nation mentioned in the Bible was black. They do not prove that this is true. They simply assert that it is so. Anyone who disagrees with them is labeled a racist.

E. It claims that the ancient Sumerians, Assyrians, Babylonians and Persians were all black. Yet, they were the cruelest oppressors known in history. For example, the Assyrians enslaved and deported entire populations. Mass murder was their favorite means of oppression. How can they be "black" when they were worse oppressors than Hitler or Stalin?

F. It claims that the ancient Egyptians were black and that the Jews were black as well. But since the Egyptians were a very oppressive society that enslaved the Jews and other minorities and conquered many surrounding nations, how can the Egyptians be "black" and oppress people at the same time?

G. Just like the KKK and other racist groups, it claims that their race is the sole source of all that is good in all cultures. But this is a two-edged sword. If the blacks are responsible for all the good in the world, then they are equally responsible for all the evil. To claim that the black man can do no wrong and that the white man and yellow man can do no good, is absurd as well as racist.

H. It claims that the ancient Greeks were black and thus Greek philosophy was created by blacks. But then it also says that the white Greeks stole their philosophy from African blacks. How can the Greeks be black and white at the same time? But if they were all blacks, then what is wrong with blacks sharing ideas?

I. It claims that the Greeks stole their ideas from black Africans and thus all the good in Western culture comes from blacks. But if this is true, how can it condemn Western culture on one hand and then claim that it came from blacks on the other hand?

J. It also claims that all the good in Oriental culture came from

African blacks. The Orientals thus stole their culture from the blacks. But, if this is true, why are African motifs missing in Oriental philosophies and art?

K. Its authors claim that the Egyptian word Kemet means "the land of the Blacks." In reality, the word actually means "the black land" referring to the dark soil along the flood plain of the Nile. It is used in Egyptian literature in opposition to the word Deshret that literally means "the red land," a reference to the color of the dirt or sand in the desert.

VIII. Black Liberal Theology Contradicts The Bible

In order to make everyone in the Bible black, it takes passages out of context, ignores the grammar of Hebrew and Greek, and then attacks anyone who disagrees with them as "racist" or "white." But it violates several clear Scriptures.

1. Acts 17:26 "He made from one all the nations of mankind to live on all the face of the earth." The Bible teaches that there is only one race –the human race– regardless of size, shape or color. Thus there is no "black" or "white" blood. There is only human blood that can be transfused from one man to the next regardless of color or race. It contradicts this by talking about "black blood."

2. Rom. 2:11 "There is no partiality with God." God does not treat people any differently because they are red, yellow, black or white. They are all precious in His sight. But Black Liberal Theology claims that God is partial to blacks! This is just as wrong as the Nazis who claimed the same thing for the Ayrian race or the KKK who claims the same for the white race.

3. Gal. 3:28 "There is neither Jew nor Greek, there is neither slave nor free man, there is neither male nor female, for you are all one in Christ Jesus." It divides the Church into different economic classes and pits them against each other. Thus they try to put asunder what God has joined together. The Body of Christ is one.

4. Eph. 4:31-32;5:1-2 "Let all bitterness and wrath and anger and

clamor and slander be put away from you, along with all malice. And be kind to one another, tender-hearted, forgiving each other, just as God in Christ also has forgiven you. Therefore be imitators of God, as beloved children; and walk in love, just as Christ also loved you, and gave Himself up for us, an offering and a sacrifice to God as a fragrant aroma." It preaches bitterness, wrath, anger, clamor, slander and that blacks should seek revenge instead of taking the path of forgiveness.

5. 1 Sam 16:7 "But the LORD said to Samuel, "Do not look at his appearance or at the height of his stature, because I have rejected him; for God sees not as man sees, for man looks at the outward appearance, but the LORD looks at the heart." It looks only at the outward appearance.

Conclusion

Black liberal theology is not of God but of the devil. It is nothing more than "white liberal Marxist religion" and is used by white theologians and politicians to keep blacks down in order to use them as cannon fodder for a Marxist revolution. Black liberal theologians are the slaves of their white Marxist masters to bring about a violent revolution that would guarantee that all men, blacks included, would always be poor and oppressed.

The only answer to Black Liberal Theology, regardless of the color of those who teach it, is personal salvation through the Lord Jesus Christ. Once you have experienced the love of God in Christ, you do not have any room in your heart for the self-hate and racist rage upon which it feeds. The black community needs a revival– not a revolution; Jesus–not Marx; biblical Christianity –not liberalism. Jesus is the only One who can change the hearts of all men and set them free.

CHAPTER TWENTY-FOUR

World Religions

Left Picture: Sati Ceremony, circa 1800, author unknown. The above picture depicts the practice of sati (suttee), or widow-burning in India where the widow was sacrificed by being thrown onto the funeral pyre with her dead husband.

Right Picture: Human sacrifice (an Aztec ritual) as shown in the <u>Codex Magliabechiano</u>, Folio 70. Heart-extraction was viewed as a means of liberating the *istli* and reuniting it with the Sun: the victim's transformed heart flies Sun-ward on a trail of blood. (Created in the 16th century.)

Introduction

Universities and colleges today draw students from all over the world and, as a result, you will encounter religious systems that deny and contradict what the Bible says about God, man, the world, sin and salvation. While it is "politically correct" to pretend that all religions worship the same God and are fundamentally one and the same, this is nothing more than a lie and gross ignorance. It not only disrespects Jesus Christ who said He was the ONLY way, the truth, and the life (John 14:6), but also shows disrespect for all other religions who have their own ideas on what to believe and how to live.

Evangelical Christians believe in the Gospel because it is true. It is not true because they believe it. The Jesus of history was the long-awaited Jewish Messiah who actually died on the cross for the sins of His people. He actually rose bodily from the dead and ascended into heaven and will one day return in glory to judge the world in righteousness.

In this section we will deal with those major world religions that do not pretend in any way to be "Christian."

The situation is difficult with Roman Catholicism and Eastern Orthodoxy. We will deal with Roman Catholicism in Appendix 3. We give a detailed refutation of Eastern Orthodoxy in the book *Is Eastern Orthodoxy Christian?* (www.faithdefenders.com).

The historic Protestant position is quite clear. Both Catholicism and Orthodoxy are false and apostate churches because they teach a works-based salvation and deny the Gospel that we are saved by grace alone, through faith alone, in Christ alone, according to Scripture alone.

This does not imply that there are no true Christians in the Roman Catholic Church or Eastern Orthodox churches. We know Roman Catholics and Eastern Orthodox members who trust in the person and work of Christ alone as the one and only basis of their hope of forgiveness and heaven. They do not put their trust in the worship of idols, icons, saints or Mary to merit the mercy of God.

This is why we equally condemn those Protestant churches that now deny the Gospel as false and apostate churches. Those "main-line" Protestant churches who have officially rejected their original confession of faith and replaced them with a works-based social gospel and no longer believe in the inspiration, inerrancy, and authority of Scripture are false and apostate churches.

What we are saying is not something new or novel but we are simply affirming the historic Evangelical position. Modern neo-Evangelicals are usually honest to admit that when they accept Catholics, the Orthodox, neo-orthodox theologians, liberals, etc. as fellow Christians, they are not in line with the Reformation. Those who reject sola scriptura and preach a works- based salvation are preaching "another gospel" and are under the condemnation of Gal. 1:8. Since we have dealt at length with false churches elsewhere, we refer the readers to those treatments.[56]

Hinduism
Introduction

Hinduism is one of the oldest pre-Christian pagan religions still viable in the world today. While we think of it as the faith of Mother India, it actually traces its origins to a mysterious tribe of Europeans called the Aryans who invaded and conquered Northern India from 1500 BC to 500 BC. The light-skinned Brahmins of Northern India claim to be their physical and spiritual descendants.

The Aryans

The Aryans brought with them their sacred writings called the Vedas. They were originally fire worshippers and this is why they believed in cremation instead of burying their dead. They also invented the theory of soul-transmigration in which at death you do not go to heaven or to hell but you are reborn into another body on earth. This next body could be animal, vegetable or human depending on whether you were good or bad. Your past behavior catches up with you in your present life due to the law of karma.

You could in your next reincarnation end up a clam, a carrot, a bush or a human being. The highest rebirth you could wish for was to be born as one of the white-skinned Brahmins who by virtue of their color were considered the "higher" class.

The Ugly Reality of Racism

The inherent racism of historic Hinduism is thus blatant. You were judged by the color of your skin, not the content of your character, skills or talents. The darker your skin, the lower your caste and rank in Hindu society. The whiter your skin means the higher your caste and rank. The Brahmins prided themselves on their white skin while despising the darker skinned "untouchables" who were often viewed and treated as sub-humans.

This explains why Hindu gurus are more than willing to travel to the West to convert rich white Europeans to Hinduism BUT never travel to black Africa to make converts. The truth is, they don't want black people whose skin color is an indication of bad karma. As long as they can sucker rich white people into giving them money ("Money is evil. So give it all to me.") why bother with darker skinned people?

This can be documented by the statements of many of the gurus who have reaped riches in the West. When one guru was asked on TV what he was doing to help the poor, he responded, "Let the Christians take care of them. I am here to help the rich."

The Caste System

The terrible caste system was invented in order to protect the white Brahmins from polluting their sacred whiteness with black blood. You had to marry and to labor in the caste into which you were born. The lines were clearly drawn and no one was allowed to move from one caste to another by marriage or trade.

The mechanism of the caste system is tied to the Hindu theory of soul-transmigration in which your rebirth determines your caste. Your rebirth was predetermined by your karma. Your karma was in turn determined by how you lived in your past life. For example, if you were born with a dark skin to untouchable parents, your life of misery and poverty is your punishment for being evil in your previous life. In other words, you are getting what you deserved.

The poor, the sick, the disabled, the dark-skinned, etc. are what they are because of their own fault. They deserve their suffering because they did something bad in a previous life and their karma has caught up with them. We should not interfere with their suffering because if we do, we will doom them to experience it in the next life. Thus the kindest thing to do is to leave them alone so they can get their suffering over and hopefully have a better rebirth the next time around.

On the other hand, if you were born with white skin to Brahmin parents, your life of wealth and pleasure is your reward for good deeds done in your previous life. You deserve to be rich and white. You earned it. Thus you have no moral obligation to help those less fortunate than you.

The social inequities of Hinduism ultimately led millions of lower caste Indians to abandon Hinduism for Buddhism, Islam, Sikhism or Christianity because those religions did not lock them into a rigid caste system. Social and financial mobility required a change of religion. Of course, if you were a rich white Brahmin, why would you convert to a religion that would strip you of your social status and wealth?

Social Evils

Being originally fire worshippers, Hinduism developed the grisly practice of burning a widow alive on the funeral pyre of her husband (suttee). If she did not willing jump into the fire, she was often thrown into it by the mob gathered to watch her burn to death.

Child sacrifices to animal gods such as sacred crocodiles were common until this Hindu practice was criminalized by the British. The ritual murder and burial of travelers by the Kali cult (the thugees) is another example of Hinduism's inherently demonic nature and inspiration.

Other immoral practices of Hinduism included using children as sex slaves in Hindu temples. They not only served the sexual perversions of the priests and gurus but were used as prostitutes to bring in money. The poorest of the poor who often could not afford to keep a new child, left the baby in a temple assuming that the child would have a better life with the priests than with its parents. They doomed their child to a life of pain and misery.

The tourist who travels to India's many temples is often shocked by wall art that depicts sodomy, child sex, orgies and bestiality of the grossest kind. Yet, all this is part of what lies at the core of Hinduism.

The same shock is received when tourists see Hindus drinking urine from animals and humans and smearing dung in their hair and on their body. The smell that emanates from the gurus, monks and holy men of Hinduism is enough to warn us that Hinduism is rotten to the core.

Why are we beginning our discussion of Hinduism with such ugly topics as racism, the caste system, burning of widows, ritual child abuse and gross immorality? To see the true nature of Hinduism we must study what it produces in those societies where it is the dominant religion. Thus a mere abstract philosophic presentation of Hinduism in the classroom will give a false view of it. Hinduism is far more than a list of abstract dogmas. It is actually a social program that seeks to organize a culture according to Hindu concepts of soul-transmigration, karma, race and caste.

The Philosophic Failures of Hinduism

1. Hinduism denies the existence of the infinite/personal triune God of the Bible who exists independent of and apart from the universe that He created out of nothing. It is atheistic in this sense.
2. Hinduism never solved the problem of the One and Many or the infinite/personal dichotomy.
3. Those Hindus who emphasize the One over the Many, teach Monism (All is One) and pantheism (All is God), erasing any distinction between Creator and creation. "God" is an impersonal infinite force or power which manifests itself as the universe around us. The "things" we see around us do not really exist per se. They are only illusions of the One. This is what the high caste Hindus teach the Westerners who come to India in search of "enlightenment."
4. The vast majority of Hindus do not follow the Brahmin doctrine of monism. Instead of emphasizing the One over the Many, they emphasize the Many over the One and practice the most vile forms of polytheism imaginable in which they worship millions of gods and goddesses. It is said that the Hindus worship more gods and goddesses than the total number of Hindus who exist today. They

worship snakes, monkeys, elephants, crocodiles, cats, insects and other absurdities.

5. As a worldview, Hinduism fails to answer crucial questions:

a. Why does the Universe exist as opposed to not existing? Since it cannot answer this question, Hinduism simply denies the existence of the world around us. It is an illusion (maya) or dream.

b. Is the universe eternal or did it have a beginning? Hinduism has always taught that the universe is eternal. But this has been successfully refuted by modern science. This also exposes an inherent contradiction within Hinduism. If the universe does not exist but is illusionary in nature, how then is it eternal? How can Hinduism speak of the universe going through eternal cycles if the universe does not exist?

c. Why does the Universe exist in such a form that predictability and science are possible? By denying the existence of the world around it, Hinduism did not develop science and cannot explain why it works.

d. What is evil? Once again, since Hinduism could not answer this question, it simply denied that evil existed.

e. Why does evil exist? Hinduism cannot answer this question.

f. What is man? Hinduism denies that we actually exist.

g. How can we explain the uniqueness of man? Hinduism cannot explain why man is distinct from the world around him.

h. Why do we do evil? Hinduism cannot answer this question.

i. What is sin? Because it does not have a concept of a personal/infinite Creator, Hinduism has no concept of "sin" per se.

j. How do we obtain forgiveness for our sins? There is no forgiveness in Hinduism. You will have to suffer in the next life for the evil you do in this present life. This answer exposes an inescapable contradiction within Hindu philosophy. If the universe, evil, and man do not actually exist but are only illusions (Maya), then on what grounds does karma exist? If it does not actually exist either, then on what grounds does reincarnation happen?

k. On what basis can we explain man's desire for meaning,

significance, justice, morals, truth and beauty? Hinduism has no answer to these questions.

 1. How can we provide a sufficient basis for meaning, significance, justice, morals, truth and beauty? Hinduism cannot provide a philosophic basis for any of these things.

Conclusion

Hinduism cannot answer the essential philosophic questions that always arise wherever and whenever the human intellect matures. It has been weighed on the scales of truth and has been found lacking.

Even more importantly, Hinduism has no concept of a Creator God, the Creation, the Fall of man into sin and guilt, a Day of Judgment, atonement or forgiveness, or a Savior who redeems us from our sins by the sacrifice of Himself in our place.

It did not produce democracy, science or equality among different races and ranks of mankind. Instead it produced great social evils that afflict the Indian people to this day. As a religion and a philosophy, Hinduism is a complete failure and cannot provide a basis for meaning, significance, justice, morals, truth and beauty.

Buddhism
Introduction

Buddhism is an Eastern religion that has gained many followers in the West especially among movie stars. It is only appropriate that we examine this ancient pagan religion.

The Buddha

Buddhism is supposedly built upon the teachings and example of a Hindu guru who was called the "Buddha," i.e. Enlightened

One. The problem we face is that this guru did not write down any of his teachings. Neither did any of his early disciples. A few manuscripts appear four to five hundred years after his death! But most of the manuscripts do not appear until nearly 1,000 years after his death. This gives plenty of time for legends and myths to arise that falsify the life and teachings of the guru.

This problem is further complicated by the development of two contradictory literary traditions: Pali and Sanskrit. These divergent literary traditions produced hundreds of Buddhist sects that disagree with each other on many major points.

No Primary Sources

Because of the lack of primary source materials for the history of Buddhism, modern scholars seriously doubt the reliability of the traditional legends about the Buddha. As a matter of fact, if he were alive today he would not recognize the religion that bears his name! Since Buddhists themselves disagree on the "facts" of the life and teachings of their guru, there is more than adequate reason to cast doubt on the entire history of the "Buddha."

What We Know

There are only a few facts about this Hindu guru that are agreed upon by most scholars. He was born around 563 B.C. in what is now called Nepal. His name is not known for certain. The ones that history preserved are spelled differently. One variation is Siddhartha Gautama. Although this name is doubted by many scholars, we will use it for lack of a better alternative.

It is universally agreed that Siddhartha did not intend to start a new religion. He was born a Hindu. He lived as a Hindu. And he died a Hindu in 483 B.C. The myths and legends that gradually built up around him over the centuries are no safe guide to what he really believed or practiced.

As Buddhism evolved over the centuries, many different authors from varying cultures set forth their own ideas in the name of the Buddha. As a result, Buddhism developed inherent contradictions. When this was realized, Buddhism embraced these contradictions as a badge of honor. Thus the making of self-contradictory statements has become one of the pronounced features of Zen and other esoteric forms of Buddhism.

The Myths

The many conflicting and fascination legends about his early life, marriage, wanderings and enlightenment are unreliable. Siddhartha was supposedly born into a wealthy family and grew up isolated from the poverty and suffering in the surrounding culture. Some legends exaggerate the wealth of his family and even make them into royalty. But these legends are obvious embellishments and there is no historical evidence to back them up.

He was married and had one infant child by the age of 29. Disobeying his father's wishes, he went out into the world and for the first time saw the pain and suffering of the unwashed poor and the untouchable. Their suffering made him feel guilty over his life of ease and luxury.

As he became psychologically obsessed with guilt, instead of doing something positive to alleviate human suffering, like setting up a hospital or giving food to the hungry, Siddhartha decided to increase human suffering by abandoning his family and taking up the life of a Hindu beggar/monk. By making his family suffer as well as himself, he only added to human suffering. This is one of the great defects of both Hinduism and Buddhism. They increase human suffering with their belief systems.

For six years Siddhartha wandered around the countryside begging and abusing his body in the attempt to purify his soul. But his suffering did not profit anything for anyone including himself. The legends state that he was sitting under a fig tree when it dawned on him that the source of all his suffering was his failure to find a Middle Way between pleasure and pain, wealth and poverty, etc. He had gone from one extreme to another and both experiences had left him dissatisfied with life.

Then a new idea came into his mind. His real problem was that he had DESIRES. When his desires were not met, he became dissatisfied. Thus the way to avoid frustration and the suffering it caused, is to arrive at the place where he had no desires for anything, good or evil. For example, he should have no desire to see his wife or child or to help the poor and needy. Desire qua desire must be eradicated.

With these insights (sic), Siddhartha was proclaimed a "Buddha," i.e. Enlightened One. Did this mean he went back to his family and fulfilled his moral obligation to his wife and child? No, his wife and child remained abandoned. Siddhartha's so-called "enlightenment" was intensely self-centered and inherently selfish. This is still one of the main problems of Buddhism.

Now that he was a "Buddha," he should not have any desires to be or do anything. We would therefore expect him to withdraw to a cave and die in isolation. But his desire to preach sermons and make converts was apparently alive and well. He set forth preaching his new message to all who would hear him.

According to the legends, from his enlightened lips came the four Noble Truths, the Eightfold Path, the Ten Perfections, and many other sophisticated teachings. But Siddhartha never really taught any of these things. They were developed many centuries after his death and his name was invoked in order to give them the air of authority.

No God

Siddhartha never taught that he was a god or that he should be worshipped as a god. He did not even claim to be a saint or an avatar. As a Hindu, he believed in millions of finite gods and goddesses. But being finite deities, they were of little consequence and could be ignored except when you needed their assistance. Thus most Buddhists call upon the gods only when they need something.

The Evolution of Buddhism

The starting point for any analysis of Buddhism is Hinduism. Scholars have long pointed out that Buddhism was intended to be a reform movement within Hinduism, not a separate religion. Indeed, much of Buddhism is a reaction to be the sociological evils spawned by the Hindu commitment to such things as the caste system with its millions of untouchables. The following charts summarize the unity and diversity between Hinduism and Buddhism.

Unity	
Hinduism	Buddhism
1. Human autonomy 3. Idealism 5. Enlightenment	2. Monism 4. Karma 6. Reincarnation

Diversity	
Hinduism	Buddhism
1. Brahmanism 2. caste system 3. The Vedas 4. enlightenment for only a few 5. group 6. polytheistic 7. eternal soul	rejected rejected rejected enlightenment for all individual atheistic no soul per se

Christianity and Buddhism

Buddhism is inferior to Christianity in many ways:

A. "Southern" Buddhism is polytheistic involving the worship of idols including the Buddha (a huge, fat, smiling, pot-bellied man sitting in the lotus position). Some rub his stomach for good luck. Sacrifices are presented to him.

B. The OT prophets pointed out the defects of polytheism and the folly of worshipping what we make with our own hands. My book *Battle of the Gods* has two chapters on the philosophic defects of polytheism.

C. "Northern" Buddhism is more atheistic than polytheistic. If any god is acknowledged, it is the "god" within us. Buddhists deny the existence of the personal/infinite Maker of heaven and earth. They are atheistic in this sense.

D. Having no infinite/personal Creator, Buddhism cannot provide any basis for truth, justice, meaning, morals or beauty. It cannot answer the riddles of the origin or goal of life.

E. Its inward orientation made the development of science impossible.

F. Its concept of suffering prevented them from alleviating human suffering.

G. Their concept of karma and reincarnation compounded the problem of evil by adding more suffering to it.

H. Because Buddhism teaches that man's problem is primarily ignorance, it never developed a way to gain forgiveness for sin.

I. Because it strives only for enlightenment, Buddhism offers no plan of salvation.

J. Its goal is not to glorify God or to make a positive contribution to humanity but the extinction of individual consciousness in the ocean of nothingness called Nirvana. Its failure to find a purpose and meaning for life that is greater than life itself is one of its greatest defects.

K. Because of its narcissistic and self-centered nature, Buddhism appeals to those who seek justification for living a selfish lifestyle. This is why Hollywood movie stars are drawn to it.

L. Buddhism fails the test of history by being based on groundless myths and legends. It thus has no basis in history and is built on lies and deceptions set forth in Buddha's name.

The Answer to Buddhism

1. The Biblical Doctrine of Creation: The universe is not eternal as Buddhism teaches. It had a beginning and will have an end. Man is created in the image of an infinite/personal Creator. God created matter as well as mind, and both are good. Buddhism fails the test of science with its idea of an eternal universe.

2. The Biblical Doctrine of the Fall: Man's problem is moral and not metaphysical. He has sinned against God's law by violating its commands and failing to live up to its standards. Our problem is not that we have a body or that we are conscious of our individual existence. Our problem is that we are sinners in need of salvation. Buddhism fails the test of morals because it fails to address the sin problem.

3. The Biblical Doctrine of Redemption: God so loved us that He sent His son to die for our sins on the cross. His atoning work renders karma and reincarnation unnecessary. The goal is to retain our individual consciousness for all eternity in service to God and others. Buddhism fails the test of salvation because it provides none.

Conclusion

Buddhism is legendary while Christianity is historical. Buddhism is irrational and attempts to escape logic and reason. But Christianity is the very essence of logic and reason. Buddhism is a death-wish philosophy and is not mentally healthy. It does not really enable people to cope with the real world but tries to escape reality and live according to illusion and fantasy. In every respect if fails the tests of truth. Jesus Christ alone is the Way, the Truth and the Life. We cannot go to the Father without Him.

Modern Judaism

Introduction

The first thing we must understand is that Judaism is not a race but a religion. In fact, most Jews today are not believers in or members of any of the various sects of Judaism. Almost 80 percent of the Jews in America do not belong to any Jewish religious organizations.

Part 1

The Biblical View

The second error we must correct is the idea that "Judaism" does not accept Jesus as the Messiah. This is erroneous because what we call "Christianity" is actually "Messianic Judaism." The early Christian Church was only one of many Jewish sects. They even met in the synagogue (James 2:2).

Acts 24:5: "For we have found this man a real pest and a fellow who stirs up dissension among all the Jews throughout the world, and a ringleader of the sect of the Nazarenes."

Acts 24:14: "But this I admit to you, that according to the Way that they call a sect I do serve the God of our fathers, believing everything that is in accordance with the Law, and that is written in the prophets."

Acts 28:21: "And they said to him, 'We have neither received letters from Judea concerning you, nor have any of the brethren come here and reported or spoken anything bad about you.' "

Acts 28:22: "But we desire to hear from you what your views are; for concerning this sect, it is known to us that it is spoken against everywhere."

Acts 28:23: "And when they had set a day for him, they came to him at his lodging in large numbers; and he was explaining to them by solemnly testifying about the kingdom of God, and trying to persuade them concerning Jesus, from both the Law of Moses and from the Prophets, from morning until evening."

The third fact to remember is that if you are a Gentile who has accepted Jesus as the Messiah, then you are a believer in Messianic Judaism. This means that you are now Jewish in religion.

Rom 2:28: "For he is not a Jew who is one outwardly; neither is circumcision that which is outward in the flesh."

Rom 2:29: "But he is a Jew who is one inwardly; and circumcision is that which is of the heart, by the spirit, not by the letter; and his praise is not from men, but from God."
Phil. 3:2: "Beware of the dogs, beware of the evil workers, beware of the false circumcision."

Phil. 3:3: "For we are the true circumcision, who worship in the Spirit of God and glory in Christ Jesus and put no confidence in the flesh."

Gentiles must remember that they are wild branches grafted on the tree of Judaism, while those Jews who reject Jesus are broken off the tree and are thus no longer part of Judaism.

Rom. 11:13: "But I am speaking to you who are Gentiles. Inasmuch then as I am an apostle of Gentiles, I magnify my ministry."

Rom. 11:14: "If somehow I might move to jealously my fellow countrymen and save some of them."

Rom. 11:15: "For if their rejection be the reconciliation of the world, what will their acceptance be but life form the dead?"

Rom. 11:16: "And if the first piece of dough be holy, the lump is also; and if the root be holy, the branches are too."

Rom. 11:17: "But if some of the branches were broken off, and you, being a wild olive, were grafted in among them and became partaker with them of the rich root of the olive tree."

Rom. 11:18: "Do not be arrogant toward the branches; but if you are arrogant, remember that it is not you who supports the root, but the root supports you."

Rom. 11:19: "You will say then, Branches were broken off so that I might be grafted in."

Rom. 11:20: "Quite right, they were broken off for their unbelief, but you stand by your faith. Do not be conceited, but fear."

Rom. 11:21: "For if God did not spare the natural branches, neither will he spare you."

The tree = Biblical Judaism
The Jews = the natural branches in the tree
The Gentiles = branches from wild trees
Unbelieving Jews = branches broken off the tree
Believing Jews = branches still in the tree
Believing Gentiles = branches grafted on the tree

Part 2

The Modern Meanings of 'Judaism'

The word "Judaism" has many definitions. Not even the Jews have a unified definition. If you ask two Jews, they will give you three opinions! The following definitions of Judaism reflect the massive confusion that exists on the subject.

1. The original religion of mankind.

Judaism is thus the first and oldest religion. Adam, Eve, Abel, Seth, and all true believers in God before the Flood were part of Judaism.

2. The covenant with Noah.

The present day Jewish cult called B'nai Noah, the Noahides or Sons of Noah, led by J. David Davis, reduces Judaism to the laws established by Noah after the Flood.

3. The covenant with Abraham.

The blessings, promises and curses connected with the Abrahamic covenant are sometimes identified as Judaism.

4. The covenant with Moses.

We now come to what most people assume to be Judaism. The Mosaic laws governing the civil, ceremonial, and cultic aspects of the national and religious life of the nation of Israel are often what people think when they hear the word "Judaism."

5. Jewish life during the diaspora.

After the destruction of the temple, the synagogue became the center of Jewish religious life instead of the temple. The rabbi instead of the temple priest became the teacher of the Law. Many different Jewish sects arose that contradicted each other on fundamental doctrines:

Scribes	The Apocrypha
Pharisees	The Pseudepigrapha
Sadducees	The Targums
Herodians	The Septuagint
Zealots	The Midrash
Hellenists	The Dead Sea Scrolls
Apocalypticists	
Essenes	

6. The Talmudic period.

After the temple was destroyed in A.D. 70, the oral traditions had to be written down or they would be lost. The Mishnah, the Jerusalem Talmud, and the Babylonian

Talmud were written. Since without a temple or its ceremonies, the Mosaic covenant was impossible, a system of legalistic rules about food, drink, etc., were substituted for the Mosaic covenant.

7. The Cabalistic occult period. During the Middle Ages in Europe, many Jews practiced witchcraft, magic, and the occult sciences called the Cabal. Much of modern witchcraft is derived from the Cabal. The Golem is an example of this occult brand of Judaism.

8. The Rationalistic period. After the Industrial Revolution, many European Jews adopted a secular humanistic worldview. A rationalistic Judaism arose that was anti-supernatural in nature. The Mosaic authorship of the Pentateuch and the historicity of miracles were rejected.

9. The Zionistic period. When the Jews returned to Israel, there was a small revival of Talmudic Judaism. But most Israelis are still secular humanistic in outlook. Yet many of these secular Jews feel that the old geographical boundaries of biblical Israel should be set up again.

10. The Messianic period. As more and more Jews accept Yeshua as the Messiah, there is a growing movement to reclaim Jesus as a Jewish prophet.

Part 3

How to Graft Broken Branches Back on to the Tree

1. Don't assume that the Jew you are talking to believes in God.
2. If he does believe in "God," realize that he is usually pantheistic in outlook.
3. If he believes in a personal God, don't assume that he believes in the Bible.
4. If he says he believes in the Holy Scriptures, realize he only means the five books of Moses, the Torah. He does not believe the Writings of the Prophets are inspired.
5. Realize that he believes that Christianity was created by Paul—not Jesus, and that Paul derived it from Greek paganism—not Judaism.

6. Understand that he believes that the Catholic Inquisition killed millions of Jews and that this is what Christians do: kill Jews. He blames Christianity for the crimes of Roman Catholicism.
7. Once you get through all these hurdles, share with him that true Christianity is Jesus. Show him that Jesus fulfilled the Old Testament:

Old Testament	New Testament
Unfilled prophecies	Fulfilled
Unsatisfied longings	Satisfied
Incomplete destiny	Completed
Unexplained ceremonies	Explained

Question: Is Historic Judaism in its Biblical and Rabbinic Forms Exclusive or Inclusive of Other Religions?

Introduction

I debated the head of "Jews for Judaism" on ABC national radio. The rabbi started out with a great deal of anger: "How dare you say that Jesus is the only way! We Jews do not believe that our religion is exclusive. Jesus is OK for Gentiles but not for Jews. You are intolerant if you say that your religion is the only true religion. To say that means you are anti-Semitic and a hatemonger."

While the rabbi was in line with the popular relativism of the day, he was out of line with the historic Judaism found in the Hebrew Scriptures and in the writings of Rabbinic Judaism. In effect, he had denied what his religion has always stood for and was no longer a "Jew" theologically.

When Christians say that there is only one way to heaven, they are simply repeating what the Law and Prophets and the rabbis taught. We must remember that the word "Christian" was invented by Gentiles who did not understand who we were. All Christians, regardless of ethnic background or color, have actually joined Messianic Jews who have accepted the long-awaited Messiah in the person of Jesus. They are Gentile by race but now a Jew by grace.

Proposition 1: The Torah (Law), the Prophets, the Rabbis, Rabbi Yeshua and the Apostles were all exclusive of other religions.

a.   The Torah: No other gods!

"You shall have no other gods before Me" (Exo. 20:3).

b.   The Prophets: NO other Savior!

"I, even I, am the LORD; And there is no savior besides Me" (Isa. 43:11).

c.   The Rabbis were united on this point:

"In virtue of the commandment, 'Thou shalt have no other gods' Israel will have a claim to be remembered favorably as exterminators of idolatry" (Midrash Rabbah [IX. 45] Numbers I, Vol. V., p. 320).

"Know this day, and lay it to thy heart, that the LORD, he is God in heaven above and upon the earth below beneath; there is none else (ib. iv, 39). Not only that, but we have sworn to our God that we will not exchange Him for any other god" (Midrash Rabbah [I.16] Deut., Vol. VII, p. 131).

d.   Rabbi Yeshua (Jesus): No other Way!

Jesus said to him, "I am the way, and the truth, and the life; no one comes to the Father, but through Me (John 14:6).

e.   The Apostle Peter: No other Name!

"And there is salvation in no one else; for there is no other name under heaven that has been given among men, by which we must be saved" (Acts 4:12).

f.   The Apostle Rabbi Saul: No other Mediator!

"For there is only one God, and only one mediator also between God and men, the man Christ Jesus (1 Tim. 2:5).

Proposition 2: All the gods of other religions are either nothing or demons.

a.   The Torah:

"They sacrificed to demons who were not God, To gods whom they have not known, New gods who came lately, Whom your fathers did not dread " (Deut. 32:17).

"And they shall no longer sacrifice their sacrifices to the goat demons with which they play the harlot. This shall be a permanent statute to them throughout their generations" (Lev. 17:7).

b.   The Prophets:

"For all the gods of the peoples are idols, But the LORD made the heavens" (1 Chron. 16:26).

"They have cast their gods into the fire, for they were not gods but the work of men's hands, wood and stone. So they have destroyed them"

(2 Kings 19:18).

"Have you not driven out the priests of the LORD, the sons of Aaron and the Levites, and made for yourselves priests like the peoples of other lands? Whoever comes to consecrate himself with a young bull and seven rams, even he may become a priest of what are no gods" (2 Chron. 13:9).

"Has a nation changed gods, When they were not gods?" (Jer. 2:11).

"Why should I pardon you? Your sons have forsaken Me And sworn by those who are not gods" (Jer. 5:7).

"But they are altogether stupid and foolish In their discipline of delusion—their idol is wood! Beaten silver is brought from Tarshish, And gold from Uphaz, The work of a craftsman and of the hands of a goldsmith; Violet and purple are their clothing; They are all the work of skilled men. But the LORD is the true God; He is the living God and the everlasting King" (Jer. 10:8-9).

"Can man make gods for himself? Yet they are not gods!" (Jer. 16:20).

c.   The Rabbis were united on this point:

"I am not called 'the god of idolaters,' but 'the God of Israel' "(Rabbah Midrash, Exo. 29:4-5).

"But is not burning incense to a demon idolatry?" (b. Talmud, San. 65a).

"And they shall no more offer their sacrifices unto demons" (b. Talmud, San. 61a).

d. Rabbi Yeshua (Jesus):

"that they may know Thee, the only true God" (John 17:3).

e. The Apostles:

"No, but I say that the things which the Gentiles sacrifice, they sacrifice to demons, and not to God; and I do not want you to become sharers in demons" (1 Cor. 10:20).

"However at that time, when you did not know God, you were slaves to those which by nature are no gods (Gal. 4:8).

Proposition 3: To worship any God other than YHWH was a capital crime in Israel to be punished by death.

a. The Torah:

"He who sacrifices to any god, other than to the LORD alone, shall be utterly destroyed" (Exo. 22:20).

"You shall also say to the sons of Israel, 'Any man from the sons of Israel or from the aliens sojourning in Israel, who gives any of his offspring to Molech, shall surely be put to death; the people of the land shall stone him with stones" (Lev. 20:2).

"As for the person who turns to mediums and to spiritists, to play the harlot after them, I will also set My face against that person and will cut him off from among his people" (Lev. 20:6).

"You shall not allow a sorceress to live" (Exo. 22:18).

"Moreover, the one who blasphemes the name of the LORD shall surely be put to death; all the congregation shall certainly stone him. The alien as well as the native, when he blasphemes the Name, shall be put to death" (Lev. 24:16).

"If your brother, your mother's son, or your son or daughter, or the wife you cherish, or your friend who is as your own soul, entice you secretly, saying, 'Let us go and serve other gods'…you shall surely kill him; your hand shall be first against him to put him to death, and afterwards the hand of all the people" (Deut. 13:6-9).

"You shall bring out that man or that woman who has done this evil deed, to your gates, that is, the man or the woman, and you shall stone them to death" (Deut. 17:5).

"Seize the prophets of Baal; do not let one of them escape." So they seized them; and Elijah brought them down to the brook Kishon, and slew them there" (1 Kgs. 18:40).

"But rather, you are to tear down their altars and smash their sacred pillars and cut down their Asherim" (Exo. 34:13).

b.   The Rabbis were united on this point:

"Our Rabbis taught: Seven precepts were the sons of Noah commanded: social laws; to refrain from blasphemy; idolatry; adultery; bloodshed; robbery; and eating flesh cut from a living animal" (b. Talmud, San. 56).

Footnote (1), p. 382: "These commandments may be regarded as the foundation of all human and moral progress. Judaism has both a national and a universal outlook in life…it recognizes that moral progress and its concomitant Divine love and approval are the privilege and obligation of all mankind. And hence the Talmud lays down the seven Noachian precepts, by observance of which all mankind may attain spiritual perfection, and without which moral death must inevitably ensue. That perhaps is the idea underlying the assertion that a heathen is liable for death for the neglect of any of these."

"R. Huna, Rab Judah, and all the disciples of Rab maintained: A heathen is executed for the violations of the seven Noachian laws" (b. Talmud, San. 57a).

"He who sacrifices to any god, other than to the LORD alone, shall be utterly destroyed" (B. Talmud, Gitten 57b).

"The Torah decreed that such a charmer is to be stoned" (b. Talmud, San. 65a).

"There is no severer penalty than incurred for idolatry, for God himself is jealous of it, as it is said, 'Thou shalt have no other gods before me, etc.' (Exo. Xx, 3); as it is written, 'For the LORD thy God is a devouring fire, a jealous God' (Deut. Iv, 24)...the penalty for idol worship is so severe..." (Midrash [II.18] Deut., Vol. VII, p. 45).

"He who engages in idol worship is executed. It is all one whether he serve it, sacrifice, offer incense, make libations, prostrate himself, accept it as a God, or say to it, 'Thou art my God'" (Mishnah 60b).

"The necromancer and the charmer are subject to the death penalty of stoning, so is a sorceress also subject to the penalty of stoning" (b. Talmud, Yebamoth 4a).

"Our Rabbis taught: Thou shalt not suffer a witch to live: this applies to both man and woman....How are they executed?...stoning...The sorcerer who insists on exact paraphernalia works through demons" (b. Talmud, San.

67a).

"Our Rabbis taught....The inclusion of heathens, to whom blasphemy is prohibited just as to Israelites, and they are executed by decapitation; for every death penalty decreed for the sons of Noah is only by decapitation" (b. Talmud San. 56a).

Conclusion

Rabbi Yeshua and the Apostles taught that no physical violence was to be used in evangelism or church discipline. The Church set up by Jesus can only exclude from her membership rolls: idolaters, pagans, cultists, occultists, homosexuals, lesbians, heretics, apostates, and those who commit beastiality.

When the Roman Catholic Church used violence to force pagans, Jews and Protestants to convert and then tortured and killed those who refused, this was not New Testament Christianity. There is no historical evidence of Evangelical Christians using violence in this way. We use the moral persuasion found in the Gospel instead of brute force. We believe in missions, not missiles; Bibles not bullets. Messianic Jews believe in religious freedom for all.

Islams

We refer to "Islams" in the plural because there are many different religions each claiming to be the "true" Islam. They differ from each other in belief and practice to such a degree that they have waged war on each other. The Shiite and the Sunni Islams are examples of this reality. Thus there is no such thing as "Islam" in a monolithic sense. There are competing groups each claiming to be "Islam."

The teachings of Muhammad are making their way into Western society. In years past, contact between Muslims and

Christians was limited to Black Muslims selling newspapers on a street corner or Muslim students coming here to study. But two things have radically changed this situation.

First, every year thousands of Muslims are immigrating to the West from such places as Pakistan, Egypt, etc. They are here to stay and they need our respect and acceptance.

Second, oil-rich Middle Eastern countries such as Saudi Arabia are using billions of oil dollars to convert Westerners to Islam. They have been building thousands of mosques all over the United States, England and Europe in anticipation of millions of converts. They are giving a thousand dollars to any South African black who converts to Islam, and then pay him even more money for each person he brings with him! See my ground-breaking book, *Islamic Invasion*, for the documentation.

The Issues

The issues that divide biblical Christianity and Islam are very clear. When the historical and factual errors of the Qur'an and the shortcomings of Muhammad are pointed out by scholars, this should not be taken as a personal insult by Muslims. When Muslims contradict the Bible and state that Jesus Christ was not the Son of God, that Jesus was never crucified and that Jesus cannot save anybody, should their attacks on Christianity be taken as a personal insult by Christians? We hope not! After all, to disagree with someone is not the same as to insult someone.

1. Muhammad taught that Christians believe in three gods named the Father, The Mother (Mary), and the Son (Jesus) (Sura 116). Yet, the truth is that no Christian church has ever taught such a doctrine. Christians have always believed in one God eternally existing in three persons: the Father, the Son and the Holy Spirit. How can Muhammad be an infallible prophet and the Qur'an inspired by God when they make such a blunder remains one of the great problems facing Islam.

2. Muhammad also denied that Jesus was the Son of God, that Jesus died on the cross and that Jesus was the Savior. He taught that

Jesus was only one of many prophets of which he, Muhammad, was the greatest. Yet, how could he be greater than Jesus Christ? Jesus was born of a virgin and was sinless in nature and the doer of mighty miracles such as raising the dead. But there was nothing superior about Muhammad's birth or life. He never made the lame to walk, the blind to see or the dead to live. Allah even commanded him to repent of his many sins. How then can he be greater than the Christ?

3. The contrast between Jesus and Muhammad could not be greater. While Jesus forbade the use of force to convert people (Matthew 26:51-54), Muhammad commanded his followers in the Qur'an (Sura IX.5) to force people to accept Islam by war, plunder, slavery or the threat of death!

4. The Qur'an itself is filled with every kind of self-contradiction, historical and scientific error known to man. In Sura XVIII. 82-98, the Qur'an tells us that Alexander the Great was a believer in the one true God, and that he lived through two generations of men. Since Alexander was a pagan and died when only 33 in 323 B.C., the Qur'an is obviously in error.

The use of circular reasoning on the part of Muslims cannot erase these errors. To argue, "the Qur'an is inspired, therefore it cannot contain any errors," is to put the cart before the horse. A rational person cannot accept the Qur'an or any other "bible" if it has historical and factual errors. This holds for Christians, Mormons, Jews or Hindus as well as for Muslims. Thus our Muslim friends should be willing to let the evidence decide the Truth.

5. Most Western scholars have always stated that Muhammad had mental problems. He was given to fits and spells as a child, during which he claimed to have seen and talked to desert spirits including a goddess. See my book, *Islamic Invasion* (www.faithdefenders.com) for the documentation.

6. He married over a dozen women, including taking another man's wife under "divine" command (Sura XXXIII. 37-38). He even married a little girl 6 or 7 years of age. That Muhammad had 13 wives is not denied by Muslim scholars. That Muhammad took a girl 6 or 7 years old as one of his wives is admitted by such Muslims historians as:

Ibn Hisham (vol. Iii, p. 94)
Ibn Athir (vol ii, pp. 117,118)
Mishkat (pp. 262, 272)

7. As to taking another man's wife, Muslim writer Kausar Niazi admits: "The Holy Prophet never married another man's wife except that of Zayd" (*Islam and the West*, p. 17).

8. In terms of his beliefs, Muhammad held a strange combination of ideas from the Old Testament, the New Testament and his own pagan background. He never freed himself from such pagan rituals as running seven times around the "Black Stone" in Mecca. This stone is a rock that the pagans in Muhammad's day worshipped as a god who "fell" from Heaven. This is not known by most Muslims.

Haykal's *The Life of Mohammed*, which is a Muslim work, states that the "black rock" or Ka'bah was "a pantheon full of statues for idol worship." The rocks "appeared to have Fallen from Heaven" and were "worshipped as divinities" (p. 30).

The pagan ceremony included a pilgrimage to the rock, running around it seven times and praying toward it. This is what all Muslim scholars admit. That Muhammad took a pagan ceremony and changed its meaning does not alter the fact of the pagan origin of why Muslims pray toward Mecca, make a pilgrimage to it and run around it seven times. This is also stated in the *Encyclopedia Britannica*, vol. 15, p. 152, under "Mecca."

9. While a Muslim must work his way to paradise by repeating the Muslim prayer five times a day, fasting, giving money and going on a pilgrimage to Mecca, the Christian believes he is saved by grace alone through faith alone in Christ alone.

The United States is a great country because it has a Constitution that guarantees civil rights to all beliefs. Islamic law does not recognize non-Muslims as having any civil rights. This is why the death penalty is mandated for any Muslim who chooses to convert to some other religion. This is why Jews and Christians are often put to death and their goods plundered in many Muslim countries such as Egypt.

Conclusion

America has room for all religions as long as they respect the lives, properties and rights of others. The conflict between Christ and Muhammad cannot be ignored. Either Jesus is Lord or Muhammad was a false prophet. But Muhammad is dead, while Jesus is alive forevermore.

Atheism

Introduction

As a worldview, atheism must justify itself intellectually just like any other worldview. It makes many faith-based statements about the universe, man, and God, which it expects us to accept as true by blind faith. In this sense it is a world religion.

Atheistic faith assertions must pass the same tests for truth that judge any and all such assertions. Atheism is thus not exempt from having to prove its truth claims.

I. The creed of classical atheism is as follows: "In the entire universe, there has never been in the past, there is not now in the present, and there will never be in the future, any god, gods or goddesses of any size, shape or description." See my book, *The New Atheism* And *The Erosion of Freedom* (www.faithdefenders.com) for the documentation.

We will now examine the creed of atheism to see if it passes the tests of truth.

I. The first question is this: Is the creed of classical atheism logically valid or invalid? If it is invalid according to the laws of logic, then it is irrational and unacceptable to the educated mind. The atheist's creed clearly violates the laws of logic and is thus irrational in nature.

A. It is impossible to prove a universal negative. When an atheist makes the assertion, "There is no god anywhere at any time," he is making a universal negative, which he cannot prove. Since he cannot prove or demonstrate his assertion, he is being irrational.

B. The second logical problem is that the only way he could prove his assertion that there is no god is to become God.

    1. He would have to be everywhere in the universe at the same time, i.e. he would have to be omnipresent and infinite.

    2. He would have to travel throughout the past, the present and the future at the same time, i.e. he would have to be eternal.

    3. He would have to know all things, i.e. he would have to be omniscient.

    4. In order to be infinite, omnipresent, eternal and omniscient, he would also have to be omnipotent.

C. Thirdly, if only an infinite and eternal God can logically say there is no infinite and eternal God, this itself would be a self-contradictory statement and, hence, irrational.

II. The creed of post-modern atheism is not as dogmatic as classical atheism. It does not claim to know that God does not exist because it does not claim to know anything at all. It has no truth to defend, no morals to follow, no meaning to cherish. Thus they do not attempt to refute the existence of God or claim to be able to defend their own beliefs. I debated on the radio a post-modern atheist named George Smith. He wrote a book entitled *The Case Against God.* At the outset of the debate I demanded he set forth his case against God. What evidence and arguments did he marshal to shoot down the idea of God? I asked him to set forth his case against God. Smith's reply is indicative of modern relativists. He responded that he did not have a case against God because he did not know if God existed or not. He did not believe anything and thus did not have to defend anything. A transcript of the debate can be found in my book, *The New Atheism And The Erosion of Freedom.* His hypocrisy was exposed when I pointed out that in one chapter he denied there any moral absolutes and then in the very next chapter he spoke of "the evils of Christianity." You can't have it both ways. You cannot condemn belief in God, Christianity or the Bible as "evil" or producing "evil" if you do not belief in good and evil as absolutes! He replied that he did not claim that he could prove that God did not exist. His form of atheism is not un-belief or dis-belief but "lack of belief." I responded that a rock has "lack of belief." How then was he different from a rock? He could not answer. I went on to point out that atheism has not produced any great art or music. It has always produced totalitarian governments that deny people basic human rights and civil rights. It is morally bankrupt, economically corrupt, aesthetically impotent, and politically disastrous. With such a blitzkrieg, he quit the debate and ran away.

Conclusion

Modern atheists do not have the courage of their conviction. They believe that God does not exist. But they do not want to defend that belief. Thus they pretend not to know anything. People with such beliefs should not write books.

CHAPTER TWENTY-FIVE

The Occult and Parapsychology

The downward-pointing pentacle is often used to represent Satanism.

The occult has to do with those rites, ideas, practices and miraculous feats connected with witchcraft. The word "occult" itself means hidden or unseen because it was used to refer to those satanic rites that were forbidden by law during the Middle Ages. Those who desired to practice witchcraft had to do so while hidden or unseen in order to escape civil prosecution.

Its Recent History

At the beginning of the 19th century, Theosophy renamed "spiritualism" or "spiritism" as "psychic forces" or "psychic power." Later, the Society of Psychical Research (SPR) redefined witchcraft and sorcery as scientifically neutral and representing the "natural" mental abilities of man.

When the theory of evolution became popular the idea arose that perhaps the human race was evolving in terms of psychic powers so that what formerly was done only by a witch or sorcerer could now be done by everyone.

It was J.B. Rhine in the 1950's who made "psychic power" a subject of valid research in the scientific community. He was the one who invented the term Extra-Sensory Perception or E.S.P. What was formerly known as sorcery was now labeled as E.S.P.

Rhine had been introduced to the occult through Arthur Conan Doyle who was one of the most dynamic representatives of the Society of Psychical Research. It was Rhine's hope to demonstrate scientifically that what was formerly understood to be satanic or witchcraft was only man's natural psychic powers.

Today witchcraft and sorcery are called "parapsychology." But we must remember that a rose called by any other name smells the same. What the Bible condemns as witchcraft and sorcery is nothing more than what is called E.S.P. or parapsychology today.

While modern humanists are willing to view such things as bending spoons or levitating objects as being representative of "psychic forces," the Christian knows that this is simply the same old occult that has plagued the world since man's Fall into sin. For a detailed history of the occult, see my book, *Death and the Afterlife*, (www.faithdefenders.com).

Why People Get Into the Occult

Why do people become involved in the occult? Some people become involved in the occult because they want to communicate with dead loved ones. Perhaps a favorite aunt or uncle has died and they wish to contact them. Or their husband or child has died and they feel lonely without them.

Secondly, some people become involved because they want to know the future. They want to know if they will marry or have children in the future. They want to know the stock market or what the commodities market will yet bring.

Thirdly, some people go into the occult because they want power. They want the power to heal themselves, to cast spells on other people or to get rich. Of course, they must pay with their immortal soul to get it.

Fourthly, some people want to contact Satan or the demonic host through the occultic rite. They desire to be in his service and will do acts of blasphemy and sign contracts in their own blood in which they sell their soul to Satan. Satanism is widespread today and is growing at a dangerous rate.

Fifthly, some people get involved with the occult simply to satisfy their curiosity or their need for excitement. When they play with the Ouija board or go to a séance, this gives them a thrill because it is a frightening experience. But what they do not understand is that playing with the occult is like juggling nitroglycerin. They just might destroy themselves.

The Origin of the Occult

Where does the occult derive its power? God has never been interested in doing parlor tricks in order to amuse people. He does not have the slightest interest in making tables dance or bugles float in the air. He will not make a spoon bend in order to entertain an audience. When Jesus was asked to perform miracles to entertain King Herod, He refused (Lk. 23:8–12).

Neither Jesus nor the Apostles viewed the miracles they did as coming from some kind of "inner psychic force" (see: John 5:19; Acts 3:12–13). Even the Old Testament prophets acknowledged that the miracles they did came from God and not from their own power (Gen. 41:16). This refutes modern parapsychologists who claim that the miracles of the Bible were simply the results of natural human powers.

On the other hand, the authors of Scriptures clearly indicate that they viewed all supernatural feats that did not come from God as coming from Satan himself (Acts 16:16–18). Those who were controlled by demonic forces could do miraculous feats (Matt. 24:24).

This was the perspective of Scripture because Satan has always tried to counterfeit God's miracles by producing his own miracles (Matt. 24:24; 2 Thessalonians 2:9; Revelation 13:11–17). The magicians of Pharaoh sought to match Moses miracle for miracle (Exo. 7–9).

The Important Thing to Remember

The important thing to remember is that just because something is real does not mean that it is good. Just because some supernatural event took place does not mean that God is behind it.

Some people are so foolish as to believe such statements as, "All healing comes from God" or "All miracles come from God." There is another power or force in this universe of which the Bible speaks. This power is evil and very dangerous.

We must also remember whatever diseases or sicknesses Satan has inflicted on someone, he can readily remove. This is the kind of counterfeit miracle Satan does. Just because something is a miracle or a demonstration of power, does not mean that God did it. Be not deceived.

All occult practices are condemned in Scriptures as being satanic in origin and power (Deut. 18). Thus they are an abomination to God and forbidden to His people.

The Christian must also be prepared for much fraud in this area. A competent magician or illusionist can reproduce most of the so-called "miracles" or "psychic" feats of those who claim paranormal abilities. They can bend spoons by trickery and make objects appear to float around in mid-air. There are even Christian illusionists who have debunked well known religious con artists who were duping people with common magician's tricks.

Conclusion

Christians should not engage in any parapsychological experiments to develop their E.S.P. powers. As a matter of fact, they do not need E.S.P. because they have H.S.P. (Holy Spirit Power)!

The Christian does not fear Satan for "Greater is He that is in us than he that is in the world" (1 John 4:4). God's truth and God's kingdom will ultimately triumph over the kingdom and lies of the devil. Don't become entangled in the forces of darkness under the guise of the "science" of parapsychology.

Questions for Discussion

1. What is the occult and how does it relate to modern parapsychology?
2. If a psychic feat is not a fraud, where did its power come from?
3. Should Christians live in fear of the devil?
4. Who invented E.S.P.?
5. Did the prophets, apostles or Jesus use E.S.P. to do their miracles?
6. Should Christians get involved in parapsychological experiments?
7. What does Deut. 18 say about the occult?
8. What important point should be remembered?

CHAPTER TWENTY-SIX

The New Age Movement

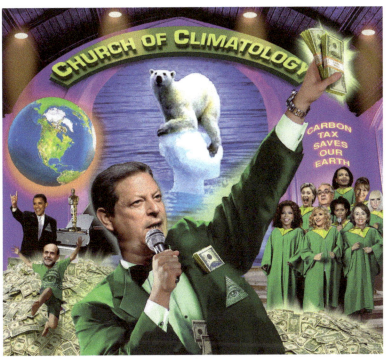

Church of Climatology by DDees.com

Introduction

From time to time, the New Age Movement (NAM) makes the daily newspaper by claiming:

- "Christ" has returned!

- We are all gods and Christs!

- A "New Age" has dawned.

The present popularity of astrology, reincarnation, crystal balls, tarot cards, séances, Ouija boards, channeling, psychics, gurus, astral-travel, pagan groups, witchcraft, Satanism, devil worship, ESP, UFOs, numerology, good luck charms, crystals, TM, Eastern religions, "mind" cults and Gnostic mystery religions show the effectiveness of the NAM.

We must look beyond the surface to the underlying concepts, political goals and programs of the NAM. We must not spend too much time on nut-cases or con-artists. The NAM is far more serious than gurus, Zen-masters, and psychics ripping off the gullible and the naive. The success of the NAM constitutes a clear and present threat not only to the Church but also to the nation. We must look beyond its Surface Sensationalism to its Underlying Concepts, Goals, and Programs.

I. The Terminology of the NAM.

A.   The NAM is Not "NEW" in the sense of not previously known. The concepts of the NAM are very old. The same ideas and practices were called the occult or witchcraft not too long ago. For example, what once was called "mediumship" by a "witch" is now called "channeling by a psychic friend."

B.   "New" as opposed to "Old:"

Age of Pisces	Age of Aquarius
The Old	The New
Christianity	New Age Movement

C. "New AGE" in the sense of an idealistic utopianism: the belief that history is moving toward an ideal age in which harmony and peace will prevail over all the earth. This was originally a biblical concept involving the Return of Christ, the Resurrection and Judgment Day. But instead of Jesus making a "new heavens and a new earth," the NAM says man will bring it about by his own powers.

Utopianism	
Christian	**Humanistic**
Jesus at His return to earth.	Man will bring it about.

Humanistic Utopianism	
Secular	Religious
Materialistic	Spiritualistic
Marxism	NAM
Dialectic	Event/evolution

Both Marxism and the NAM are Christian heresies in this sense.

II. What is the NAM?

It is a religious form of Humanism: the belief that man is the measure of all things and thus the Origin and Judge of truth, justice, morals and beauty. Man is his own "god" literally or figuratively.

Humanistic Utopianism	
Secular	Religious
No God	No God
No absolutes	No Absolutes
Autonomy	Autonomy
Subjectivism	Subjectivism
Materialism	Spiritualism
All is matter	All is mind
Rationalism	Mysticism
"Science"	Parapsychology
Anti-Christian	Anti-Christian

III. The NAM is religious atheism:

It denies the existence of an infinite/personal God who exists outside of and independent of the universe.

IV. The NAM Misuses the word "God."

The NAM takes the word "God" and applies it to the universe. The problem with this is that the attributes of the universe and God are opposites.

God	The Universe
Infinite	Finite
Eternal	Limited by time
Omnipresent	Limited by space
Omnipotent	Limited in power
Omniscient	Limited in knowledge
Sovereign	Limited in control
Immutable	Mutable
Perfect	Flawed/imperfect
Good	Evil/good
Independent	Dependent

V. The NAM's solution:

It denies the existence of the universe! The world we see around us is an illusion! Our body does not exist. Evil does not exist. Pain, sickness and death are all illusions! We are not limited or finite in any way. "Mind" or "consciousness" is all that really exists.

VI. The NAM's worldview leads to:

A. solipsism, egoism, selfishness

B. no concern, compassion or help for the sick, handicapped, old or dying. The NAM does not build hospitals or nursing homes.

VII. When did the NAM begin?

It began in the 1950's with J. B. Rhine. It became popular in the 1960's and led to drugs, rebellion, the Beatles, Gurus, free sex, Cayce, Dixon, cults, ESP, etc.

VIII. Why did it become popular?

A. The failure of secular humanism to provide a materialistic basis for truth, justice, morals or beauty. Man was reduced to an animal, machine, a meaningless accident in a backwater without dignity/worth/meaning.

Man → a dog

B. Because of the failure of secular atheism, many '60s humanists became religious atheists. Example: John Denver.

C. Humanism has always swung between two poles:

materialism	**spiritualism**
"man is a dog"	"man is a god"

D. Humanism is doomed to swing back and forth because it is reductionistic, i.e., man is reduced to only one element: body/mind, matter/spirit.

E. When humanism is the dominant world view in any culture, the culture swings back and forth from materialism to spiritualism.

Ancient Greece	
Materialism	Spiritualism
Heraclitus	Parmenides
Matter	Mind
Empiricism	Mysticism
Aristotle	Plato

19th Century	
Early:	Late:
Materialism	Spiritualism

20th Century	
Early:	Late:
Materialism	Spiritualism

F. The popularity of humanistically based religions depends on whether the culture is in a materialistic or spiritualistic phase.

Popular Forms of Materialism	
Secular	**Religious**
Atheism	Neo-orthodoxy
Agnosticism	Paul Tillich
Skepticism	"God is dead"
Marxism	Soul sleep
Anti-Miracle	Annihilationism
Anti-ESP	SDA
Anti-God	WT
Rationalism	Armstrong

Popular Forms of Spiritualism	
Secular	Religious
ESP	Spiritualism
Parapsychology	Occult
SPR	Witchcraft
Psychics	NAM

G. This explains WHY the NAM is so popular at this time. Western humanistic culture is swinging toward its spiritualistic pole.

IX. **Only when a culture is dominated by the Christian worldview does it escape from both materialism and spiritualism.**

The Biblical Worldview	
Reality is matter/visible	Spirit/invisible
Man is body/flesh	Mind/spirit

X. **The NAM will lose its popularity when the culture swings back to its materialistic pole.**

Psychism always becomes boring. The rip-offs, con-games and frauds run it into the ground. You can only pretend that "There is no pain" until you are in pain! To say "There is no death" never stopped anyone from dying! Ex.: Mary Baker Eddy. The mere act of stubbing one's toe tends to vanquish all claims to divinity! When you have kids you find out that you are not omniscient or omnipotent. Is it any wonder that the NAM is primarily composed of affluent singles!

XI. How wide spread is the NAM?

It has invaded every area of society and has thousands of organizations in an international network:

religion	sports	music	sales
science	psychology	art	business
education	cartoons	movies	police
military	medicine	politics	UN

XII. Is the NAM dangerous? Yes!

1. It is psychologically damaging.

2. It is socially worthless.

3. It is financially disastrous.

4. It is scientifically fraudulent.

5. It is spiritually delusive.

6. It is biblically satanic and demonic.

XIII. Why should we be concerned?

The goals of the NAM call for the destruction not only of the Church but also the nation. In search of its monistic ideal of "ONENESS," the NAM wants three things:

A. **A ONE-WORLD GOVERNMENT** run by a charismatic leader trained in the occult arts of psychism. The NAM names Hitler as their first attempt! The U.S. constitution must be destroyed. The UN must take over.

B. **A ONE-WORLD RELIGION** run by a NEW AGE CHRIST who will be forced on all religions. There will be NO FREEDOM OF RELIGION.

C. **A CENTRALIZED CONTROL** of money, food, goods, jobs and births. If you do not accept their one-world government or religion, you will be denied money, food, jobs, goods and the right to have children. "Illegal" babies will be murdered as in Communist China. People who resist "re-education," i.e., NAM teaching, will be denied work. There will be no human or civil rights: No freedom of religion, speech, assembly or of the press!

THIS IS THE DARK SIDE OF THE NEW AGE MOVEMENT.

XIV. Our greatest fear:

The NAM is the final fulfillment of the biblical prophecies about the anti-Christ and the end of the world. What is scary is that there is a direct correspondence between the biblical anti-Christ and the NAM!

A. NAM doctrines: I John 2:18-23; 4:1-4; II John 7-11; II Thess. 2:1-5.
B. NAM miracles: II Thess. 2:9-12; Rev. 13:12-15.
C. NAM goals: A one-world government and religion dedicated to the destruction of the Bible and Christianity: Rev. 13:3-18.

The so-called "Green Movement" and so-called "Global Warming" heresy are examples of humanistic anti-Christian worldviews that have nothing to do with reducing pollution or protecting the earth. They are politically motivated attempts to justify the redistribution of wealth by stealing it from those who worked hard to earn it and giving it to those who will not or cannot work. We deal with the Christian view of the earth and society in the book, *The Bible, Natural Theology and Natural Law: Conflict or Compromise?* (www.faithdefenders.com).

CONCLUSION

Since the essence of Humanism is rebellion against God, it has always sought to destroy the people and worship of God. Be it materialistic Marxism in the Communist World or the spiritualistic New Age Movement in the West, the Church faces its greatest challenge today as it proclaims the Gospel to a lost and dying world.

CHAPTER TWENTY-SEVEN

Biblical Evangelism

Elymas the Sorcerer is struck blind before Sergius Paulus (Roman Proconsul). Apostle Paul was preaching the Gospel of Christ to the Roman Proconsul and Elymas was opposing Apostle Paul (Acts 13). Painting by Raphael from the Raphael cartoons (1515).

God's Goal-Matthew 16:18

I. God wants His church to grow (Dan. 2:35; Matt. 13:32; Acts 2:47).
II. True church growth is by conversions, not by transference.

The Problem: Too many Christians follow tradition instead of Scripture. Jesus clearly laid down the law that whenever tradition was in conflict with the Bible, the Bible must always win: Matt. 15:2, 6, 9.

EVANGELISM

QUESTION	TRADITION	THE BIBLE
Who?	The pastor is supposed to do it.	Every believer and every member (Matt.28:18-20; Acts.1:8; 8:1-4; I Thess. 1:7-10).
Why?	He is paid to do it. It is his job.	Christ commands all His disciples to reproduce themselves by converts (Matt. 28:19).
Where?	Within the walls of the church buildings by the pastor in his sermons.	Outside the walls of the church building in homes, at work i.e.,

		everywhere (Acts. 2: homes; 8: roadside; 16: marketplace).
The people's responsibilities?	Invite sinners to church to hear the pastor's sermon.	To lead sinners to Christ and to disciple them in the things of God (Matt. 28:19, 20).
The pastor's responsibilities?	To make the church grow.	To equip the saints that they will make it grow (Eph. 4:11-13).
If few are converted?	The pastor is at fault. Trade him in for a new man.	The people are at fault if the pastor has taught them the truth.
Origin and motivation?	The duty, responsibility	Maturity and growth

	and salary of the pastor.	(Eph. 4:15-15; Heb. 5:11-14; I Pet. 2:1-3). (Eph. 4:11-13).
How is it to be carried out?	The pastor is to preach, teach and visit.	The believers are to witness, teach and visit (Acts 8:4; Matt 25:34-40; James 1:27; 2:14-26).

SUMMARY

The goal of the church's evangelistic program is to equip all believers to be faithful evangelistic priests. While the word "preaching" is almost always used to describe the evangelistic activities of all believers, the church's primary responsibility is summed up in the New Testament by the word "teaching."

While sinners are called to receive Christ as an aspect of the teaching ministry of the Church, evangelism is not the "Alpha and Omega" of the mission of the Church. Evangelism needs to be viewed as a responsibility of all Christians and not just the task of "paid" professionals.

CHAPTER TWENTY-EIGHT

The Missionary and the Poor

**Food distribution to poor people in Galicia (Sanok), Poland
by Jan Gniewosz (10/24/1847)**

When a Western missionary goes to a Third World country, one of the first things that creates an enormous cultural shock is the visible presence of the poor. Robert Kreider relates his experience.

> We visited the Bihari refugee camp on the edge of Dacca, Bangladesh. Three hundred refugees live together in an area no larger than a small basketball court. As we entered the area, dozens of thin, but bright-eyed, curious children crowded around to see, to touch, to

hear. Adults came up and angrily tried to chase them away. Approached by beggars on the ferry boat, in the street, literally everywhere, we were haunted by the admonition of our Lord: "Give to him that asketh." The hundreds of people sleeping on the concrete floor of Hawrath Railroad Station in Calcutta evoked the image of the Son of Man having no place to lay His head.

We saw people carrying enormous loads on their heads and backs and heard the Scriptural Injunction: "Bear ye one another's burdens." And in noting others carrying heavy loads from a yoke borne on the shoulders, we remembered Christ's words: "Take my yoke upon you."[57]

The sadness at seeing the poor and the sick everywhere is soon overwhelmed by a sense of utter helplessness. What can one missionary do to help the poor and the sick? Should he spend his time organizing relief programs? Should he petition the national government to redistribute the wealth in that society? Should he give away his own food and clothing? What should he do?

The obvious but hard answer is that Christ did not call him or her to fight poverty per se, but to preach the Gospel. One person cannot solve all the problems of the poor. As soon as he has met the needs of a few, the many come looking for what has already been given away. To put it bluntly, there are too many poor for poverty to vanish from the face of the earth. Did not Jesus say, "Ye have the poor always with you" (Matt. 26:11)?

The utopian dream of a world free of hunger, poverty and injustice is one of humanism's optimistic leaps into the dark. The Bible tells us that poverty and injustice will continue as long as sinners live on earth. Only at the Second Coming of Christ shall a new earth be created where there will be no place for sorrow, death or pain.

Even though biblical Christians do not entertain vain utopian hope and dreams, they have done more to erase poverty, hunger and injustice than any other force in history. Those nations that embraced biblical Christianity during the Reformation have developed the highest living standards and the freest societies on earth. The sociological benefits of having a Reformation basis or background have been pointed out by Dr. Lorraine Boettner.[58] He demonstrates that a nation's religion will affect its standard of living.

India's problems are not rooted in having too many people. Other countries, such as Holland, have more people per square mile than India! India's problems are rooted in its false religion. Its poverty and starvation flow out of its Hinduism. Her religion is the greatest hindrance to her prosperity.

The same can be said for Latin America's ignorance and poverty. Such things flow out of Roman Catholicism. A nation's religion will directly affect its living standard. That Reformation countries have highest literacy rates is the fruit of the Reformation.

This is why those who are concerned with the poverty and injustice on the mission field feel that the greatest need in the Third World is a massive turning to Reformation Christianity. Only upon this base could these nations overcome poverty and injustice, as did the Western Protestant nations. Without a Christian basis, a Third World country may be doomed to international panhandling (i.e. foreign aid).

Thus, the Gospel missionary who feels with the poor will realize that salvation is what Third World people need most of all. The Gospel will do more for the poor than bread, clothing or bullets. Did not Jesus say that He came to "preach the Gospel to the poor" (Lk. 4:18)?

Jesus did not build houses for the homeless or overthrow governments by violence. He knew that the root of injustice could be cured only by the preaching of the Gospel; for wherever the Gospel is received, there follows godliness, cleanliness and prosperity.[59]

Even though a religious and moral explanation of the Third World's poverty is obvious, the non-Christian world (including the World Council of Churches) is furious at even the slightest suggestion that biblical Christianity produces a superior lifestyle and standard of living. In an age in which the World Council of Churches is trying to convince everyone that all religions are one, the superiority of Christianity over the pagan religions is absolutely rejected as not even being a consideration.

The non-Christian community, in league with the World Council of Churches and Marxist ideology, has sought to place the full blame of the world's poverty and injustice on the Western countries and, in particular, the United States. The Marxists reject religion and morals as being the explanation of the ills of this world and, instead, point to world economics. One non-communist but Marxist-influenced church leader put it this way: 10,000 persons died today because of inadequate food. One billion people (more than one fourth of all persons living today) are mentally or physically retarded because of poor diet. The problem, of course, is that the world's resources are not evenly distributed. We in the West are an affluent island amid a sea of starving humanity. North America, Europe and Australia have only one fourth of the world's population, but they greedily consume one half of the world's available food. The average income per person in India is about $70 per year; in the U.S. about $4,000. We now have almost 60 times as much as our brothers over there and the difference will continue to widen.[60]

Such people evidently assume that a "redistribution of wealth" is the answer to poverty. This is an old Marxist theory that has never worked even in communist countries. It is interesting to note that those people who talk about "redistributing wealth" never distribute *their* wealth. They always want us to give away what we worked hard for while they continue to be the idle rich. Jane Fonda, the Kennedys and many other idle rich come readily to mind as an example. Until they "redistribute" all of their wealth, their words are hollow.

Harold B. Kuhn points out the Marxist thinking behind much of the "liberation theology" being developed in Latin America.

Latin liberation theology appeals largely to Marxist models. This accounts for its simplistic assumption that all human ills grow out of the misdoings of one class, which is regarded as the bearer of all evil. In the radical form of this theology, North American capitalism is seen as the sole cause of injustice and misery in Latin America. Its advocates can thus easily adopt the myopic stances of the United Nations World Population Conference in Bucharest and the World Food Conference in Rome, both held in 1974, and close their eyes to the problems raised by burgeoning populations and tradition-hindered ways of agriculture. This is a source of great confusion.[61]

Anyone who understands the doctrine of total depravity or human psychology knows that if all the wealth of the world was redistributed, within one year there would once again exist the poor, the middle class and the rich. Some people will not work and are addicted to poverty. Others are unscrupulous and will heap dishonest wealth to themselves. Others will prosper through honest toil.

Of course, when Marxist-influenced missiologists, theologians and politicians began screaming about "the American fascist capitalist pigs" who are single-handedly responsible for the poverty and injustice in this world, they completely ignore the fact that communism generates immense poverty and injustice through its totalitarian denial of basic human rights.[62]

Are we then to do nothing for the poor? No, we are not saying that. Just because the Gospel gets to the heart of the problem because it deals with the hearts of the people is no excuse for individual Christians and churches not to do what they can to help the poor, heal the sick and feed the hungry.[63] The Gospel has the first place but not the only place.

Ministering to the poor in material things is a handmaid to the Gospel. Missionaries have always done what they could to raise the living standard and lengthen the life-expectancy of the people to whom they ministered. Even though they have been accused of being "culture- busters," they have done for the Third World what it could not do for itself. In the past, missionaries have helped people climb out of their poverty by teaching them better agricultural techniques. Mission hospitals and schools were built to deal with body and mind. Even things like concrete factories or exporting of native art objects have been developed by concerned missionaries. The half has yet to be told of all the wonderful and tremendous things that fundamental

Bible-believing missionaries have done to raise the living standards of the poor for the cause of Jesus Christ. The love and compassion of Jesus moved missionaries in the past and will move them in the future to take pity on the poor and the oppressed.

What definite steps have missionaries taken to deal with the poor?

Step No. 1: They have won disciples to Jesus Christ and planted local national churches. As Arthur Glasser put it: "There is but one acid test that should be applied to all activities that claim to represent obedience in mission. Do they or do they not produce disciples of Jesus Christ?"[64]

Step No. 2: They have worked with these disciples in developing proper attitudes and skills that will help them become self-supporting. Why work with Christians and not just non-Christians at large? The Bible tells us to do good "especially to those of the household of faith" (Gal. 6:10).

Biblical Christians reject the present popular doctrine of universalism, which is the motivation of most of the World Council of Churches projects. Some have assumed that the poor and the oppressed belong to the church or that all men are the children of God.[65]

Kuhn points out:

> One peril that shows through the literature of liberation theology is an uncritical use of the biblical models. The major model currently in use is that of the Exodus. Rather too easily, in my opinion, Latin American theologians assume that today's oppressed people are the heirs of God's Exodus—that they are the present-day counterparts of the Israelitish people in Egypt. Attempts to domesticate God have not been particularly successful in the past and there is little reason to suppose that this current form will be any more effective. It is precisely this form of idolatry that

343

emerges as any group assumes for itself a "people of God" role. It is disturbing that liberation theologians do not give more attention to building a set of common values and adequate symbols among their peoples. Without these, any liberation by violence will probably lead only to a change of oppressors. Mere oppression neither makes any people to be "the people of God" nor guarantees that a victory by force will produce lasting liberation. A second peril grows out of the first. Some liberation theologians suggest that the Exodus is a model by which all oppressed peoples, regardless of their plight, find deliverance from their miseries. It may be questioned whether the Bible can be used indiscriminately to justify all political and economic struggles. A third peril lies hidden in the rationale advanced for this position. Hugo Assmann, Gustavo Gutiérrez and Juan Luis Segundo, may be regarded as a spokesman for Latin liberation theology, highlights this aspect of the problem. In his Theology for a Nomad Church, Assmann makes clear the movement's assumption that the purely "Salvationist" understanding of the Christian mission has been rendered obsolete by what Guitiérrez calls "the unvarnished affirmation of the possibility of universal salvation."[66]

Step No. 3: Once the national church becomes self-supporting and self-ruling, it can begin its own deaconate ministry in which it will attempt to meet the needs of its own community. The nationals can become involved in political appeal and in the struggle to overcome injustice. The missionaries should be a moral force only and not political activists.

Poverty can be overcome, not by theft, which is the true meaning of the "redistribution of wealth", but by Third World people becoming Reformation Christians.

CHAPTER TWENTY-NINE

A Biblical Political Science

The great Oliver Cromwell (04/25/1599 – 09/03/1658) between two pillars as Lord Protector—Cromwell was a Puritan who defeated the corrupt Charles I with his army of godly Puritans, which included John Owen. (1658 Engraving.)

"What is the Biblical view of political science?" This question is particularly important today because state universities indoctrinate students with socialist or Marxist ideas that violate biblical doctrine. The Christian student who applies the Lordship of

Christ to all of life must understand and articulate the Christian view of political science in opposition to all the humanistic views that are dominant today.

The following material is merely an outline of a series of lectures on a Christian view of political science. It is hoped that it will provoke Christians to develop it further.

A Christian View of Government (the State)

The Christian world and life view is based upon Creation, Fall, and Redemption. When we apply Creation, Fall, and Redemption to the state, this gives us the Christian view of the state. I define, document, and define this view in my book, *When Is It Right To Fight?* (www.faithdefenders.com). This book is essential reading for any Christians studying political science and the right of revolution when Christians must overthrow the existing government by any means necessary.

Introduction: Six Foundational Biblical Principles:

Before we apply Creation, Fall, and Redemption to political science, there are six foundational biblical principles that put the issue in the scriptural context.

1. All authority resides in God alone. He is the Origin and Source of all authority. (Dan. 4:28-37; Matt. 28:18)
2. All human authority is delegated authority. "Delegated authority" means that God will hold the person or institution accountable to Him for the way they used the authority He gave to them (Rev. 20:11-15).
3. It also means that no person or institution has absolute or intrinsic authority. They cannot do as they please (John 19:10- 11).
4. Delegated authority is valid only when it operates according to Scriptural guidelines and functions within Scriptural limits.

5. The Scriptures recognize four sovereign spheres of authority.

FAMILY	CHURCH	BUSINESS	STATE
Eph. 5:22-29 Eph. 6:1-4	I Thess. 5:12-13 Heb. 13:17, 24,	Eph. 6:5-9 I Pet. 2:18-19	Rom. 13:1-7 I. Pet. 2:13-17

6. While the spheres are interrelated and do interact with each other, they must not invade each other in the attempt to take over the authority or responsibilities that God delegated to other spheres.

The Lordship of Christ Over the State

I. The Creation

1. God is the Origin of the state, not man. The state is thus not a fluke of a meaningless chance-driven evolutionary process.
2. Human government is a Creation ordinance and was instituted by God in the Garden of Eden along with marriage for the benefit of mankind.
3. Human Government is part of God's plan for man.
4. The authority of the state is delegated and limited by God in Scripture (Rom. 13:1-7).
5. The functions and responsibilities of the state according to Scripture are found in such passages as Rom. 13:1-7; I Tim. 2:1-2; I Pet. 2:13-17, etc.

   a. To protect and promote the general welfare of the nation.
   b. To punish evil doers.
   c. To reward the good.

d. To promote unified cultural tasks.

e. To administer justice.

f. To implement just civil laws for the good of all.

g. To maintain peace, unity, and order in society.

h. To insure all civil rights for all citizens including religious freedom.

i. To protect the life of citizens including the unborn, the handicap, the infirm, and the elderly.

j. To safeguard the borders of the country against illegal immigration and invasions by foreign powers.

k. To provide for the poor who cannot care for themselves.

l. To punish those who abuse the welfare system.

m. To maintain an army to protect the nation from attacks by other nations.

n. To maintain local police and prisons to protect citizens from criminals.

o. To maintain national and state avenues of transportation for people, goods, and services.

p. To ensure that all citizens have the same access to the political process and can run for office.

q. To ensure that all citizens have equal standing before the law.

r. To protect citizens from terrorism by any means necessary.

Note: As an example of how God provided for the poor and needy, consult Lev. 19:9-10; 23:22; Deut. 19-22. The practical outworking of the biblical safety net is the Book of Ruth where two widows could glean the fields for food.

6. The right of private ownership is inviolate according to Scripture. The Ten Commandments condemn stealing. Theft happens when someone takes or uses your personal property without your permission. The state and the church do not have any right to confiscate your private property (1

Kings 21:1-10; Acts 5:4).

II. The Fall

1. The Fall explains the origin of totalitarianism, socialism, communism, fascism, and all political systems that violate the inalienable rights given by God to all human beings.

2. Any government that violates the dignity and freedom of human beings is not ordained of God and can be overthrown by any means necessary. This was the theological basis of the American Revolution and explains why so many clergymen were at the forefront of that violent revolution.

3. The breakdown of government (i.e. anarchy) during which people do whatever they want, is condemned in Scripture (Judges 21:25; 1 Cor. 14:33).

4. The state is not to intrude into the other sovereign spheres and take over their authority or responsibilities.

    a. The state has no Scriptural authority to intrude into the sphere of religion. It must not choose the religion of its citizens. It cannot judge who can preach or what is to be believed. A Christian must rebel against the state the moment the state violates his religious freedom (Acts 4:19).

    b. The state has no Scriptural authority to intrude into the sphere of the family. It cannot make the father's headship illegal, make all children the wards of the state, or legislate against such disciplines as spanking.

    c. The state has no Scriptural authority over the education of children. The parents bear that responsibility alone. The parents can home school their children, put them into parochial school, a private school or a public school.

    d. The state has no biblical authority to intrude into the sphere of business by nationalizing and running all businesses. Neither should the state forbid private ownership or enterprise. The more the state interferes with and regulates the business community, the poorer the economy and the lower the living standards become. Socialism has always been a disaster.

III. Redemption: The Responsibilities of Christians to the State.

A. To recognize the priority of their heavenly citizenship over their earthly citizenship (Phil. 3:20; Heb. 11:13-16). Versus:
   1. Blind nationalism is anti-Christian.
   2. National racism is anti-Christian.
   3. Militaristic Imperialism is anti-Christian.
B. Pray for the leaders (I Tim. 2:1-2).
C. Pay taxes (Rom. 13:6.)
D. Show respect to officials (Rom. 13:7; I Pet. 2: 17).
E. Obey all valid laws (I Pet. 2: 13-17).
F. Support "law and order" (I Tim. 2:2).
G. Work for freedom (religious rights, civil rights, etc.).
H. Work for justice for the oppressed (widows, orphans, etc.)(James 1:27)
I. Obey ordinances (salute flag, etc.) (I Pet. 2: 13).
J. Put righteous people in office by getting involved in politics (voting, campaigning, etc.).
K. Use all available legal means to secure freedom or protection (Acts 22:25-29; 25: 11).
L. Preach the Gospel to leaders (Acts 24: 1-27).
M. Be involved in the defense of your country when it is involved in a just war. (Judges 2: 16; 3: 12-30).
N. Be prepared to overthrow an evil government or alien power who takes over your country. When a state no longer functions according to Rom. 13:1-5, that government is no longer ordained of God. This is particularly relevant when a government persecutes the church. A Christian as a good citizen will have to revolt against corrupt governments. Examples:

- Reformation wars by Christians

- Attempted Assassination of Hitler by Christians
- Freedom movements in communist countries.
- Civil rights and women's rights in US history.

Conclusion

Christ has the preeminence over all things, including the state. Thankfully, Christians in America still have equal standing before the law and equal access to the political system by running for office or voting. Thus there is no biblical justification for Christians to engage in acts of violence against the government or citizens of this nation. There is no biblical justification for the murder of abortion doctors or blowing up family planning clinics.

As Francis Schaeffer pointed out, if any country denies the civil liberties of Christians, those Christians have a moral obligation to overthrow that government by any means necessary. This particularly applies to Christians suffering in Muslim and socialist countries. We should help them overthrow all despotic regimes that persecute the church. Dr. Peter Hammond's work in Africa is a modern example of how to help Christians overthrow political leaders that persecute Christians. (Dr. Peter Hammond is a missionary serving persecuted churches in Africa and the Director of *Frontline Fellowship* located at https://www.frontline.org.za/.)

**Picture above: *The western front of the United States Capitol.*
The Neoclassical building is located in Washington, D.C. on top of Capitol Hill at the east end of the National Mall. The Capitol was designated a National Historic Landmark in 1960.**

Picture below: *The coat of arms of the United States of America.*

Note: Beware of the phony *left* vs. *right* dichotomy of Democrats and Republicans in the United States Congress and Presidency. Yes, there are some real differences when it comes to social issues and the 2nd Amendment (see *When Is It Right To Fight* radio interview on " RemantXRadio" in 2015 based on my book with the same title above that shows biblically that Christians can defend themselves with firearms and refutes the false doctrine of pacifism; listen to the 4 part audio interview series on *Faith Defenders* website located at http://www.faithdefenders.com). However, the deception takes place when a so-called *conservative* or a so-called *liberal* is running for office and is funded by the same powerful globalists/one-worlders who support so-called free trade agreements such as *North American Free Trade Agreement* (NAFTA) that was passed by a Republican Congress and signed by President William J. Clinton (Democrat & 42nd U.S. President: 1993 - 2001) on 12/08/93 and took effect in 1994. Free trade agreements such as NAFTA have decimated the base of American manufacturing by off-shoring jobs and factories that resulted in the importation of cheap foreign-made products—a free trade agreement is trade regulated by unaccountable regional government bodies that operate outside of the American judicial system; the free trade agreements are used by the global elite as stepping stones for a socialistic global government under the United Nations.

It should be mentioned that President Donald J. Trump (Republican & 45th U.S. President: 2017 - present), an honorable man, also opposes these so-called free trade agreements, the "Deep State" and is anti-globalist.

The *Trans-Pacific Partnership* (TPP) is another example of a bad trade agreement proposed for America and the passage of the *Trade Promotion Authority* (TPA) in 2015, which relinquished what is constitutionally, under Article II, Section 2, Clause 2, Congress' power to provide advice and consent to the president in order to make treaties—TPA relinquished this power to the executive branch. Any political candidates that support these trade agreements are controlled by the globalists.

The globalists/one-worlders also promote *illegal immigration* (no borders), *exploiting the poor* (slave labor), *unjust wars* (see my book *When Is It Right To Fight*), *the Federal Reserve* (a private bank), *Carbon Taxes, UN Agenda 21/Sustainable Development, Common Core* (besides dumbing down our students, it is an integral part of UN Agenda 21), *Worldwide Internet Censorship*, which would occur under TPP, *Social Justice* (code word for Anti-Americanism, Anti-Christian positions such as abortion, same-sex marriage, etc.; there is no moral cause) and so on.

In addition, the globalists want the *confiscation of firearms* and *mass migration of Muslim jihadists* into Europe and the U.S. to destroy *Western Culture & Christianity* (see my book *Islamic Invasion*). In reference to the *confiscation of firearms*, Democide (Murder by Government) always preceded gun control and gun confiscation. Dr. Rudolph J. Rummel (October 21, 1932 – March 2, 2014) was professor emeritus of political science at the University of Hawaii and estimated that there were over 262 million people murdered by their own governments in the 20th century (see his book *Death By Government*); for further information on the "Second Amendment," see *New Jersey Institute for the Advancement of Truth (NJIAT)* located at http://www.njiat.com/second-amendment.html.

Also, the globalists were able to pass into law dangerous bills that undermine our American Republic such as the *USA PATRIOT Act* (a violation of the 4th Amendment) that was signed into law by President George W. Bush (Republican & 43rd U.S. President: 2001 – 2009) on 10/26/01 and was extended by President Barack Hussein Obama II (Democrat & 44th U.S. President: 2009 – 2017), who signed the *PATRIOT Sunsets Extension Act of 2011* into law. In addition, President Obama signed the *National Defense Authorization Act (NDAA)* into law on 12/31/11 for fiscal year 2012 (and continuously renewed since that time) that decimated the *Constitution* and *Bill of Rights* such as the *writ of habeas corpus* (a civil right so fundamental to Anglo-American common law history that it predates the Magna Carta) which is now voidable upon the command of the president of the United States; the 6th Amendment right to counsel is also revocable at his will.

Furthermore, the globalists that control large multinational corporations have adopted a *fascist political & economic ideology,* promote a one-world government via the United Nations and no longer believe in the *Constitution* and *Bill of Rights* and have no fear of God. They also promote and sponser the ungodly LGBT activist agenda. A God-fearing populist/patriot is always rejected. (For further information on "Politics & Economics" from a Christian perspective, see *New Jersey Institute for the Advancement of Truth (NJIAT)* located at http://www.njiat.com/politics.html & http://www.njiat.com/finance.html.)

CHAPTER THIRTY

Ten Campus Curses

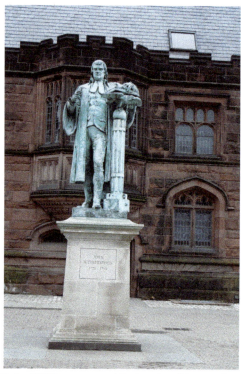

Statue of John Witherspoon at Princeton University (01/27/07)

Introduction

Why does the Christian Church lose 75 to 90 percent of its young people who go off to college? Even though they were raised in Christian homes, taken to church from infancy, and even sent to Christian schools, they often lose their faith after a year or two in college. Why? The main reason we lose so many students is to be found in the churches and Christian schools they attended. The thousands of students who lose their faith in college every year are the unpaid bills of the Christian Church and its schools. These students were not intellectually prepared to defend their faith. They were entertained - not educated.

When Christian students attend a state college or university, they will have to deal with ten campus curses. If they overcome these curses, they will continue steadfast, unmovable, always abounding in the work of the Lord.

I. The Bankruptcy of Ignorance (Hos. 4:6)

Christian young people have never been more ignorant of the Bible, theology, apologetics, and philosophy than today. They do not know what they believe or why they believe it. They do not know anything about doctrine. Why?
    a. Anti-intellectualism from the 1920s
    b. Anti-creeds/confessions/catechisms
    c. Anti-social/political concerns
    d. The search for personal peace
    e. Entertainment-centered services
    f. Baby-sitting youth ministries
    g. Stupid Sunday Schools (S.S.S.)

II. The Plague of Gullibility (1 Chron. 12:32)

Because we are sincere in our religion and tell the truth about what we believe, we assume that all other religious people have the same attitude. But Jesus warned us about religious deception (Matt. 7:15; 24:4, 5, 11, 24) and we are exhorted to be critical thinkers like the Bereans (Acts 17:11).

III. The Scourge of Cowardliness (Eph. 6:10-18)

We have raised a generation of wimps who will not stand up for the faith when it is attacked. They "give way" to ridicule and peer pressure. They often feel inferior and helpless in the face of evil. They whine and complain, and then flee to self-centered pietism. We need young men and women with backbones who will be strong for the Lord.

IV. The Insanity of Isolationism (1 Tim. 6:12)

Instead of viewing college as a wonderful opportunity to win sinners to Christ and to take over school offices, clubs, newspapers, and activities, and then use them to teach the Christian view of things, too many Christian students retreat into isolationism.

V. The Wickedness of Mediocrity (1 Cor. 10:31)

Too many students ask, "What is the least I have to do and still get by?" instead of striving to be and do the best they can for the glory of God. We don't need any more "balanced" people. What we really need are more fanatics for Jesus.

VI. The Cult of Popularity (Lk. 6:26)

Too many of our young people want everyone to "like" them. Thus, they do not stand up for Christ when push comes to shove. But Jesus warned that if everyone like us, this is not a blessing, but a curse!

VII. The Curse of Spiritual Apathy (Rev. 3:15-16)

We face an apathetic group of young people today. They are not interested in doing or learning anything concerning the things of God. They are neither hot nor cold, but lukewarm. They need to be on fire for God.

VIII. The Happiness Syndrome (2 Tim. 3:1-5)

One of the greatest curses today is that too many students are seeking after happiness instead of holiness. If you seek holiness, you will get happiness as a by-product. But if you seek after happiness, you will end up with neither.

IX. The Deception of Wealth (1 Tim. 6:9-10)

Everyone wants to enjoy the lifestyle of the rich and the famous. Personal peace and affluence is their god. There is no concept of sacrificial giving to the cause of Christ.

X. The Problem of False Assurance (1 John 2:19)

1 John 2:4 tells us that if someone says he is saved, but he is

living a disobedient life, he is a liar. Instead of confronting young people with the truth that they are probably on their way to hell, we make far too many excuses for them.

Conclusion

Young people need to be strong in the Lord and the power of His might; to stand alone and stand up for Jesus when all around oppose them. We need to go into the world as victors— not as victims; as overcomers—not underachievers.

PART TWO

CHAPTER THIRTY-ONE

Introduction to Apologetics

Apostle Paul in Athens (a.k.a. Mars Hill) refuting Greek philosophy & presenting the Gospel (the Apostle was not finding common ground, but "argued from Scripture," Acts 17) by Raphael (1515)

Christian apologetics is not the art of apologizing for being a Christian. Neither is it a special calling reserved only for a few Christian "intellectuals." Rather, it is an activity in which all Christians should be engaged in the normal course of their day to day witnessing for Christ in a world of unbelievers. All Christians have been commissioned by Christ and empowered by the Holy Spirit to be Christ's witness bearers (Matt. 28:19, 20; Acts 1:8). And one very vital and important aspect of witness bearing is the task of apologetics.

God's vision of what every Christian should be doing includes apologetics. Just as God envisions every believer as being "competent to counsel," even so He envisions every believer as being "competent to counsel," even so He envisions every believer as being "competent to defend the Faith" (Jude 3). The average believer must not rob himself or herself of the joyous task of apologetics by assuming that it is best to let "clerical George" do it. *All* Christians are called to this task. When this truth finally dawns upon the 21st century church, perhaps we shall recapture the aggressiveness of the Protestant Reformation.

While there are several good books on apologetics, few of them are simple enough for the average high school or college student. When you try to find something especially written for them, you run into great difficulty.

It is to this need that this book is directed in the hope that it will introduce the average Christian to the subject of apologetics and, at the same time, serve as a catalyst to spur him on to do further research on the subject. The first thing we should observe is that apologetics involves two different kinds of activities:

1. The *defensive* work of the believer is to defend the faith when it is attacked (Jude 3). The apostle Peter also states that our defense of the faith should not be sloppy but it should be an intelligent reply (1 Peter 3:15).

Example: An anti-Christian bigot made a public attack on Christianity by claiming that it is the cause behind the present ecological crisis (Lynn White, "The Historical Roots of our Ecological Crisis", Science, vol. 155, pp. 1203-1207, 10 March 1967). According to White, Christianity breeds disrespect for the environment and leads to the wanton destruction of the earth. Pollution is the result of the acceptance of Christian beliefs. This is a deliberate attack on the Christian faith.

My dear friend, Dr. Francis Schaeffer, accepted White's challenge and refuted his charges in his book, *Pollution and the Death of Man: The Christian View of Ecology*, Tyndale, House, Wheaton, 1970. Schaeffer demonstrates that biblical Christianity is **not** to blame for causing pollution.

2. The *offensive* work of the believer is to demonstrate that the

non-Christian philosophies and religions are false and that only Christianity answers the ultimate questions of life.

Example: After the bigot attacked Christianity by laying the blame for pollution on it, he then stated that the only way to deal with the crisis is to embrace the religions of the East and, in particular, the doctrine of pantheism. According to him, only by turning to Eastern religions such as Zen-Buddhism can we solve the present ecological problems.

Dr. Schaeffer also accepted this challenge and demonstrates in his book on pollution that the Eastern religions do not and, indeed, cannot give a sufficient basis upon which to deal with the present environmental crisis. Dr. Schaeffer goes on to prove that only biblical Christianity can provide a true basis for working out the environmental problems.

Thus Dr. Schaeffer did two things in his book. He *defended* Christianity and *defeated* the anti-Christian attack. Schaeffer was both negative and positive in his apologetics. Our goals in this study on apologetics are:

1. To survey briefly the many ways in which the various non-Christian systems or world-and-life views fail.

2. To put forth the different ways in which the Christian can challenge and refute non- Christian systems of thought.

3. To set forth several illustrations of how the Christian world-and-life view can be developed in various areas of life.

Discussion questions:

1. Are all Christians commanded by God to defend the gospel?
2. What should I do when my faith is attacked on campus or in the classroom?
3. Am I faithful in defending what I believe by showing why I believe it?
4. Is something true because I believe it?
5. Or should I believe something only if it is true?
6. What two activities comprise apologetics?

CHAPTER THIRTY-TWO

The Preparation of the Life

A Hunterdon Central High School Graduation held on the football field (Class of 1982).

"But sanctify Christ as Lord in your hearts, always being ready to make a defense to every man who asks you to give an account for the hope that is in you, yet with gentleness and reverence; having a good conscience" (1 Peter 3:15–16).

In the above passage we find not only the call to do apologetics but also the necessary preparation that apologetics requires, for we are told to "sanctify Christ as Lord" in our hearts before we can "make a defense." The sanctifying of Christ as Lord involves two things.

I. *Receiving Christ as the Lord of your life in terms of salvation.* In order to do Christian apologetics you must be a *bona fide* Christian. The issue of personal salvation is very important in apologetics for several reasons.

First, if the apologist is not saved, the Holy Spirit will not empower his witness with true boldness. Apologetics is then reduced to a mere intellectual debate. It becomes composed of mere words and will not be given or received "in power and in the Holy Spirit and with full conviction" (I Thess. 1:5).

Second the unregenerate apologist stands a good chance of being "converted" to the non-Christian position. Too many young people become excited about apologetics and end up losing their faith because their faith was actually an empty profession (I John 2:19).

Let the reader stop and ask himself, "Have I ever really received Jesus Christ as my own personal Lord and Savior? Do I see and do others see in my life definite clear-cut evidence that I am born again?" Self-examination is a biblical responsibility that is an absolute necessity for apologetics (2 Cor. 13:5).

II. Sanctifying Christ as Lord also involves *obeying Christ as the Lord of your life in terms of holiness.* Without holiness of life, the Christian will not be effective in witnessing no matter how "intellectual" or "airtight" his apologetics may be. Obeying Christ as Lord in the Christian life involves several things.

A. The Christian must deal with his own personal sins. He must not hide or rationalize them away. He must repent of and confess his sins or he will not prosper in witnessing (Prov. 28:13; I John 1:9). It is very important that the apologist should never engage in defending the faith until he has confessed his sins afresh to God. There must not be a single conscious controversy between the apologist and God because He will not hear you if sin is retained in the heart (Ps. 66:18).

B. The Christian who would do apologetics must consistently read the Scriptures, and constantly test his ideas by biblical truth in order to grow personally and to be guided in the ways of God.

C. The importance of prayer cannot be overstressed. The prayer-less Christian is the power-less apologist. Not only must you pray before you witness, but during and after the witness, prayer should be constantly ascending to God. It is good to ask God quickly for wisdom when handling any difficult questions (James 1:5–8). If you are engaged in a group effort at apologetics where any of the brothers or sisters are speaking, then constant prayer must be made for them while they present the Christian position. If they are not supported by prayer, it is not likely that many true conversions will follow.

D. There must be the preparation of a proper attitude before the believer can engage in apologetics. The apostle Peter said to defend the faith "with gentleness and reverence." As Paul states in II Timothy 2:23–26, refuse foolish and ignorant speculations, knowing that they produce quarrels. And the Lord's bond-servant must not be quarrelsome, but be kind to all, able to teach, patient when wronged, with gentleness correcting those who are in opposition, if perhaps God may grant them repentance leading to the knowledge of the truth, and they may come to their senses and escape from the snare of the devil, having been held captive by him to do his will. Christians must deal with the problem of pride because "God is opposed to the proud, but gives grace to the humble" (James 4:6). If the unbeliever senses that you are filled with contempt or an air of superiority, he will not listen to you.

E. Lastly, the apostle Peter also points out the necessity of a "good conscience." A good conscience is a clear conscience void of offense toward God or man (Acts 24:16). There cannot be any unresolved conflicts between you and God or between you and others. Clear your conscience by following the procedure laid out in Matthew 18:15–19 or Matthew 5:23–24. Seek to maintain a good conscience at all times. Boldness before others is rooted in maintaining a good conscience.

Discussion Questions:

1. When and where did I accept Jesus as my Lord and Savior?
2. Do I affirm Christ's Lordship over my life every day?
3. If I fail to defend my faith, is Jesus really the Lord of my life?
4. Is popularity on campus more important than obedience to Christ?
5. Do I fear the professor more than I fear God?
6. How important is the Lordship of Christ in my life today?

Pictures: Two Teenage Cousins on their Yamaha Motorcycles (1979)

Note: Two former Flemington, New Jersey residents (both cousins) had the skill and endurance to be professional *Motocross* riders—however, the Supreme Ruler of the Universe (Yeshua Ha-Mashiach) had different plans for them. They became *born again/born from above* Christians a few years later. Three pieces of advice from the cousins for young Christian students: (1) you should fear God; (2) learn sound doctrine to be able to discern false doctrine from true doctrine; and (3) study apologetics in order to defend the faith (Jude 3; I Peter 3:15). High school and college students will find *A Christian Student's Survival Guide* a true blessing—the cousins wish they had a book like this when they were students.

CHAPTER THIRTY-THREE

Two Ways to Defend the Faith

There are two major schools of apologetics: Biblical Apologetics and Natural Apologetics, sometimes called "Natural law" or "Natural theology." See my book, *The Bible, Natural Law, and Natural Theology: Conflict or Compromise?* (www.faithdefenders.com), for the documentation.

I. *What they have in common*: They both claim the same goals: to defend Christianity, to refute the non-Christian systems and to demonstrate that Christianity is the only valid way of living and believing.

II. Where they differ:

      1. They differ as to the *Origin* of their apologetics.

Simply put: Biblical apologetics begins from above with God as the Origin of truth, justice, morals, meaning, and beauty while natural apologetics begins below with man as the Origin of truth, justice, morals, meaning, and beauty. For the Biblical apologist, God is the measure of all things while for the natural apologist man is the measure of all things.

2. They differ as to the *method* they use to do their apologetics. The Biblical apologist understands that if you do not begin with God as the Origin and Measure of all things, "all is meaningless." It is impossible to base truth, justice, morals, meaning, and beauty on Rationalism, Empiricism, Mysticism or Fideism because they all collapse into the mire of relativism.

Most Natural apologists appeal to their own reason, feelings, experience, and faith as the ultimate standard of truth and morals. They look within themselves for truth. A few appeal to something called "Common Sense," which they never define, thus their apologetics is a waste of time. But they all pretend there are "universal, self-evident, intuitive" truths, laws or principles somewhere out there in "Nature," independent of and apart from God and His revelation in Scripture. But no one can define those terms. Not even the so-called "laws" of logic have any validity unless they are first grounded in the God who is revealed in Scripture.

III.   The Biblical apologists takes into account the following things:

1. The *person* who invented the worldview, religion or philosophy is the foundation of that system. For example, Buddha, Moses, Jesus, Muhammad, Joseph Smith, Marx, etc. are the founders of a worldview or religion. Is the founder worthy of your trust and commitment? Did he or she do what they told others to do? Were they a good moral example for your children to follow? If a founder is an immoral murderer and thief, why follow them? If they were hypocrites because they violated their own teachings and commandments, it would seem foolish to believe and obey them.

2. The *faith* that underlies the presuppositions needs to be

examined, for at the bottom of every system there is faith. Did the founder assume doctrines, rituals, and superstitions from his culture that are obviously in error today?

3.　We must examine the *presuppositions* that underlie a system and from which the concepts are developed.

4.　Next comes the *individual concepts* or *ideas* that make up the bulk or substance of the system.

5.　In the last section we come to the logical conclusion of the system, for if we are consistent, the system will take us somewhere. Where it will take us is the crucial question. Now that we have examined the diagram in general, let us apply it to typical non-Christian systems of thought.

The following are challenging questions that we have a right to apply to any system of thought. Thus they should be posed to each section of any non-Christian system of thought.

Discussion questions:

A.　*When we witness to an unbeliever, are we dealing with someone created in God's image with dignity and worth or only an animal as humanists claim?*

1.　This question deals with our attitude towards non-Christians. We should view them in love as being very important and significant to us because they are image-bearers.

2　This question reveals to us who they really are and what they know deep down in their heart of hearts. From Romans chapters one and two, we learn that all men know three immutable facts:

a.　That God exists (Rom. 1:18–25). This they see from the *creation* around them.

b.　That they are sinful creatures (Rom. 2:12–16). They experience guilt feelings when they do what they believe is wrong.

c.　Even though all men know the above by virtue of the image of God within them, Romans 1:18 states that all men "suppress" or "hold down" the truth in unrighteousness. Because of sin, men will deny what they know in their heart of hearts.

B. *Aren't we dealing with someone who is totally depraved as a result of Adam's fall into sin and guilt?*

1. *Intellectually*, the non-Christian will reject and oppose biblical Christianity because his heart is darkened (Rom. 1:21) and his mind is blinded by Satan (II Cor. 4:4). Thus, non-Christians are spiritually incapable of understanding the truth (I Cor. 2:14). The gospel is foolishness to them (1 Cor. 1:18). They suppress the truth that is in their hearts (Rom. 1:18).

2. *Morally*, they are wedded to their sins and they really do not want to repent of their sins. Did not our Lord Himself give us this very realistic truth in John 3:19–20? "And this is the condemnation, that light is come into the world, and men loved darkness rather than light, because their deeds were evil. For every one that does evil hates the light, neither comes to the light, lest his deeds should be reproved."

3. *Volitionally*, without the new birth, they cannot see, enter or receive the kingdom of God (John 3:1–5; 6:44) for in their hearts they actually hate God (Rom. 1:30; 8:7; John 3:20).

Example: The unbeliever's hatred of God is most visible when he curses using God's name whenever anything goes wrong. It is helpful at times to ask the unbeliever if he ever used God's name in vain. If truthful, he will answer in the affirmative. Then read Exodus 20:4–7, which shows that all sin is ultimately rooted in man's hatred of God.

4. *Sin renders man ethically insane or irrational*. Because of sin man will act at times just like a mindless unfeeling animal. *Example*: The biblical concept of man's depravity supplies us with the only way to understand the inhuman atrocities that Hitler committed against the Jews and that the Muslims now perpetrate against the Christians.

C. Isn't the real problem moral and not intellectual?

    1. True faith will not come through argumentation (II Tim. 2:23, 26).

    2. There is more than enough evidence on every hand from every department of human experience and knowledge

to demonstrate that Christianity is true. The light is shining and the music is playing but the non-Christian shuts his eyes and plugs his ears and then pretends that there is neither light nor sound.

3. Because the basic problem is moral, our approach must be given in terms of a confrontation. We need to confront sinners lovingly with the fact of their sin and boldly and authoritatively to proclaim repentance and faith. We must never believe or act as though Christianity is just one option among many. It is God's *only* answer to man's moral dilemma.

D. *Shouldn't the gospel be our main subject?*

Apologetics may prepare the way for, accompany or follow the gospel, but never let apologetics displace the gospel. Too often apologetics becomes an "ego trip" because the apologist is more concerned with winning the argument than with winning the person.

IV. Questions concerning the *faith* that underlies the presuppositions.

A. *Does this faith have any grounds in the world around us or in man himself? Is it subjective in its content as well as in its commitment?* The faith of the non-Christian is externally and internally groundless. They are the ones who leap into the dark. Some, like Kierkegaard, have admitted this. *Example:* The 21st century abounds with atheistic humanists who have a utopian faith about man's future. On every newsstand there are humanistic utopian science-fiction books that picture man as evolving into a love-filled creature who no longer makes war and where all mankind lives as one family without greed, crime, hatred or selfishness. There is manifestly no evidence for such utopian hopes in (1) man's nature or (2) in the history of the world.

B. *Isn't this faith ethically directed?*

1. We must emphasize that there is no neutrality-not even in science. Objectivity is a myth. Gordon Clark demonstrates this in his book, *Religion, Reason and Revelation*, Craig Press, Nutley, NJ, 1964.

2. Some anti-Christian concepts are believed simply because they are anti- Christian.

371

Example: Some scientists openly admit that they believe in the theory of evolution because *the only alternative is creation.* They admit that evolution as a theory has never been proven and that there is much evidence against it. Mathematically, Polini and others have proven that evolution is impossible. The M.I.T. computers have confirmed this to be true. Given up to six billion years, chance, and matter—what is the probability that the complex earth that now exists could have evolved to its present state by pure chance? The mathematical answer is zero probability. Here is one illustration that Polini developed to demonstrate the problem the evolutionists have to deal with. Imagine that as you travel into Wales by train, you see at the border on a hillside the words—"Welcome to Wales"—arranged out of white stones. It is more probable, statistically speaking, for those by stones by chance to pop out of the earth by themselves, by chance to develop a white exterior, by chance to roll together and spell out the words "Welcome to Wales" than it is for the evolutionary theory to be true.

V.   Questions concerning the *presuppositions.*

A.   *What are your presuppositions—assumptions—starting points? Example:* You meet a non-Christian who tells you, "I do not believe that Jesus arose bodily from the grave." It is obvious that the real problem behind this man's rejection of Christ's resurrection is his presuppositions. When you examine his presuppositions you find out why he rejects the resurrection. *Unless you deal with his anti-Christian presuppositions, all the evidence in the world will not convince him of the bodily resurrection of Jesus Christ. He assumes the following things.*

1.   The universe is a self-contained, closed system.
2.   Everything happens according to natural law and can be explained by natural law.
3.   No miracles or supernatural intervention are possible. Therefore, he concludes, the resurrection of anyone including Christ is impossible.

B.   *Are there common presuppositions that are generally shared by most non- Christian systems? Yes!*

1.   *Human Autonomy*: The assumption that man starting

from himself by himself without any outside special revelation can arrive at a true understanding of himself and the world around him with all the inter-relationships involved.

2. *Ontological Thinking*: The assumption that whatever is "thinkable" to you exists and whatever is "unthinkable" cannot exist. Reality corresponds to what you think it to be.

3. *Monism*: The assumption that ultimate reality is of one kind or essence of being, i.e., there is no qualitative difference between objects. Things differ only quantitatively in terms of a different arrangement of general being. Reality is viewed in terms of a scale of being.

VI. Questions concerning the *individual concepts* of the non-Christian system.

A. Are there any concepts here that are borrowed from the Christian system? Yes.

B. Are these concepts consistent with non-Christian presuppositions? No.

Example: You meet a non-Christian who believes in civil rights and in the dignity and oneness of mankind. You challenge his right to believe in such things because he has certain presuppositions that contradict these ideas. He assumes that the theory of evolution is true and that man is an animal who has fought his way to the top by the survival of the fittest. He rejects the biblical account of Adam and Eve. You press him until he admits that on the basis of his evolutionary presuppositions, the different races are probably different species of animals that evolved from different ancestral origins. Once he admits this, he must recognize that he cannot believe in the equality, dignity and oneness of mankind and believe in evolution at the same time.

C. Are these concepts consistent with each other? No.

Example: Sartre and the Algerian Manifesto (1960) are good illustrations of conflicting concepts. On the one hand, he believed that, since God did not exist, there was no infinite point of reference from which meaning could be given to particulars. Thus there are no absolute moral laws. On the other hand, Sartre signed the Algerian Manifesto, which was a protest statement against the Algerian War. It is obvious that you cannot say that God does not exist and that any war is wrong at the same time. Without God there is no day of judgment, no ultimate justice, and no ultimate standard for right or wrong. We do not have any sufficient basis to say that anyone is wrong or right and reject God at the same time.

D. Are these concepts coherent? Are they understandable as a whole and in their parts? No.

Example: When the pre-Socratic Greek philosopher Cratylus was asked what he believed, all he would do was wiggle his little finger. He would not speak a single word. Thus whatever he believed, it certainly was not comprehensible.

One friend was disturbed because, while he was high on certain drugs, he thought he was writing tremendous philosophical essays and composing brilliant pieces of music but when he was finally down and sober he always discovered complete confusion and incoherence. Reality demands coherence while fantasy can play around with the absurd.

E. Are these concepts cohesive? Do these concepts hang together? No. Example: A box of pearls do not manifest any order or meaning. But if we put them on a string, then they can become something meaningful like a necklace or a bracelet. In the same way, many people do not try to correlate their ideas. They simply pick up an idea here and there without any attempt to relate them to each other or to bring any cohesiveness to these ideas.

F. Are these concepts self-refuting? Do they carry within themselves the seeds of their own destruction? Yes.

Example: Hegel destroyed himself by his concept of the dialectic process of truth. If truth is not found at any point of the thesis-antithesis-synthesis process but is only found at the ultimate end of the process, then Hegel's own philosophy is not true because it is only a part of the dialectic process. If Hegel is right—he is wrong!

G. Can these concepts stand up to a rigorous exposure to the Law of Contradiction? No.

Example: Hegel logically established the Law of Contradiction when he denied it, for to deny anything you must use the Law of Contradiction.

H. Can those who hold to these concepts believe what they live and live what they believe? No.

Example: The famous modem musician John Cage believes that chance underlies reality. Therefore music should reflect this contingency. Yet, he picks mushrooms as a hobby. It is obvious that he would not live very long if he picked and ate mushrooms on the basis of chance. He cannot live what he believes.

I. Are these concepts verifiable? Do they correspond with what is there? Can we investigate the claims of these concepts? No.

Example: Behaviorists claim that "man is a mechanized animal and everything he does is predetermined, by chemical and environmental factors." This concept of determinism is set forth by many modem scientists. Yet, this theory does not correspond with the evidence.

1. We can point to art since machines and animals do not produce art.
2. Others point to the lack of factual evidence for determinism.
3. Others point to psychological evidence that proves that man is not a machine and that man is ultimately free.

VII. Questions concerning the *logical outcome* of the system.

A. *Where will this system ultimately take us if we follow it to its logical conclusion?*

In the Christian view of reality there exists God, angelic beings, man, animals, plants, and things. In the non-Christian system, once the biblical God is rejected there begins a destructive process that ultimately brings man down to the level of an impersonal object such as a rock or stone. For example, once we say, "God is dead," there is no reason to believe in angels, no reason to see man as unique and apart from the animals, no reason to separate animal life from plant life, and no reason not to look at all things including man merely as material objects that are either "useful" or "in the way" of the upward evolutionary process.

The destruction of hope, love, morals, meaning and

significance is complete once man is reduced to the level of a machine. The theories and actions of the godless communists must be understood in this light. When they murder millions of people who are in their estimation "unproductive" and "reactionary," they are just being consistent.

Clarification by way of diagram #1

There are two ways to sink a ship: torpedo it from below or blow it to pieces with guns from above. *The Presuppositionalists argue from "presuppositions." The Evidentialists argue from "evidences."* Both methods can be used to reach the same goal: defend Christianity, refute non-Christian systems and present the Gospel of Christ. Of course, as explained in this chapter, it is either Biblical Apologetics or Natural Apologetics. Natural Apologetics is a waste of time and unbiblical.

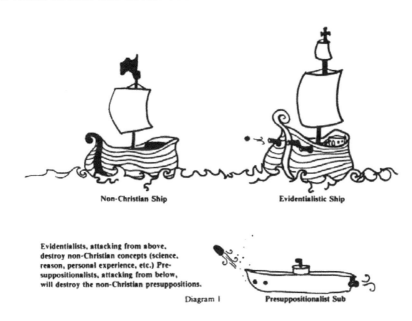

Non-Christian Ship

Evidentialistic Ship

Evidentialists, attacking from above, destroy non-Christian concepts (science, reason, personal experience, etc.) Pre-suppositionalists, attacking from below, will destroy the non-Christian presuppositions.

Diagram I

Presuppositionalist Sub

CHAPTER THIRTY-FOUR

The Christian World and Life View

Colosseum in Rome, Italy (1981)

I. Introductory Remarks
    A. Our goal: To review briefly the Christian worldview as given in Scripture.
    B. Importance: It is not only necessary to defend the faith (Jude 3) but we must intelligently explain it to others (I Peter 3:15).
II. Discussion:
    A. *The Person*
      1.Spiritual regeneration has taken place and now the person both sees and enters the kingdom of God (John

3:1–16).

2.The mind has been opened to understand Christianity in a unique way known only to believers (Luke 24:45).

3.The heart has been predisposed by the Spirit to receive the Christian message (Acts 16:14).

B. *The Faith*

1. The Christian faith is not a humanistic leap in the dark. It is not a leap into non-reason.

2. Faith is given by the Holy Spirit (Phil. 1:29; Eph. 2:8).

3. Faith is guided by the Holy Spirit (John 16:13).

4. Faith rests on the objective Word of God, the Holy Scriptures.

C. *The Presuppositions*

1. They are revealed in the Holy Scriptures and are found nowhere else.

2. According to the Bible, Creation-Fall-Redemption are the foundational presuppositions that make up the biblical world and life view. To understand anything correctly is to view it in the light of these basic truths of the Bible.

a. These truths are put first in the Bible because they are *foundational* to all that follow. Genesis 1–3 simply unfolds the three truths of Creation-Fall-Redemption.

b. *Thematically*, everything else in Scripture is a development of these three themes. In the Old Testament and in the New Testament we are constantly reminded of these three great events.

c. *Exegetically*, these three truths serve as spectacles or glasses through which we can understand and deal with present problems and issues. When Jesus dealt with the issue of marriage and divorce, He approached it in terms of what marriage originally was at the creation and thus "ought" to be. Then He looked at the issue from the perspective of the Fall, for sin explains why divorce was granted to man (See Matt. 19:1–6).

The apostle Paul used Creation-Fall-Redemption as the spectacles through which he could examine from the biblical perspective: (1) the respective roles and functions of male and female in the context of the home and in the church (I Cor. 11:3–12; I Tim. 2:12–14); (2) whether certain foods are "evil" and should not be eaten by Christians (1 Tim. 4:1–5); (3) why the creation is in a state of "groaning and travailing" and why the Christian has hope that the creation shall be delivered from the evil effects of Adam's Fall into sin (Rom. 8:18–23)..

D. *The Concepts*

1. Starting with the given presuppositions of Holy Scripture, we can develop the Christian position on many things in direct opposition to the opposing non-Christian concepts. In the following examples the Christian position is stated and then the opposing non-Christian concept is given.

a. From the presupposition of *creation*.

(1) The world was created out of nothing versus the eternity of matter or energy.

(2) The Creator-creature distinction versus all forms of monism.

(3) The reality of matter versus all forms of spiritualism.

(4) The reality of spirit versus all forms of materialism.

(5) The goodness of matter versus the evil of matter.

(6) The fact of divine order and plan behind the creation versus the concept of ultimate chance or contingency.

(7) Beginning with the personal versus beginning with the impersonal.

(8) Man as a unique creature created in God's image with singular dignity and importance versus man as an animal kicked up by some fluke of chance in the blind and meaningless evolutionary process.

(9) The oneness of humanity versus racism.

b. From the presupposition of the *Fall*.

Definition of original sin: Man's attempt to be autonomous and independent of God. Genesis 3 reveals that man was tempted on three levels: (a) metaphysical: Satan said, "Be what you want to be," (b) epistemological: Satan argued, "Know what you want to know," (c) ethical: Satan demanded, "Do what you want to do"

(1) The creation is now sub-normal versus the world is normal.

(2) Man is now sub-normal versus man is normal.

(3) Man's problems are rooted in the ethical and not in the

metaphysical versus man's problem is his humanity and his finiteness.

c. From the presupposition of *redemption.*
(1) Salvation is something initiated, planned, and accomplished by the triune God of Father, Son and Holy Spirit versus all forms of self- saving religions.
(2) Biblical salvation concerns individuals and sees to it that they remain and retain their own unique personality versus impersonalism and nihilism.
(3) Salvation is cosmic in scope versus soul saving only (Rom. 8:21; 2 Peter 3; Rev. 21).
2. The biblical world and life view meets all the tests of a valid system. The Christian concepts are:
a. Consistent with each other as well as being consistent with their presuppositions.
b. Coherent and cohesive.
c. Not self-refuting and self-destructive.
d. In full accord with the Law of Contradiction because the Law of Contradiction itself is based upon the biblical view of God's ontological nature. Since God cannot lie (Titus 1:2), the Law of Contradiction is an aspect of God's very being.
e. Verifiable and do, in fact, correspond with what is there.
f. Livable. The Christian is the only one who can live what he believes and believe what he lives. Everything in his life corresponds exactly to the biblical world and life view.

E. *The logical conclusion of the Christian system*
1. Ultimate meaning and significance for all things including man versus existentialism's meaninglessness.
2. Absolute ethical standards versus all forms of relativism and situational ethics.
3. Brings hope, love and life to light through the gospel of Jesus Christ versus ultimate despair.

CHAPTER THIRTY-FIVE

Applications of the Christian World and Life View

Tucson, Arizona (05/17/09)

The following applications are not intended to be exhaustive studies of any of the topics examined. The following examples are suggested outlines that illustrate how to apply the Christian perspective of Creation, Fall, and redemption to all of life. It is hoped that these illustrations will motivate others to do exhaustive treatments of important topics from the Christian perspective.

    I. A Christian View of Ethics

        A. In view of the creation of both the world and man

            1. Christian ethics is based upon the Creator-creature relationship.

                a. Man was created dependent upon God his Creator for all things.

b. Man was not created autonomous, i.e., independent of God and dependent only upon himself. He was not created to be a truth-maker or an ethic-maker. He was made to think God's thoughts after Him, i.e., to be a truth-receiver. He was made to be an ethic-receiver, i.e., to reflect ethically God's moral character as God's image-bearer.

c. All apostate ethical theories assume that man is autonomous. They assume that man can create or discover his own ethics by starting with himself and from himself and that man does not need any outside special word revelation.

2. The importance of pre-Fall special Word revelation

a. Since man was created dependent upon his Creator, it is not surprising to find that Genesis 1–3 reveals that *God spoke to man in words that man could understand.* God told Adam what man's task in life was and ethically what his duty was and what was forbidden. *From the very beginning of creation, man was dependent upon special word revelation for his ethics.* God spoke to man because God never intended man to make or discover his ethics solely from:

(1) general revelation

(2) the image of God

(3) his moral image (conscience)

(4) his reason or logic

(5) instinct or intuition

(6) insight into the situation that would reveal supposed "laws" of nature or creation "norms."

b. Apostate ethical theories either deny or ignore pre-Fall special Word revelation because they want man to be free from any supernaturally revealed absolute ethical standards. They base their ethics on the assumption that man can discover or create his own ethics apart from special revelation by looking to one, some or all of the six sources listed creation as knowing instinctively, intuitionally, or by insight into general revelation what his task in life was, and that he was not to eat of the tree of the knowledge of good and evil and that to eat of the other trees was ethically good. They attempt to free man from revealed ethical standards in order to establish human autonomy.

B. In view of the Fall of man into sin and guilt.

1. The Fall supplies us with the only valid explanation of the present ethical confusion and tension. The existence of sin, evil, death, war, pain, etc. can be and must be understood in terms of the historical Fall of Adam and Eve into sin.

2. The biblical doctrine of total depravity reveals that:

    a. Man is alienated from God's revealed ethical standards because he hates God and His law and will not submit to it and, indeed, he no longer has the spiritual ability to obey the law from the heart (Rom. 8:7–8).

    b. Man is now predisposed to choose the wrong, believe the false, and feel the evil and wicked (John 3:19–20).

    c. Man will seek to escape God's revealed ethics by:

        (1) rejecting the idea of revealed absolutes;

        (2) saying that God's law was only for the people to whom He revealed the law and that it has no bearing today on our ethics;

        (3) pretending that we can discover God's ethics by looking into the creation or the situation using the light of love and reason to reveal man's ethics. Some have pretended that God did not actually reveal the law to Moses by *talking* to Moses and by actually *writing* the law on the tablets with His own finger. But, rather, they say that Moses got the law by "insight" into the creation and into the situation in which he found himself. Thus we can discover ethics for today by "insight."

3. The Fall did not do away with God's revealed ethics for man. But, instead, it made necessary more and greater special revelation that would show man in detail how and in what ways he is to be an image-bearer of God. The moral law of God is simply God's revelation of the ethical aspects of His own being that man is to reflect. *Example*: Since God does not lie, man is told not to lie (Titus 1:2; Exod. 20:1.

4. Apostate theories of ethics usually assume the following things.

Major premise: What is, is normal.
Minor premise: What is normal, is right.
Conclusion: What is, is right.

The biblical truth of the Fall reveals the Fallacy of the major premise; for what is, is not normal, since what is, is not what once was; and neither is it what it shall be. What is, is not "right," for it is not what "ought" to be. "Oughtness" belongs to what man was at creation when he was perfect in righteousness, holiness, and knowledge. The "ought" and "right" of creation is the standard that judges and condemns what is now.

5. If man in the original creation needed special word revelation to give him his ethics, how much more does Fallen man need and depend upon God's special Word revelation—the Holy Scriptures! In the Bible we find moral absolutes that are binding on man the image-bearer at all times.

6. Apostate ethical theories that claim to be "Christian" will often state that special revelation was given only because and after man fell into sin. They tell us that man does not need special Word revelation as *man* but as *sinner*. But this is manifestly false because man as man was the recipient of special Word revelation from the very moment of creation. *The Fall into sin did not bring special revelation into being. Rather, it was the rejection of special revelation that brought the Fall into being* (Gen. 3:1–6). Satan's plan to tempt man to sin against God began by casting doubt on the absolute and universally binding character of God's revealed ethic for man. "Hath God said?" (Gen. 3:1).

7. The Fall makes necessary a full disclosure of man's sin. God's revealed law ethic for man has as one of its functions the driving of sinners to Christ for forgiveness. The law exists to show us that we are sinners in order to bring us to Christ (Rom. 3:20; 7:7; Gal. 3:24).

C. In view of redemption

1. Christ Jesus came and perfectly obeyed God's revealed law ethic for man in order to fulfill all righteousness (Matt. 3:15; 5:17; Gal. 4:4, 5). His obedience to the law is the basis of justification. Through union with Christ we are declared ethically perfect and without guilt (Rom. 5:1).

2. The Holy Spirit comes into the heart of the believer and causes him to love the law and to obey it from the heart. Love for God does not negate the law or substitute for it. Jesus said, "If you love me *you will keep my commandments*" (John 14:15; cf. I John 2:3, 4).

3. Redemption does not do away, with special word revelation but, instead, it makes greater and more detailed special word revelation necessary, for the gospel cannot be found in general revelation. True saving faith can come only through hearing the written Word of God, the biblical gospel (Rom. 10:17).

4. Apostate ethical theories that claim to be "Christian" will sometimes teach that redemption does away with revealed ethics and man is now to derive his ethics from his "insight" into the "laws" or "norms" in the given situation. The law of God is now supposedly supplanted by love. But this is manifestly false for redemption was not accomplished to make conformity to God's ethical or moral character no longer necessary as if man's purpose is no longer to bear God's image. Rather, redemption comes so that we may be recreated in God's image and conformed to the moral law that reveals how man may ethically reflect God's character in this world. Man was once perfectly conformed to God's ethic. The Fall made man a sinner who hates God's ethic and who seeks to set up his own ethical standards. Redemption comes to enable man to once again render perfect obedience to the law of God out of love (Rom. 8:4).

Note on Situation Ethics

1. While the Fallacy of situation ethics can be demonstrated by pointing out the anti- biblical presuppositions that underlie it and the invalid method of arguing from highly irrelevant stories and situations, the death blow to all forms of so-called "Christian" situation ethics is found in I Corinthians 10:13, which says that because God is faithful we will *never* find ourselves in a situation where we *must* sin but there will *always* be a way to escape. We never have to sin to make grace abound (Rom. 6:1). God never puts us in a situation or calls upon us to break one of His revealed ethical laws in order to keep another one of His laws. A Christian must never say or feel that he "must" or "ought" to break God's laws. The Bible does not teach that anyone in any situation "ought" to sin.

2. The situation ethics people will respond by trying to picture a situation in which they feel that they "must" sin because it is what they "ought" to do. Once the sin is viewed as a "must" and as an "ought," it is justified and magically transformed into being "good."

3. A Christian view of ethics will reject each of the constructed situations that the situational ethicist puts out because the situation described does not take into account several things.

a. God's sovereignty is not taken into account. Since no one knows the future and what God may do even in terms of extraordinary providence, no one can say that "unless you sin these people will die." God will always make a way for the people of God to escape sinning. His sovereignty guarantees it. God is still alive today.

b. The power of the Holy Spirit is never taken into account. The believer does not have to worry about what he would say if he found himself in any of the weird and highly unlikely situations that are put forward by situation ethics proponents because he has the promise of Jesus, "do not be anxious about how or what you will speak; for it shall be given you in that hour what you are to speak. For it is not you who speaks, but it is the Spirit of your Father who speaks in you" (Matt. 10:19–20). We are to "trust the Lord with all our hearts and lean not to our own understanding." As we do this in the area of ethics, as in all of life, we will find that "He will direct" our path (Prov. 3:5, 6).

  c. Even though God is faithful in making a way for us to escape sinning, the believer to his shame is not always faithful in using the escape and thus he sins. The believer is then directed by Scripture to seek forgiveness through the cleansing blood of Jesus (I John 1:7–2:2). But situation ethics never points you to the blood of Jesus Christ. Instead of leading men to the cross, situation ethics rationalizes the sin away. They seek to hide their sins by pretending that they "had" to sin or they did what was "necessary" and what "ought" to be done. Since the sin was "necessary," they are not really responsible! Thus God will not judge them for it. So why confess it? There is no place in situation ethics for the necessary blood atonement of Christ, the need to come before God for forgiveness or the pain of repentance and confession. Situation ethics is but one sad and tragic attempt of rebellious sinners to overthrow God's revealed ethic and to escape the judgment on the Last Day.

  d. Situation ethics is actually blasphemy because it pictures God as being either ignorant or stupid. God is ignorant in that He did not foresee that His laws would contradict each other at times and that His people would have to break one law in order to keep another. Or, God is stupid because He foresaw that His laws would contradict each other and that they would force His people to sin that grace may abound but He could not figure out any way to deal with the problem.

II. A Christian View of History

  We must begin by making the distinction between history and the study of history. History is the unfolding of God's plan; the study of history is man's attempt to record and interpret what has happened in the past.

  A. History

    1. *In View of Creation*

      a. History has a beginning and an end versus cyclical views of history.

      b. History is the unfolding of God's plan versus

history as an aimless and meaningless evolutionary process.

   c. History has ultimate meaning and significance since all history will glorify God versus history viewed in terms of meaninglessness, operationalism, utilitarianism, pragmatism, etc.

  2. *In View of the Fall*

   a. History reflects the chaos and crime of man's sin.

   b. History reflects the existence of evil (war, death, floods, etc.).

   c. History reflects the judgment of God upon man for his sin (the flood, Canaan, etc.).

  3. *In View of Redemption*

   a. a. God acts in history as a true agent versus the popular modern supra-history theories. Example: Karl Barth's salvation history theory.

   b. History is moving to a redemptive climax, for the world that now exists will be destroyed, and a new earth will be created versus the theory that the earth will continue as it always has.

   c. God orders history for the good of the elect (Rom. 8:28).

B. The Study of History

  1. Man as God's image-bearer can have a finite but true knowledge of history versus history as unknowable.

  2. The study of history is one of the sciences that covers all other sciences (history of math, history of society, history of economics, etc.).

  3. No science is objective or neutral. Therefore the study of history is guided by one's presuppositions.

  4. The study of history primarily concerns man as a culture-former in his reactions to God, his fellow man and the world around him. It includes God's intervention into human affairs.

  5. We must avoid all reductionistic historical methods. *Example:*

   a. Hegel reshaped history to conform to his thesis-antithesis synthesis model.

b. Communistic economic reductionism reshapes history into class struggles. c. Fall of Rome. What caused it? Typical reductionistic reasoning will ascribe Rome's fall to only one of the following causes:

(1) Political—pagans caused it.

(2) Economic—inflation caused it.

(3) Cultural—slavery caused it.

(4) Religious—Christianity caused it.

The Christian approach avoids the reductionistic thinking by stating that:

(a) Ultimately, Rome fell simply because God willed it (Dan. 4). God's sovereignty should be stressed.

(b) There were many things that God used to accomplish His plan. Thus some of the reasons given above are valid.

6. Moral judgments concerning people and their actions are possible only upon a Christian basis. *Example:*

a. Hitler was evil.

b. Greed drove the Spanish to explore South America for gold while religious persecution drove the Pilgrims to North America for God.

7. We must reject the pretended historical neutrality and objectivity of humanistic historians even though the myth of objectivity has a stranglehold on most modern historians. Christian historians must be radical enough to escape the influence of this myth. God did and still does act in history. God did raise up Luther and Calvin. When humanists and misguided Christian historians accuse great Christian historians such as D'Aubigne of writing "biased" and "purple-prose" history, they reveal that they themselves are actually the real

myth-makers who are pretending that God did not act in history. D'Aubigne represents the highest standards for Christian historians who have not been duped by the myth that scholarship means neutrality.

III. A Christian View of Psychology

A. Your *anthropology*, i.e., your view of man's nature, origin and relationship to the rest of the creation, will determine your view of the nature, function and methods of human psychology.

Example 1. Typical non-Christian anthropologies view man as being an animal produced by the evolutionary process. Thus some non-Christian psychological theories seek to explain human behavior in terms of comparative animal behavior and evolution. The behavior of primates, mice, etc., is assumed to be the key in the explanation and interpretation of human behavior.

Example 2. Christian anthropology views man as being a unique creature created in God's image. As such, he relates to the divine as well as to the earthly.

In that man is created in God's image, he has an immortal personal soul, but in that he is finite and has a body, man will be similar in some bodily functions to animals (which do not have personal souls).

Although there are comparative bodily and mental functions between man and animals due to both having finite bodies, human psychology cannot be explained simply by the observation of the actions of animals. A man is not a monkey or a mouse and it is foolish to think that man can be explained simply by observing animals in laboratory experiments or in the wild.

B. Human psychology must take into account the fourfold state of man.

1. *In View of Creation:* Adam and Eve did not have any psychological problems within themselves or any problems relating to God, other people, or the world around them.

2. *In View of the Fall*: Because of (a) moral alienation from God through hatred in his heart toward God, (b) inward conflict due to lust, pride, envy, etc., and (c) problems relating to other sinners and the hostile world around him, man is beset by many

psychological ills. All psychological problems are rooted either in sin or in the effects of sin. Thus the basis of man's problems is moral and not his humanity. Even chemical, glandular, or physical problems are rooted in the effects of the Fall because all pain, sickness, and death came to be through sin.

3. *In View of Redemption:* When salvation takes place, man's moral alienation from God is removed and the love and peace of God is shed abroad in the heart by the Holy Spirit who comes to dwell with the believer and his problems. After all, does the unbeliever have the indwelling Spirit? Is his conscience renewed? Is he convicted of sin by God? Does the blood of Jesus wash away the guilt and defilement of his sin? It is a shame that even supposedly Christian psychologists lump Christians and non-Christians together in their theories and therapy. (The English Puritans had great insights into the psychology of the believer.)

4. *Man after Death:*

    a. The saints in heaven: once again there are no psychological problems. The process of being conformed to Christ that was begun in regeneration and carried on in sanctification is now completed in heaven. There needs to be a psychology of the blessed.

    b. The wicked in hell: the weeping, wailing, cursing, gnashing of teeth, etc., which Jesus and the apostles used to describe the agonies of hell should lead to a psychology of hell.

C. The Scriptures supply us with a good amount of material on many psychological topics.

Example: A psychology of atheism and unbelief can be developed from Romans 1, 2, 8 and I Corinthians 1–4, etc. The Christian should explore the psycho-spiritual causes behind the unregenerate's rejection of the gospel. See my book, *The New Atheism and the Erosion of Freedom.*

IV. A Christian View of Marriage

A. Marriage in view of Creation:

The biblical account and concept of creation supplies us with the only valid way of understanding the origin, purpose and significance of marriage.

1. The origin of marriage: According to the biblical account and concept of creation, marriage is not a social contract or institution that developed in human culture through a blind and meaningless evolutionary process. Marriage is the creation of God and is, therefore, a divine institution.

As a divine institution, marriage and the family belong to God. Thus God has a right to set up or structure marriage and the family any way He pleases. The original marriage of Adam and Eve constitutes the standard for all future marriages. We can now state that what marriage "ought" to be should be patterned after what it originally was in the Garden of Eden. The first marriage is the prototype for all future marriages.

2. The purpose of marriage: Marriage was instituted by God as being the best way of ordering human relationships that would give God the most glory and man the most good. Marriage is for God's glory.

Marriage should reflect the beauty and harmony that is in the triune Godhead. As the heavenly family of Father, Son, and Holy Spirit work together in wondrous harmony born out of their infinite love for each other, even so the human family should reflect the love, harmony, and intimate communication within the Trinity.

It is also obvious that marriage was instituted by God to be the stable context within which human sexuality could be fulfilled in the procreation of children. When God created Eve and gave her to Adam, we must realize that this marriage was the only way to fulfill the cultural mandate to fill the earth with mankind. Adam and Eve were the first husband and wife and then, as God intended, the first parents.

Marriage was instituted in order to make man complete, for God said, "It is not good that the man should be alone; I will make him an help meet for him" (Gen. 2:18). Adam needed a companion who would share all of life with him. Thus we must say that God never intended for anyone to be alone and lonely. For every person there should be a companion for life.

If the world would have continued in sinless perfection, there would never have been any lonely or unloved people. Every person would know the joy of loving and being loved as God intended.

It is only upon the basis of Christian theology that marriage and the family can be viewed as having dignity, validity and true significance. As Hebrews 13:4 states, "Marriage is honorable; let us keep it so, and the marriage-bond inviolate; for God's judgment will fall on fornicators and adulterers" (NEB).

3. The significance of marriage: The first marriage took place when Adam and Eve reached maturity in every area of their lives. When they reached sexual maturity and puberty, they were also ready for all the responsibilities of married life. Thus neither of them experienced sexual frustration or desired sexual deviation. Since marriage and family belong to God, we must follow the structure of marriage that God instituted in the Garden. Adam was the head of the family and Eve was submissive to his headship. This structure is what "ought" to be in every marriage. Thus the Women's Liberation Movement is in open violation of God's creation ordinance of marriage when it denies the man's headship over the woman.

While the male and female are equal in terms of their *being* or *nature*, seeing that they are both (1) equally created in God's image, (2) equally sinners before God and, (3) recipients of the same benefits of salvation, nevertheless, the Scriptures also teach that they are not equal in terms of *function* or *office*. Man's headship did not arise because of the Fall or as a result of Hebrew culture. Man was the head of the woman at creation as a direct institution of God Himself (I Cor. 11:3, 7-9; 1 Tim. 2:12, 13).

The first marriage as it came from God's hand was perfect in every respect. There were no problems in the marriage. Therefore we must look to the Fall as the origin of marital problems.

B. Marriage in view of the Fall

The Fall of man into sin and guilt gives us the only valid way of understanding all the problems that now beset marriage.

1. Sin disrupted man's relationship with other people in every area of life. Thus Jesus in Matthew 19 traces divorce to the sinful nature of man. He carefully pointed out that although divorce "is," it is not what "ought" to be, for it was not in the beginning at the creation.

2. All marital problems are rooted in either sin or the effects of sin. It is not "human" to fight or to be selfish. Some marriages reflect

hell instead of heaven because the ones involved in the marriage are unredeemed sinners. The institution of marriage is not at fault.

3. Part of the divine curse upon man was that the woman's "desire shall be unto her husband and he shall rule over you" (Gen. 3:16). A careful study of the Hebrew text reveals that the KJV mistranslated the passage. A better translation would show that the curse was that the woman would try to dominate the man and that the man would tyrannize the woman. This is evident by examining the parallel construction in Genesis 4:7 where sin's "desire" is to dominate Cain.

C. Marriage in view of redemption

Personal salvation through faith in the Lord Jesus Christ supplies us with the only basis upon which we can restore marriage to what it "ought" to be, i.e., what it once was in the Garden of Eden.

1. Redemption does not negate the structure of marriage God originally set up in the Garden. Rather, it now gives the power and motivation to restore marriage to its original condition.

2. Since Christians are to marry "only in the Lord" (I Cor. 7:39), they must not marry non-Christians (II Cor. 6:14).

3. In God's plan of salvation, He set forth a redemptive pattern for marriage in Ephesians 5:22–23. The man is again established by redemption as the head of the family even as Christ is head of the church. The woman is to submit to the man as the church is to submit to the authority of Christ.

4. Since man is to view his relationship to his family in terms of Christ's relationship to the church, he must take upon himself the threefold office of prophet, priest, and king.

As a prophet to his family he must teach them the truth and protect them from error. As a priest he is to lead them in the worship of God, teach them to pray to God and intercede before God on their behalf. As a king he is to provide for them, protect and guide them.

5. The key to successful marital life is the filling of the Holy Spirit since the apostle gives detailed exhortations concerning family living as examples of the way Spirit- filled Christians should live (Eph. 5:18–6:9).

6. In view of (1) the difficulties that are caused by the distress of persecution, (2) the shortness of life, (3) the nearness of Christ's

return, and (4) the greater amount of work that a single person can do for Christ, the apostle Paul declares that God decrees that some of His people will be single all their days (I Cor. 7:7–9, 26–35). In view of God's plan of redemption, the single person has true dignity if he or she uses this freedom from the responsibilities of marriage to be more zealous and productive in the service of Christ.

Discussion questions:

1. Does the Lordship of Christ extend to all of your life or are there "secular" areas where you are lord?
2. If Jesus is not the Lord of all of your life, are you really a Christian?
3. Have you tried to think about your academic courses in terms of the biblical world and life view?

Conclusion

One of the greatest challenges that we face today is the development of a distinctive *biblical* (not humanistic) world-and-life view. The Biblical perspective needs to be developed in detail in every area of life, practical or academic. The whole counsel of God needs to be applied to the whole man in the entirety of life. Every square inch of this world must be claimed and conquered for Christ. It is to this end that this monograph is dedicated in the hope that it will stir up the minds of believers to fulfill their covenantal responsibility to obey the cultural mandate in whatever calling into which God has called them.

CHAPTER THIRTY-SIX

Snappy Answers to Stupid Objections

Frist Campus Center, Princeton University (05/22/09)

Dr. Francis Schaeffer pointed out that most "objections" to the Gospel were really veiled challenges and not sincere questions at all. The Bible tells us to answer a fool according to his folly. Sometimes a snappy answer that is humorous can disarm a hostile unbeliever.

In the chart below many common objections are traced to the real problem, the presupposition that is the root issue. Then a snappy Christian answer is given. The chart should be memorized in order to trace surface objections back to the hidden presuppositions.

SURFACE OBJECTIONS	PRESUPPOSITIONS	CHRISTIAN ANSWERS
"SCIENCE HAS DISPROVED THE BIBLE. I BELIEVE IN SCIENCE."	Science and scientists are "neutral" and "objective," with no prejudices or presuppositions. *Scientific theories are always based on facts.*	Science continually changes its theories according to the presuppositions of the culture in which it exists. Science is not "neutral," or "objective." The scientist is controlled by his presuppositions, as well as his world and life view. Scientists make mistakes and produce false theories. As a matter of historical record, scientific *facts* have never disproved one word of Scripture. The theories of various scientists may contradict Scripture, but there is no evidence against Scripture.

SURFACE OBJECTIONS	PRESUPPOSITIONS	CHRISTIAN ANSWERS
"CHRISTIANITY IS TOO NARROW"	The best religion is one that makes everyone happy and secure. It assures all that everything is "going to be all right." *No* religion should offend people by saying that it is the only *true* religion.	Logically, since all religions contradict each other, there are only two options open to us. Either they are *all* false, or there is only *one* true religion. If there is only *one* God, there will be only *one* religion. The person who objects is "too narrow" to accept the truth.
"I CAN'T BELIEVE A LOVING GOD WOULD SEND PEOPLE TO HELL!"	God is too good, and man is too good, for God to send man to hell. This person assumes that God thinks, feels, and acts as *man* does. "If *I* would not send people to hell, neither would God!"	God is not a man. Neither does God think, feel, or act as a man would. His ways and thoughts are above ours. The real problem is that this person wants a "god" created in his own image … a "god" he can live with comfortably, while sinning. God loves justice, holiness, and righteousness so much that He created hell. The

SURFACE OBJECTIONS	PRESUPPOSITIONS	CHRISTIAN ANSWERS
		love of God for His own nature, His law, His universe, and His people, makes hell a product of love as well as justice.
"IT DOESN'T MATTER WHAT YOU BELIEVE, AS LONG AS YOU ARE SINCERE."	Sincerity is more important than truth or morality.	This is not logically or morally defensible. No one can live according to this belief. Who would excuse sincere Satanists, who make human sacrifices? Was not Hitler sincere in his belief that all Jews should be exterminated? Sincerity cannot displace truth or morality; you can be sincerely *wrong,* and also *sincerely immoral!*

SURFACE OBJECTIONS	PRESUPPOSITIONS	CHRISTIAN ANSWERS
"JESUS WAS A GOOD MAN AND A GREAT TEACHER … THAT IS ALL HE WAS."	Jesus was a great human being. No one can deny this… *but He was not God* or the Christ.	This statement is self-refuting. If Jesus was a good man and a great teacher, then we must accept what He taught about Himself, … i.e., that He is God the Son, the Savior of the world. If He is not who He claimed to be, He was either a liar or a lunatic. If he was a liar or a lunatic, He was not a good man *or* a great teacher!
"MAN IS NOT EVIL, BUT GOOD."	People are basically good. It is their environment that makes them bad. Give them good education, housing, and jobs, and people will be good.	This statement does not correspond to reality. History and psychology give irrefutable proof that man is corrupt in his very nature. No one need teach children to lie, steal, cheat, etc. Hitler's Germany was the most highly

SURFACE OBJECTIONS	PRESUPPOSITIONS	CHRISTIAN ANSWERS
		educated country in the world. The Scriptures are verified by *all* data when it says, "The heart of man is deceitful and desperately wicked" (Jer. 17:9)
"CHRISTIANITY IS A PSYCHOLOGICAL CRUTCH."	People accept Christianity because it meets some psychological need in them. Thus, it cannot be the true religion.	Christianity is shown to be true because it *does* meet all the needs of man, including his psychological needs. Since God created man, He knows what man needs. Thus, it is only logical to assume that the religion that God reveals will meet those needs. This position actually proves what it set out to refute.

SURFACE OBJECTIONS	PRESUPPOSITIONS	CHRISTIAN ANSWERS
"I'M AN ATHEIST. I DO NOT BELIEVE IN GOD."	They assume that they are competent to come to this position. They feel that there is no deity of any shape, size, or form.	The only person who can be an atheist is God Himself. To say dogmatically, "There is no God!" requires one to know all things, to be all places at the same time, and have all power. Thus, you would have to be omniscient, omnipresent, and omnipotent, … i.e., God! Atheism is a theological absurdity. It is self-refuting.
"IF CHRISTIANITY WORKS FOR YOU AND MAKES YOU FEEL GOOD, FINE … BUT DON'T BUG ME WITH IT!"	Everyone should do their "thing." As long as they don't bother others, it's okay. Truth and morality are not important. Only the individual pursuit of pleasure is right!	This is crude selfishness. The Christian's task is to "bug" others! Hedonistic lifestyles have always led to disaster. Just because something "feels good" does not make it right. Psychotic killers "feel good" as they murder their

SURFACE OBJECTIONS	PRESUPPOSITIONS	CHRISTIAN ANSWERS
		victims! This position is unlivable.
"CHRISTIANITY IS NOT RELEVANT."	It is not relevant to *me* in *my* life. It is not practical; … it's "pie in the sky, by and by."	True Christianity is relevant and practical. The Bible is concerned with *all* of life, and not just with *"soul saving."* This person has been exposed to defective forms of Christianity.
"WE ARE ALL A PART OF GOD. WE ARE ALL CHILDREN OF GOD."	This person assumes that "ultimate reality is of one being, and that man is part of this "world soul," or "cosmic force." It ends up *in pantheism* (all is God, God is all), or "paneverythingism" (all is Mind/ Energy; Mind/ Energy is all).	We are not a part of God. "God" is the personal, infinite Being who created this universe, not out of His own essence or being, but *out of nothing*. The Creator is quantitatively and quantitatively distinct from the creation. Pantheism and "Paneverythingism" lead to loss of

SURFACE OBJECTIONS	PRESUPPOSITIONS	CHRISTIAN ANSWERS
		identity and despair.
"I TRY TO KEEP THE GOLDEN RULE. I DON'T KICK MY NEIGHBOR WHEN HE IS DOWN. I DO THE BEST I CAN."	This statement is based on the assumption that God's acceptance of us depends on our person and performance. God will grade "on a curve" on the Judgment Day. If your good deeds outweigh your bad deeds, you will be all right!	God accepts sinners on the basis of the person and performance of Christ. Christianity is the only religion with a sub-stitutionary atonement. We can never *work* our way to heaven. There is no "scale" to measure our good and bad deeds, for either salvation or condemnation. Salvation is by *grace alone*, through faith alone, in Christ alone! (Eph. 2:8, 9)
"BUT, CHRISTIANS ARE AGAINST SEX. WHAT'S WRONG WITH SEX? IT IS NATURAL, SO IT IS RIGHT!"	They assume: What is, is normal. What is normal, is right. THEREFORE, what *is*, is *right*. Also ... "If it feels good, *do it.*"	The Fall of man into sin and guilt has made man subnormal, and the world abnormal. What is, is *not* normal. We have desires that are

SURFACE OBJECTIONS	PRESUPPOSITIONS	CHRISTIAN ANSWERS
		natural to our Fallen nature, but not *normal* to human nature as it was originally created. Sex is not wrong if it is "normal," i.e., if it is practiced where and when God originally planned.
"I TRIED CHRISTIANITY ONCE, AND IT DIDN'T WORK FOR ME."	Christianity is an emotional "high" that does not last. There is no "real" conversion experience. Because their conversion was false, *all* are false. They judge everyone else by their own experience.	It is possible to have a false conversion experience. Whatever they tried, it was not real! However, one false conversion does not make *all* conversions false. This is not logically defensible, and does not correspond to reality.

SURFACE OBJECTIONS	PRESUPPOSITIONS	CHRISTIAN ANSWERS
"I AM NOT A SINNER."	A "sinner" is a social outcast ... a whore, a drunkard, etc. This person is self-righteous, upright, and morally respectable.	All people are sinners, though in various degrees. A "sinner" is one who has not done all he should, and who has done what he should not have done. Sin is guilt before God. God demands 100% of us keeping 100% of the law, 100% of the time. Anything less is sin.
"I'M TOO EVIL FOR CHRISTIANITY. GOD WOULD NEVER ACCEPT ME."	Christianity is for good, respectable people, not for "sinners." God can never forgive really *bad* people.	According to the Bible, "good people" go to hell, and "bad" people go to heaven! Jesus said that He did not come to call *righteous* people, but *sinners*. Christianity holds out hope only for those who sense their unworthiness and sinfulness. To such, Christ says, "Come unto me!"

SURFACE OBJECTIONS	PRESUPPOSITIONS	CHRISTIAN ANSWERS
"I DON'T BELIEVE THAT JESUS ROSE FROM THE DEAD."	The universe is a closed system, controlled by the laws of nature, which are absolute and unbreakable. Since the resurrection of Christ is a miracle, it is *impossible*, since miracles *cannot* happen.	The universe is not "run" or "held together" by any so- called "laws." God is personally upholding and running the universe (Col. 1:17, Eph. 1:11). Miracles do not violate "laws," because "laws" are simply human observations of the ways God upholds the universe. Modern science now rejects the Newtonian mechanistic world and life view that lies behind the objection.
I DON'T ACCEPT THE BIBLE."	Human autonomy ...man starts *from* himself, by himself. *without* any outside special revelation. In that condition, man *can* understand himself and the world around him with all the interrelationships involved. This has	The history of philosophy shows that human autonomy ends in total skepticism. If we start with man, we end in total confusion. Only as we start with God is the universe intelligible. The

SURFACE OBJECTIONS	PRESUPPOSITIONS	CHRISTIAN ANSWERS
	always been the vain hope of the humanists.	surface objection does not correspond with reality. (See Francis Schaeffer, *The God Who Is There*, Inter-Varsity Press.)
"EVERYTHING IS RELATIVE THERE ARE NO ABSOLUTES."	Everything is relative *to the speaker's mind*! Man is the measure of all things. Might makes right. They assume that no moral judgments can be made on anyone for anything.	The above statement is self-refuting. To say, "Everything is relative," or, "There are no absolutes," is to give an absolute statement that is not to be taken in a relative way! The statement is also unlivable. Hitler and child rapists would have to be approved. No moral judgments could be given. But, *all* people make moral judgments. No one can escape this aspect of life.

SURFACE OBJECTIONS	PRESUPPOSITIONS	CHRISTIAN ANSWERS
"I CAN'T BELIEVE IN GOD. WHEN I SEE WHAT HITLER DID TO THE JEWS…AND SEE ALL THE PAIN AND SUFFERING IN THE WORLD. I CANNOT BELIEVE THERE IS A GOD."	We *can* make a moral condemnation of people, such as Hitler, without an absolute standard of morality and ethics. "God" is not necessary for making moral judgments.	The statement is not logically defensible. If there is no God, there is no absolute standard of morality, and no basis for "justice". The problem of evil requires the existence of God. It does *not* negate God. The statement is also unlivable. The existence of God is essential to discern evil, in order to condemn it. Without God, there is no "evil" *or* "good".
"EVOLUTION IS TRUE. WE CAN'T BELIEVE IN THE BIBLE ANYMORE."	Evolution is "fact" and not *theory*. All evidence supports it. There is no evidence to prove creation. All scientists believe in evolution. No intelligent person can disagree with evolution. It is the best rational explanation of the universe. Creation is only a belief, a superstition.	Evolution is a mixed bag of many different, conflicting theories. Evolutionary *theories* are theories put forth by *some* scientists. None of these theories stands up to a rigorous scientific or philosophical examination. Creation has the

SURFACE OBJECTIONS	PRESUPPOSITIONS	CHRISTIAN ANSWERS
		evidence, while evolution has only a dogmatic faith. See Shute. *Flaws in the Theory of Evolution* (Presbyterian & Reformed Publishing Co.), for a rigorous scientific refutation of evolutionary theories.
"THE CHURCH IS FULL OF HYPOCRITES."	Hypocrites receive God's blessings, and will go to heaven when they die. All Christians must be perfect! One slip, and they are hypocrites. There are no hypocrites in the bars, discos, or business world. The person giving the objection assumes that he/she is *not* a hypocrite.	All hypocrites are condemned by God, according to Matthew 23:13, 33. Isn't it better to put up with them in the church for a few years instead of spending eternity in hell with them? Christianity is a "sinner's religion." It is wrong to think that Christians have to be perfect. Besides, there are hypocrites in every organization and group within society. Look to *Christ* to become a Christian!Christians

SURFACE OBJECTIONS	PRESUPPOSITIONS	CHRISTIAN ANSWERS
		may fail you, but Christ never fails.
"ALL RELIGIONS ARE THE SAME. ALL ROADS LEAD TO GOD. THEY ALL WORSHIP THE SAME GOD. IT IS UNKIND TO SAY THAT CHRISTIANITY IS THE WAY TO GOD!"	They assume that if there is a God. He does not care what people think of Him, or how He should be worshiped. This "God" never revealed Himself to man, or made His will known. Also, they assume that all religions teach the same doctrines about "God," "Sin," "World," "Man." and "Salvation." If they *do* all teach the same things. Christianity is the only *one* way among many ways.	God has revealed His own nature, and how He is to be worshiped. Christianity stands unique and apart from all other religions by its doctrines. Each religion has its own "God" or "god." The Christian Bible, and the religion that flows from it, is the only way to God that *God* has revealed! Jesus Christ is the only way to God (John 14:6). It is not unkind to tell people the truth lovingly.

SURFACE OBJECTIONS	PRESUPPOSITIONS	CHRISTIAN ANSWERS
"CHRISTIANITY IS NOT RATIONAL OR LOGICAL."	Most people actually mean their *own* "common sense" when they use the words "logic" or "reason." They are victims of thinking that reality must be whatever they *think* it to be. If something is not "logical" to *them*, they assume it cannot exist.	If you begin with your *reason* or *common sense* as the absolute authority, you end in skepticism. Usually the people who make this objection have faulty views of Christianity: i.e., a straw man of their own making. The Christian system is in accord with the Law of Contradiction. (See G. Clark, *Religion, Reason, and Revelation* (Presbyterian & Reformed Publishing Co.), for a logical demonstration of Christianity.

SURFACE OBJECTIONS	PRESUPPOSITIONS	CHRISTIAN ANSWERS
"WHAT ABOUT THE HEATHEN?"	The heathen have never received any revelation from God. The heathen are not to be viewed or treated as sinners, because they are ignorant. They are "noble savages." We are "lost" when we reject Christianity ... but since they don't know anything about it, they can't be "lost" for rejecting it.	The heathen are lost because they are sinners, who have transgressed the general revelation found in the conscience and in the creation. They are "without excuse" according to Romans 1:20, and under condemnation (Rom 2:12). We are lost because of what we *are*, not because of what we *know*.

Conclusion

The Christian student today has a great opportunity to influence his generation for Christ. In the 21st Century, the Gospel is fast becoming the "only game in town" that offers hope to a lost humanity. The secular world views have nothing to offer people. All they can do is to deny the existence of God, the inspiration of the Bible, the historicity of Christ, and the Christian values and morals on which Western civilization depends. Their anti-morality "free-sex" crusade has resulted in a plague of V.D., AIDS, teen pregnancies, abortion, child molesting and rape.

Now is the time for Christian students to take over their campus for Christ. As soldiers of Jesus Christ they must be tough-minded.

They must throw off any feelings of inferiority. After all, they have the truth, the whole truth and nothing but the truth! Why should they be intimidated by the humanists, cultists and pagans on campus?

They need to stand up and speak out for the cause of God and truth. They must not allow the anti-Christian forces to deny their civil rights to say what they believe. The pagans do not hesitate to say what they believe. Christians have just as much a right to defend Christianity as pagans have to knock it.

If thousands of authentic Christian students would submit to the Lordship of Christ over all of life, then we will experience a mighty Reformation in which millions of people will come to know the Lord Jesus Christ and Western culture would be reclaimed for Christ. It can be done if we are willing to obey God's Word.

PART THREE

APPENDIX ONE

Open Letter to Muslims

Al-Masjid al-Nabawi (the Mosque of the Prophet) in Medina, Saudi Arabia

Dear Muslim Friend,

In an age when most people do not believe that Truth exists or that it is worth their time and effort to seek it, the mere fact that you have sought us out reveals that you want to know the Truth about who and what God is and how to find acceptance before Him.

The Truth is important because it sets us free from ignorance and superstition. And, once free from these things, Truth can then set us free from the fear of death and bondage to sin.

We too share the same desire and love of the Truth that you have. Let us then search for the Truth together as fellow travelers on the road of life.

Religious Truth Claims

All religions make Truth claims; they all claim to tell us the Truth about God, man, salvation, and the universe. Yet, they do not make the same claims. One religion may claim that man is God or that the universe is God, while another religion may claim that God created man and the universe and that they are not God or gods at all. One religion may claim that there is only one God while another religion may claim that there are millions or billions of gods.

Obviously, the religions of this world make different Truth claims. In fact, they contradict each other on almost every point. This is a sad but true fact of life that we both already understand and believe. Yet, we all know people who claim: "All religions worship the same God." How foolish! How naive! The Hindu who worships millions of gods and goddesses is not worshipping the Allah of the Muslims. The Christian who worships one God in three Persons: the Father, the Son, and the Holy Spirit, is not worshipping the Allah of the Muslims, either. Each religion makes its own unique claim about the nature of deity.

What Is A Religion?

By definition a religion is a worldview that tells us what to believe and how to live. It is composed of ideas, doctrines, values and morals. A religion wants us to accept certain ideas as the True explanation of all that is. Intellectual assent to these ideas is what constitutes "faith."

A religion not only wants our intellectual assent that certain ideas or concepts are true; it also wants us to obey a list of commands and prohibitions. In other words, a religion expects us to obey its laws and observe its rites and rituals.

Is Islam A Religion?

Is Islam a religion? Of course it is. Islam puts forth various ideas that it claims to be the Truth, and it demands that all men believe them. It also demands that all men obey its laws and observe its rituals.

Common Ground

In order for us to dialogue, we have to begin with ideas that we both accept as true. The common ground that we have is the truth that "Islam is a religion." Do you accept that statement? We do. It seems self-evident to us that Islam is a religion. If you do not accept this first point, then the rest of this letter will be a waste of time.

Question #1: Is Islam a religion? Yes____No____

Islam's Truth Claims

Since we all agree that Islam is a religion, then we must also agree that it asks us to believe certain ideas or concepts as the truth. These ideas are its Truth claims. In other words, the teachings of Islam are either true or they are false. There is no middle ground. They are either one way or the other.

Question #2: Does Islam put forth various teachings that it expects us to accept as the Truth? Yes____No____

Blind Faith Will Not Do

Truth claims should not be accepted by blind faith. The issues are far too important for us to make a leap into the dark and just believe something because we were told to believe in it by our parents, a religious leader, the state, or our culture.

If we are all supposed to maintain whatever religion our parents taught us, then no one should convert from it to any other religion. But no one really believes this. Hindus accept converts from other religions just as Muslims do. As a matter of fact, people are changing religions all the time. We personally know Muslims who became Christians, Christians who became Jews, and Hindus who became Buddhists. Some people go from one religion to another as easily as they change cars.

Question #3: Do you know of people who left the religion they were raised in and converted to a different religion? Yes____No____

People can and do change their religion. This is simply a fact of life that we must all deal with. Our own children may leave our religion and convert to another religion. It happens all the time. Only a fool would deny this.

Why would someone convert to another religion? Some people change religions because of marriage. They fall in love with a person of a different religion and they give up their religion to marry that person. It happens all the time.

Other people change religions due to coercion such as threats of violence or bribes of money, sex, or political advantage. If you change your religion because someone threatens to kill you if you do not accept their religion, this is not good. If you convert to a religion in order to obtain money, sex, or a job, this is not good either.

The only moral reason to change your religion is on the basis of the Truth. If you find out that your former religion was not telling you the Truth, then you should leave it. To continue to believe in a religion that you know to be false is to live an intellectually dishonest life.

If you find that another religion is telling you the Truth, then you should be willing to join it no matter the price or consequences. To find and follow the Truth is the only way to get to ultimate reality.

The issue is thus reduced to whether you really care about Truth. To believe in a religion for any other reason than Truth is to cheat yourself. Convenience, habit, upbringing, fear, or greed do not constitute a sufficient basis for belief in any religion. Something is not true simply because you believe it. You should believe in something because it is true.

Question #4: Is your desire for Truth so strong that you would be willing to leave your present religion if the Truth led you to do so? Yes____No____

This is where the 'rubber meets the road.' This is the ultimate test of your character and love of the Truth. If you are not willing to follow the Truth if it leads you to leave your present religion, then you do not really care about the Truth. If your attitude is, "Don't confuse me with the facts, my mind is already made up," then you do not really want the Truth.

If you feel that you must blindly follow what your parents taught you until the day you die, then you will never know if what they taught you is really true or a lie. Why? For you it is irrelevant if it is true or a lie. It doesn't really matter to you. You were born a Muslim and you will die a Muslim. That is all you care about.

How sad to live your entire life without ever seeking the Truth, and to have a closed mind that will not accept anything that contradicts what you want to believe. An unexamined faith is a worthless faith. It is no better than no faith at all for it comes from prejudice and ignorance instead of the joyous search for and the acceptance of the Truth.

Question #5: Could Islam be false in its teachings and rituals? Yes____No____

This question lays all the cards on the table, "All things are possible." This means that you must accept the fact that what you have believed all your life could be a lie.

If this is not even a possibility to you, then why pretend that you want the whole Truth and nothing but the Truth? A deep commitment to finding and following the Truth regardless of where it takes you is the only attitude consistent with intellectual honesty and integrity.

Face it, Islam could be a false religion. Two thirds of the people on this planet think so. Are you even open to this fact? If not, then why are you reading this letter? It is addressed to open minded Muslims who are willing to examine the evidence against Islam with objectivity and intellectual honesty.

Question #6: Are you willing to examine the Truth claims of Islam? Yes____No____

Question #7: Are you willing to entertain the possibility that Allah is a false god, Muhammad a false prophet, and the Qur'an a false book? Yes____No____

If you react to these questions by getting angry, what does this reveal about you? Are you open or closed to the Truth? If Islam is false, why in the world would you want to continue to believe in it?

If you are still with us at this point, hopefully you feel the same as we do: There is nothing more important in this life than the Truth, is it worth whatever price we have to pay. We will follow it wherever it leads us.

The Importance of Questions

How can we test the Truth claims of Islam to see if they are true or false? By honestly seeking the answers to crucial questions we can find out if Islam is true or false. Remember, the Truth is never afraid of the light of research.

The following questions require you to think objectively about Allah, Muhammad, and the Qur'an. Don't just answer them off the top of your head without doing any research. Cheap answers will always cheat you out of the Truth. Instead, go to a library and look up the answers in encyclopedias and dictionaries. Find history books on Arabia and on Islam that answer these questions. We found them, so can you.

Crucial Questions

1. The Qur'an refers to people, places, things, and events that are nowhere explained or defined within the Qur'an itself? True____False____

2. These things were not explained because it was assumed that the people hearing the Qur'an already knew of them? True____False____

3. Some passages in the Qur'an would be unintelligible without recourse to pre-Islamic history? True____False____

4. All Islamic scholars use pre-Islamic history to explain parts of the Qur'an? True____False____

5. Thus it is both legitimate and proper to use pre-Islamic history

to explain the Qur'an? True____False____

6. Yusuf Ali does this when it comes to such things as the she-camel, the elephant army, the twelve springs, the youths in the cave, the blind man, and many other things found in the Qur'an? True____False____

7. Mecca was a pre-Islamic pagan center of worship? True____False____

8. The Kabah in Mecca was a pre-Islamic pagan temple filled with 360 idols? True____False____

9. Archeologists found three other ancient Kabahs in Arabia? True____False____

10. The pre-Islamic pagans prayed by bowing down toward Mecca several times a day. True____False____

11. The pre-Islamic pagans made a pilgrimage to Mecca. True____False____

12. When the pre-Islamic pagan idolaters got to Mecca, they ran between two hills. True____False____

13. The pre-Islamic pagans ran around the Kabah seven times. True____False____

14. The pagans kissed and caressed a large black stone on the wall of the Kabah. True____False____

15. The pre-Islamic pagan idolaters sacrificed an animal. True____False____

16. pre-Islamic pagans threw a magical number of stones at a pillar of the Devil. True____False____

17. The pagans held their public meetings on Friday instead of Saturday or Sunday. True____False____

18. The pre-Islamic pagans fasted during the day and feasted at night for one month. True____False_____

19. The pre-Islamic pagan fast began and ended with the Moon in its crescent phase. True____False_____

20. The pre-Islamic pagans gave alms to the poor. True____False_____

21. The pre-Islamic pagan idolaters performed ritual washings before prayers. True____False_____

22. As one of their washings before prayer, the pre-Islamic pagan idolaters snorted water up and then out of their nose. True____False_____

23. The pre-Islamic pagans cut off the hands of thieves. True____False_____

24. The pre-Islamic pagans forbade marrying sisters. True____False_____

25. The pre-Islamic pagans forbad the eating of swine's flesh. True____False_____

26. In pre-Islamic Arabian genealogies, Ishmael is nowhere mentioned as the father of the Arabs. True____False_____

27. Abraham, the father of Ishmael, was not an Arab. True____False_____

28. Hagar, the mother of Ishmael, was an Egyptian, not an Arab. True____False_____

29. Since his mother and his father were not Arabs, Ishmael was not an Arab. True____False_____

30. Ishmael could not be the "father" of the Arabs because they

already existed before he was born.   True____False_____

31. According to the historical and literary evidence, Abraham and lshmael lived in Palestine. True____False_____

32. Abraham and Ishmael never lived in Mecca. True____False_____

33. Abraham and Ishmael never built the Kabah. True____False_____

34. They never established the rituals connected with the Kabah such as the Pilgrimage. True____False_____

35. According to Arab history, Kosia, Muhammad's pagan great-grandfather, built the Kabah at Mecca. True____False_____

36. The title "Al-ilah" was used by pagan Arabs in reference to one of the gods worshipped at the Kabah. True____False_____

37. The word "Al-illah" was shortened into "Allah." True____False_____

38. The Moon-god was called "Al-ilah" and then "Allah" by some Arab pagans in southern Arabia. True____False_____

39. Al-Lat, Al-Uzza, and Manat were worshipped by the pre-Islamic pagan Arabs as "the daughters of Allah." True____False_____

40. Muhammad's father lived and died as a pagan and yet the word "Allah" was part of his name.   True____False_____

41. Yusuf Ali's translation of the Qur'an points out that pre-Islamic pagan Arabs worshiped the Moon as a god. True____False_____

42. Many of the pre-Islamic pagan rituals associated with the worship of Allah and his daughters were incorporated into the Qur'an and are now part of Islam. True____False____

43. The religion of Islam has adopted the name, the rituals, and the crescent Moon symbol of the pagan Arab Moon god. True____False____

44. Some of the material found in the Qur'an can be traced back to pre-Islamic pagan Arabian religions. True____False____

45. The people of Muhammad's day are recorded in the Qur'an as saying that Muhammad took old wives' tales and myths and put them into the Qur'an. True____False____

46. The Qur'an warns against asking questions about Islam because if the answers are revealed, you will lose your faith in Islam. True____False____

Concluding Remarks

We have discussed together some very important issues that touch upon the origins of the rituals and beliefs found in the religion of Islam. The burning question that confronted us was whether Islam was created out of preexisting pagan rituals and beliefs or was it revealed from heaven.

After studying the standard reference works on Islam, we must conclude that the rituals and beliefs of Islam are clearly earthly in origin, they were not brought down by Gabriel to Muhammad. The question of origins is the key to whether Islam is true or false. Your willingness to research this issue is an indication that you really do care about the Truth. Thank you for caring.

The Problem of Sin

While the issue of the origins of Islam is an intellectual question that can be answered only by research into the historical evidence, there is another issue that confronts us all. Regardless of your religion, there is the inescapable fact that we have all failed to live up to our religious convictions. Muslim, Christian, Buddhist, it doesn't really matter. We have all violated whatever moral standards we have adopted.

This means we have to find a way to be forgiven or cleansed of our sins. Why? If you believe in an afterlife and that there is a hell to escape and a paradise to gain, how can you gain entrance into heaven?

Two Problems We All Face

Our problem is twofold. First, our hearts are prone to evil. Thus we find it very easy to feel lust, jealousy, hatred, anger, and greed. Even when we try to be good, our own heart will betray us.

**Question: Do you admit that your heart is prone to evil?
Yes_____No_____**

Second, God is keeping a record of all our evil thoughts, words and deeds. He will hold us accountable for these evils on the Day of Judgment. On that Day we will have to face the reality of our own failures and sins.

**Question: Do you recognize that you will be held accountable for all your sins on the Day of Judgment?
Yes_____No_____**

How can you change your heart and clear your record in heaven? In order to come before a holy God with acceptance, you have to do these two things. Well, how are you going to do them?

Question: Will Good Works Help Us? Yes_____No_____

Some people think that if they do good deeds that this will change their hearts and clear their record. But can good works really change anyone's heart? We tried it and found that no matter how much good we did, evil was still present in our hearts.

Question: Haven't you found this true of your own heart? Yes____No_____

No matter how many good deeds you perform, your heart still has evil thoughts and motives. No, doing good deeds will never stop your heart from thinking or feeling evil things.

The same problem confronts us if we think that we can erase the divine record of our sins by doing good deeds. How many good deeds are necessary to balance out our bad deeds? It all depends on whether you are thinking of the evil that God sees or the evil we see in ourselves.

When we look at our own lives, we all tend to be easy on ourselves. We like to think that we are not as bad as some and better than most. We don't seem so bad as long as we compare ourselves to other people.

But what if we compare ourselves to a holy and righteous Deity? If we think in terms of all the sins that an all-knowing Deity sees and hears us do, we do not come off so well. Our sins are like the sand on the seashore, too many to count!

Question: Can doing a few good deeds really clear away the mountain of sin that is against us? Yes___No____

Question: Haven't you found it true that even when you do a good deed, you had evil motives such as pride? Yes____No_____

Question: Can evil motives cancel out a good deed? Yes____No_____

When we give money to be seen by men, this cancels out the good deed. Thus good deeds will never change your heart or clear your record.

A Mediator Needed

Since we have sinned, we are not allowed to come into the presence of a holy God. But if we cannot go to God for forgiveness, how will we obtain forgiveness? If good deeds will not work, how will we ever enter paradise?

What if someone went before God on our behalf? What if there was a mediator who could intercede on our behalf?

Question: Wouldn't a mediator solve our problem with sin? Yes___No___

Now, such a mediator must be sinless and without blame. Otherwise, he could not go before a holy God either. The mediator must be as righteous and as holy as God Himself or he cannot stand before God.

Even if this mediator could enter God's presence, how could he clear the record of all our sins? He would have to pay off our debt to justice somehow. One obvious way is for him to take upon himself the punishment due to us. In other words, in order for us to escape the fires of hell, he would have to smother the flames of hell in his own bosom.

This mediator would have to be the bridge between heaven and earth and between God and man. A mediator who is not quite God or not quite man is a bridge broken at either end. We need someone to represent God to us and us to God. This mediator has to be both God and man at the same time or salvation is not possible.

The Gospel

Have you ever heard the word "Gospel?" What is it all about? It is a word that means "good news." What is the good news? The good news is that Jesus Christ is the only mediator between God and man. He did what we could not do. He entered into the presence of God on our behalf to obtain forgiveness for us.

How could he do this? On what basis? He bore our sins and iniquities in his own body on the cross. He died for our sins according to the Gospel. This is why salvation is a gift of God's grace.

Jesus paid the price for our salvation. Thus God now offers us eternal life free of charge. We become a Christian by simply asking Jesus to be our Mediator, our Savior, and our Redeemer. You don't become a Christian by joining a church, getting baptized, or doing some other good deed. No, salvation is by grace alone through faith alone in Christ alone. He brings us into the very presence of God.

Question: Haven't you ever wondered why Allah feels so distant or far off? Yes_____No_____

Without a mediator, God is far off and distant. A distant God is only feared, not loved. He is unapproachable and seems far away.

Question: Don't you see the need for a mediator to pay off your sins and clear your record?   Yes_____No_____

Question: Does Islam offer you a mediator to take away your sins? Yes_____No_____

Question: If Islam has no mediator and no atonement, does it have any gospel, that is, good news? Yes_____No_____

The End Of The Matter

Dear Friend, Islam leaves you high and dry with no way to deal with the corruptions of your heart here on earth or the record of your sins in heaven. It does not build a bridge between you and God. It does not have a mediator who is both God and man. With no Savior and no atonement, it can never give you any sure hope of heaven.

But all these things are found in the Gospel. Stop right now and ask Jesus to be your Mediator. Ask Him to come into your heart as your Lord and Savior, Receive forgiveness through His atoning work. Pray this simple prayer.

Lord Jesus, I ask You to reveal Yourself to me. Save me and cleanse me of my sins. Pay off my debt to God. Come into my heart and save me from hell and make a home in heaven for me. I acknowledge that You are the Son of God and that You died on the cross for me and rose from the dead on the third day.

If you sincerely prayed this prayer, you have become a child of God by faith in Jesus Christ. Jesus has now cleared your record in heaven and the Holy Spirit will now come into your heart to deal with the corruptions found in it. God is no longer distant and far off. He is your Father and you are his child. Welcome to the family of God! Contact us so we can share your joy. (www.faithdefenders.com)

APPENDIX TWO

Open Letter to Jews

The Destruction of Jerusalem by the Romans under the Command of
Titus, A.D. 70, by David Roberts (1850).

Is the New Testament Jewish in its Interpretation of the Old Testament?

One of the ploys used by modern Jewish apologists is to claim that the authors of the NT inserted the Messiah in many OT passages that the Jews never considered messianic. It is further claimed that these erroneous messianic interpretations prove that Christianity did not develop out of Judaism. Instead, the true origins of Christianity can be found in Greek/Roman paganism.

Jewish apologists usually get away with making such bold

claims because the average Christian is completely ignorant of the early Jewish literature that formed the literary and theological context of the NT. But ignorance is not bliss when it comes to apologetics. We are commanded in the NT to be prepared to answer those who attack the Faith (I Pet. 3:15).

The only way to ascertain if early Judaism did or did not in fact give a messianic interpretation of the OT Scriptures that are interpreted as messianic by the NT authors is to examine the Jewish literature that existed before the NT was written. Since most of this literature is available only to scholars, it is very difficult for the average Christian to answer Jewish apologists.

Since these apologists are growing in popularity and are becoming more vocal in their attacks on the Church, we will now demonstrate that the NT was in line with the way Judaism interpreted their Scriptures. In other words, we will prove that the NT is thoroughly *Jewish* in its interpretation of the Hebrew Scriptures.

We have already demonstrated in *The Trinity: Evidence and Issues* that the NT's messianic interpretation of the OT was in line with early Judaism by examining the Midrash and the Talmuds. In an effort to supply more of this evidence, we have decided to expound upon the messianic interpretations found in the Aramaic Targums.

The Origin of the Targums

During the Captivity, many Jews lost the knowledge of Hebrew. To deal with this problem the rabbis translated the Scriptures into languages that were understandable to the people. They produced the Septuagint for those Jews who could read Greek and the Targums for those who could read Aramaic.

Since fragments of some of the Targums have been found in the

Dead Sea Scrolls and definitely date before the birth of Yeshua, they cannot be dismissed as the work of Christian scribes. The Targums are indisputably Jewish.

The Targums are not a literal word-for-word literal translation from the Hebrew text but a loose paraphrase that strives to make plain the meaning of the text. The Targums also include editorial insertions that "fill out" the text by inserting comments from the translators. These interpolations reflect traditions that are obviously older than the Targums.

For example, instead of translating Gen. 2:17, "in the day that you eat from it you shall surely die," Targum Pseudo-Jonathan: Genesis 2:35-36 paraphrases it as, "on the day which you eat of it you shall incur the death-penalty."

The translator solves the problem that since Adam did not in fact die the day he ate of the forbidden tree, the threat of God failed to materialize as promised. But instead of the threat of death, Adam was faced with the threat that he would incur the death penalty on the day he sinned. The dying would take place on another day.

Another example is found in Targum Pseudo-Jonathan: Genesis 39:1 where the translator inserts into the text crucial information as to who Potiphar was and why he purchased Joseph.

> Joseph was taken down to Egypt, and Potiphar, an official of Pharaoh, the chief executioner, an Egyptian, bought him with a surety from the Arabs who had taken him down there. For he saw that he was handsome, and he intended to practice sodomy with him; and immediately a divine decree was issued against him, and his testicles dried up, and he became impotent.

We are obviously given a great deal of information in the Targums about Potiphar that is not part of the original Hebrew text.

This information is often much more than mere commentary. We are sometimes told the origin of various aspects of intertestamental Judaism. For example, where and when did "synagogues" originate? The Targum of Ezekiel in ch. 11:16, tells us,

> Therefore, say, "Thus says the Lord God: Because I scattered them in the countries, therefore I have given them synagogues, second only to My Holy Temple, because they are few in number in the countries to which they have been exiled."

The Memra and The Word of God

Some of these interpolations form the background of the New Testament. When John in John. 1:1 referred to "the Word" who created the world, he was not referring to the Platonic Greek philosophic Logos found in Philo. He was linking Jesus to the Memra mentioned hundreds of times in the Aramaic Targums.

The Memra is introduced as the Creator of the world (Targum Neofiti 1:Genesis 1) and the One who appeared to Adam, Noah, and the Patriarchs. See particularly Targum Pseudo-Jonathan on Genesis: pages 22, 26, 31, 41, 53, 64, etc.

What is amazing is the Aramaic text in Targum Neofiti 1: Genesis: 1:1, literally reads, From the beginning with wisdom the Son of Yahweh (bar dYYY) created and perfected the heavens and the earth.

Most liberal scholars assume that this reading could not be in the original text and they correct it to read "the Memra of Yahweh created…" But the Aramaic "Son of God" Scroll found in Cave Four of the Dead Sea Scrolls demonstrates that intertestamental Judaism had already developed a doctrine of the Messiah as the divine "Son of God" before Jesus was born. (See my book, *Trinity: Evidence and Issues* for the details.)

What the Memra did in the Targums is often attributed to Jesus in the New Testament. He is the Memra of YHWH ("Word of God").

The Messiah

The Messianic expectations found in the Targums reveal a deep longing for the coming of the Anointed One, the King, the Son of David, who will deliver Israel, raise the dead, and usher in the final eternal kingdom that will encompass the entire world. Echoes of the Targums can be found throughout the New Testament.

Targum Neofiti 1: Genesis

Gen. 3:15 The serpent will be defeated "in the day of King Messiah."

Gen. 49:10-13 "Kings shall not cease from among those of the house of Judah and neither shall scribes teaching the Law from his son' sons until the time of King Messiah shall come, to whom the kingship belongs; to him shall all the kingdoms be subject. How beautiful is King Messiah who is to arise from among those of the house of Judah. He girds his loins and goes forth to battle against those that hate him; and he kills kings with rulers, and makes the mountains red from the blood of their slain and makes the valleys white from the fat of their warriors. His garments are rolled in blood; he is like a presser of grapes. How beautiful are the eyes of King Messiah; more than pure wine, lest he see with them their revealing of nakedness or the shedding of innocent blood. His teeth are purer than milk, lest he eat with them things that are stolen or robbed. The mountains will become red from his vines and the vats from wine; and the hills will become white from the abundance of grain and flocks of sheep. And Zebulun will dwell by the coasts of the Great Sea, and he shall rule over the ports of ships, and his territory shall reach as far as Sidon."

Targum Pseudo-Jonathan: Numbers

Numbers 24:17-24 "I see him, but he is not here now; I observe him, but he is not near: When the strong King from those of the house of Jacob shall rule and the Messiah and the strong rod from Israel shall be anointed, he will kill the leaders of the Moabites and make nothing of all the children of Seth, the armies of Gog, who in the future will make war against Israel, and all their dead bodies shall fall before him…The first of the nations who made was against those of the house of Israel was those of the house of Amalek. Their end in the days of the King Messiah, is to make war along with the children of the east against those of the house of Israel…And he took up the parable of this prophecy and said: "Woe to whoever is alive at the time when the Memra (Word) of the Lord is revealed, to give the good reward to the righteous ones, and to take revenge on the evil ones, and to cause nations and kings to form alliances, and to incite one against another…They shall afflict the Assyrians and subjugate all the children of Eber. Yet the end of each of these shall be to fall by the hand of the King Messiah and to be forever destroyed."

Targum Pseudo-Jonathan: Deuteronomy

Deut. 30:3-4 "his Memra will accept with pleasure your repentance and will be gracious to you and will return and gather you from all the nations where the Lord scattered you. Even though your dispersal will be to the ends of the heavens, from there will the Memra of the Lord gather you through the mediation of the King Messiah."

The Isaiah Targum

4:2 "In that time the Messiah of the LORD shall be for joy and for glory, and those who perform the law for pride and for praise to the survivors of Israel."

9:6 "The prophet said to the house of David, "For to us a

child is born, to us a son is given; and he will accept the law upon himself to keep it, and his name will be called before the Wonderful Counselor, the Mighty God, existing forever, the Messiah in whose days peace will increase upon us."

11:1-6 "And a king shall come forth from the sons of Jesse, and the Messiah shall be exalted from the sons of his sons. And a spirit before the LORD shall rest upon him, a spirit of wisdom and understanding, a spirit of counsel and might, a spirit of knowledge and the fear of the LORD. And the LORD shall bring him near to his fear. And he shall not judge by the sight of his eyes, and he shall not reprove by the hearing of his ears. But in truth he will judge the poor, and reprove with faithfulness for the needy of the people; and he shall strike the sinners in the land with the command of his mouth, and with the speaking of his lips the wicked will die. And the righteous shall be all around him, and the faithful shall be brought near him. In the days of the Messiah of Israel shall peace increase in the land, and the wolf shall dwell with the lamb, and the leopard shall lie down with the kid, and the calf and the lion and the fatling together, and a suckling child shall lead them."

14:29 "Rejoice not, all you Philistines, because the ruler who was subjugating you is broken, for from the sons of the sons of Jesse the Messiah will come forth, and his deeds will be among you as a wounding serpent."

28:5-6 "In that time the Messiah of the LORD of Hosts will be a diadem of joy and a crown of praise, to the remnant of his people; and a command of true judgment to those who sit in the house of judgment, to judge true judgment and to give the victory to those who go forth in the battle, to return them in peace to their houses."

52:13-53:10 "Behold, my servant, the Messiah, shall prosper, he shall be exalted and increase, and shall be very strong...he shall scatter many people and kings shall be silent before him...a man of sorrows and appointed for sicknesses...our iniquities for his sake will be forgiven...they shall see the kingdom of their Messiah..."

The Targum of Jeremiah

23:5-6 "Behold the days are coming, says the Lord, when I shall raise up for David a Messiah, and he shall reign as king and prosper, and he shall perform true justice and righteousness in the land."

30:9 "And they shall worship before the Lord their God, and shall obey the Messiah, the son of David, their king whom I will raise up for them."

30:21 "And their king shall be anointed from them and their Messiah shall be revealed from among them; and I will bring them near, and they shall assemble to my worship. For who is he whose heart delights to draw near to my worship, says the Lord?"

33:13 "In the cities of the mountains, in the cities of the lowland, and the cities of the south, and in the land of the tribe of Benjamin, and in the environs of Jerusalem, in the cities of the house of Judah, the people shall yet eagerly pursue the words of the Messiah, says the Lord...In those days I will raise for David a Messiah of righteousness, and he shall perform true justice and righteousness in the land."

The Targum of the Minor Prophets

Hosea 3:5 "After that, the people of Israel will return and seek the worship of the Lord their God, and will obey the Messiah, son of David their king."

Hosea 14:8 "They shall be gathered from among their exiles, they shall dwell in the shade of their Messiah. The dead shall be resurrected and goodness shall increase in the land."

Micah 4:8 "And you, O Messiah of Israel, who has been hidden away because of the sins of the congregation of Zion, the kingdom shall come to you, and the former dominion shall be restored to the kingdom of the congregation of Jerusalem."

Micah 5:1 "And you, O Bethlehem Ephrathah, you who were too small to be numbered among the thousands of the house of Judah, from you shall come forth before me the Messiah, to exercise dominion over Israel, he whose name was mentioned from of old, from ancient times."

Zech. 3:8 "Hear now, Joshua the high priest, you and your companions who sit before you, for they are men who are worthy that a sign be performed for them; for behold, I will bring my servant the Messiah, and he shall be revealed."

Zech. 4:7 "What are you reckoned, O Foolish kingdom? Are you not like a plain before Zerubbabel? And he shall reveal his Messiah whose name is told from of old, and he shall rule all kingdoms."

Zech. 6:12-13 "And you shall speak to him, saying, "Thus speaks the Lord of hosts, saying, 'Behold the man whose name is Messiah will be revealed, and he shall be raised up, and shall build the temple of the Lord. He shall build the temple of the Lord and he shall assume majesty and shall sit and rule upon his throne'…""

Zech. 10:3-5 "the house of Judah…from them will be their king, from them their Messiah…" Zech. 12:10 "…they shall mourn for him just as they mourn for an only son and lament for him as they lament for a firstborn."

Note: The Reuchlinianus marginal reading adds, "And afterwards the Messiah son of Ephraim will go out to do battle with Gog, and Gog will slay him in from of the gate of Jerusalem."

The Targum of Qohelet

7:24 "Behold, already it eluded man to know everything which was from the days of old and the secret of the day of death and the secret of the day when king Messiah will come."

The Targum of Canticles

1:8 "they will be provided for in exile, until I send them the King Messiah, who will lead them gently to their tents, that is the temple, which David and Solomon the shepherds of Israel had built for them."

1:17 "How fair is the Temple of the Lord that has been built from cedar-wood, but fairer !still will be the Temple that is going to be built in the days of King Messiah, the beams of which will be of cedars from the Garden of Eden, and its joists will be of cypress, teak, and cedar."

4:5 "Your two deliverers, who will deliver you, the Messiah son of David and the Messiah son of Ephraim, are like Moses and Aaron, the sons of Jochebed."

7:14 "When it shall be the good pleasure of the Lord to redeem his people from exile, He will say to the Messiah, '...Arise now and receive the kingdom I have stored up for you.'...'"

8:2 "I will lead you, O King Messiah, I will bring you up into my Temple, and you will teach me to fear the Lord, and to walk in His ways."

8:4 "The king Messiah will say, 'I adjure you, O my people of the House of Israel, not to be stirred up against the nations of the world, in order to escape from exile, nor to rebel against the hosts of Gog and Magog. Wait yet a little till the nations that have come to wage war against Jerusalem are destroyed, and after that the Lord of the World will remember for your sake the love of the righteous, and it shall be the Lord's good pleasure to redeem you.'..."

The Two Targums of Esther

In chapter one we are told that ten kingdoms have been destined to rule the earth:

1. The kingdom of Lord of Hosts
2. The kingdom of Nimrod
3. The kingdom of Pharaoh
4. The kingdom of Israel
5. The kingdom of Nebuchadnezzar
6. The kingdom of Xerxes
7. The kingdom of Rome
8. The kingdom of Greece
9. The kingdom of "the son of David, the Messiah"
10. The kingdom of Lord of Hosts

Conclusion

Once you add the testimony of the Targums to that of the Midrash, the Mishnah, the Talmuds, the Pseudepigrapha, and the Dead Sea Scrolls, it is clear that the New Testament's messianic interpretation of the Old Testament was in line with the Judaism of its day. Christianity is Jewish to its inner core and is the flower of which Judaism is the bud.

APPENDIX THREE

Open Letter to Roman Catholics

St. Peter's Basilica (Vatican City, Rome, Italy) - 1981

Let us state at the outset that throughout this two-part series that it is not our intent to offend those Roman Catholics who trust in Jesus Christ alone and rest their hope of salvation on God's grace alone. We gladly embrace them as fellow Christians.

But there are those Roman Catholics who trust in their own good works to get them into heaven. They openly venerate Mary and pray to the saints. And, when they do these things, they are actually following the official teachings of the Roman Catholic Church!

It is our intent to refute a visible, earthly organization called the ***"Roman Catholic Church"*** whose headquarters is at Vatican City in Rome and whose earthly "head" is the Pope, considered the "Vicar of Christ".

Please note that we are NOT attacking Catholics as people or their motives. We are dealing with those historic issues that caused the Protestant Reformation.

We did not invent these issues and we are quite aware of the fact that we will not solve them either. But we feel the time has come to clarify once again what exactly those issues are and why we are still "protesting" against the Roman system.

The first issue concerns the heart of the Gospel: **Justification by faith apart from works.** If Romanism is in error on justification, then it is preaching another gospel and cannot be described as a true Christian church.

The Biblical Doctrine of Justification

I.   The Greek verb *dikaiow* in Roman Law and society meant "to declare not guilty" or "to declare innocent of all charges" as a legal vindication in court. It was the opposite of a verdict or declaration of "guilty as charged".

II.   When it is used in a nontechnical sense, it simply meant "to be vindicated" before others. Old Testament: Genesis 44:16; Job 33:2, 32; Isaiah 43:9. New Testament: Matthew 13:37; Luke 10:29, 16:15.

III.   But when it is used in its technical or theological sense in the Old and New Testaments, this word has the same legal or forensic declaratory meaning as in Roman Law. Old Testament: Deut. 25:1; Isaiah 5:23; Micah 6:11. New Testament: Romans 8:33-34.

IV.   It is clearly in this sense that both the Father and the Son are said to be "justified". This can only mean that God is "declared innocent", "declared not guilty" or "vindicated from all charges". Old Testament: Psalms 51:4. New Testament: Luke 7:29; Romans 3:4. 1 Timothy 3:16 *Rotherham* translation says, "declared righteous" and the *Twentieth Century* "pronounced righteous".

V.   The Greek verb "to justify" is used in opposition to the word "to condemn", i.e., "to pronounce a verdict of guilty as charged." Old Testament: Deuteronomy 25:1; Job 40:8; 1 Kings 8:32. New Testament: Romans 8:33-34.

VI. Just as "to condemn" someone does not **make** him wicked, neither does "to justify" someone make him righteous.

VII. The equivalent words and phrases that are used as literary parallels to the word "to justify" mean "to declare innocent" and "to treat as not guilty". None of them means to **make** someone righteous. Old Testament: Psalms 32:2 "transgression is forgiven", "sin covered", "does not impute iniquity". New Testament: Romans 4:3 "reckoned to him as righteousness", 4:4 "reckoned", 4:5 "reckoned as righteousness", 4:6 "reckons righteousness", 4:7 "forgiven", 4:7 "sins covered", 4:8 "will not take into account (sin)", 4:9 "reckoned as righteousness", 4:10 "reckoned", 4:22 "reckoned as righteousness",4:23 "reckoned", 4:24 "reckoned", 5:10 "reconciled" (cf. vs. 9 & 10).

VIII. Man's justification before God is always based on God's grace through Christ's life, death and resurrection. Old Testament: Isaiah 53:11. New Testament: Romans 3:4, 24, 28; 4:25; 5:9; 2 Corinthians 5:21; Titus 3:7.

IX. Thus justification is a free gift and not something merited by works. New Testament: Romans 3:20-30; 4:1-12; 5:15-17; 6:23; Galatians 2:16-21.

X. The instrumental means of justification is faith apart from such works as baptism. New Testament: Romans 3:22, 26-30; 4:1-12, 16; 5:1; Galatians 3:8, 11..

XI. The Protestant view of justification is the doctrine of the early church while **the Romanist doctrine cannot be found anywhere in the early church.**

The Bible vs. Romanism:
How Romanists Try to Refute The Reformers

I.   **Romanists usually misrepresent the Reformers.**

They often claim that the Reformers taught that sinners are justified "by faith alone" in order to contrast this statement with James 2:24 "not by faith alone". But this is not what they taught.

The Reformers taught that the ungodly are justified "solely" (i.e. "only") through faith. They did not say that we are justified "by faith that is alone". They were careful to make the distinction between "only" and "alone".

They stated that the faith that justifies is "alone" but is always accompanied by all the other virtues such as love, obedience, etc. Hence, it is "not alone".

But what they did say was that the Bible makes it abundantly clear that *the sole instrumental means* by which one receives salvation is faith viewed as set apart from the other virtues such as obedience.

Why? *Faith* is the only "empty" virtue that has no merit in and of itself. Faith is not to be viewed as being the meritorious basis of salvation. *Christ's work-not ours-is the meritorious basis of salvation.*

Thus while salvation is "through" faith as its sole means of reception, it is accompanied by all the other virtues.

II. **Objection: What About James vs. Paul?**

A.   James uses the word "justify" in its non-technical sense of a personal "vindication" before man of one's profession of faith. He emphasizes that you should validate your faith before others by the kind of life you live.

B.   Thus James is emphasizing the *demonstrating* of justification and not how to achieve it.

C.   Nowhere does James use the word "justify" to

mean to **make** someone righteous.

III. **Questions Which Romanists Must Answer:**

    A. Can you produce a single verse in the Bible where the concept of grace as a "substance" is taught?

    B. Can you show us a single verse where justification is described as "infused righteousness"?

    C. Is not the concept of "grace as a divine substance infused into the soul" a medieval idea?

    D. On what basis do you ignore the legal, cultural, and exegetical meaning of the word *dikaiow*?

    E. Is there a single passage in the Bible which links baptism with justification as the means of its reception?

    F. Can you produce a single citation from the Apostolic Fathers where they taught the concept of "infused righteousness"?

The Biblical Doctrine of Authority

The Reformers did **not** say that the Bible was the **only** authority. This is why they appealed to logic, history, science, the Church fathers, tradition, councils, creeds, confessions, commentators, Greek and Hebrew scholars, etc.

But what they did say was that when it came to **doctrine**, there can be **only one ultimate authority**-the Bible.

The "buck" has to stop somewhere. Thus the "final court of appeal" is the Bible and not the Pope, councils, creeds, tradition, etc.

The other authorities (logic, history, etc.) are as good as far as they go. But they are not **the ultimate deciding factor in doctrine**. Just like the prophets, Apostles, Jesus, and the New Testament Church, Protestants appeal

to the scriptures as the "final court of appeal", i.e., the ultimate authority in all matters of faith.

    I.   **Question:** *When deciding doctrine, to what did the prophets, Jesus, the Apostles, and the New Testament*

Church appeal as their ultimate authority, i.e., what was their "final court of appeal" when seeking to establish doctrine?

Answer: They always appealed to the scriptures as the determining authority in matters of faith.

II. **Question:** *How do we know this?*

Answer: Throughout the Bible, the prophets, Jesus, the apostles, and the New Testament Church used certain key literary phrases that indicated an appeal to authority (Isaiah 8:20; Matthew 22:23-46; 1 Corinthians 15:3-4; Acts 15:12-18).

A. "as it is written" used 46 times:

1. Old Testament: 13 times (example: 2 Kings 23:21)

2. New Testament: 33 times (example: Romans 1:17)

B. "Scripture says" 7 times: (ex.: Rom. 4:3; 9:17; 10:11; 11:2)

C. "according to the Scriptures" 3times: (ex.: 1 Cor. 15:3-4)

D. "the law and the prophets" 38 times: (ex.: Luke 24:44-47)

III. **Question:** *Did the prophets, Jesus, the Apostles, or the New Testament Church ever appeal to "tradition" as the authority for their doctrines?*

Answer: Not once did the prophets, Jesus, the Apostles, or the New Testament Church appeal to tradition as the authority of their doctrines. As a matter of fact, the idea of people appealing to "tradition" instead of Scripture is condemned by the prophets (Isaiah 29:13), Jesus (Matthew 15:1-9), and the Apostles (Colossians 2:8). The only Biblical author to use the word "tradition" in a positive way is the Apostle Paul who clearly used it to refer to the handing down of scriptural doctrines such as the Gospel. Since the Church had just begun, it would be logically impossible for him to be referring to

447

"historical traditions" when the history of the Church had only just begun! How could it have any "historical traditions" when it did not have any history yet?

The Romanist View of Authority

I.   **Romanism's view of religious authority is usually based on the fallacy of circular reasoning.** They appeal to their church's authority to prove their church's authority! This is like rowing with one oar. All you do is go around in circles.

    Romanist: The "Church" is the ultimate authority.

    Protestant: Who says so?

    Romanist: The "Church" says so.

    Protestant: By what authority?

    Romanist: The "Church" is the ultimate authority.

II.   **Romanists are guilty of setting up a false dichotomy between Scripture and tradition. This is the fundamental logical error underlying their entire argument.** The moment it is admitted that there is such a thing as a "scriptural tradition" the dichotomy falls apart. For example, in 1 Corinthians 15:3-4 the Apostle Paul clearly appeals to the authority of Scripture as the basis for the Gospel. Then this scriptural teaching on the atonement is called a "tradition" to hand down to others in 1 Corinthians 11:2.

III.   **Romanists use the logical fallacy of appealing to human authority.**

    Some papists argue, "Since there are so many

denominations and interpretations of Scripture, we need someone to decide what is true. Thus we need the Pope!" Of course, we can point out that Hitler, Joseph Smith, Rev. Moon, and many other people have all made that same exact argument! We have no more reason to let the Pope do our thinking for us than to let all the other cult leaders do so!

Romanist Objection #1:

Note: Karl Keating is a Roman Catholic apologist and author of ***Catholicism And Fundamentalism,*** "Nowhere does the Bible say, 'Scripture alone is sufficient'" (Karl Keating, "What's Your Authority For That?")

Protestant Response:

First, this is a logical fallacy. The fact that the Bible does not contain the exact words "Scripture alone is sufficient" does not logically imply that the concept that underlies those words cannot be found in the Bible. For example, where does the word "Trinity" appear in the Bible? Where does it explicitly say "God in three persons?" Yet, the concept that underlies the doctrine of the Trinity can be found in the Bible even though the terminology was developed later on in Church history.

Second, this argument is self-refuting. Where does the Bible explicitly say "immaculate conception", "papal infallibility", "the mass", etc.? If this argument were valid, it would do far more damage to Romanism than to us.

Third, the Reformation doctrine simply states that the prophets, Jesus, the Apostles, and the New Testament Church always appealed to whatever written Scriptures existed in their day as the basis for their doctrines (for example, see 1 Corinthians 15:3-4). They never appealed to "tradition", "the Church", "the pope", etc.

Fourth, logically, since they only appealed to Scripture as the basis of their doctrine, then the burden of proof falls on the Romanists to demonstrate why we should appeal to anything else.

Lastly, in 1 Corinthians 4:6 we are told "not to go beyond what is written" in Scripture. This statement of Paul is the sum and substance of "sola scriptura".

Catholic Bibles:

Jerusalem Bible: "Keep to what is written."
New American Bible: "Do not go beyond what is set down."

Romanist Objection #2:

"The Bible actually denies that it is the complete rule of faith" (Karl Keating, *Catholicism And Fundamentalism*, page 136).
Protestant Response:
First, this negative argument claims, without substantiation, that the authors of Scripture explicitly knew of and then clearly denied the doctrine of "sola scriptura".
Second, please show us passages in the Bible where the authors deny that Scripture is the complete rule of faith. Protestants have been waiting several centuries for Romanists to "put up or shut up". Yet, they have never found a single text to support their argument.

Romanist Objection #3:

"The Church tells us the Bible is inspired, and we can take the Church's word for it precisely because the Church is infallible." (Karl Keating, Catholicism And Fundamentalism, page 125).
Protestant Response:
This argument is based on circular reasoning: He 'proves' the Bible by the Church and then "proves" the Church by the Bible! This is irrational to say the least!

Romanist Objections #4:

"The Church existed before the Bible. The Church made the Bible. Therefore: a) The Church made the Bible. Therefore: a) The

Church is over the Bible, b) The Church has greater authority than the Bible." (see Keating, *Catholicism And Fundamentalism,* pages 121-133 and also "How To Talk To Fundamentalists" tract).

Protestant Response:

There are major problems with this typical Romanist argument.

First, it is a logical fallacy to assume that: If x precedes y, then x has greater authority than y. In logic, chronology does not determine authority. This is the fallacy of irrelevance. For example, the Buddha came several centuries *before* Jesus. Is Buddha therefore over Jesus and does he have *greater* authority than Jesus? NO!

Second, historically, Romanism did not exist in the first century. So, how could it have anything to do with the canon of Scripture? The truth is that popery did not exist until many centuries *after* the canon was closed.

Third, Romanists are once again guilty of the fallacy of ambiguity. They speak of "the Bible" as if no part of it existed *before* the church came into existence. (See Karl Keating, "How to Talk To Fundamentalists", "…it was the Church that formed the Bible"). But a set of writings called the "Holy Scriptures" existed before the church was created. That more Scripture was added to this "set" of writings does not logically imply that the Church "made" the Bible.

Fourth, they have the chronology backwards. Faith comes through hearing the Word of God (Romans 10:11-17). The church is the community of believers that is created by the Word. It does not matter if Scripture is heard or read. Thus the Word of God creates faith and not the other way around.

Romanist Objection #5:

"But didn't the Church decide doctrine in Acts 15 on the basis of its own authority instead of Scripture?" See my DVD or CD, **Geneva vs. Rome** (www.faithdefenders.com) for a scholarly and gentlemen's debate between Roman Catholic Apologist Dr. Robert Fastiggi and myself.

Protestant Response:

In Acts 15:13-22, James appealed to the Scriptures to settle the Gentile issue. Once he quoted the Scriptures that applied to the issue, the discussion was concluded. No further words needed to be said. The Scriptures had solved the issue.

Questions That Romanists Must Answer

1. Just as "no man can serve two masters", is it not logically impossible to have *more* than one *ultimate* authority?

2. When "push comes to shove", is it not true that the Romanist's *ultimate* authority rests in the decrees of its Popes and church councils and not in Scripture or tradition?

3. Is it not self-contradictory to appeal to the Bible as your authority to prove that you should not appeal to the Bible as your authority?

4. Is it not self-contradictory to appeal to the Bible as the authority of your doctrines while saying that the Protestants are in error because they appeal to the Bible as the authority for their doctrines?

5. Is it not self-contradictory to appeal to the Bible as your authority to prove that the Pope or the "church" and not the Bible is your authority?

6. Where in the Bible did the Old Testament prophets appeal to "tradition" or any other authority than Scripture when establishing doctrine?

7. Can you show us just one verse where Jesus ever appealed to "tradition" as the basis of his authority?

8. Can you show us just one verse where the apostles ever referred to "tradition" as the basis of their doctrines?

Appendix Four

Open Letter to Witches

Title illustration of Johannes Praetorius (writer) (de)
Blocksbergs Verrichtung (1668) showing many
traditional features of the medieval Witches' Sabbath.

I see from the pentagram you wear and all your other magical charms that you believe in the power of magic. Perhaps you have attended a Wiccan gathering or you have participated in magic rituals. I don't know.

But so many questions fill my mind. Have you "drawn down the moon" yet? Have you ever felt a power come upon you? Do you

453

worship a particular goddess? Have you been initiated? Do you have a Wiccan name? Have you gone sky-cladding? Are you in the outer or the inner circle? Have you used blood in your rituals? Have you ever called forth a familiar spirit?

The reason I am writing to you is that I have studied the occult for more than 30 years and I have come to certain conclusions. I know that you will disagree with some of my conclusions because we have traveled different paths. But I have the added benefit of the testimonies of those who used magic in the highest levels possible such as the Golden Dawn and the O.T.O. (Ordo Templi Orients) and then, having come to faith in Christ, have now renounced magic.

All I ask is that you have an open mind and give serious attention to the things I now bring up.

Remember an unexamined faith is a worthless faith.

1) The fact is that magic does not work. After all the talk about the "power" that people can get from magic, I have never known a more powerless group of people.

Many of those who use magic are sick all the time. They go through multiple marriages. They have money problems. Their cars get flat tires. They get their share of the flu and colds. Even more seriously, they cannot beat their own drug or sex addition. They are usually in bondage and totally powerless to change their lives for the better.

If magic really worked, they would never be sick. They would win every horse race in town! They would own Wall Street by now! They would be able to maintain successful marriages. Witches would be picking the winning lottery numbers every week. But the fact is, when the "rubber meets the road," magic simply does not work. You can waste a lot of money and time on magic and be no better off. In fact, you will end up worse off.

2) Their lame duck excuses as to why they are sick or why they

can't keep their marriage together or why they aren't rich are weak and feeble. One psychic "healer" (a relative of mine) is sick all the time. Her first husband is dying of cancer! When she boasted to me of her magical powers, I confronted her with the rather obvious fact that her magic did not work for her or for her ex-husband. She replied that her magic will not work for herself.

But who says that you cannot heal yourself by magic? Where is this written down? And who says that your husband or wife cannot use magic to heal you? If her magic cannot help herself or her husband, then what good is it?

I could not help but also point out that she is always crying about money problems. What use is her magic if it cannot make her rich?

3) A magical world view is internally contradictory and hypocritical.

a)   To say, "There are no moral absolutes" is to give an absolute.

b) To say, "Do what thou wilt, this is the whole of the law" has been used to justify everything from black magic to human sacrifice. If there are no standards, then on what grounds can witches condemn child abuse, Hitler, murder, etc.? They can't.

c) To say, "Everything is relative" and "There is no evil," and then to turn around and say that Christianity is "evil" is contradictory.

d) To say, "Everyone has the right to believe what they want" and then to condemn Christians for what they believe is contradictory.

e) To say, "Do what thou wilt" and then to tell Christians not to do what they wilt is hypocritical.

f) To say, "It is wrong to judge/condemn others," and then to judge/condemn Christians is contradictory.

4) Magical view of life does not correspond to reality.

455

a) No magic is going to make you thin if you do not stop eating. No magic will make you rich if you do not get up and go to work.
b) The claim of modern witches that they are reviving pre-Christian paganism is not historically true. The rituals and beliefs of modern-day magic are of recent origin.
c) A close relative of mine who is into the occult told me that he was going to use magic to get himself a parking space in New York City. I in turn told him that I would ask Jesus to get me a space. He drove around for four hours before finding a place, while I found one at once and did not have to go around the block even once! His magic was not even good enough to find him a parking space!

5) A magical view of life is a cop out and it breeds irresponsibility. Instead of taking responsibility for their lives, those who use magic always blame "bad luck" or claim that someone is using black magic against them. The truth is that you are responsible for the choices you make in life--not magic.

6) It attracts people with mental problems. Sad but true. I have seen this many, many times. The state mental hospitals are filled with people who were users of magic. It appeals to nut cases.

7) They live in constant fear of the powers they draw down. Hence, they need the occult protection of the circles, towers, shields, charms, etc. What a terrible religion of fear!

8) If you depend upon trinkets such as pentagrams to protect you, you do not have any real power. To think that a stupid piece of metal or glass is going to protect you from a demon is just plain stupid.

9) The lust for blood is evil. It has led to horrible crimes. Killing animals and people for their "energy" is wicked as well as criminal.

10) Sex magic is filthy and gross beyond words and involves child abuse, bestiality, sodomy, etc. You will never have a normal

satisfying sex life once you debase yourself in sex magic.

11) Magic is for losers. The greatest magicians all ended up broke, alone and miserable. Check to see what happened to people such as Crowley. They were all losers.

12) Whenever a true Christian challenges them, the magicians always lose. I have challenged occultists to take their best shot and they always failed. On one occasion, a coven sent demons to kill me, but I did not even get a headache!

13) While there is a lot of hate and lust in magic, there is no love. If you leave the group or reveal the secrets, they will try to kill you. I helped to move a girl from Philadelphia to Florida to escape her former occult friends. If they really loved her, why did they try to kill her? If she wanted to leave the group, why did they object to her "doing what she will"?

14) There is no forgiveness, comfort or salvation in magic. It has no Savior or God who loves and cares for you. The occult is lonely, sad, cold and sterile.

15) The Bible says that the true power behind the magical arts is Satan. Those who deny this are the dupes of the devil.

Conclusion

These are just a few things that came to mind as I thought about what I have learned in 30 years of research into the occult. The Lord Jesus Christ has broken the power of the magic and has brought life, love and immortality to light through the Gospel. Jesus is Victor!

The occult has nothing to offer that compares with the love of Jesus. Turn to Him in repentance. Renounce your witchcraft as the works of the devil. Burn your magic books and smash your altars. Turn...or burn. Repent...or perish! Jesus is Victor!

Appendix Five

Atheists and Absolutes

Flag of the German Reich (1935 – 1945). Nazism was based upon mystical Hinduism that include other religious worldviews such as Nietzsche, Darwinism, Social Darwinism, the Occult, Paganism, Norse Revivalism, etc. This is why the Nazis used The *Swastika*. It was actually an ancient Hindu symbol (unity, good luck, etc.). Hinduism is a religious form of *atheism*.

Introduction

The problem of "absolutes" has plagued philosophy from the very beginning. Theists have always argued that unless you begin with God as the Infinite Reference Point that gives meaning to all the particulars of life, it is impossible to have any absolutes. Some modern atheists have denied this and claim instead that they can have "absolutes" without God. That they are in error at this point can be shown by the following points.

1. Modern atheists boldly proclaim, "Everything is relative." We have all heard this claim many, many times. They applied this idea first to morals and then to all areas of life such as science, art, etc. (see my book, *The New Atheism And The Erosion Of Freedom*).

2. An "absolute" refers to some kind of standard by which we understand or judge something as being either true/false, right/wrong, black/white, hot/cold, helpful/harmful, etc.

3. Human language cannot exist without distinctions drawn from such "absolutes." For example, "I am writing to you." The law of non-contradiction means in this case that I am not you.

4. Atheists commit the fallacy of equivocation at this point. When the theist used the word "absolute" he was referring to those standards that are:

> infinite - not finite,
> universal - not cultural,
> objective - not subjective,
> perfect - not imperfect,
> immutable - not mutable,
> eternal - not temporal

5. The atheist's claim to be able to have "absolutes" without God rests upon a very basic error in logic. He has switched the meaning of the word "absolutes" without mentioning this to the theist. The so-called "absolutes" of the atheist are finite, cultural, subjective, imperfect, mutable and temporal. This is, of course, a contradiction of terms because the atheist's "absolute" is a non-absolute!

Such relative "absolutes" would be useless so far as ethics is concerned because we can make up whatever so-called "absolutes" we want, Hitler included. Thus the so-called "absolutes" of the atheist are only the subjective projections of his personal feelings, ideas, biases, etc.

6. In logic, we cannot have a universal in our conclusion if we do not

have one in our premises. Thus a finite creature such as man can never make the leap to a universal if all he has is his own limited and biased feelings and ideas that are all particulars.

7. An infinite universal can only come from an infinite Being. Thus only the infinite God of Scripture can give us a sufficient basis for absolutes. The finite gods of paganism cannot generate any basis for universals in truth, justice, morals or beauty.

8. While some modern atheists claim to be able to have "absolutes" and "universals" without God, what they really mean is relative absolutes and finite universals. This is the same as claiming to be able to draw a round square or a square circle! Philosophically and logically speaking, it is impossible to have relative absolutes or finite universals.

9. The atheists are using the old "pea and shell" game to confuse people. They redefine such words as "absolute" to mean the exact opposite of what the word means. Thankfully, some of them are a little more honest and state that there are no absolutes in logic, mathematics, history, and science. When Albert Einstein was asked how did he know that the speed of light in a vacuum was the same everywhere in the universe, he replied,

"God does not play dice with the universe." Even such principles as the speed of light require the existence of God.

Conclusion

Without God nothing in life can have meaning because there would be no standards by which we can discern the difference between good and evil, truth and error, justice and injustice, and right from wrong. Morality and civilization vanish once man is reduced to a hairless ape.

The Juilliard School of Music (Irene Diamond Building) – 04/08/16

Illustration: Dr. Robert A. Morey debated an Atheist professor at The Juilliard School of Music in New York City (Dr. Morey led the Christian Student Association at Juilliard from 1971 to 1972)--the following is excerpted from my book, *The New Atheism and the Erosion of Freedom.*

Juilliard School in New York City

Christian students at the Juilliard School of Music in New York City were being hassled by an atheistic professor who used class time to attack belief in God and Christianity. Since he taught musicology and not philosophy, his constant attempts to convert students to atheism had progressed to the point where he was mocking the Christian students and using ridicule to score points against theism.

Feeling they had tolerated enough, the students asked him if he would like to debate the issues with a theist at one of their meetings. He agreed to debate the atheist position and even arranged for a classroom to be used. Because the students and I attended several of their meetings at Juilliard, they asked me to debate the atheistic professor. The Christians publicized the coming debate and arranged for as many students to come as possible.

The atheist was given the opportunity to begin the debate. His opening statement was:

I am so happy to have all of you together at last. You see, the Bible says that "when I was a child, I thought and acted like a child. But now that I am an adult, it is time to put away childish things." This is what I have been trying to tell you students.

You and I used to believe in Santa Claus when we were children. But we no longer believe in him, do we? It is the same way with God. God is for childish minds. No adult should believe in Him any more than believing in Santa Claus. You see, there is not God. He does not exist anymore than Santa. I know the Bible says "the fool says there is no God," but I say that only a fool believes in God.

This is all I really have to say. Atheism is simply a matter of giving up childish beliefs.

He sat down at this point and I was asked to give the theist's opening statement.

I appreciate the frankness of the Professor. It isn't every day that the cards are laid on the table so quickly in a debate. The thesis that he gave us was quite simple and clear. He said, "There is not God."

In order for me to make my presentation, I need the assistance of the professor. Would you please join me once again at the front of the classroom?

He agreed and came forward.

Would you please take this piece of chalk and come to the blackboard with me? Thank you.

We now stood at the black board. For the dialogue which

follows, "A" will denote what the atheist said and "T" what the theist said.

T: Now, would you make a dot on the blackboard. It doesn't have to be big. For the purposes of this illustration, this dot represents you. Is this all right with you?

A: Oh, I don't see why not.

T: Would you now draw a circle around that dot with the dot in the center of the circle. The inside of the circle represents what you know, what you studied or experienced, where you have been, and what you have seen and heard. The outside of the circle represents what you do not know, what you haven't studied or experienced, and where you haven't gone or seen or heard. Now, obviously in this age of specialization, there will be more outside the circle than what's in the circle. Since your degree is in musicology, would you claim to know a great deal about—let's say, nuclear physics or quantum mechanics?

A: No, I admit that I am limited in knowledge.

T: Given that this is the case, how much is outside of the circle in comparison with what's inside it?

A: Well, I can't guess that.

T: What I mean is that if you walked through the Library of Congress, how many of the subjects would you say you knew?

A: Well, I guess I would have to admit that I would know only a fraction of the knowledge that is out there.

T: You would agree that it would be in the decimal points. We would all have to say that our knowledge would be something like .00001%, but for the purposes of this illustration, we will say that you have 1% of all knowledge. Would you please write 1% in the inside of the circle? Thank you. Now, how much is outside the circle?

A: I guess that would be 99%.

T: Please write 99% outside the circle. Thank you. Now, would you please hand me the chalk? Now, remember that what's outside the circle is what you admit you do not know.

(I drew an X outside the circle.)

Is it possible for God to exist outside the circle of your experience and knowledge? Is it logically possible for God to exist outside the circle? What if "God" lived in Argentina? Have you been to Argentina?

A: I would have to admit that I have never been to Argentina. But I don't think that this is fair.

T: You see, the point of my opening statement is that it is philosophically and logically absurd to state such a universal negative as, "There is no God."

The only one who can say that there are no gods of any size, shape, or form in the universe throughout all of time is God!

You would have to have been all places at the same time with perfect knowledge of all of time to know that God doesn't exist.

In short, you have to be omnipresent and omniscient to have such knowledge. And in order to pull off the whole thing, you would have to be omnipotent as well!

Now, I asked you, "Is it possible for God to exist outside the circle of your limited knowledge and experience?"

A: Well, I would have to admit that God could exist outside the circle.

But I think that it is impossible to know if He does.

This debate isn't fair. I didn't know that I would have to deal with this man.

T: You said, if I heard you correctly, that it is logically impossible to say that God doesn't exist?

A: Yes, I admit it. You see, I am really not an atheist. I am an agnostic. I don't know if God exists.

T: Well, then I have won the debate. You have presented yourself to these students as an atheist all year long and now you have admitted in front of them that atheism isn't logically possible.

You agreed that it is a false theory. Instead, you now claim to be an agnostic.

A: I didn't know that this is what I was going to get into when I agreed to come to your meeting. I don't think this is fair at all.

T: Since we have refuted atheism together, perhaps you would be willing to discuss agnosticism? That would be a totally new debate. Would you be willing to discuss agnosticism?

A: I don't know if I care to discuss the issue with you.

T: At least tell us what kind of agnostic you are.

A: What kind?

T: Yes, there are two basic kinds: The ordinary agnostic says, "I don't know if God exists, but if you can show me from the circle of my own knowledge and experience that God exists, I will believe in Him." This is in opposition to the ornery agnostic who dogmatically states, "I don't know if God exists and you don't know if God exists because no one can ever know if He does or doesn't. It is impossible to know if God exists."

A: Well, I hope that I am an ordinary agnostic.

T: Then you are willing to look inside the circle of your knowledge and experience to see if there are any evidences of God's existence? This means that you won't make any leaps of faith to abstract ideas that we cannot experience.

A: What do you mean?

T: For example, if we begin to discuss the relationship between cause and effect, you won't up and say that there are "causeless effects" or that you now believe in "cause and effect."

After all, you have never experienced something that was without a cause, have you? If you hear a noise in your house in the middle of the night, you get up and investigate its cause. You don't roll over and go back to sleep, saying that the noise doesn't have a cause. Or, if I appeal to the principle that something has to get the ball rolling, you won't say that motion can be eternal and without a cause, for you have never experienced a causeless and eternal motion.

If you walk into a room and see a pool ball rolling across the table, you would never in your right mind say that the ball either started rolling all by itself or has been rolling around on the table for all eternity.

Or again, if I appeal to the Second Law of Thermodynamics, in which the universe is running down, you won't say that the universe has been running down for all eternity and need not have a beginning. Have you ever had a clock that ran down that had not been first wound up? In other words, we will limit ourselves to what you have really experienced and leave off abstract ideas that simply don't conform to life as it is.

A: I don't care to continue the debate any further. It is over so far as I am concerned.

T: Then in terms of your original position of atheism, you admit defeat?

A: I don't admit anything. (He walked out of the room at this point.)

T: I hope the audience enjoyed my debate with the professor. In terms of his original thesis, he had to admit that it was logically and philosophically absurd to say that there is no God. I was willing to go on and debate agnosticism and the theistic proofs. But, seeing that he has left the room in a hurry, perhaps you can persuade him that a second debate is necessary.

The professor later refused my offer, but at least he stopped hassling the students for the rest of the semester.

Appendix Six

"Standing on the Cross"
An Interview with Dr. Robert A. Morey
by B.K. Campbell of The Christian Thinker

If you do not know this person, you should get to know him. He is your top Christian theologian and apologist in the world with over 60 books published.

QUESTION:

Dr. Morey, we at The Christian Thinker do not believe that anti-intellectualism is exclusive to our time; we believe this obstacle must be overcome in every generation and in every culture. We believe this because man's nature is set against the "intellectual" truth of God. It is easier to distract the mind than it is to think with the mind. You have often referred to anti-intellectualism in your books. Perhaps, you can tell us why anti-intellectualism poses such a threat to the stability of the Church?

DR. MOREY:

Theologians and philosophers used common words and phrases, the meaning of which depends on how each individual author defines those words. The term "anti-intellectualism" is a good example of how a phrase can have different meanings.

To the rationalist, anyone who holds to the Reformation principle of sola scriptura is "anti- intellectual" in the sense that Scripture is placed above the human intellect, i.e. above human reason. Anyone who believes that the Bible is the final authority in all matters of faith and morals is "anti-intellectual" in this sense.

When a rationalist wants to dismiss Christian thinkers like Schaeffer or Van Til, he will hurl the term "anti-intellectual" as an ad hominem slur on their character. Thus the phrase "anti-intellectual" is often used in an emotive sense as a way to dismiss a theologian with the wave of the hand. While it is a cheap shot, it does avoid having to deal with the arguments of your opponents.

On the other hand, those who look to God as the Origin of truth, justice, morals, meaning, and beauty, view rationalism as "anti-intellectual" in that absolute truth and morals are not possible if you make man's intellect (i.e. reason) the Origin and Measure of all things. If you begin with yourself, you will eventually fall into the abyss of the unrelated and quagmire of relativism.

One of the themes of Jonathan Edwards' Great Awakening was the insufficiency of human reason and general revelation. [1] When Princeton Seminary was established, in his inaugural speech, Archibald Alexander argued against the exaltation of human reason above the authority of Scripture.

"We must unequivocally deny to reason the high office of deciding at her bar what doctrines of Scriptures are to be

received and what not."[2]

Instead of bowing before the idol of reason, Alexander stressed that we must,

> *"insist that all opinions, pretensions, experiences, and practices must be judged by the standard of the Word of God."[3]*

In his speech, Alexander stated that the two greatest threats he saw in his day to the church were rationalism and mysticism. The Bible was the final answer to both errors.

Today, once again, the errors of rationalism and mysticism dominate the Evangelical and liberal theological landscape. Be it the rationalism of William Lane Craig or the mysticism of James Taylor, either road does not lead to the one true God who has spoken in Scripture. Rationalism cannot justify its own validity on the basis of human reason because one man's reason is another man's idiocy. What is or is not "intellectual" is more psychological than philosophical. You may "feel" a certain doctrine is "intellectual" in the morning, but, by Noon, "feel" it is "anti-intellectual."

Rationalism has generated the seeker-church movement, the emergent and emerging church heresies, the Open View of God, the New Exodus, the New Perspective, and a host of other plagues that have harmed the Body of Christ. The root problems are rebellion against the authority of Scripture and *reasonolatry*. Pro. 3:5-6 warns us "do not lean on your own understanding." Instead, we should lean on divine revelation.

The consistent theist views the human "intellect" as the gift of God which He created to *receive* truth and morals from the Creator. Man was not created to be a truth-maker or a morals-maker because he is not the Origin of truth, justice, morals, meaning or beauty. God is the Origin and Measure of all things. Thus to be truly "intellectual" is to submit to divine revelation.

The other error that faces us today is mysticism. Instead of looking within themselves to their intellect, the mystic looks within himself to his feelings (i.e. "heart") to tell him right from wrong and truth from error. Scripture tells us that the heart is continually evil (Gen. 6:5) and "out of the heart come evil thoughts, murders, adulteries, fornications, thefts, false witness, and slanders" (Mat.15:19). Pro. 28:26 warns us that only a fool would trust his heart to tell him truth and morals.

Mysticism has produced the madness seen on TBN, which we have nicked named "The Babylonian Network." The "health and wealth" prosperity movement's extravagant claims of healings, revivals, resurrections, gold fillings, limb replacements, holy laughter, vomiting, dancing, visions, dreams, 90 ft. Jesus, and tongue speaking have made "Christianity" a subject of derision on Saturday Night Live! Positive thinking, positive confession, blab it/grab it, contemplative prayer, imaging, inner godhood, and other New Age ideas have filled stadiums and hell.

To the theist, it is the rationalist and the mystic who are guilty of "anti-intellectualism" in that by beginning only from themselves, with themselves, and by themselves, they have destroyed any hope of ever finding truth, justice, morals, meaning or beauty. The Apostle Paul put it this way, "Let God be true even if it means that every man is a liar."(Rom. 3:4)

QUESTION:

I find your perspective on anti-intellectualism most compelling. Where most would be inclined to refer to anti-intellectualism as merely a mystical and emotional threat, you have touched on the reality of another kind of anti-intellectualism (one not as easily seen); the anti-intellectualism of the rationalist who hides behind the appearance of truth and logical consistency. And yet, he is so man-centered in his thinking that he refuses to think Biblically. If ideas do not conform to his self-ascribed theory of knowledge then [for him] they cannot be true; scripture is judged at the bar of human reason. So, if I have understood you correctly, then you are saying, that reason must always be subject to scripture?

471

DR. MOREY:

It is important to begin by noting that the biblical Hebrew and Greek languages do not have a noun that is equivalent to our English noun "reason" because there was a different anthropology (i.e. view of man) in the Bible that has nothing to do with the modern Western European Renaissance view of man.

Our modern English word "reason" is a noun that refers to an idealized and romanticized faculty within man that is infallibly capable of discovering truth and morals apart from and independent of God and His Law/Word. It is loaded with philosophical baggage that grew and developed with the twists and turns of Western European philosophy. The science of hermeneutics warns us not to take such modern ideas and insert them into the ancient Jewish Scriptures.

The Rationalists during the Renaissance looked within themselves and abstracted and absolutized the ability of man to string ideas together in such a way that one idea seemed to lead to another idea until we come to a conclusion. The rules/laws of what was or was not a valid string of ideas came from Aristotle via Aquinas. The validity of these rules/laws was not questioned until recent times, which is why there are now non-Aristotelian rules/laws.

These rules/laws sometimes contradict each other or are self-refuting. For example, one rule says that all appeals to authority as the basis of truth or morals are invalid. Yet, if you ask on what basis is that rule itself valid, it is based on the authority of Aristotle!

The Renaissance Rationalists capitalized the letter "r" in "reason" and changed it to "Reason." The capital "R" emphasized that they viewed human "Reason" as the Origin of truth, justice, morals, meaning, and beauty. Using the error of reductionism, they reduced all knowledge to what was obtainable through thinking as opposed to any knowledge coming from experience or feelings. They assumed that reality must conform to what they thought it to be because the real was the rational and the rational was the real.

When explorers returned from Australia for the first time, they described an animal that had a bill like a duck, fur like a beaver, claws like a bird, lived in water, laid eggs, and yet was a mammal. The Rationalist pronounced that such a creature could not exist. When later explorers brought back the skins of these animals, they were denounced as clumsy frauds created by sewing together body parts of several different animals. Only after a live duckbilled platypus was taken back to Europe did the Rationalists finally admit that such a strange creature existed.

Reasonolatry reached its climax during the French Revolution when an actress was carried into the Notre Dame Cathedral and enshrined as the goddess of Reason. Everything must conform to the demands of the goddess of "Reason." Everyone (including God) must stand before her judicial Bar and she alone decided right from wrong, good from evil, truth from error, the ugly from the beautiful, etc.

The authors of the Bible never heard of the Renaissance concept of "Reason." Their view of man was different. Man's thinking about things was not absolutized into some "thing" that existed within man. Faculty psychology, in which man is divided into reason, experience, and feelings, is a modern Western philosophic concept that was unknown to the biblical authors.

In the Bible, man "reasoned," i.e. thought and argued about things, but he did not have a "Reason" *per se*. This is why the verb "reasoning" has parallels in both biblical Hebrew and Greek but there is no noun that refers to what the High Renaissance called human "Reason." Thus the prophets and apostles never referred to the "demands of Reason," the "bar of Reason," etc. and never claimed that their ideas were "reasonable" or "rational," i.e. in line with what Renaissance man thought was true and good.

When I am asked, "Is Scripture above Reason or Reason above Scripture," I begin by saying that the question assumes there is such a thing as "Reason." Now, I can pick up the Bible and hold it in my hand. Thus I know it exists. But I cannot hold "Reason" in my hand because it does *not* exist. It is a mere figure of speech or metaphor for man's limited, fallible, and often mistaken attempt to string ideas together in order to arrive at a valid conclusion.

But stringing ideas together according to someone's rules/laws does not mean that you will always end with truth. Something that is correct twice a day is to be preferred to something that is never correct. Does that sound "reasonable" to you? That proposition meets Aristotle's rules/laws. But this means that a stopped watch is to be preferred to a watch that runs a minute slow or fast! The rules/laws that Aristotle set up would have you wearing a stopped watch!

Having taught both high school and college students, I do not have any romantic ideas that all men and women have an infallible thing inside of them called "Reason" that enables them to discover truth and morals. IQs differ and, be it math or logic; most students struggle to get it right. While I believe in reasoning, I do not believe in "Reason."

The Renaissance concept of Reason led to the rise of Rationalism. But it collapsed as a philosophy because it could not justify itself according to its own rules/laws. While Rationalism no longer exists as a viable philosophy in Western thought, its language, such as the "demands of reason" and the "bar of reason," etc. still haunt the halls of academia as the ghosts of a long dead European epistemology.

God, not man, is the Origin of truth, justice, morals, meaning, and beauty. The biblical view of !God, the world, and man is absolute and infallible. God is there and He has not been silent. He has spoken in the Written and Living Word. If we begin with God, we will end with truth and morals. But, as the book of Ecclesiastes demonstrates, if you begin only with yourself, by yourself, and from yourself, you will end in "meaningless, meaningless, utter meaningless."

QUESTION:

Dr. Morey, your answer touches on an important point, the fact that we should not merely assume definitions outside the context of scripture. As Christians we have a set of presuppositions, which should ultimately determine the outcome of our definitions. It is not enough to simply speak of "reason" as an abstraction, but we must define what reason is. Indeed, we must always define what we mean when we use a word to explain a concept. This brings us to the idea of the non-believer's linguistic construction; can he or she really find objective meaning in words if those words are founded on a *"blank" conception of reason? Is it possible for the non-Christian to defend the authority of his or her definitions? And after all, isn't every theoretical position dependent upon the authority and sustainability of the words which make up that system?*

DR. MOREY:

A. We must remember that "words" are only linguistic symbols used to express ideas. The symbols change from language to language because they are relative to time, culture, religion, and worldview. Thus "Dios" in Spanish or "God" in English are different symbols but each refers to the same idea. Thus systems are not built on "words" per se but on the ideas those symbols express. "Words" are not objective but relative to the speaker or writer. For example, the word "is" can have fourteen different meanings.

B. All systems (theological, philosophical, scientific, mathematical, etc.) begin by assuming certain ideas are true. These ideas are called "foundational truths," "axioms," "first principles," or "givens." A "system" is a chain of ideas that is supposedly derived from or deduced from the foundational ideas when applied to various issues. But not all systems are created equal. Some are good, some bad, and far too many are ugly.

C. Some systems are inconsistent and include ideas in the chain that contradict the foundational ideas. For example, Joe assumes that evolution is a fact and that man is only an animal. But he also believes in human rights, equal rights, women's rights, etc. But, if man is only a primate, he cannot have any rights beyond that of any other animal. This is why Skinner wrote *Beyond Freedom & Dignity*. Given his foundational ideas, a consistent humanist cannot believe in "man" any more than he can believe in God. Man died the day God died.

D. It does not matter if someone responds that he does not believe in presuppositions. He has just given you his presupposition!

E. The Christian should derive his foundational ideas from the Bible - not the world (Rom. 12:1-2). It is not hard to see what they are. Genesis chapters one through three give us the three ideas that the authors of Scripture use throughout the rest of the Bible to interpret all of life.

> **1.** Creation *ex nihilo*,
> **2.** The radical Fall of man into sin and guilt,
> **3.** Redemption by grace.

F. These three foundational ideas form the basis of the biblical worldview. From Genesis to Revelation these three ideas are brought up over and over again as the basis of, or rationale of, this or that doctrine. For example,

> **a.** In terms of Creation, because all people are created in the image of God, all people have dignity and worth. Man is not junk.
> **b.** In terms of the Fall, the universality and inevitability of sin is the result of the imputation of the sin and guilt of Adam's sin to all his posterity. All have sinned and all are falling short of the glory of God.
> **c.** In terms of Redemption, the Father designed and initiated a plan of salvation for sinful man through the vicarious blood atonement of His Son in which He could be just and the justifier of those who believe in Jesus. Salvation is by grace alone, through faith alone, in Christ alone, according to Scripture alone.

G. The non-Christian has his own presuppositions or foundational ideas. In order for a Christian to challenge the unbeliever's belief system, the Christian must look beyond surface ideas to the foundational ideas such as Monism, rationalism, evolution, etc. We need to lay the axe against the roots of unbelief instead of picking its leaves. As long as the roots survive, the leaves will grow back.

H. Someone can be a "Christian" in his "heart," but humanistic in his "head," i.e. his worldview is humanistic. This happens when a professing Christian has foundational pagan ideas. For example, many "Christians" assume the humanistic dichotomies of mind/matter, form/essence, nature/grace, nature/freedom, etc., when they believe in the secular/sacred dichotomy. For example, art is divided into sacred art and secular art. But all of life is sacred according to Scripture (1 Cor. 10:30). The Lordship of Christ is over all of life. There is no "secular" realm of life where God is absent.

I. Christians must become epistemologically self-conscious of their foundational ideas and bring them into conformity with Creation, Fall, and Redemption.

QUESTION:

Dr. Morey, the role of scripture is, no doubt, central to your method. What does it mean to believe and apply the authority of scripture? And, if you would be so kind as to explain, why is this authority superior to all other authorities?

DR. MOREY:

The definition of the word "authority" is the first task before us. For something or someone to function as an "authority" over you means that the thing or person is "greater" than you in some sense. The "lesser" must always bow before the "greater." Second, we must make the distinction between "power" and "authority." Someone may have power over you but no authority to exercise such power. For example, a rapist may have the power to violate you sexually because he has a gun to your head. But, he has no authority to have sex with you. The state has God-given authority to levy just taxes but no God-given authority to steal from you by unjust taxation. You have to have God-given authority to exercise power.

Third, there are different spheres of authority. God ordained the state, the family, and the church as three sovereign spheres, each with its own set of delegated duties and the divine authority to fulfill those duties.

The spheres overlap in a few places. For example, my son is a citizen, my child, and a member of my church. The state has the duty and authority to protect his life and health. Thus I cannot, as his father or as his pastor, put him to death. But the state cannot interfere with my duties as a father or as a pastor. Thus I have the God-given right to educate my son in the ways of the Lord, and I have the God-given right to discipline him as a church member if he falls into heresy or immorality.

But one sphere must not usurp the authority of the other spheres. The state cannot usurp the spheres of the family or the church. Thus the state has no God-given authority to tell fathers or pastors to contradict their duties as given in Scripture. When the state told Peter what to preach, he refused to submit to the state (Acts 4:19-20). The church has no authority from God to control the government or the family. The family has no divine authority to take over the state or the church.

1. The State: The state has God-given "authority" (i.e. legal power) to tell you what to do and not to do in all matters pertaining to the common good. It does not require you to respect, love or even like government authorities. While we respect the office, we may despise the man or woman who holds it.

  a. The state has the authority (i.e. legal power) to make laws and levy taxes on you. The state can set the speed limit and require all kinds of permits.
  b. The military officer whose rank is above your rank has authority (i.e. legal power) over you. This means that he can

order you to do things that he feels are necessary. He has the power and the authority to send you into harm's way. It is not necessary for you to even like your superior officer. You simply have to obey his orders.

c. The police have the power and the authority to order you to do things. When the police tell you to stop, you acknowledge their authority by stopping.

d. Judges and the courts have "authority," i.e. power over you. They can send you to jail and even put you to death.

e. In the area of state education, someone is an "authority" if he is your teacher and you are his student; if he has higher degrees in the area than you; if his peers acknowledge him as the expert on the issue. The student should acknowledge the authority of his teacher by doing what he says in terms of papers, projects, tests, etc.

f. Your employer or supervisor at work has "authority" over you. They can hire or fire you. They tell you the work you are to do.

2. The Family: In marriage, the husband is the head of his home. Thus he has God-given authority over his wife and children. The parents have God-given authority over their children. We reject the heresy that the state owns our children. They are given to us as a stewardship to raise in the fear and admonition of the Lord and we will be held responsible for this task on the Day of judgment.

3. The Church:

a. First, councils, creeds, confessions, theologians, constitutions and bylaws, ecclesiastical courts, denominational leaders, church discipline, pastoral decisions, official resource works, etc. have God-given authority to rule over the doctrines and morals of the members of said church. The pastor/elders are "over" the members and the members are to obey and to submit to their doctrine and discipline (Heb. 13:17). Members are to highly respect them in love for their work's sake (1 Thess. 5:12-13).

b. Second, the Reformation doctrine of sola scriptura says the Bible is the final authority in all matters of faith and practice in the sense that it is the last court of appeal and the final judge of truth and morals. We do not believe in solo scriptura but sola scripture.

c. Third, this means that, while we acknowledge lesser "authorities" in the church (i.e. its councils, creeds, confessions, constitution and bylaws, past and present noted theologians, church history, standard reference works, elders, pastors, etc.), the Bible is the greatest authority and it alone is the final test of truth and morals. When a church contradicts the clear teaching of Scripture it is apostate and becomes a false church.

d. Lastly, while we acknowledge the God-given authority of the state, the family, and the church to function according to their respective spheres, the authority of Scripture is absolute above all three spheres because it is the verbal, plenary, inspired, infallible, inerrant, written word of God. What Scripture says is what God says (Rom. 9:17, 25; 10:11; 11:2; 15:10). Scripture does not change and is unaffected by contemporary cultural or philosophical trends.

It is the rock on which we stand and the beginning and end of what we believe and how we live.

QUESTION:

Dr. Morey, what do you think about compromise? More specifically, when should we as Christian's compromise? I mean, haven't many believers been wounded by the "politically correct" Christian who is afraid to offend or stand against the grain and atmosphere of the world? Haven't many Christians been wounded, by those who profess faith in Christ, but refuse to stand for Christ?

DR. MOREY:

What do I think about compromising truth or morals? To compromise truth or morals is a betrayal of the Lordship of Christ. It is sheer wickedness and high treason against the King of glory.

Today, personal peace and affluence has tempted many theologians and pastors to compromise truth and morals. The applause of the world, the riches of Egypt, and the pleasures of sin for a season have corrupted many. The lust for popularity, friendship with the world, and the fear of rejection has stumbled many. The way of the cross is hard and few there be that take that road today.

A well-known seminary professor came to my home and offered me the position of Head of their practical theology department. They particularly wanted me to set up an Islamic Studies Department to handle the cults and the occult. The only fly in the ointment was that I had to sign a statement that I believed in a certain prophetic doctrine that was in their statement of faith. Faculty members had to sign it each year. When I pointed out that I could not sign the statement in good faith, they were surprised. The professor explained that he did not believe the doctrine either but signed anyway. I objected that this is the game played by liberals. He looked at me and said, "Morey, if you don't compromise, you will never succeed." I replied, "I would rather be a failure in the eyes of man, and pastor a small church, than compromise my faith by signing something I did not believe."

The true child of God is a soldier of Christ who announces to one and all, "I will not retreat; I will not sell out; I will not back down; I will not compromise; but I will fight on in the service of my King until He calls me home. To this end, I will run the race set me before me looking unto Jesus, the Author and Finisher of my faith."

QUESTION:

Dr. Morey, you mentioned Islam, and this brings me to another point. Many readers will be familiar with your book Islamic Invasion I find it interesting that you wrote about the threat of Islam long before it had been recognized. I wonder if you might tell us what you see as the historical threat of Islam- the threat that Islam always presents to a civilization?

DR. MOREY:

We are witnessing what is historically called a "people movement." It happened to Europe once before when millions of Muslims moved into Europe and turned churches into Mosques. If you remember your history, Islam took over Eastern Europe and Southern Spain. If you do not know what I am talking about, you must read *Jihad in the West: Muslim Conquests from the 7th to the 21st Centuries* by Paul Fregosi.

How did Europe solve the problem of the massive immigration of Muslims into their lands? They went to war and forced them out by the sword. The kings and queens of England, France, Spain, Austria, Bulgaria, Yugoslavia, Transylvania, Hungry, Greece, etc. did not stop the forceful ejection of Muslims until all of Europe was free of Islam. The Muslims were forced back to Africa and Turkey.

Gleason Archer and I teamed up and wrote a book on the issue and we agreed that unless the politicians do not stop all legal and illegal immigration of Muslims, it is only a matter of time before Islam becomes the majority religion and Sharia law displaces Western law. Freedom of religion and all other freedoms will be gone. By the year 2050, Europe will become at least 50% Muslim and, some say, 60%.

I do not believe that the present politicians of Europe, Canada, America, South America, Australia, and Sub-Sahara Africa have the will or the courage to forcibly expel millions of Muslims from their countries. The election of Obama has emboldened terrorists around the world. The insanity of political correctness is destroying the last vestiges of our Christian heritage. The legalization of gay marriage will lead to the legalization of Muslim polygamy. We are witnessing the death of the West with our own eyes.

This issue is intensely personal to me. My speaking against Islam and warning about Jihad has led to a terrorist attempt on my life, being put on a death list by Hamas, and the Pakistani secret police infiltrating my ministry in the attempt to get me to visit Pakistan - where I was to be killed. Thankfully, the FBI warned me in time to prevent my murder.

The seminary in Pakistan, which honored me with a D.D. in Islamic Studies, was taken over at gunpoint and the Board and faculty thrown out. The government put in Muslim sympathizers who first denied that the degree had been given. But pictures of the ceremonies with Carl Macintyre being present refuted that lie. The Pakistani Christian community still stands with me against the terrorists who stole the seminary.

The Christian world has yet to understand the threat we face. Seminaries are not training pastors to deal with Islam. Bible colleges do not have courses on Islam and how to convert Muslims. The church is asleep while Islam is growing.

I had the opportunity to discuss this issue with Patrick J. Buchanan after his book *The Death of the West: How Dying Populations and Immigrant Invasions Imperil Our Country and Civilization*, was published. I gave him *Islamic Invasion and Winning the War Against Radical Islam*. He was surprised that I had written on Islam's threat to Western Civilization in the 1980's. He appreciated my documentation that Allah was originally the pagan Arabian Moon god, al-ilah. We both agreed that Europe is doomed. I also interviewed Bat Ye'or who wrote *Eurabia: The Euro-Arab Axis*. She also felt that Europe is doomed.

I attended a high security "invitation only" meeting on Islamic Terrorism with government and private experts on terrorism. I was honored by several attendees as one of the few scholars who warned about this in the 1980's. An FBI agent congratulated me on exposing several important terrorists who were either arrested or deported. I told them, "I am thankful that you guys are now getting the death threats that I used to get all the time. Since I am no longer alone in sounding the warning of terrorism, the Muslims no longer concentrate just on me. Thanks."

The only thing that can save us now is a New Reformation. To this end I have been laboring night and day for almost forty years. I will continue to fight Islam and promote a New Reformation until my last breath. The first Reformation took place when Islam invaded the West. May God grant us another Reformation as we face another Muslim invasion.

QUESTION:

Dr. Morey I was somewhat aware of your Islamic persecution for taking a stand, and have always had a deep respect for your work and courage. I don't think people quite understand just how easy it is to be targeted by Islamic extremists. My prayers are with you, in that I hope the Christian community catches onto this great threat. What can you tell those Christians who are afraid to confront Islam? What can you tell future generation who may face the greater force of this threat?

DR. MOREY:

Many years ago, Dr. John Frame encouraged me to write a book on the fear of God. It took me ten years to do so as there were more pressing issues to address. But the book *Fearing God* was finally published. It analyzes all the Hebrew and Greek words for "fear" and exegetes all the pertinent passages where "fear" is found in Scripture.

Several key passages come to mind in answer to your question:

1. God commands us not to panic when the wicked threaten to assault us.

Do not be afraid of sudden fear, nor of the onslaught of the wicked when it comes (Pro. 3:25)

2. If you let the fear of man control you, it will bring you into spiritual bondage just as surely as the cords of a snare entangle a bird.

The fear of man brings a snare (Pro. 29:25)

3. The first antidote to the poison of the fear of man is to trust in God. The word "trust" means to place your ultimate confidence and hope in the Lord and to rest in that confidence that He knows what is best for you and your family. The sovereignty of God is the rock on which the child of God stands. Solomon goes on in Pro. 29:25 (via Hebrew parallelism) to say, but *he who trusts in YHWH will be exalted.*

4. The second antidote to the poison of the fear of man is the fear of God. To the degree you fear God is to the degree you will not fear man. The smile of God must be more important to you than the frown of man. Jesus warned us, And I say to you,

"My friends, do not be afraid of those who kill the body, and after that have no more that they can do. But I will warn you whom to fear: fear the One who after He has killed has authority to cast into hell; yes, I tell you, fear Him!" (Lk. 12:4-5)

5. As I document in Fearing God, the triumph of the Transcendental Movement in New England during the 19th century led to the feminization of American Christianity.

- God was feminized by denying the doctrine of hell. Thus there was nothing about God that we should fear him. The love of God excluded the fear of God.

- Jesus was feminized by depicting him as an effeminate white male with a pale complexion and womanly hair. He was so "sweet" that he would never harm a fly. He would never throw anyone into hell and there was nothing to fear from him.

- Hymns were feminized by sentimental unmarried women hymn writers who used erotic imagery and language to describe their relationship to Jesus. They sang of "falling in love" with Jesus, resting in his arms or bosom, Jesus was their "lover," etc. Sticky sweet love songs to Jesus could just as easily be sung to your sexual lover. "You light up my life" is a modern example of "hymns" that are erotic in nature.

- The clergy was feminized. Preaching hell fire and damnation sermons was frowned upon. People were not rebuked for sin or warned of hell. Pastors were reduced to reading poetry at the Ladies afternoon tea. Laws were passed forbidding pastors from holding public office or fighting in the military. Manly pastors who dared to discipline sinners in the congregation were slandered as "mean" and "unloving." "Meekness" was interpreted to mean weakness.

- Christian men were feminized by the heresy of passivism. They were told that they could not be a policeman or a soldier because Christians were forbidden to use physical violence. Evangelicals resigned from the police force and handed it over to the Irish whose Catholicism did not condemn the use of force. Hunting, boxing, and other manly arts were frowned upon as unchristian. Men were told that Christians could not defend themselves even when assaulted!

The reason I give this historical survey of the feminization of Christianity is that it gives us the context that explains why modern pastors and laymen refuse to confront Muslims. One pastor told me, "Morey, you're crazy for getting the Muslims upset. They will kill you and your family. I would shut up if I were you."

For years only Anis Shorrosh and I did public debates with Muslim apologists. Attempts were made on our lives. Acid was thrown at our cars. We had to travel under false names. We were threatened with death. One Muslim even wrote a book in which he said, "Dr. Morey, are you ready to die for your faith in Jesus Christ?" The FBI and the police had to be called upon at times to protect us. But we feared God more than we feared the Muslims. They could only kill the body but could not harm our souls.

Modern feminized Evanjellyfish are afraid of death because they do not believe in the absolute sovereignty of God, the doctrines of sovereign grace that flow from that grand truth, and thus they fear man more than they fear God. This is why the Evangelical world has fallen to pieces. No one is bold enough to stand up for King Jesus and go toe to toe in battle over the truth as it is in Jesus. Compromise and cowardliness are the rule of the day.

This is why the book I just finished writing, _The Bible, Natural Theology and Natural Law: Conflict or Compromise?_, is politically incorrect because I dare to call heresy _heresy_ and name the heretics who are denying _sola scriptura_ and promoting _sola ratione_. The dunghill idol of _Reasonalotry_ is rebuked and God's Word is exalted. It is bold, blunt, and confrontational.

I know ahead of time that many will ignore my arguments against naturalism, and _ad hominem_ attacks will be made against me personally. But this is how Job, Moses, Isaiah. Jeremiah, Jesus, the apostles, the Reformers, Spurgeon, etc. were attacked. But I trust in the Living God, whom I serve day and night, that He will give me the grace to endure whatever the world or the apostate church throws against me. The smile of God is more important to me than their frown.

QUESTION:

Dr. Morey it would be a shame to conclude our interview without finding out about your study habits. In your book "Practical Christianity" you tackle just about every major and controversial issue of the Christian life- this includes thought as well as practice. Your answers are intelligent and well researched. How do you proceed when you set out to write a book?

DR. MOREY:

The gifts and calling of God often go hand in hand. Because my family moved every year of my early life and I went to six different elementary schools, three different junior highs, and two different high schools, I excelled in academics instead of sports. I was an "egg head" with pens and a slide rule in his shirt pocket and not "cool" at all. Teachers made me their "pet" because they could always count upon me to answer their questions if no other student would or could.

In the 10th grade three things happened. I rated 3rd year college level in reading and comprehension; I was chosen by Yale

University to be part of their S.M.S.G. advanced mathematics program; and I "found grace in the eyes of the Lord."

My father was an agnostic when sober and an atheist when drunk. He was horrified that I had become a Christian and told me that if I did not renounce religion, he would throw me out of the house. Thus at the age of 16, I packed my bags and left home. I had to choose between my family or Jesus. I chose Jesus.

Being raised a skeptic made me question the evangelical world. I was thrown out of Columbia Bible College for the sin of intellectualism and for asking too many questions. When Professor Sanders claimed in class that he had lived without sin for two years, I raised my hand and asked, "May I talk with your wife?" When he asked why I wanted to talk with his wife, I said, "If you have sinned in the last two years, she will know." He became furious, turned bright red, and yelled, "You are not allowed to talk with my wife." He was the one who pushed for me to be thrown out.

I found that my questions were not answered at CBC and I was castigated for merely asking them. I began to doubt Christianity, as no one could or would answer my questions. There were four men who literally saved me from going liberal: Walter Martin, Gordon Clark, Francis Schaeffer, and Cornelius Van Til. These men took the time to answer my questions and did not put me down for asking them. They became my heroes and role models.

Of my four mentors, Francis Schaeffer was the best. Edith made my wife and me feel at home at L'Abri in Switzerland. She sent me out to pick snails off the trees and out of her garden so she could cook them. There was a wonderful retired opera star that was staying there. I will never forget Schaeffer assuring me with tears in his eyes that it was not wrong to ask questions. True humility is to acknowledge that all good in you and all the good done by you, you owe to God and to others.

The study habits of my heroes were such that they did not stop researching an issue until they had the answer. They were all prolific writers and worked day and night to defend the faith. My *modus operandi* is as follows.

Step 1

I fly to Washington, D.C. and read everything in the Library of Congress on a given subject. This is why it takes around two to three years to produce a major works such <u>Death and the After Life, Islamic Invasion, Battle of the Gods, The Trinity</u>, etc. I do not stop until there is nothing more to read on the subject.

Step 2

I organize the research material into files. For example, all the photocopies on Arianism would be placed in its own file folder.

Step 3

Once all the research has been filed, I work on an outline that is pedagogically arranged in such a way that each chapter naturally leads to the next chapter. You cannot understand chapter three unless you first understand chapters one and two. Thus the chapters interrelate and work in unison driving the reader to the conclusion.

Step 4

Once the chapters are "mind- mapped," I get up around 4:00 AM each morning and begin writing. I use the files to plug in the citations I gleaned from the Library of Congress. It takes around one or two years to write the manuscript, depending on the size of the book. My new book, refuting *Natural Law and Natural Theology*, took me two years of research and two years of writing. It is around 500 pages in length. One chapter is over 65 pages and has 148 footnotes with multiple references cited in each note.

Step 5

I rewrite and edit the manuscript three times and then give it to several scholars to proof read. Once I have all their suggestions and corrections,

I rewrite it one last time.

Step 6

The finished manuscript is handed to the publisher for them to format, add indexes, and prepare for publishing. Several men have accompanied me to the Library of Congress to learn how to research a topic. I am sad to say that they got tired by the third day and quit. They could not take the unceasing grind of research. But I love it.

QUESTION:

Dr. Morey, what advice do you have to give to those of us who believe in asking questions; to those of us who believe that the life of the mind is important, who believe that we must defend the faith and witness for Christ at all costs. What can you share with future generations of the Church? How can we fight for truths survival?

DR. MOREY:

After Walter Martin died, I was asked to speak in his place at a major apologetic conference in Rockford, IL. The title of my lecture was, "*The Cost of Discernment.*" It has proven to be very popular for those who have been attacked for asking questions and defending the Faith.

1. There is a personal cost. Truth becomes all consuming, and the most important thing in your life. You cannot simply accept what people say without checking it out.

2. There is a family cost. Your wife, husband, parents or children will attack you. They will tell you that you need to be more "positive" and "accepting."

3. There is a financial cost. You will spend countless thousands of dollars on books, references works, DVDs, CDs, etc. in your pursuit of the truth.

4. There is a friendship cost. Friends will desert you because you are too "negative."

5. There is a church cost. You will find it hard if not impossible to find a church that shares your love of apologetics. Many pastors will not like you and may view you as a troublemaker. They will pray and hope that you will move on to another church. They value money, buildings, and numbers while you value truth, justice, and righteousness.

6. There is a reputation cost. You will be maligned, slandered, and put down as mean, nasty, unloving, unkind, etc. You get tired of fighting the good fight.

7. There is a professional cost. Since you will not compromise; call good evil and evil good; are bold to condemn heresy; name names; and warn people against false popular false teachers, you will not be hired at most seminaries or called to pastor big churches.

8. There is a spiritual cost. Your spirit will be grieved over all the heresy being taught today. You are tempted to become depressed and discouraged. You live in an age where truth is not valued. No one seems to understand why you care about truth and holiness. Thankfully, the godly have always faced this same situation: We are,

"Afflicted in every way, but not crushed; perplexed, but not despairing; persecuted, but not forsaken; struck down, but not destroyed." (2 Cor. 4:8-9)

We must keep in mind 1 Cor. 15:58,

"Therefore, my beloved brethren, be steadfast, immovable, always abounding in the work of the Lord, knowing that your toil is not in vain in the Lord."

The smile of God is all you need to endure the frown of man.

Footnotes-------

[1] Thabiti M. Anayabwile, The Decline of African American Theology, (Downers Grove: IVP, 2007), ibid, p. 24.

[2] Archibald Alexander, A Sermon Delivered at the Opening of the General Assembly of the Presbyterian Church in the United States May 1808.

[3] Ibid.

Soli Deo Glori
Dr. Robert A. Morey
www.faithdefenders.com

A Partial List of other Books
Written by Dr. Robert A. Morey,
who is the Author of Over 60 Books.
(For a more complete list, go to www.faithdefenders.com)

1. The Biblical Discipleship Program for Women by Dr. Anne Morey
2. The Bible: Intelligent Design or Chance?
3. How to Answer a Mormon/How to Answer a Jehovah's Witness (two books in one)
4. Horoscopes and the Christian/Reincarnation and Christianity (two books in one)
5. The Bible, Natural Theology and Natural Law: Conflict or Compromise?
6. The End of the World According to Jesus

7. Experiencing God in the Psalms
8. The Trinity: Evidence & Issues
9. How the Old & New Testaments Relate to Each Other
10. Studies in the Atonement
11. A Bible Handbook on Slander and Gossip
12. The Encyclopedia of Practical Christianity
13. The Nature and Extent of God's Knowledge
14. Is Eastern Orthodoxy Christian?
15. When is it Right to Fight?
16. Islamic Invasion (United States and Europe was warned about Islam in the 1980s by Dr. Robert Morey -- do people remember the *Battle of Vienna on 09/11/1683*? The Islamic Turks were poised to overrun Europe, but were defeated.)
17. Winning the War Against Radical Islam (Dr. Robert Morey has been debriefed by both the **FBI** and **Naval Intelligence** on the meaning of Jihad and his vast knowledge of Muslim terrorism in the United States. It is unfortunate that government officials in the United States on the highest levels are funding Islamic groups such as **Al-Qaeda** and **ISIS** for their foreign policy objectives, while Russia is actually fighting the Islamic terrorists -- the back cover of this book has a picture of a **Russian FSB Officer** (The Alfa Counter-Terrorism Unit).)
18. Fearing God: The Key to the Treasure House of Heaven
19. Exploring the Attributes of God (An Apologetic for the Biblical Doctrine of God)
20. Battle of the Gods
21. Death and the Afterlife
22. The New Atheism and the Erosion of Freedom
23. The Truth about Freemasonry (the book is recommended by many high degree Masons such as *Senator Jesse Helms (33rd Degree Mason, 10/18/1921 – 07/04/2008)* because it gives a fair and accurate presentation)
24. Satan's Devices: Breaking Free from the Schemes of the Enemy
25. Worship: It's Not Just Sunday Morning

Endnotes

[1] Tom Sorell, *Scientism: Philosophy and the Infatuation with Science*, (London: Rutledge, 1991).

[2] Helen Longino, *Science as Social Knowledge*, (Princeton: Princeton University Press, 1990).

[3] Larry Laudan, *Science and Values*, (Los Angeles: University of California, 1984)

[4] Thomas Kuhn, *The Structure of Scientific Revolutions*, (Chicago: University of Chicago Press, 1963). See also: A. Rupert Hall, *The Revolution in Science* 1500-1750, (London, Longman, 1983).

[5] Karl Popper, *Conjectures and Refutations*, (London: Routledge, 1963).

[6] Solomon, *The Book of Ecclesiastes*.

[7] Edgar Zeller, *Outlines of Greek Philosophy*, (NY: Meridian Books, 1967) pgs. 18-19.

[8] Robert Morey, *Battle of the Gods*, (Millerstown, PA: Christian Scholars Press, 2008).

[9] Zeller, ibid., p. 20.

[10] ibid.

[11] ibid.

[12] See the article on Wilson in Isaac Asimov, *Asimov's Biographical Encyclopedia of Science and Technology*, (New York: Doubleday & C., 1882).

[13] Robert Morey, *Horoscopes and the Christian*, (Millerstown, PA: Christian Scholars Press, revised, 2008).

[14] David Hume, *Enquiry Concerning Human Understanding*, (London: Clarendon, 1966), Book IV, section 4. Also: Popper, ibid.

[15] Max Jammer, *Einstein and Religion*, (Princeton: Princeton University Press, 1999), pgs. 68-69.

[16] Ibid, p. 32.

[17] Ibid, p. 58.

[18] Ibid, pgs. 46-58, 74, 81, 85, 92.

[19] Ibid, p. 57.

[20] Ibid, pgs. 46-58, 74, 81, 85, 92.

[21] Stephen Hawkins, *A Brief History of Time*, (NY: Bantam Books, 1996).

[22] Ibid, pgs. 53f.

[23] Ibid, p.53.

[24] See: Rodney Stark, *The Victory of Reason*, (New York: Random House, 2005) and J. Budziszewski, *Written on the Heart, The Case for Natural Law,* (Downers Grove: IVP, 1997).

[25] Ibid, pgs. 259f.

[26] Francis Schaeffer, *The God Who Is There*, (Downers Grove: IVP, 1968).

[27] Bernard Ramm, *Protestant Christian Evidences* (Chicago: Moody Press, 1966), pp. 59, 60.

[28] Michael Cosgrove, *The Essence of Man* (Grand Rapids: Zondervan, 1977), p. 34.

[29] Ramm, ibid., p. 58.

[30] Guy Zukav, *The Dancing Wu Li Masters: An Overview of the New Physics* (New York: Bantam Books, 1979.)

[31] See my analysis and refutation of materialism in *Death and the AfterLife*, (Millerstown, PA: Christian Scholars Press, 2008).

[32] Fritjof Capra, *The Tao of Physics: An Exploration of the Parallels between Modern Physics and Eastern Mysticism*, (Boston, MASS: Shambhala Publications:1999)

[33] Guy Zukav , ibid.

[34] Tony Rothman, *Instant Physics: From Aristotle to Einstein, and Beyond*, (NY: Byron Preiss Publications, 1995)

[35] Frank Ramsey, *Philosophical Papers*, (Cambridge: Cambridge University Press, 1999. Most helpful was: *Cambridge and Vienna: Frank P. Ramsey and the Vienna Circle* (Vienna Circle Institute Yearbook), ed. Maria Galavotti, (Netherlands: Springer, n.d.).

[36] Keil, Carl Friedrich; Delitzsch, Franz: *Commentary on the Old Testament*. (Peabody, Mass : Hendrickson, 2002, S. 6:242).

[37] Spence-Jones, H. D. M. (Hrsg.): *The Pulpit Commentary: Proverbs*. (Bellingham, WA: Logos Research Systems, Inc., 2004, S. 309)

[38] Gordon H. Clark, *The Philosophy of Science and Belief in God*,

(Jefferson, MD: Trinity Foundation, 1987). See also: Abraham Kuyper, *Lectures on Calvinism*, (Grand Rapids: Eerdmans, reprint: 2000), chapter IV. And Vern Sheridan Poythress, *Redeeming Science: A God-Centered Approach*, (Wheaton, IL: Crossway, 2006).

[39] *The International Standard Bible Encyclopedia*, ed. James Orr, (Peabody: Mass: Hendrickson, 1996) I:420.

[40] The biblical view of art has never received much attention. I am much indebted to my friends Francis Schaeffer and Hans Rookmaaker for their instruction on Christian art. To investigate this subject further, see:
Abraham Kuyper, *Lectures on Calvinism*, (Grand Rapids: Eerdmans, reprint: 2000). Robert Morey, *Introduction to Defending The Faith*, (Millerstown, PA: Christian Scholars Press, 2007). John P. Newport, *Christianity and Contemporary Art Forms*, (Waco, TX: Word, 1970). Hans R. Rookmaaker, *Modern Art and the Death of a Culture*, (Downers Grove : IVP, 1975). Francis Schaeffer, *Art and the Bible*, (Downers Grove: IVP, 1974).

[41] Robert Morey, *Is Eastern Orthodoxy Christian?* (Millerstown, PA: Christian Scholars Press, 2008).

[42] A. R. Fausset, *Bible Dictionary*, (Grand Rapids: Zondervan, 1979) p. 1310.

[43] *International Standard Bible Encyclopedia*, ed. James Orr, (Grand Rapids: Eerdmans, 1986), III:1174.

[44] Carl F. Henry, *The Biblical Expositor, The Living Theme of The Great Book, with General and Introductory Essays and Exposition for each Book of the Bible in Three Volumes*, (Philadelphia: Holman,1960), I:58.

[45] Keil and Delitzsch, *Commentaries on the Old Testament* (Grand

Rapids:Eerdmans, n.d.), p. 46.

[46] Henry, Matthew: *Matthew Henry's Commentary on the Whole Bible : Complete and Unabridged in One Volume*. Peabody : Hendrickson, 1996, c1991, S. Ge 1:1.

[47] John Peter Lange, *Lange's Commentary on the Holy Scriptures* (Grand Rapids: Zondervan, 1960), I:71-72.

[48] Ibid, p. 71.

[49] Leupod, H. C., *Exposition of Genesis*, (Grand Rapids: Baker, 1950) pgs. 27f.

[50] The definitive work is Jan Gulllberg, *Mathematics: From the Birth of Numbers*, (NY: Norton, 1997).

[51] Henry, Matthew: *Matthew Henry's Commentary on the Whole Bible : Complete and Unabridged in One Volume*. Peabody : Hendrickson, 1996, c1991, S. Ho 6:1.

[52] Henry, Matthew: *Matthew Henry's Commentary on the Whole Bible : Complete and Unabridged in One Volume*. Peabody : Hendrickson, 1996, c1991, S. 1 Co 15:1.

[53] Spence-Jones, H. D. M. (Hrsg.): *The Pulpit Commentary: 1 Corinthians*. Bellingham, WA: Logos Research Systems, Inc., 2004, S. 484.

[54] Garret, Duane A.: *Hosea, Joel*. electronic ed. Nashville : Broadman & Holman Publishers, 2001, c1997 (Logos Library System; The New American Commentary 19A), S. 158.

[55] For documentation, see: www.heretical.com/cannibal/china.html

[56] See: *Is Eastern Orthodoxy Christian?* and *A Reformation View of Roman Catholicism*: available from Christian Scholars Press,

PO Box 240, Millerstown, PA, 17062 (www.faithdefenders.com).

[57] Robert Kreider, "To Give But to Receive," pp. 3-4.

[58] Loraine Boettner, *Roman Catholicism*, Presbyterian Reformed Publishing Co., Philadelphia, 1969.

[59] The difference between the Hindu and Christian sections of India are like night and day. The Christian sections of India are clean and prosperous, while the Hindu sections are filled with filth and poverty.

[60] Ron Sider, "The Graduated Tithe," Partners in Mission.

[61] Harold B. Kuhn, "The Evangelical's Duty to the Latin American Poor," *Christianity Today*, Feb. 4, 1977, pp. 537-538.

[62] Kuhn, ibid., p. 537.

[63] Howard A. Snyder, *The Problem of Wine-Skins*, InterVarsity Press, Downer Grove, Ill., 1977, p. 46.

[64] Arthur F. Glasser, Mission Trends, No. 1, editors Gerald H. Anderson, Thomas F. Stransky, Paulist/Eerdmans, 1974

[65] One example of the heresy of universalism is found in Feeding the Hungry: Mission by Congressional District (Bread for the World, Christian Citizens' Movement).

[66] Kuhn, ibid., p. 538.

9 781545 647431